CANADA AT A CROS

Boundaries, Bridges, anu Laissez-Faire
Racism in Indigenous-Settler Relations

Drawing on group position theory, settler colonial studies, critical race theory, and Indigenous theorizing, *Canada at a Crossroads* emphasizes the social psychological barriers to transforming white settler ideologies and practices and working towards decolonization. After tracing settlers' sense of group superiority and entitlement to historical and ongoing colonial processes, Denis illustrates how contemporary Indigenous and settler residents think about and relate to one another. He highlights how, despite often having close cross-group relationships, residents maintain conflicting perspectives on land, culture, history, and treaties, and Indigenous residents frequently experience interpersonal and systemic racism. Denis then critically assesses the promises and pitfalls of commonly proposed solutions, including intergroup contact, education, apologies, and collective action, and concludes that genuine reconciliation will require radically restructuring Canadian society and perpetually fulfilling treaty responsibilities.

JEFFREY S. DENIS is an associate professor of sociology at McMaster University and a settler Canadian of mixed European ancestry living on the lands of the Anishinaabe and Haudenosaunee nations in Dish with One Spoon territory.

Canada at a Crossroads

Boundaries, Bridges, and Laissez-Faire Racism in Indigenous-Settler Relations

JEFFREY S. DENIS

UNIVERSITY OF TORONTO PRESS
Toronto Buffalo London

© University of Toronto Press 2020
Toronto Buffalo London
utorontopress.com
Printed in Canada

ISBN 978-1-4426-4654-4 (cloth)   ISBN 978-1-4426-6601-6 (EPUB)
ISBN 978-1-4426-1447-5 (paper)   ISBN 978-1-4426-6600-9 (PDF)

Library and Archives Canada Cataloguing in Publication

Title: Canada at a crossroads : boundaries, bridges, and laissez-faire racism
   in Indigenous-settler relations / Jeffrey S. Denis.
Names: Denis, Jeff, 1980–, author.
Description: Includes bibliographical references and index.
Identifiers: Canadiana (print) 20200156594 | Canadiana (ebook) 20200156756 |
   ISBN 9781442646544 (cloth) | ISBN 9781442614475 (paper) | ISBN
   9781442666016 (EPUB) | ISBN 9781442666009 (PDF)
Subjects: LCSH: Whites – Ontario – Rainy River (District) – Relations with Indians. |
   LCSH: Racism – Ontario – Rainy River (District) | LCSH: Rainy River
   (Ont. : District) – Race relations.
Classification: LCC FC3099.R34 Z7 2020 | DDC 305.8009713/117 – dc23

Cover art: Niiyobinaasiik (Danielle H. Morrison) is of the Sturgeon clan and a member of the Anishinaabeg of Naongashiing. Her cover artwork is inspired by the theme of building bridges, reflected in the coming together of two beings through the practice of ceremony and prayer. In Anishinaabe tradition, every mindful process starts with a smudging ceremony. It cleanses and prepares the spirit for our daily work. It is grounding in times of difficulty. In this depiction, two strands of smoke are intertwined as they carry the prayers and intentions of the two figures to the vastness above, where the Great Spirit sits. In a world that is wrought with tensions and conflict, mutual understanding is found through the coming together and sharing of space and time. Relationship building is the way forward.

This book has been published with the help of a grant from the Federation for the Humanities and Social Sciences, through the Awards to Scholarly Publications Program, using funds provided by the Social Sciences and Humanities Research Council of Canada.

University of Toronto Press acknowledges the financial assistance to its publishing program of the Canada Council for the Arts and the Ontario Arts Council, an agency of the Government of Ontario.

Canada Council   Conseil des Arts
for the Arts   du Canada

ONTARIO ARTS COUNCIL
CONSEIL DES ARTS DE L'ONTARIO
an Ontario government agency
un organisme du gouvernement de l'Ontario

Funded by the   Financé par le
Government   gouvernement
of Canada   du Canada

Contents

Illustrations

Figures

Tables

Acknowledgements

This book is a result of many years of hard work and (un)learning. Writing it would not have been possible without the assistance and support of many individuals and groups.

First and foremost, I would like to acknowledge all residents of the Rainy River District who contributed to this project and who made me feel welcome in the Fort. Thank you to the Fort Frances Chiefs Secretariat, the Sunset Country Métis Council, and the Grand Council Treaty No. 3 for allowing me to conduct research in your territories. I am especially grateful to all interviewees and photovoice participants for generously sharing your time, knowledge, experiences, opinions, and stories. Although some may disagree with some of my interpretations and conclusions, I sincerely appreciate your trust in me and hope that you will find this book useful for working towards a more just and sustainable world.

Several residents deserve special recognition for their role in offering support and guidance at various stages. Some acted as gatekeepers or provided essential documents; others taught me cultural protocols for interacting with Anishinaabe Elders and chiefs; still others invited me to participate in fishing trips, sweat lodge ceremonies, backyard barbecues, birthday parties, and other events. The following people contributed in such critical ways: Gary Allen, Wanda Botsford, Pam Cain, Clint Calder, Cuyler Cotton, Hugh and Robin Dennis, Rhoda Dickson, Naomi Field, Elaine Fischer, Giiwetinoong Binecke (Lori R. Flinders), Dorothy Friesen, Andrew George, Dawn Hayes, Janice Henderson, Bebaamweyaazh (Robert Animikii Horton), Mashkawegaabo (Al Hunter), Sandra Indian (Spirit Horse), Candace Jourdain, Glenn Jourdain, Janet Loney, Peggy Loyie, Bessie Mainville, Mark McCaig, Ed and Betty McLeod, Ed Morrison, Dan Morriseau, Naa-Gaabiinegee-zhig (Calvin Morrisseau), Mona-Rose Morrisseau, Rick Nielson, Paul Pirie,

Joseph Shebagegit, Gilbert Smith, the late Gene Stoltzfus, Mary Ann Swain, and the Right Relations Circle. (It should *not* be inferred that all these individuals were formally interviewed.) The United Native Friendship Centre kindly provided space for photovoice meetings. The Métis Community Hall in Fort Frances, Knox United Church in Emo, and Fort Frances Public Library hosted public presentations of drafts of this manuscript.

The following agencies and organizations provided financial support for research, writing, and photovoice: the Frank Knox Memorial Fellowships, the Harvard University Native American Program, the Multidisciplinary Program in Inequality and Social Policy at John F. Kennedy School of Government, the National Science Foundation, the Social Sciences and Humanities Research Council of Canada, the University of Toronto/McMaster University Indigenous Health Research Development Program, and the Weatherhead Center for International Affairs, Canada Program.

Although I conducted every interview and edited every transcript, the following persons assisted by transcribing one or more interviews: Victoria Boquiren, Rachel Bruner, Romeo Colobong, Rystle Enverga, Tazeen Hasni, Michelle Kellaway, Sandra Kimber, Kasia Krzyzanowski, Doris Liaw, Shana Maracle, Elizabeth McCarville, Jenn Pritchard, Eloisa Sarmiento, Elysse Schlein, Fadek Taki, Linda Zhang, and the Cambridge Transcription Company.

Drafts of various chapters were presented at the following conferences and workshops: American Sociological Association, Canadian Sociological Association, Culture and Social Analysis Workshop (Harvard University), Craft of Ethnography Workshop (Columbia University), Eastern Sociological Society, Harvard-Oxford-Stockholm Aage Sorensen Memorial, Harvard University Native American Program Colloquium, Inter-Ivy Sociology Symposium, National Gathering of Graduate Students in Aboriginal Health Research, Responses to Discrimination and Racism: Comparative Perspectives Symposium (Harvard University), and Qualitatives. I was also invited to present earlier versions of the book manuscript and received helpful feedback from members of the departments of sociology at Lakehead University, McGill University, and McMaster University, and at Reconciliation Kenora's inaugural AGM.

On a copyright note, an earlier version of chapter 5 was published in *Ethnic and Racial Studies* (2012) and an earlier version of chapter 7 in *American Sociological Review* (2015). Excerpts from chapter 9 were published in *Reading Sociology: Canadian Perspectives*, 2nd edition (2011).

The publishers have granted permission to include these materials in the book.

The following scholars and colleagues provided valuable feedback on drafts of book chapters or related presentations: Billie Allan, Christopher Bail, Kerry Bailey, Brent Berry, Amy Bombay, Martin Cannon, Stephen Cornell, Kathy Edin, James Fenelon, Tina Fetner, Crystal Fleming, Victoria Freeman, James Frideres, Eva-Marie Garroutte, Greg Hooks, Anthony Jack, Jiwook Jung, Matt Kaliner, Krista Maxwell, Neil McLaughlin, Wapskhaa Ma'iingan (Aaron Mills), Nissim Mizrachi, John Myles, Dennis Norman, Tony Puddephatt, Howard Ramos, Dean Ray, Jeffrey Reitz, Vic Satzewich, Todd Theringer, Van Tran, Jason Turowetz, Vanessa Watts, and Jana Rae Yerxa.

I am ever grateful to my PhD supervisory committee members – William Julius Wilson, Lawrence Bobo, Michèle Lamont, Mary Waters, and Frederic Wien – for all your advice and support. Mary asked difficult questions that led me to pursue the puzzle of how contact coexists with racism. Larry articulated the theoretical framework (group position theory) on which I most directly build to answer this and related questions. Fred offered thoughtful comments on earlier versions of the manuscript and alerted me to funding sources. And Bill and Michèle meticulously read long and detailed drafts, provided timely and constructive feedback, and pushed me to think both more deeply and more broadly. Thank you.

Special thanks to Neil McLaughlin for being an incredible post-doctoral mentor, for reading every page of this manuscript (often more than once), for providing wise editorial and framing advice, and for offering constant encouragement.

Thank you to Angela Pietrobon for your skilful editorial assistance and moral support, and to Nancy Wills and Nicholas Martino for indexing assistance.

Thank you to University of Toronto Press for supporting this book, to Doug Hildebrand and Jodi Lewchuk for seeing potential in the manuscript, and to Janice Evans for seeing it through to completion. Thanks also to the anonymous reviewers for forcing me to clarify theoretical and methodological details and to be more concise.

Thank you to my parents, Andrzej and Bonnie Denis, for teaching me the values of hard work and perseverance. Along with my brother Derek, you have always encouraged me to pursue my dreams and believed in my ability to achieve them.

Thank you to my father-in-law, Ross Jackson, for driving me and my boxes of field notes all the way back to Toronto in forty-below weather, including a memorable pit stop in Cochrane.

Most of all, thank you to my wife, Lisa Jackson, for taking a chance on a six-month contract in a small town we could not previously locate on a map. You have supported this project from start to finish, with all its ups and downs, from karaoke sing-a-longs to frozen water pipes in the dead of winter. I am eternally grateful for your insights, your patience, your willingness to discuss (and re-discuss) ideas, your keen editorial eye, and your constant love and support. I could not have done this without you.

And finally, thank you to our son, Dylan, who inspired me to complete this book, which I began writing long before you were born and which I hope will contribute in some small way to making a better world for you and your generation and the generations yet to come.

Preface

My body shivered – not from the crisp spring air, but from the realization that I, as a settler-Canadian, am complicit in colonization. This was my first reaction as Mashkawegaabo (Al Hunter), published poet and former chief of Rainy River First Nations, explained the doctrine of discovery. I had come to interview him about the "boundaries and bridges" between Indigenous and non-Indigenous people in the Rainy River District, northwestern Ontario. But as we sat amid the poplar, birch, and spruce trees behind Al's house, listening to the chirping sparrows, feeling the cool breeze, my own assumptions were challenged. What does "equality" mean? Can racism be understood apart from ongoing settler colonialism? Perhaps the "solution" to Indigenous struggles involves more than compensating for past injustices and eliminating the barriers to participation in mainstream Canada. Perhaps it also means honouring treaties and respecting Indigenous self-determination. But why had I learned so little about these topics in school or elsewhere?

Born and raised in the Toronto suburbs, I am a white male settler. Although my parents were not rich or politically connected, I grew up in a pleasant middle-income neighbourhood, across the street from a lush and expansive ravine where I would hike, bike, and sometimes search for Indigenous artefacts. I wore a Chicago Blackhawks jacket and laughed along at racist and sexist jokes in house league hockey locker rooms. It seemed normal.

When I was ten, vivid images of masked Mohawk warriors confronting Canadian soldiers during the Oka Crisis/Kanehsatake Resistance flashed across our TV screen. I had little idea what the conflict was about, but I remember my dad saying that, ultimately, the Indigenous people were right: "It's their land." I didn't know exactly what he meant, but I thought it significant. My parents were generally apolitical. They were also very nurturing and stressed the value of education; I believed that working hard and doing well in school was key to success.

Yet throughout my education I learned virtually nothing about residential schools, treaties, or colonization in Canada. As an undergraduate at the University of Toronto, I was drawn to sociology because it promised tools for understanding social problems such as racism and inequality and seemed to offer insight into the possibilities for creating a more just world. But little was said about Indigenous peoples in Canada. When I attended Harvard on a graduate scholarship, I planned to study racial/ethnic diversity in big cities. But when my (white female) partner Lisa took a public health job at the Northwestern Health Unit in Fort Frances, new opportunities arose.

Lisa frequently told me about the anti-Indigenous racist comments that some white residents routinely made. One even warned her to avoid the reserves, lest the "Indians" send the dogs after her. Yet when I visited her for the first time in 2006, travelling on the (now cancelled) bus from Thunder Bay, I noticed that one had to drive through Couchiching First Nation to get into town. Shopping at Safeway, we saw Indigenous and non-Indigenous residents mixing and mingling together. We soon learned that most Indigenous and settler children attend the same schools and that intermarriage has long been common in the region. But the racist comments continued. How could this be? Thinking this would make a compelling case study of intergroup relations, I discussed it with my PhD supervisor, William Julius Wilson, and he approved.

When I first began this research, then, I had a vague sense that Indigenous peoples had been treated unjustly. From sociology courses, I was aware of the over-representation of Indigenous people in poverty, crime, and suicide statistics, and I knew this had something to do with social inequality. But that was it.

Since 2006, I have learned much from books, articles, and films, especially those of Indigenous scholars and activists. I have learned even more from my interviews and fieldwork with the Indigenous and non-Indigenous residents of northwestern Ontario (Treaty No. 3 Territory) who were kind and patient enough to mentor and teach me. They did not have to do this, and I am truly grateful for their assistance. I am also aware that I am still (un)learning and that this is an ongoing process. I accept responsibility for any errors or oversights that follow.

That said, I am also responsible for telling the following story. As one Anishinaabe interviewee said (paraphrasing), "I'm glad you're doing this research because if I spoke to white people about racism, they'd probably just see another Indian, but if you – as a white guy from a prestigious university – say the same things, some of them might listen." I realized this was a problem and resolved to use whatever power or privilege I have – including the knowledge gained through research – to combat racist and colonialist mentalities and to work with Indigenous peoples for social and environmental justice.

The intended audience for this book, therefore, is not only specialists in sociology or Indigenous studies, but the wider Canadian public. While this is the story of one town and region, many of the processes described here are also evident in other parts of the country. It is a very Canadian story.

My goal is to illustrate how the social psychological underpinnings of racism and colonialism operate today at both interpersonal and community levels, through everyday attitudes, perceptions, and interactions, and to provide an empirically informed account of promising ways forward. Much of what I say will be common sense to many Indigenous people, but I hope that some of them read it too. If my story resonates with them, while also making theoretical contributions and enhancing settlers' understanding, opening new vistas for them and inspiring willingness to take constructive, decolonial action, then I'll know I have done my job.

A Note on Terminology

The appropriate term(s) to identify the original inhabitants of Canada and their descendants is contentious. When I first began this research, I mainly used the term "Aboriginal" because it was the standard term in Canadian law to refer to First Nations, Métis, and Inuit peoples, all of whom are recognized as having "Aboriginal rights" in Canada's Constitution Act (1982). However, this is not the term preferred by many "Aboriginal" peoples themselves. It is a state-imposed concept that seeks to homogenize and assimilate (Alfred and Corntassel 2005). As "a gesture of respect," scholars increasingly use "Indigenous-language terms of self-identification" (Maxwell 2011, x). In northwestern Ontario, First Nations people often refer to themselves as "Anishinaabe(g)"[1] ("The People" in Anishinaabemowin, the Anishinaabe language) or Saulteaux/Boundary Waters Ojibwa (a branch of Anishinaabe from the Rainy Lake and Lake of the Woods area). Many of the local Métis are "Red River Métis" who fled from Manitoba after the 1870 Resistance.

During this study, however, the terms "Aboriginal" and "Native" were widely used by Indigenous and non-Indigenous residents alike. Some residents even used terms such as "Indian" and "half-breed" as a matter of self-definition – sometimes tongue-in-cheek. Given this diversity of language use, I do not prioritize any single term. When writing generally about the original peoples of North America (Turtle Island), I tend to follow most Indigenous scholars and use "Indigenous." When citing my own interview questions, as originally formulated, I sometimes use "Aboriginal" or "Native." More precise terms (such as "Anishinaabe" or "Métis") are used when the distinction is important for making a theoretical or empirical point. And in quoting and describing research participants, I use the labels that they preferred in defining their own identities.

The appropriate term for Canadians whose ancestors arrived within the past five hundred years is not clear-cut either. Some oppose the term "non-Native" because, they say, they were "born here too." Possible alternatives (to which no interviewees objected) include "non-Aboriginal" and "non-Indigenous." Many Indigenous and critical Western scholars use the terms "settler" or "settler-descendant" to highlight the history and ongoing realities of colonization (e.g., Lowman and Barker 2015; Lawrence and Dua 2005). Although I did not use "settler" during my fieldwork, and it was rarely used by interviewees, I am increasingly drawn to this term, mainly as a marker of structural position, not necessarily self-identification. Still, the criteria for defining settlers are contentious; different settlers have different relationships to Indigenous peoples and lands and may experience varying levels of colonial privilege and complicity depending on their class, race, gender, sexuality, and so on. (For more on these debates, see, e.g., Phung 2011, Thobani 2007, Veracini 2010, and Vowel 2016.) Within northwestern Ontario, many Anishinaabe distinguish themselves from "mainstream" Canadians. While at times I use some of the above-mentioned terms, given the relevance of racialization to this book and the fact that 99 per cent of the non-Indigenous residents in this research setting were of European descent, I often refer to them – as they often referred to themselves – simply as "white." Yet I also recognize that definitions of whiteness, like definitions of settlers, are contentious and have shifted across time and place (Maghbouleh 2017; Roediger 1991). In citing earlier studies, I generally retain the original terminology (e.g., "Indian" and "white" in Braroe 1975).

CANADA AT A CROSSROADS

Boundaries, Bridges, and Laissez-Faire
Racism in Indigenous-Settler Relations

Boundaries and Bridges in Indigenous-Settler Relations

On Friday, 15 February 2008, it was revealed that six white girls at Fort Frances High School, all members of the esteemed Muskie girls' hockey team, had filmed themselves dancing to powwow music, holding liquor bottles, and mimicking Indigenous accents. They posted their video on Facebook. It later appeared on YouTube, with a new title ("Disrespect"), and spread throughout the Internet.

This now notorious "video incident" provoked uproar among Indigenous communities, not only in northern Ontario but across North America. Within days, the high school principal received phone calls from as far away as Arizona complaining about "the racist video." On the Friday in question, there were fistfights in the halls. Local First Nations removed their students from school and held emergency community meetings. The girls who made the video were sent home and suspended from the hockey team, just weeks before the playoffs.

When the video incident struck, many white residents I spoke with denied and minimized the racial implications: "It's just some girls being silly"; "they didn't mean anything by it"; "it wasn't racist!" Such phrases circulated like wildfire. Other residents – including school officials – acknowledged that the video was insensitive, but nevertheless called it "an isolated incident" perpetrated by "a few bad apples"; in their view, the alleged problem of "racism" had been "blown out of proportion" by the media and troublemaking activists.

Although some Indigenous residents agreed with such interpretations, the majority (along with a few settlers) perceived the video as another sign of the systemic and interpersonal racism that Indigenous peoples continue to face in twenty-first-century Canada. Regardless of the girls' intentions, the video triggered painful memories of residential school abuse and an earlier era of more overt racism, including the criminalization of powwows and other ceremonies by the federal government.[1] For many Anishinaabe and Métis, the video was a collective insult. Something had to be done.

As residents exchanged heated words on the streets and in online discussion boards, as Indigenous and non-Indigenous youth assaulted each other at school, and as friendships and marriages began to break apart over the video, a few Anishinaabe Elders intervened, arranging healing circles with the girls and their parents. After several private sessions, the entire community was invited to a larger healing ceremony. On 4 March 2008 at the Couchiching First Nation Recreation Complex, approximately seventy-five Indigenous and twenty-five non-Indigenous residents sat in a circle with a drum at the centre. Five of the six girls attended. They listened as Anishinaabe of all ages described the cultural significance of the powwow and why the video was offensive. The girls were given a chance to apologize. While denying hurtful intentions, they said they were sorry. They were then forgiven, and a drum song was played to honour them.

In retrospect, some Anishinaabe described the video as "a gift" because it opened a much-needed dialogue on racism and colonialism and provided an opportunity for all residents to learn and grow. Once the healing ceremony had concluded, however, the status quo was quickly restored, and the broader issues were once again swept under the rug.

Not "an Isolated Incident"

I use the video incident as a vehicle to begin this investigation of the state of Indigenous-settler relations in contemporary small-town Canada. The incident's sociological significance lay not so much in the video itself as in the underlying tensions it exposed and the systematic ways in which each group responded. Whatever their intentions, and whether they realized it or not, the girls who made the video found themselves in the middle of a long-standing struggle for power, status, recognition, and resources that has been unfolding between Indigenous and settler peoples for centuries. In part, the uproar was about the insensitivity of the video itself. As some residents suggested, its highly public nature may have motivated local First Nations to defend their honour on behalf of all Indigenous peoples. However, closer analysis of intergroup relations in the Fort Frances area shows that more was at stake. The tensions expressed during and after the incident went far beyond the video and may be best understood in terms of the shifting "sense of group positions" (Blumer 1958; Bobo 1999) between Indigenous peoples and settler-Canadians – a transformation sparked by wider political, economic, demographic, and cultural trends, and by a repeated local testing of intergroup boundaries.

Drawing on eighteen months of fieldwork (between 2007 and 2009), 160 in-depth interviews and surveys, and a photovoice project with First Nations, Métis, and non-Indigenous (primarily white) residents in the Rainy River District, this book investigates the underlying sources of conflict and cooperation in a twenty-first-century small-town Canadian context. After briefly analysing how the sense of group positions developed historically, I ask: How do Indigenous and non-Indigenous residents today perceive, construct, and negotiate "boundaries" (things that divide) and "bridges" (things that unite)? How does racism get reproduced and contested in daily attitudes and interactions and in critical incidents like the Fort High video and its aftermath? What are the possibilities and limitations of commonly proposed solutions, such as contact, education, apologies and reparations, and collective action?

Theoretically, this work seeks to combine social psychological and sociological approaches to the study of intergroup relations, while also dialoguing with and learning from critical Indigenous perspectives and the growing field of settler colonial studies. It emphasizes how individual thoughts, feelings, and behaviours are structured by wider cultural processes of meaning-making and historically rooted power dynamics. At the same time, it shows how basic social-cognitive and micro-interactional mechanisms serve to reproduce and sometimes challenge – and potentially transform – those larger structures.

My initial theoretical goal was to assess the degree to which general theories of race relations developed in other contexts (such as histories of slavery and segregation or immigrant exclusion) improve our understanding in this case or require revision. I sought to clarify the utility and limitations of the classical psychological, realistic conflict, group positioning, and cultural-sociological models of race and racism.[2] In general, I argue that group position theory offers a useful framework for understanding Indigenous-settler relations because it integrates a concern for identities *and* interests, historical processes *and* contemporary relations. Nevertheless, the theory can and should be enhanced by specifying how a variety of social-cognitive, political-strategic, and cultural mechanisms – suggested by the other models – help to maintain, challenge, and potentially transform the sense of group positions itself.

As my research progressed, I also became increasingly aware of the limitations of all four models and the need to bring them into closer dialogue with settler colonial studies and critical Indigenous scholarship – entire fields that were virtually ignored in my sociological training. As we will see, group position theory offers a better explanation for white attitudes and behaviours than for those of Indigenous peoples. Group positioning dynamics also must be contextualized by the historical and ongoing realities of settler colonialism and Indigenous resurgence.

On a practical level, the future of Canadian society depends on the ability of Indigenous and non-Indigenous peoples to repair their relationships and collectively heal from colonization. In 2008, as the video incident divided Fort Frances, and as long-simmering land disputes proliferated across the country, Prime Minister Stephen Harper formally apologized in the House of Commons, on behalf of all Canadians, for the Indian residential school system and promised to forge a new relationship based on mutual respect. The following year, the Truth and Reconciliation Commission of Canada began its monumental task of documenting the history and effects of residential schools, educating the public, and promoting reconciliation. In 2012/13, the Idle No More movement for Indigenous self-determination and environmental protection took Fort Frances, Canada, and (briefly) the world by storm, pushing questions about Indigenous-settler relations increasingly onto the public radar.

Underlying Idle No More, at least for some Anishinaabe, was the eighth fire prophecy – something I first became aware of when, at the healing ceremony for the high school girls, an Anishinaabe man in his thirties handed me a film called *The 8th Fire*, featuring Anishinaabe Elder and spiritual advisor Dave Courchene Jr. (Pickard and Pickard 2007). As also explained in a 2012 CBC documentary of the same name hosted by Wab Kinew of Onigaming First Nation (ninety-five kilometres northwest of Fort Frances), Anishinaabe medicine people prophesied long ago that after seven historical phases ("fires"), including colonization and its devastating consequences, a "New People" (Oshkimaadiziig) would arise and revive their traditions. They would come to "a fork in the road" where they would have to choose between the current path of materialism, greed, and competition – where some individuals get rich amid widespread poverty and polluted air, water, and soil – or an alternative spiritual path of working together to find new ways of living that restore balance to both social relations and the ecosystems on which we depend. If we choose correctly, an eighth fire will be lit, heralding a new era of peace, justice, and harmony (see Benton-Benai 1988; Simpson 2011). Many Anishinaabe believe that Canada is now at the crossroads.

Towards a Decolonized Group Position Theory: Theoretical Models

Classical Social Psychology

Starting out, I collected data relevant to four broad theoretical models for understanding racism and racial conflict. The first is the classical psychological model, developed by Gordon Allport (1954) and colleagues.

In this model, the basic problem is negative individual beliefs and feelings about the "other" that have been learned through socialization. Stereotyping and prejudice are seen as irrational or pathological. The proposed solution is a combination of intergroup contact and education. As individuals acquire information about and familiarity with one another, they will recognize their common humanity, misconceptions will dissipate, tensions will be resolved, and intergroup attitudes and behaviours will improve. Hundreds of studies, based on large-scale surveys and laboratory experiments, have offered support for the contact hypothesis (Pettigrew and Tropp 2006). Social psychologists also have identified mechanisms whereby intergroup contact/interaction might reduce prejudice, including changes in the social representations of in-groups and out-groups, out-group knowledge, intergroup anxiety, empathy, perspective-taking, collective guilt, and self-disclosure (see Brown and Hewstone 2005; Dovidio, Gaertner, and Kawakami 2003).

While this approach should be commended for its empirical rigour and precise measures of individual-level variables, it also tends to neglect issues of power imbalance and material conflict (Bonilla-Silva 2003; Dixon, Durrheim, and Tredoux 2005; Jackman and Crane 1986). As Dixon et al. (2005, 702–3) put it, not only do "contact interventions leave intact the collective and institutionalized bases of discrimination," they also may be "vulnerable to ideological exploitation"; that is, "the political and economic reforms that are essential to the reduction of racism may be deferred in favour of policies designed to give divided communities the opportunity to 'get to know one another.'" Much the same can be said about approaches that emphasize education – particularly teaching settlers about Indigenous peoples – to the neglect of structural transformation (Lee and Yerxa 2014).

Realistic Group Conflict Theory

An alternative approach to studying race relations is the realistic group conflict model, which outlines the basic problem as being political or material conflict (Levine and Campbell 1972; Sherif et al. 1961). Here, racial groups have real competing interests for power, money, and land. Racism is essentially rational for the dominant group, and discrimination and exclusion are strategic behaviours that protect their objective interests. As social norms shifted in the post–Second World War period and as (overt) biological racism was discredited and condemned, long-standing hierarchical racial structures – including inequities in political, economic, educational, and health outcomes of Indigenous and white people in Canada – remained largely intact.

Thus, while agreeing that racial groups have underlying conflicting interests, some neo-Marxists have sought to reveal the more covert forms of racial domination and the ideological bases of persisting structural inequality (Bonilla-Silva 2003, 2010; Gallagher 2005), including how dominant groups often seek to *avoid* conflict in order to protect their privileges (Jackman 1994). From this perspective, "actors' views stem from a racial ideology expressing their collective group interests" (Bonilla-Silva 2003, 63). Bonilla-Silva analyses the "frames, styles, and stories" whereby actors *"explain and justify* (dominant race) or *challenge* (subordinate race or races) *the racial status quo"* (65; italics in original) in an ongoing process of "racial contestation." Since racial conflicts are fundamentally political, "not an exercise in personal logic," the only solution, he says, is to redistribute resources (66).[3]

This approach has been criticized for reifying "race" and ignoring the social processes whereby groups themselves are constructed (Loveman 1999). In Bonilla-Silva's defence, it is often necessary to set aside one problem to examine another.[4] However, an important but related limitation of the realistic conflict and neo-Marxist approaches is that they tend to neglect issues of identity and recognition. Given the history of cultural genocide and forced assimilation in the Americas, Indigenous peoples may value symbolic resources (such as a strong sense of self) as much as material resources (such as access to homelands); in holistic Indigenous worldviews, the two are inextricably linked (Little Bear 2000; Smith 1999).

Group Position Theory

While the above models have their merits, the approach that I find most useful is Herbert Blumer's (1958) group position theory, especially as developed by Bobo (1999) and colleagues. This approach incorporates aspects of the classical psychological and realistic conflict models, but it goes beyond them in important ways. It recognizes the significance of ethno-racial or ethno-national *identities* (including emotional attachments to one's group), but also the tangible and intangible *interests* (such as control of land) that become associated with such identities once they have been institutionalized, and it emphasizes the *historical and relational* dimensions of group conflict. In this model, prejudice is conceived as a *sense of group position*, "a general attitude or orientation involving normative ideas about where one's group should stand in the social order vis-à-vis an out-group" (Bobo 1999, 449). The essential features are a feeling of superiority on the part of the dominant group, a feeling that the subordinate (or marginalized) group is inherently different and alien, a sense of entitlement to higher status and resources, and a perception of threat from marginalized group members who seek a greater share of (material or symbolic) resources. In this view, prejudice is most forcefully expressed when the marginalized group is perceived as "getting out of place," or as threatening the dominant group's power, privileges, or livelihood (Blumer 1958, 4).

This sense of group positions is also a constituent element of racial ideologies that defend and justify structural inequalities (Bobo 1999). Although Canada is often portrayed as a liberal democratic, peaceful, and multicultural society, it is also characterized by a substantial degree of *systemic racism*: "laws, rules, and norms woven into the social system that result in an unequal distribution of economic, political, and social resources and rewards among various racial groups" (Henry and Tator 2006, 55). Since Europeans began colonizing the Americas in the sixteenth century, "racist practices, perspectives and institutions" have been "foundational" (Wingfield and Feagin 2010, 6–7). Like the United States, Canada remains a settler colonial state, "premised on the diminishment of tribal nations and a denial of Indian rights" (Steinman 2012, 1120). Yet the ideologies that sustain racial inequities "need not be based on overtly negative views about [Indigenous peoples] in order to be effective" (Bonilla-Silva 2003, 74).

In contemporary Canada, the ideological framework within which group position processes operate may be best described as *laissez-faire racism* (Bobo, Kluegel, and Smith 1997). This concept – originally developed to explain the emergence of the dominant configuration of white attitudes towards African Americans in the post–civil rights era, and which I extend to an Indigenous-settler relations context – entails probabilistic (not categorical) stereotyping of Indigenous peoples, blaming of Indigenous poverty and social problems on Indigenous people (not historical or structural factors), and "resistance to meaningful policy efforts to ameliorate [Canada's] racist social conditions and practices" (Bobo 1999, 464).[5] As Bobo says, these views are "rooted in perceptions of threat and the protection of collective group privileges" (ibid.).[6]

In a rare application of group position theory to Indigenous-settler relations, Bobo and Tuan (2006) analysed white Wisconsinites' racial attitudes and behaviours during the 1980s–90s Chippewa fishing rights dispute. Using multivariate analyses to assess five theories of prejudice, they found that perceived group competition (such as agreement that "protecting the rights of Indians hurts whites") and perceived political threat (such as negative evaluations of Indian leaders) were the best predictors of opposition to treaty rights and participation in anti-treaty protests. Moreover, perceptions of group competition and political threat were strongly correlated with and largely accounted for the effects of anti-Indian stereotypes, anti-Indian affect, and self-interest (such as hunting or fishing interests) on treaty rights opposition. Thus, group position theory offered the most complete, coherent, and parsimonious explanation of white attitudes and behaviour among the theories tested. As Bobo and Tuan (2006, 217) put it, "When the Chippewa defied state fish and game regulations" and exercised their treaty rights, many whites perceived this as a "declaration of intent to alter the prevailing group positions ...These actions, when finally upheld as legal by the courts, occasioned powerful feelings of violation among most white Wisconsinites, regarding their 'sense of group position.'" In short, they felt *threatened* by the perceived narrowing of the gap between the Chippewa and themselves.

While the theoretical power of this model is impressive, it also faces limitations. First, it has difficulty accounting for the minority of whites who do *not* feel "violated" or "threatened" by the legal enforcement of treaties and who actively support Indigenous rights. Do these individuals express an alternative sense of group position? If so, how did they develop it?[7]

Second, Bobo and Tuan (2006) examined only half of the equation – the sense of group position among whites. They did not investigate how the Chippewa understand their own position or attempt to challenge whites' sense of superiority/entitlement. Although some past research has examined minority group perceptions of competitive threat, the focus has been on African Americans and recent immigrants in multi-ethnic urban contexts (Bobo and Hutchings 1996). Given the unique history and cultural resources of Indigenous peoples, the fact that they are *nations* and not merely racial/ethnic groups, and the dynamics created by the small-town Canadian setting, group position theory may require modification in this context.

Third, although Blumer's original focus was on meaning and interpretation, most empirical applications of group position theory take a survey-based quantitative approach. While this is useful for establishing overall trends and statistically significant relationships (such as the correlation between perceived group threat and conservative racial policy orientations or, in the Wisconsin case, participation in anti-treaty protests), there is still a need to examine, with qualitative data, how the sense of group positions is actively constructed and maintained (or challenged and transformed), both on a routine basis – in daily interactions and conversations – and during critical incidents (like the video incident) that test intergroup boundaries and threaten the status quo. In this book, I show how some basic social-cognitive and political-strategic mechanisms (including subtyping, conflict avoidance, and victim-blaming) suggested by the first two models help reinforce and sometimes challenge the dominant sense of group positions.

Cultural Sociology of Boundary Work

Bobo and Tuan (2006, 220) also promote "a more explicit linking of cultural-sociology approaches to race and the social psychology of race and prejudice." Specifically, they highlight the relevance of "boundary work," or processes whereby individuals create, maintain, negotiate, and challenge social categories (including racial categories) and membership criteria (Lamont and Molnar 2002). The fourth model I draw upon, therefore, is the cultural sociology of boundary work. In this view, actors construct social identities using culturally available repertoires (shared symbols, stories, and myths) to draw *symbolic boundaries* between "us" and "them" and thereby uphold their moral worth. Analysis of these processes often shows an "intermingling" of "group comparisons," "moral condemnation" of the other, and a "sense of loss and threat" – all essential elements of group position theory (Bobo and Tuan 2006, 221). Such us/them distinctions are often used to create and justify *social boundaries*, or "objectified forms of social difference manifested in unequal access to and unequal distributions of resources and opportunities" (Lamont and Molnar 2002, 168). In other words, as social identities are institutionalized, they often become associated with tangible and intangible interests; group members begin to feel entitled to certain (material and symbolic) resources and may attempt to solidify or create new boundaries (such as segregation laws) to counteract perceived "threats" from out-group members. Thus, although the group position and boundary work models use somewhat different language, the social processes they describe – whereby actors define and protect their identities, statuses, and interests – are similar. Cultural sociology's focus on how individuals interpret the world in and through social interaction is also consistent with Blumer's emphasis on meaning and interpretation, but is enriched through the application of such concepts as "frames" (interpretive lenses for organizing experience and guiding action; Benford and Snow 2000) and "toolkits" (socially learned habits, skills, and styles; Swidler 1986), which provide a more explicit bridge between macro and micro levels of analysis.

Ultimately, I suggest, the prevailing sense of group positions is constituted, reinforced, and potentially transformed by how group members *frame* their relationships with one another, and conceive of and evaluate intergroup boundaries and bridges. However, the capacity of such framing processes to shape social relations is mediated, in part, by adherence to the *interaction norms* that reproduce social boundaries. For example, Eliasoph (1999) shows how political avoidance norms in many civic settings deter individuals from talking about race or, especially, voicing antiracist sentiments, thereby reproducing the racial status quo regardless of their private beliefs. Along with boundary work and framing, therefore, interaction norms (or the breaching of such) may serve as additional mechanisms that constitute and reinforce (or challenge) the dominant sense of group positions.

Bringing in Settler Colonialism

What none of these models considers, however – with the partial exception of Marxist conflict models, which examine processes of primitive accumulation and economic exploitation (Coulthard 2014) – is the ongoing context of *settler colonialism*. As I have come to appreciate through my fieldwork and through more recent immersion in settler colonial studies and critical Indigenous studies, the settler colonial system is a primary source of whites' sense of group position and is fundamental to the status quo that laissez-faire ideologies seek to uphold (see chapter 1). In settler colonialism, colonizers "come to stay" – as opposed to governing from a far-off imperial centre (Bell 2014; Lowman and Barker 2015; Tuck and Yang 2012; Veracini 2010; Wolfe 2006, 388). As part of this process, Indigenous peoples are displaced from their land; colonizers assert sovereignty over the land and expropriate "natural resources" for their own benefit; and there is an ongoing attempt to erase Indigenous ways of life and replace them with those of the colonizer (via such institutions as boarding schools). In practice, however, Indigenous peoples are not necessarily eliminated; aspects of Indigenous cultures may be appropriated by settler society, partly to distinguish it from the "mother country" (Wolfe 2006, 389). What does this mean for group position theory?

The driving motive behind settler colonialism is said to be access to land and resources. Acting on this motive and imposing settler state rule, however, presumes that settlers are *entitled* to the land and its resources and that their social systems are *superior* to those of Indigenous peoples. While these presumptions may not always be fully conscious (or even necessarily accepted by all who participate in the system), I suggest that they are a crucial part of the "background" or "common sense" (Rifkin 2013) that enables the daily reproduction and naturalization of settler occupation of Indigenous lands. Thus, when Indigenous peoples make claims to land or exercise their treaty rights or even merely assert their presence, settlers may feel threatened and seek to keep Indigenous peoples in their place.

Indeed, settler colonialism operates not only through formal political and economic structures, but also through everyday cultural practices in which all settlers are implicated, though we do not all participate in the same way or benefit to the same degree (Furniss 1999). Macoun and Strakosch (2013, 433) summarize some of the narratives that circulate in and legitimize settler institutions, such as the notions that Indigenous society is inferior and in need of help, that the settler state is universal and benevolent, and that colonialism is in the interests of Indigenous people, has ended, or is inevitable. They also identify common emotions among settlers that support such narratives, including a feeling of authority over definitions of Indigeneity, fear of Indigenous people, fear of displacement and dispossession, and frustration at Indigenous people who will not "get over it" (434). Similarly, Tuck and Yang (2012, 10) describe settler "moves to innocence," or strategies to relieve "feelings of guilt or responsibility without giving up land or power or privilege." These include settlers convincing themselves that colonization is in everyone's interest and using "decolonization" as a metaphor for liberal social justice initiatives. Notwithstanding these insights on the role of discourse, emotions, and settler subjectivity, much settler colonial theory (SCT) remains abstract and focused at the macro-structural level. Group position theory, by contrast, draws attention to the complexities and subtleties of everyday perception and interaction, and how these are linked to power dynamics. It also stems from a more empirically grounded tradition that can be easily applied to case study research. As such, it provides insight into social psychological dynamics that complement SCT and helps illuminate how Indigenous-settler relations play out on the ground.

One potential discrepancy is that while SCT emphasizes a logic of elimination (Veracini 2010), group position theory emphasizes exclusion. The settler colonial desire to assimilate Indigenous peoples differs from black-white dynamics in the United States (the context where group position theory originated), where whites have typically sought to segregate and stigmatize blacks. However, the drive to assimilate Indigenous peoples is often half-hearted and derives from the same premise of white/settler supremacy. In fact, I suggest, both logics coexist in Canada: while Indigenous polities are erased or subsumed within the settler state, Indigenous persons remain a foil for the colonial psyche and face a double bind: "you must be like us, but you can never be like us."[8] In other words, Indigenous people are encouraged to assimilate, and those who do so may be conditionally accepted, but, unless they completely renounce their Indigeneity (or at least their Indigenous land and rights), they can never fully be one of "us" because they are still, ultimately, Indian. This contradictory logic *positions* settlers as superior, entitled, and normal.

It is also important to acknowledge here the large and growing literature on Indigenous resurgence, which, rather than seeking settler/state recognition, advocates for restitution (especially the return of land), the regeneration of politically autonomous Indigenous nations, and the creation of sustainable alternatives to hetero-patriarchal colonial-capitalism (Alfred 2005, 2009; Corntassel 2012; Coulthard 2014; A. Simpson 2014; L. Simpson 2011, 2017; Tuck and Yang 2012). Although this is not my primary lens, as a settler scholar I do consider (especially in chapter 10) some of the implications of Indigenous resistance and resurgence for group positioning, and I intend for my work to complement this literature.

To be clear, then, this book primarily uses group position theory to explain how residents construct intergroup boundaries and bridges and how racism gets reproduced in daily attitudes and interactions. Although group position theory cannot explain everything, and Indigenous-settler relations are complex and fraught, group positioning is a crucial and largely overlooked dimension that helps shed light on why racism is such a persistent problem that cannot be eliminated simply by contact, education, apologies, or any other "magic bullet" solution. I also use empirical data to qualify the theory, identifying limitations and supplementing it with other critical perspectives. Settler colonialism is an ongoing process (Wolfe 2006) and will remain so without the "repatriation of Indigenous land and life" (Tuck and Yang 2012, 21). Interrogating the sense of group position that holds settlers together vis-à-vis Indigenous peoples is essential for tackling the social psychological barriers that mediate both racism and settler colonialism.

Indigenous-Settler Relations in Small-Town Canada: A Brief Review of Prior Research

Surprisingly little recent research has examined contemporary locally situated relationships between Indigenous peoples and settler-Canadians. On one hand, there have been outstanding historical analyses of Indigenous-settler relations; insightful critiques of Canadian laws, policies, and institutions affecting Indigenous peoples; thoughtful studies of identity politics, media representations, Indigenous social movements, and the praxis of decolonization and Indigenous resurgence; and comprehensive overviews of the political, economic, and demographic conditions of Indigenous peoples, including class and gender dynamics. There are also growing fields of research on Indigenous health and healing, Indigenous feminism and violence against Indigenous women, urban Indigenous experiences, Indigenous knowledge and pedagogy, Indigenous law, settler solidarity, and Indigenous community economic development, among other areas.[9] However, field studies of Indigenous-settler relationships in concrete community settings have been in short supply since the publication of some classics in the 1970s. Below, I consider four of these classics and two more-recent studies.

First, in his study of "Crow Lake,"[10] northwestern Ontario, Stymeist (1975, 5–7) described a sharp separation of Indigenous peoples from English, French, Italian, Ukrainian, and Chinese Canadians: "They were different in a way that was more significant than the general differences between members of other ethnic constellations ... In the community's terms, the Indians were seen as failures ... who would not help themselves." Rejecting explanations rooted in irrational prejudice, cultural difference, or the social disorganization of Indigenous communities, he argued, from a structural Marxist perspective, that whites' attitudes reflect and legitimize their economic dominance. In other words, white racism stems from and reinforces paternalistic relationships whereby many whites earn their living by "helping" downtrodden Indians through the provision of health care and social services.

The same year, Braroe (1975) published his ethnography of Indian-white relations in a Canadian plains community in southern Alberta. Like Stymeist, he described an almost complete separation of "Indian and white" social, spatial, and moral worlds. Very few Indigenous people lived in town, they were not involved in community organizations, and they were "tacitly forbidden" access to restaurants, parks, and hotels (42); conversely, "whites [were] seldom present on the reserve" (61). On rare occasions when they did interact, there was a logic of "mutual exploitation": each group acted in ways that reinforced their image of the other as "morally inferior" (186). Perhaps most relevant for the present study, Braroe argued that

> the attainment of a morally defensible self for both Indian and White occurs at the expense of the other, and in an atmosphere in which each represents a moral threat to the other. The failure, or refusal, of Whites to extend assistance of some kind to Indians is taken by them as evidence of their moral superiority, but is taken by Indians as proof of White moral failure. Conversely, sharing among Indians is seen by them as a reflection of their moral worth, whereas Whites see it as evidence of the Indians' greediness and as a cause of their low economic and moral status. (186–7)

Building on some of these ideas, Dunk's (1991) ethnography of white male working-class culture in Thunder Bay, Ontario (350 kilometres east of Fort Frances), included an insightful chapter on cognitive classifications and moral evaluations of Indigenous peoples. From a cultural Marxist perspective, he described six local images of "the Indian" (noble savage, backward simpleton, victim of external forces, moral degenerate, welfare bum, and whore) and the meanings that working-class white men attributed to them. He also described a process of regional alienation whereby Indigenous peoples were thought to receive special treatment from the "external white power bloc" (in big southern cities), making them "both the object of derision and the object of envy" (103). Feeling powerless to prevent their own economic exploitation by resource-extraction companies, working-class white men positioned themselves as morally superior to both urban elites and Indigenous neighbours, and stubbornly defended their material privileges over the latter. In other words, Dunk suggests two underlying motives for anti-Indigenous racism: (1) competition for scarce resources (such as the use of tax dollars), and (2) the desire to define a moral hierarchy that justifies existing power relations. This argument is compatible with group position theory. But while it provides a nuanced analysis of the diverse images of Indigenous peoples in the context of white male working-class resistance, Dunk's study was situated in a larger, more diverse setting than Fort Frances and did not consider the perspectives of white women or Indigenous peoples.

Meanwhile, Lithman's (1984) study of an Ojibwa reserve community in Manitoba offered a helpful model of intergroup interaction, based on relative situational power. In this case, most interactions followed the pattern of white segregation (such as exclusion of Indigenous people from desirable paper mill jobs) or white dominance/Indian submission (a retail store in which Indigenous customers were expected to defer to the white owner). Far rarer were bargaining (Indigenous leaders negotiating with federal bureaucrats) and Indian segregation (Indigenous youth making sexual remarks in their own language as white girls passed on the street). Although theoretically possible, no cases of Indian dominance/white submission were observed in two years of fieldwork, a reflection of the vast power imbalance. While this study provided a focus on interaction that was lacking in some of the others, Lithman's emphasis on Indigenous peoples' alleged "opposition culture" and desire to live on reserve and rebuild their own institutions skirted the issue of the roots of white racism, overlooked the impact of forced assimilation on Indigenous attitudes, and led to the pessimistic conclusion that "Indians in the future will probably decrease their contacts with White society ... so that no substantial reasons for change can be seen" (5).

Despite their theoretical differences, all four studies described extreme spatial and social segregation. Only Braroe and Lithman paid sustained attention to the views of Indigenous people, but these authors lacked a critique of the wider context of colonization. More recently, Furniss (1999, 11) examined Indigenous-settler relations in the BC interior, emphasizing how power "resides not only in the policies, practices, and ideologies of state institutions and their officials," but also in the "everyday cultural attitudes and practices of 'ordinary' rural Euro-Canadians." By analysing historical representations, political discourse, private conversations, and community festivals, she illustrated the pervasive operation of a "frontier cultural complex ... in which the categories of Indian and white are mutually exclusive and oppositional and in which Euro-Canadian cultural superiority, material privileges, and political authority are taken as unquestioned truths" (16–17). In short, Furniss elucidated how, even amid relatively high levels of intergroup contact, "common-sense" racist assumptions and control over public definitions of histories and identities perpetuated "an ongoing system of colonial domination" (11). She also documented Indigenous peoples' diverse strategies of coping and resistance. Apart from promoting "reflexive self-awareness," however, her study provided little clue as to how to decolonize settler society.

In her multisite ethnography, Mackey (2016, 4) focused more directly on "conflicts over Indigenous land rights in Canada and the United States." Drawing on settler colonial theory, she highlighted settlers' "deep sense of entitlement ... to own and develop property/land" and the anger and anxiety they felt when their expectations were "unsettled" by Indigenous land claims (8). She traced settlers' "fantasies of possession and entitlement" to European Enlightenment ideas and showed how "Western philosophy, law, and land claims policy have all sought [certainty] for settler projects" (9–10) and how opponents of Indigenous land rights, while making contradictory arguments, consistently drew on colonial assumptions about the certainty of Crown sovereignty and property ownership. But she also showed how these "logics of settler colonialism" were being challenged by Indigenous peoples and solidarity activists and exhorted settlers to "let go of the desire for certainty" and embrace their role as treaty partners (190).

Although these recent studies provide critical insights into ideas and practices that sustain settler colonial structures, a more explicit look at boundary (and bridge) work and group positioning will provide a deeper understanding of the social psychological underpinnings of these processes. Group position theory, for example, draws attention to how settlers' sense of superiority and entitlement gets reproduced (and challenged) in specific perceptions and interactions, including in, but not limited to, land disputes. Appreciating how these social psychological barriers function, even in the face of intergroup contact, education, apologies, and Indigenous-led social movements, seems prerequisite to charting a decolonial path forward. Given this, as well as other recent theoretical developments in social psychology, cultural sociology, and settler colonial studies, the need for theoretical integration, and major practical developments in Indigenous-settler relations since the earlier field studies – including the entrenchment of Aboriginal and treaty rights in the Canadian Constitution (1982),[11] the Oka Resistance (1990), the Royal Commission on Aboriginal Peoples (1996), the Indian Residential School Settlement Agreement (2007),[12] the Truth and Reconciliation Commission (2009–15), and ongoing conflicts over land and treaty rights – more empirical fieldwork was needed.

To what extent do ordinary Indigenous and non-Indigenous people, in concrete settings, still live in separate spatial, social, and moral worlds? How is the sense of group positions reproduced and challenged in small-town Canada today? And how, if at all, is the national discourse on truth and reconciliation playing out in local communities?

To begin to address these questions, I investigate a case where Indigenous and white residents have long had intimate contact – through school, church, and intermarriage – and examine the views and behaviours of both groups. Nevertheless, I find that many of the same social processes described in the classic ethnographies – including paternalistic attitudes, moral distinctions, and regional alienation – persist in twenty-first-century northwestern Ontario and are fully consistent with the revised group positioning framework outlined above.

Setting

The study is set in Rainy River District, a long southern strip of northwestern Ontario, comprising ten rural municipalities and ten First Nation communities (see figure I.1), which is part of Treaty No. 3, an agreement signed between the Crown and twenty-eight Anishinaabe communities in 1873 (see figure I.2).[13] Although the region is rich in natural resources (water, timber, minerals), many economic benefits have been appropriated by multinational corporations, and residents tend to be economically disadvantaged relative to the rest of Ontario, with geographically remote First Nations experiencing disproportionate poverty. The population, sparsely settled over vast distances, includes

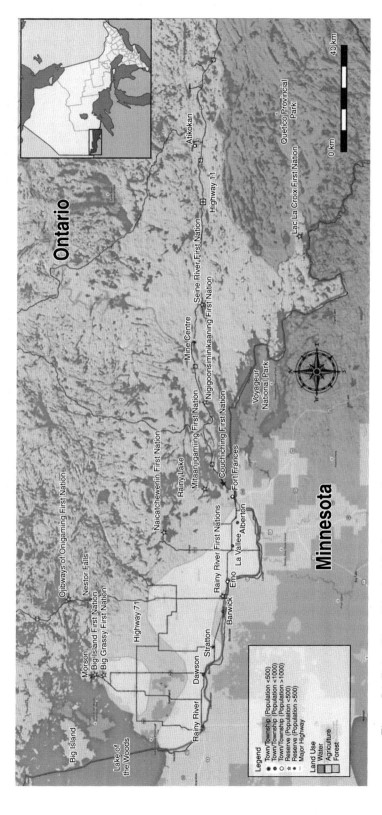

Figure I.1 Rainy River District, Northwestern Ontario. Image provided by Dean Ray.

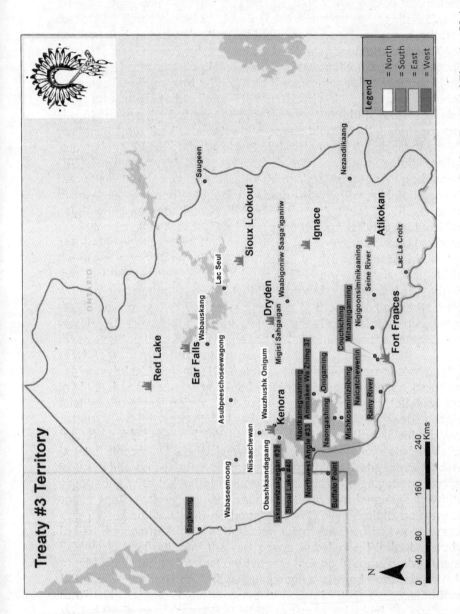

Figure I.2 Treaty No. 3 First Nations. Image provided by Lucas King, water resources specialist, Territorial Planning Unity, Grand Council Treaty No. 3.

Figure I.3 Fort Frances Pulp and Paper Mill. For more than a century, forestry has been the backbone of the local economy. As of 2008, the AbitibiBowater pulp and paper mill (pictured above) employed more than seven hundred residents. Less than 2 per cent identified as Indigenous. Photo courtesy of the author.

mainly descendants of European settlers and a large and growing Indigenous population. The largest town in the district, Fort Frances, has long been known as a mill town (see figure I.3).[14] As of the 2006 census, it had a population of 8,103, with 17 per cent of its residents identified as Indigenous (First Nations or Métis) (Statistics Canada 2007).[15]

Fort Frances is an ideal setting for studying Indigenous-settler relations for at least three reasons. First, the history of the fur trade and the relative absence of non-European immigration have combined to create three distinct groups – Anishinaabe, Métis,[16] and white – which both simplifies and accentuates the intergroup dynamics. Second, although 83 per cent of residents identify as white/Euro-Canadian, the town is located directly beside Couchiching First Nation (with a population of about seven hundred) and within an hour's drive of several other First Nation reserves and predominantly white farming communities. As the only major service centre in a two-hundred-kilometre radius, Fort

Frances is the site of daily intergroup contact, providing many opportunities to observe how Indigenous and white residents interact. Finally, before the video incident, the town had never been in the spotlight for racial tensions, making it a conservative test case. Unlike Kenora (a larger mill town 220 kilometres northwest) or Thunder Bay (whose epidemic of racial violence has been documented by Talaga [2017]), Fort Frances had a local reputation for racial harmony, a source of pride for many residents. The video incident briefly cracked this collective self-image, revealing a darker "underlayment" (Winship 2004) that I sought to explore in my research.

Data and Methods

While the main data source analysed in this book is a series of in-depth interviews with First Nations, Métis, and non-Indigenous (primarily white) residents, I also conducted ethnographic fieldwork and a photovoice project.[17]

Between 2007 and 2009, I lived in Fort Frances for eighteen months, participating in local voluntary groups (such as the Right Relations Circle, a small group of Indigenous and non-Indigenous residents seeking to improve intergroup relations), community events (hockey, karaoke, powwows), and private gatherings (barbecues, fishing trips). While doing so, I took detailed field notes on front- and back-stage behaviours and meanings (those expressed publicly versus only in the presence of trusted others) that are difficult to ascertain through surveys. Although the initial gatekeeper was my partner Lisa, I also developed independent contacts, including at a food bank, a church, and an Anishinaabemowin language workshop. Reactions to my presence varied. Some whites initially expressed racist views, but when told I was studying Aboriginal–non-Aboriginal relations they often avoided the topic; some stopped inviting me to gatherings. In contrast, many Indigenous residents spontaneously shared stories of encounters with racism and invited me for dinner, ceremonies, and recreational activities. In general, I tried to keep a low profile and observe residents in their natural settings.

This fieldwork provided important insight into Indigenous and white identities, public interaction norms, intergroup boundaries and bridges, and the dynamics of interpersonal racism and antiracism in local contexts. It also enabled me to get to know some of the same individuals in multiple settings and see their relationships and perspectives develop over time. Moreover, it was helpful for building the trust necessary to conduct more formal interviews and surveys.

To supplement my fieldwork, I interviewed 160 residents, including 68 First Nation (Anishinaabe),[18] 14 Métis, and 78 non-Indigenous (76 white) people. Interviews were conducted in participants' homes, offices, or public places of their choosing.[19] Using a snowball technique with multiple independent starting points (Biernacki and Waldorf 1981), I chose interviewees based on their special knowledge about a subtopic or other theoretically relevant characteristics. Since I also sought to maximize the range of perspectives and experiences represented, I interviewed both community leaders and ordinary men and women from major economic sectors (forestry, agriculture, education, health) and local Indigenous and settler communities. Although the sample is reasonably representative of the regional adult population,[20] the more important point is that it satisfies the conditions of "theoretical sampling," including natural cases with the necessary conditions to evaluate theoretical assumptions (Wilson and Chaddha 2009). For example, given the hypothesized influence of community leaders and interest groups in shaping the sense of group positions (Blumer 1958; Bobo and Tuan 2006), I oversampled such figures as federal, provincial, and municipal politicians, church leaders, school administrators, senior managers in the forestry sector, First Nation chiefs, Métis Nation of Ontario leaders, and antiracist activists. As the research progressed, to compare racial attitudes I also deliberately interviewed some couples who were intermarried and others who were not.[21]

Through semi-structured interviews, I asked participants about their identities and values, intergroup friendships, boundaries and bridges between Indigenous and settler communities, experiences with racism, and opinions on issues such as the Indigenous-white poverty gap, treaty rights, and the federal government's 2008 residential school apology.[22] When other issues arose or responses were ambiguous, I posed follow-up questions. Interviews ranged in length from under forty minutes to more than four hours, with an average of seventy-seven minutes for non-Indigenous and ninety-two minutes for Indigenous participants.[23] (For selected demographic characteristics of interviewees and residents of Fort Frances and the Rainy River District, see table I.1).

After each interview, participants completed a written survey,[24] which gathered basic demographic information (such as age, education, and employment status) and quantitative measures of key variables of interest, including intergroup contact, racial attitudes, and experiences with discrimination. For example, participants were asked the race/ethnicity, gender, and occupation of their spouse (if relevant) and "five best friends" (proxies for contact). Standard measures of prejudice, including indicators of the sense of group position (Bobo and Tuan 2006),

Table I.1 Selected Demographic Characteristics of Indigenous and Non-Indigenous Interviewees and Residents of Fort Frances, Rainy River District, and Canadian Populations

Characteristic/ variable	Indigenous interviewees (N = 82)	Non-Indigenous interviewees (N = 78)	Indigenous residents, Fort Frances	All residents, Fort Frances	Indigenous residents, Rainy River District	All residents, Rainy River District	Indigenous residents, Canada	All residents, Canada[1]
Population size (% of total population)	N/A[2]	N/A	1,330 (16.8)	8,103	4,615 (21.7)	21,564	1,172,785 (3.8)	31,612,897
% male	55	55	47	48	49	49	49	49
Median age (in years)[3]	50	53	27.4	42.3	27.3	41	26.5	39.5
% First Nation	83	1.3	49	8.3	69	15	60	2.2
% Métis	17	0	49	8.2	29	6.3	33	1.2
% visible minority (non-white, non-Indigenous)	0	2.6	0	<1.0	0	<1.0	0	16.2
% living in Fort Frances	39	65	100	100	29	38	<1.0	<1.0
% living on reserve	49	3.8	0	0	54	11.6	50	1.7
% who grew up in northwestern Ontario	92	77	N/A	N/A	N/A	N/A	N/A	N/A
Formal education								
% less than high school diploma	27	14	33	24	39	30	48[4]	24
% post-secondary diploma or degree	27	51	28	34	26	30	20.5	40
% attended residential school	19	0	N/A	N/A	N/A	N/A	N/A	N/A
Mainstream labour force participation								
Unemployment rate (%)[5]	6.1	3.8	12.8	7.3	13.2	7.9	14.8	6.6
Median household income ($)	N/A	N/A	49,375	54,859	44,233	51,476	43,261	53,634

Characteristic/variable	Indigenous interviewees (N = 82)	Non-Indigenous interviewees (N = 78)	Indigenous residents, Fort Frances	All residents, Fort Frances	Indigenous residents, Rainy River District	All residents, Rainy River District	Indigenous residents, Canada	All residents, Canada[1]
Poverty rate (%)[6]	N/A	N/A	N/A	7.0	34.0[7]	6.6	24.6	8.4
% ever directly employed in forestry	12	19	N/A	N/A	N/A	N/A	N/A	N/A
% of employed labour force in economically fragile industry[8]	5	28	18	27	23	33	N/A	N/A
Household and family characteristics								
% overcrowding	N/A	N/A	N/A	N/A	N/A	N/A	14.7	2.9
% married or common law (15 years and older)	73	77	51.4	58.2	52.4	67.1	48.2	58.4

Sources: Statistics Canada, 2007, 2008. Unless otherwise specified, the information in the last six columns is derived from the 2006 Canadian census.

[1] A more apt comparator to the Indigenous data may be "non-Indigenous residents" rather than "all residents." However, such data are not readily available for some of the key characteristics. The data shown here therefore represent a conservative estimate of Indigenous/non-Indigenous disparities.

[2] Not available/unknown.

[3] The median age of interviewees is substantially higher than that of the general population because I did not interview children.

[4] The education data in the "Indigenous Residents, Canada" column are for First Nations only (see Wien 2009).

[5] Not working but looking for a job (i.e., excludes individuals who are full-time students, retired, disabled, on medical leave, or not seeking paid employment).

[6] The prevalence of persons fifteen years and over falling below Statistics Canada's "low-income cut-off" *after* tax. In this row, the figure for Indigenous residents is for First Nations only (Wien 2009).

[7] One (non-random) survey of 578 Aboriginal residents of Rainy River District found 34% were earning less than $20,000 per year (Newton-Taylor and Larion 2009). The study also found that 24% of all respondents were unemployed, 40% were without a high school diploma, and 20% had a post-secondary degree.

[8] This category includes forestry, small-scale agriculture, and related industries. It is somewhat difficult to estimate the percentages using census data; my approach was to combine all those working in "agriculture and other resource-based industries" and "manufacturing and construction industries" and divide by the total currently employed labour force, fifteen years and older.

and a well-tested self-report measure of experiences with discrimination (Krieger et al. 2005), were also included (for more details, see chapter 4). Although the survey data provide quantitative evidence to support (and sometimes qualify) my arguments, the methodological strength of this study is the rich qualitative data, which illustrate some of the core social processes in action.

The final data source was a photovoice project (Wang and Burris 1997) in which I invited a dozen Anishinaabe, Métis, and white residents to take and discuss pictures on the themes of identity ("Who am I? Who are we?") and boundaries and bridges (sources of division and cooperation). After our group discussions, participants wrote their own captions or asked me to do so based on their descriptions. This project offered unique data, including visual representations of residents' conceptions of boundaries and bridges (inserted throughout the book to help substantiate my arguments)[25] and lively debates about what those images meant. These data not only deepened understanding of theoretically pertinent social processes, such as political avoidance (see chapter 7), but also offered new insights that may not have been obtained through conventional research methods, such as how treaties may be considered both a boundary and a bridge (see chapters 3 and 6). Although photovoice is not an Indigenous research method, it is consistent with many Indigenous research principles (Castleden, Garvin, and Huu-ay-aht First Nation 2008; Kovach 2010). In this case, photovoice was a way of engaging residents in the co-construction of knowledge, developing ongoing relationships, and "giving back" to the community. Participants received free digital cameras and photography skills training from a local Anishinaabe photographer (Joseph Shebagegit, Jr.) who was hired to co-facilitate the project. They also had the opportunity to visualize and voice their concerns, meet new people,[26] and build intergroup bridges. In March and April 2010, the results of this project were displayed at the Fort Frances Museum, an exhibit attended by 750 individual visitors, 12 large groups, the local member of Parliament (John Rafferty), and several First Nation chiefs.[27]

Overall, my methodology was both deductive and inductive. While many of the survey and interview questions were designed to tap theoretically relevant variables from the start, the more open-ended nature of participant observation and photovoice helped generate new ideas that would build on and challenge the theoretical models. My analytic approach varied somewhat depending on the specific research question. In general, however, the interview transcripts, selected field notes, and photovoice captions were coded in ATLAS.ti in an iterative process of back and forth between the three data sources and existing literature. In some cases, grounded codes were developed and new analytic categories created (Charmaz 2006). In others, widely accepted concepts (such as subtyping and laissez-faire racism) were used or modified where appropriate. Reliability and validity were established by triangulating among data sources and by checking interpretations with community members.

Ethical Considerations

A study such as this raises important ethical considerations. For instance, any research involving First Nations, Métis, or Inuit peoples requires community engagement, as per chapter 9 of the Tri-Council Policy Statement on Ethical Research Involving Humans (CIHR, NSERC, and SSHRC 2018). Before conducting interviews or organizing the photovoice project, I therefore met with the Fort Frances Chiefs Secretariat (elected leaders of seven local First Nations) to present my research proposal and seek community feedback and consent.[28] In doing so, I was fortunate to be accompanied by a local Anishinaabe man whom I had befriended and who guided me on cultural protocols for approaching chiefs and Elders (such as offering tobacco). Some chiefs quickly granted approval, others consulted widely with community members before doing so, and one (who was not at the meeting) never responded to my phone calls or emails.[29] I also met separately with the president of the Métis Nation of Ontario's Sunset Country Métis Council. Another Anishinaabe man took me to a sweat lodge to ensure I underwent the necessary ceremonies to pursue this research in a good way. Upon completing the core research, I publicly presented the main findings and arguments to obtain community feedback and then incorporated residents' suggestions into the story that follows.[30] I have also kept in touch with many residents, some of whom emphasized that doing this research meant my entering ongoing relationships with them.

Another ethical issue, especially given the small-town setting and complex local relationships, is confidentiality. I decided to use the town's real name for two reasons. First, as Duneier (2001, 178) writes, disclosing the setting holds the researcher to "a higher standard of evidence. Scholars and journalists may speak with these people, visit the site ... or replicate aspects of my study ... others who were there or who go there [should] recognize [my interpretation] as plausibly accurate." Second, as a Canadian sociologist, I have a moral commitment to identify societal problems and promote social justice. As a settler, I also have a responsibility to honour treaties. I do not intend to label Fort Frances as an especially "racist town" (racism exists across Canada) or to "out" prejudiced individuals. Instead, I seek to show how racist ideologies and systems get reproduced even in a place where intergroup contact is relatively common.

At the individual level, I have sought to protect participants' confidentiality as much as possible. Interviewees and photovoice participants were informed about the risks and benefits of participating in this study before signing the consent form. Although I promised not to link their names to the information they provided (unless they requested to be named), they were aware that the stories they told or references they made could indirectly reveal their identities. Beyond removing names and other identifying information, or using pseudonyms, I sometimes checked with participants to ensure they were comfortable with the material being included. In a few cases, I altered peripheral details of interview quotations or field notes to mask participants' identities. That said, the public nature of some of the stories described in this book means the identities of participants are already well known. Public figures, such as elected politicians, were not promised confidentiality. Moreover, some Indigenous participants requested to be named in part to ensure credit for their ideas (given the unscrupulous history of settler academics taking credit for Indigenous peoples' knowledge). I have made every effort to honour participants' requests and to write this book in a responsible manner. Although some of my findings and arguments may be unsettling, the purpose is to shed light on the challenges to help point the way to a more just, equitable, and sustainable future for all residents of Treaty No. 3 territory.

Overview of This Book

The book is made up of three major sections. First, I investigate how the sense of group positions among Indigenous and settler residents has developed and changed over time, by tracing the history of colonization (and anticolonial resistance) in the region. I then examine how group positions were expressed in the early twenty-first century in the divergent ways in which Indigenous and white residents perceived their relationships, including intergroup boundaries and bridges, and in the laissez-faire and paternalistic attitudes of many settlers, which served to justify their power and privileges. Finally, I evaluate some commonly proposed remedies.

Chapter 1 shows how the balance of power and the concomitant sense of group positions between Indigenous and settler peoples in the Rainy River District have shifted over time from the first days of contact and the fur trade era to the signing of Treaty No. 3, colonial impositions, and accelerated resource-extraction and settlement, to the more recent trends of Indigenous resurgence, regional economic decline, and settler uncertainty.

The next set of chapters analyses how Rainy River District residents perceived intergroup relations and how their perceptions reflected and reinforced their sense of group positions at the time of my research. Chapter 2 shows that white residents were more likely to describe local Indigenous-settler relations in positive terms ("good," "cooperative," "integrated"), whereas Indigenous residents were more critical, using terms such as "strained," "conflictual," "two-faced," and "hostile."

Chapter 3 examines residents' perceptions of intergroup boundaries (sources of division). Despite variations within and between groups, there was a salient conflict in how Indigenous and white residents tended to frame boundaries: whereas many whites viewed treaties, land claims, and self-government as boundaries to better relations, many Anishinaabe and Métis said the "real" boundary was whites' lack of understanding of and respect for their histories, rights, and worldviews.

Chapter 4 looks at one prominent boundary: anti-Indigenous racism. It shows that although old-fashioned prejudice (overt categorical hostility) was rarely expressed in the Rainy River District, more subtle expressions of a sense of superior group position and justifications for racial inequity were widespread. Despite often having Indigenous friends and family members, many white residents blamed Indigenous social problems on Indigenous people themselves, rejected follow-up action on the residential school apology, and resented Indigenous activists.

Taking a more ethnographic approach, Chapter 5 turns to a specific critical encounter between Indigenous and white residents, analysing the strategies and tactics that each group has used to defend or challenge their positions. In this case, the proposed relocation of an Anishinaabe child welfare facility – the Weechi-it-te-win Family Services Training and Learning Centre – to the predominantly white rural township of Alberton (directly west of Fort Frances) provoked heated backlash and boundary-maintenance mechanisms. This chapter shows how the entrenched laissez-faire attitudes of a critical mass of whites, as well as the practical constraints of small-town living, may limit the choice and effectiveness of strategies for change.

Chapter 6 investigates what, if anything, can be done about group positioning, by examining residents' perceptions of intergroup bridges (sources of cooperation). Overall, I found more consensus about what brings Indigenous and non-Indigenous people together than about what divides them. However, white and Indigenous residents also tended to frame bridges in ways that reflected and reinforced their sense of group positions. Whereas many whites conceived of bridges in terms of Indigenous people's willingness to assimilate, for example, Indigenous residents highlighted opportunities to learn about and experience Indigenous cultures.

The final four chapters take a closer look at four potential bridges and assess their strengths and limitations in this small-town, settler-colonial context. Chapter 7 evaluates the claim that if Indigenous and non-Indigenous people just get to know each other, everything will be fine – a simplified version of the contact hypothesis (Pettigrew and Tropp 2006). It shows that, unlike in towns studied in earlier field studies, in Fort Frances there has been widespread intergroup marriage and friendship and frequent interaction between Indigenous and non-Indigenous people. Yet this extensive contact has coexisted with pervasive prejudice and discrimination. I investigate how this paradox has been sociologically constructed and maintained, via mutually reinforcing mechanisms such as subtyping (Indigenous individuals who violate stereotypes are viewed as exceptions) and political avoidance (racism is treated as the elephant in the room).

Chapter 8 evaluates another commonly proposed bridge: education. With more accurate information, many assume, settlers will reject stereotypes and embrace egalitarian principles. Many also believe that improving education for Indigenous children will enhance their opportunities and acceptance in Canada. While there may be a kernel of truth to these views, as with contact, the situation is more complex, and education is limited as a remedy for structural inequity.

Chapter 9 examines Indigenous and settler perspectives on the federal government's 2008 residential school apology. Although the apology was arguably well crafted and delivered – including virtually all the contents and stylistic elements of an "effective" apology, as defined by sociolinguists and psychologists (Blatz, Schumann, and Ross 2009) – Indigenous and white residents interpreted it in divergent ways: many whites saw it as a final act of "closure," whereas most Indigenous residents saw it as an early step in an ongoing "healing journey."

If contact, education, and apologies are insufficient, what else can be done to transform the sense of group positions and tackle racism and colonialism? Chapter 10 shows that although organized protest and other forms of collective action frequently temporarily exacerbate perceptions of group threat (among other risks and limitations), they are often necessary to gain attention, bring governments to the table, and generate meaningful change in Indigenous-settler relations. Such actions are becoming increasingly common in the Rainy River District and elsewhere in Canada, as demonstrated by the Idle No More movement.

Ultimately, I suggest, a combination of all four strategies – and more – will be necessary to overcome the prevailing sense of group positions and the systems of racism and colonialism that it supports. Reconciliation (or anything resembling it) will require ongoing dialogue about what it means to be treaty partners and a willingness to act as such. As the Anishinaabe say, the eighth fire is upon us. We have come to a fork in the road. The path that we – Indigenous and settler peoples in the Rainy River District and beyond – collectively choose will determine the future of Canada and of our relationships to one another and the land.

Chapter One

Colonization and the Development of Group Positions: A Brief History of Indigenous-Settler Relations in the Rainy River District

Now you see me stand before you all; what has been done here to-day has been done openly before the Great Spirit, and before the nation ... and in taking your hand, I hold fast all the promises you have made, and I hope they will last as long as the sun goes round and the water flows, as you have said.

Mawedeponais (quoted in Morris 2009 [1880], 73)

Chief Mawedopenais of Long Sault Rapids, just west of Fort Frances, spoke these words to Alexander Morris, lieutenant-governor of Manitoba and Crown representative, upon signing Treaty No. 3 at the Northwest Angle, Lake of the Woods, on 3 October 1873. This event, and the Crown's subsequent neglect of Anishinaabe understandings of the treaty, marked a pivotal transition in Indigenous-settler relations in the Rainy River District.

As Blumer (1958, 5) says, group positions are a "historical product ... set originally by conditions of initial contact," including power (i.e., material resources, military force, numbers), self-conceptions, aims, and opportunities. Subsequent interactions, especially in the political-economic arena, "may mould the sense of group position in ... diverse ways" (5). Yet as group positions become "entrenched" in the "prevailing social order," they are not constructed anew at whim, but rather carried forward by shared memories and institutions, and only rarely modified by "big events" that capture public attention, "awaken strong feelings of [group] identification," and "raise fundamental questions about relations" (6–7).

Understanding how the sense of group positions developed and changed over time, including why, at the time of my research, many white settlers in the Rainy River District expressed a sense of group superiority/entitlement and perceived threat, requires tracing the history of colonization (and anticolonial resistance) in the region. This chapter shows how the balance of power between Indigenous and settler peoples shifted over time from the first days of contact and the fur trade era to the signing of Treaty No. 3, colonial impositions, and accelerated resource-extraction and settlement, to the more recent Indigenous resurgence, regional economic decline, and (increasing) settler uncertainty. The story here is local, but similar dynamics have occurred across the country at various times.

In this case, the Anishinaabe had the upper hand early on, playing fur trade companies against one another, charging tolls, and evicting miners. They bargained hard during treaty negotiations. But Canadian governments soon ignored Indigenous understandings of the treaty and imposed a new social order. "Free land" was given to settlers, old-growth forests were gutted, gold was mined, and primarily white towns flourished, while First Nations communities were forcibly relocated, segregated on reserves, or "extinguished," and Indigenous children were taken to residential schools. Over the past few decades, however, the tables have started to turn again. As many white residents struggle with mill, mine, and farm closures and population decline, Indigenous communities are healing, growing, and rebuilding, and the balance of power and sense of group positions is increasingly in flux.

What follows here is not a complete history of the region or its political economy, but rather a general overview of major developments and turning points. My aim is to set the context for subsequent chapters that will examine in more detail how Rainy River District residents make sense of their relationships, interact with one another, and reproduce or challenge historically rooted structural inequities and racist ideologies.

Early Contact and the Fur Trade Era

Indigenous peoples have lived in what is now northwestern Ontario for at least nine thousand years. The Anishinaabe – specifically, the Saulteaux tribe, or Boundary Waters Ojibwa – likely arrived in the northern Great Lakes region between the fourteenth and sixteenth centuries. According to Anishinaabe Elder Edward Benton-Benai (1988), they migrated from the eastern seaboard, stopping at various locations, over a period of about five hundred years, following prophecies to move west ("where food grows in the water") (see also Warren 1984 [1885]; Willow 2012).

An independent, self-governing nation, the Anishinaabe had their own (Algonquian) language, laws, institutions, economic system, social organization, and cultural and spiritual practices. They followed a

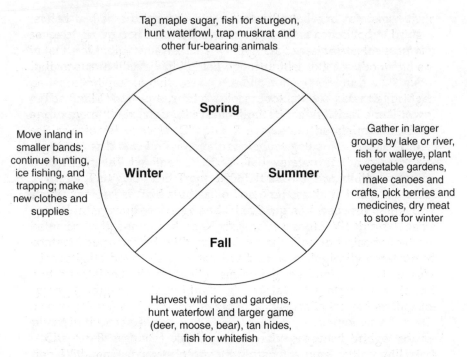

Tap maple sugar, fish for sturgeon,
hunt waterfowl, trap muskrat and
other fur-bearing animals

Spring

Move inland in
smaller bands;
continue hunting,
ice fishing, and
trapping; make
new clothes and
supplies

Winter

Summer

Gather in larger
groups by lake or river,
fish for walleye, plant
vegetable gardens,
make canoes and
crafts, pick berries and
medicines, dry meat
to store for winter

Fall

Harvest wild rice and gardens,
hunt waterfowl and larger game
(deer, moose, bear), tan hides,
fish for whitefish

Figure 1.1 Traditional Anishinaabe Seasonal Rounds. Illustration adapted from McQuarrie 2003 and Waisberg 1983.

patrilineal clan (*doodem*) system, had a Grand Council and Midewiwin (Grand Medicine Society), and practised a semi-nomadic lifestyle, travelling to specific locations each season to harvest the available resources (see figure 1.1). They lived in wigwams, travelled by birchbark canoe and snowshoe, and traded with other Indigenous nations. Individuals and bands retained significant autonomy, and leaders governed by "influence and respect rather than institutionalized coercive force" (Willow 2012, 28).

The first contact with Europeans in the region occurred in 1688 when French explorer Jacques de Noyon travelled west on Lake Tecamamiouen (later named Lac la Pluie, or Rainy Lake) on a mission to persuade the Anishinaabe to trade directly with the French, rather than with the English through Cree (Nehiyawak) intermediaries. At this time, Cree and Assiniboine peoples also lived in the region, and the Anishinaabe were at war with the Sioux to the south.

By 1731, when the nephew of Pierre Gaultier de Varennes, sieur de La Vérendrye, established Fort St Pierre at what is now Fort Frances –

making it "the oldest continuous [non-Indigenous] settlement west of Lake Superior" (Bray and Epp 1984, 13) – the Anishinaabe were in firm control of the region. Although wary about the post being built on their summer camp grounds without consultation, they developed peaceful trade relations with the French, trading beaver pelts and other furs for guns, knives, kettles, cloth, and other goods.[1]

After the Seven Years War (1756–63), the British gained control of all French holdings in North America. Scottish fur traders replaced the French, but the Anishinaabe, having supported the French, mistrusted the Scots; when they arrived, they were "denied passage ... and forced to turn back" (McQuarrie 2003, 14). The Montreal-based traders therefore turned to Frenchmen who had been living among the Anishinaabe, learning their language and skills and earning their respect. In 1779, a new trading post, Fort Lac la Pluie, was built downstream from the Koochiching waterfall, close to where the Anishinaabe harvested sturgeon each spring and whitefish each fall. Employing twenty to forty men at a time, many of whom married and had children with local Anishinaabe women, Fort Lac la Pluie soon played "a vital role in the vast fur-gathering empire of the North West Company" (16). It was a relatively large settlement, with living quarters, warehouses, gardens, and wheat fields, and a crucial resting and transfer point.

In 1792, the Hudson's Bay Company (HBC) established a competing post at Manitou Rapids (about fifty kilometres downstream). As local historian Neil McQuarrie (2003, 16) says, "The Anishinaabe took every advantage, expertly playing the two companies off against each other" and ensuring good prices. After the HBC took over the North West Company in 1821, the fur trade declined in many regions, but remained profitable here well into the 1860s. Although the old fort was abandoned, a newer HBC post (Lac la Pluie House) still overlooked the falls, and competition continued with the American Fur Company post across the river at International Falls. Once again, the Anishinaabe of the Rainy River District "relished their position of power between the two sets of traders" (McQuarrie 2003, 21).

In 1830, HBC governor Sir George Simpson and his wife, Lady Frances, visited the area; the Town of Fort Frances was named in her honour. A decade later, Governor Simpson met with an assembly of over five hundred Anishinaabe in Fort Frances who threatened to withhold wild rice, "'the staple article of provision' for Lac la Pluie traders, unless the company ceased its attempt to end the liquor trade in the district" (Holzkamm, Waisberg, and Lovisek 1995, 179). Recognizing their strength, Simpson complied: "I consider it good policy to avoid any difficulty or dispute with them," he said (ibid.). Indeed, the fur trade in this region was generally cooperative and mutually beneficial, but largely proceeded on Anishinaabe terms.

In the mid-nineteenth century, the Anishinaabe of the Rainy River District had "an expanding population [more than tripling between 1821 and 1875], national gatherings, independent tribal government ... and large-scale athletic competitions" (169). They were described by Euro-Canadian officials and religious leaders as "tall, strong, and well built" (Reverend Peter Jacobs 1852, quoted in Holzkamm, Waisberg, and Lovisek 1995, 173), and "saucy and independent of the Hudson's Bay Co." (Dawson 1859, 26). Nevertheless, the wider political-economic environment was changing, and with the influx of settlers across the continent, the Confederation (and expansion) of Canada, and the signing (and violation) of Treaty No. 3, the local balance of power and sense of group positions also was transformed.

Treaty Negotiations

In 1869, two years after Confederation, the Hudson's Bay Company surrendered its charter over Rupert's Land and the North-Western Territory[2] to the British Crown. Under the Royal Proclamation of 1763, however, the Crown was still obligated to purchase these lands or obtain a legal surrender from the Indigenous peoples. Now wishing to open said lands for settlement, agriculture, and large-scale resource extraction, and expand the Dominion of Canada, the federal government initiated a series of eleven Numbered Treaties between 1871 and 1921. As a strategically located gateway to the west, the Rainy River District was among the government's first priorities. Yet the process of treating with the Anishinaabe took a challenging four years and more than a little coercion.

Although the Royal Proclamation recognized a limited form of Indigenous land rights, it also assumed the crown's right to purchase Indigenous lands or extinguish "Indian title" whenever it saw fit. This sense of entitlement was rooted, at least in part, in the doctrine of discovery, a set of fifteenth-century papal decrees stating that the first European Christian nation to "discover" uninhabited lands, or lands not being put to "productive use" (however European Christians defined it), was "legally justified in assuming full, sovereign ownership" (Henry and Tator 2006, 107).[3] The Anishinaabe begged to differ.

In 1859, the government sent Simon Dawson, an engineer/cartographer, to survey the territory between Lake Superior and the Red River Settlement to determine its suitability for agriculture and transportation routes west. Upon arriving in Fort Frances, he was invited to a

Grand Council meeting, grilled on the purpose of his expedition, and told by Anishinaabe chiefs that he was allowed to explore the country on the condition of no more settlement "without their being consulted" (McQuarrie 2003, 24). The chiefs also said they would be willing to meet with Canadian leaders to discuss their relationship, "as they wished to be friends" (ibid).

The construction of the Dawson Route was prompted by the Red River Resistance in 1870 when Prime Minister Macdonald ordered Colonel Garnet Wolseley and twelve hundred troops to quash the Métis uprising.[4] Starting from Fort William, they followed Dawson's route, and, along the way, built "roads, bridges, portages, and blockhouses for storage," and stopped in Fort Frances where they "left a surplus of supplies" and "started a 36-bed hospital" (Fort Frances [FF] Museum Permanent Exhibit 2006/07). Over the next decade, the Dawson Road was further improved and became the main route west until the Canadian Pacific Railroad was completed in the 1880s, passing through Dryden and Kenora instead.

Anishinaabe leaders (such as Chief Wabinogigok of Seine River) continued to regulate access to their lands and charged tolls for passage over their waterways. The Wolseley expedition was no exception, and they heeded Dawson's advice to take a "cautious and delicate approach" (Chute and Knight 2006, 110). On multiple occasions, the Anishinaabe blocked the establishment of Christian missions. In 1872, Chief Blackstone and his band (east of Fort Frances) evicted American miners and demanded compensation for wood. As Reverend Salt at Rainy Lake wrote in his journal in 1855, the Boundary Waters Ojibwa were adamant about their "claim [to] not only territorial but sovereign rights" (Waisberg and Holzkamm 1998, 3).

Thus, when approached about entering a treaty with the Crown in 1870, the grand chief of the Grand Council responded:

> We want ... much that the White man has to give, and the White man on his part wants roads and land. When we meet next summer, you must be prepared to tell us where your roads are to pass and what lands you require ... do not bring settlers and surveyors amongst us, to occupy and measure our lands, until a clear understanding has been arrived at, as to what our relations are to be. (Waisberg and Holzkamm 1998, 4)

The first two attempts to negotiate a treaty in 1871 and 1872 failed because the government considered Anishinaabe terms to be too "extravagant." Yet Chief Mawedopenais of Manitou Rapids emphasized the value of his people's land and their inherent rights to it:

The sound of the rustling of the gold is under my feet where I stand; we have a rich country; it is the Great Spirit who gave us this; where we stand is the Indians' property, and belongs to them. (Morris 2009 [1880], 62)

Meanwhile, the Red River Resistance was suppressed, Métis leader Louis Riel fled to the United States, and Treaties No. 1 and 2 were signed in Manitoba. Simon Dawson persuaded the government to return to negotiations and approve higher compensation, given the importance of the region and the military strength of the Anishinaabe.[5] As Reverend George Grant wrote on an 1872 expedition through the Rainy River Valley:

[The Anishinaabe] surely have rights to this country, although they have never divided it up in separate personal holdings ... And now a foreign race is swarming over the country, to mark out lines, to erect fences, and to say "this is mine and not yours" 'til not an inch shall be left the original owner. All this may be inevitable. But in the name of justice, and of the sacred rights of property, is not the Indian entitled to liberal, and if possible, permanent compensation? (McQuarrie 2003, 25)

In response, the federal government appointed Alexander Morris, a Conservative lawyer and lieutenant governor of Manitoba, the North-West Territories, and Keewatin, to lead the negotiations, and authorized somewhat better terms. Although the Anishinaabe wished to meet at Fort Frances, their political headquarters, Morris insisted on the Northwest Angle, which offered a quicker escape route to Manitoba. He was accompanied by a large militia, Simon Dawson, Robert Pither (HBC factor and Indian agent at Fort Frances), and George McPherson ("an intelligent half-breed trader" and interpreter), among others, while the Anishinaabe contingent included twenty-two chiefs and approximately eight hundred men, women, and children.

Discussions began with the Anishinaabe demanding compensation for timber cut on their lands since 1868, accusing Dawson of breaking promises during the Wolseley expedition, and questioning whether the government could be trusted again. During three days of intense debate, proposals and counter-proposals, the chiefs reiterated that "it was the Indian's country, not the white man's" (Morris 2009 [1880], 59). As reported by Morris, Mawedopenais insisted:

All this is our property ... the Great Spirit has planted us on this ground where we are, as you were where you came from ... The white man has robbed us of our riches, and we don't wish to give them up again without getting something in their place. (62–3)

In response, Morris told the Anishinaabe that if they did not accept his terms "the conference was over" and he would tell the queen that they "refused to make a reasonable treaty." With a paternalistic flourish, he added, "I shall go away feeling sorry for you and for your children that you could not see what was good for you and for them" (50).

After this threat, the chief of Lac Seul, a northern community that had begun to struggle from the dwindling supply of game (due to the fur trade) and the lack of arable land and throughways (unlike the fertile Rainy River Valley), said he was still interested in a treaty. Exploiting these divisions, Morris exclaimed that he knew the chiefs were "not all of one mind" and "your interests are not all the same," but that "he would make a treaty with those bands that were willing to accept his terms" (64–5). The chiefs then assembled separately for five hours. Métis interpreters held "a very lengthy and exhaustive discussion" with them. According to the Manitoban newspaper account reported by Morris, on 3 October 1873 the Anishinaabe ultimately agreed "to accept the Governor's terms, with some modifications" (66).

The proceedings concluded with Mawedopenais stating that the agreement would stand "as long as the sun goes round and the water flows" (73). Upon shaking his hand, Morris replied that he would "keep all my promises, in the firm belief that the treaty now to be signed will bind the red man and the white man together as friends for ever" (73).

The precise terms of the treaty have always been contentious. According to the Crown's "official" text, the treaty meant that twenty-eight Saulteaux bands (Anishinaabe communities) in what is now northwestern Ontario and southeastern Manitoba "surrendered" 55,000 square miles (88,500 square kilometres) of land in exchange for reserve lands, annual annuities, other goods and services (such as fishing nets, ammunition, farming tools, and schools on reserve), a ban on liquor sales, and the right to continue hunting and fishing in their traditional territories. Even in this version, the terms were more generous than the previous two treaties, including larger reserves (640 acres per family of five, rather than 160 acres), higher annuities (five dollars per person per year, rather than three dollars), agricultural equipment and supplies, and harvesting rights (Miller 2009). Given the government's "take-it-or-leave-it approach," these concessions were impressive (Dickason 2006, 177). They also forced the government to revise Treaties No. 1 and 2 and set the precedent for future treaties.

According to the Anishinaabe, however, the treaty was an agreement to *share* the land in "peace and friendship" (Morris 2009 [1880], 72); it enabled Canadian settlement in their territory on condition that the Anishinaabe received just compensation and were able to continue their traditional ways of life (for Anishinaabe interpretations, see Mainville 2007; Mills 2017). The Paypom Treaty, which is based on the notes of Joseph Nolin, a Métis interpreter hired by the chiefs, and which corresponds more closely with Anishinaabe oral history, contains striking differences from the government's text.[6] It says nothing about land "surrender." Nor does it mention the "taking up" clause, whereas the government's text says Indigenous harvesting rights are "subject to such regulations as may, from time to time, be made, and saving and excepting such tracts as may, from time to time, be required or taken up for settlement, mining, lumbering, or other purposes." By contrast, the Paypom document states, "The Indians will be free as by the past for their hunting and rice harvest" (see Willow 2012, 42–9). Moreover, it has been alleged that Canadian government officials may have written the treaty text beforehand, based on previous negotiations (Daugherty 1986). These conflicts have never been resolved and, as of this writing, remain at the root of ongoing land claims and other legal actions.

The development of a treaty between the Anishinaabe and the crown potentially provided the foundation of a equitable, cooperative, and mutually beneficial relationship. From an Anishinaabe perspective, however, the treaty was quickly and repeatedly violated, and relations deteriorated (at least at the government-to-government level). Over the next few decades, the regional balance of power shifted dramatically, turning the sense of group positions on its head.

Colonial Settlement and Treaty Violations

After the signing of Treaty No. 3, the first non-Indigenous Canadians with the intention of becoming permanent settlers (as opposed to explorers, missionaries, or traders, some of whom intermarried and remained in the district) began travelling to Fort Frances via the Dawson Route. Major advertising campaigns promoted the influx of settlers. As Frank Yeigh of the Department of Crown Lands wrote in 1892, perhaps embellishing somewhat given the long, cold winters and relatively short growing season:

> No part of the Dominion offers better advantages to the farmer-immigrant or the man who desires to hew out a home in a new country, than the Rainy River District ... in its agricultural capabilities ... its ... navigable

waterways ... its healthful and equable climactic conditions ... the comparative ease with which the virgin land can be cleared and tilled ... the remunerative employment ... in connection with the extensive lumbering operations [and] great mineral wealth ... the free granting of farm lands by the government; and ... the building of colonization roads and bridges ... the District presents attractions possessed by few and certainly not surpassed by any other part of Canada. (Yeigh 1892)

Under the Rainy River Free Grants and Homestead Act (1886), the Ontario government surveyed the district, laying out twenty square townships and dividing them into 160-acre plots that were "granted free of charge" to each adult male settler willing to build a house and cultivate the land (FF Museum Permanent Exhibit 2006/07).[7] Settlers could also purchase up to 80 more acres, including riverfront lots, at one dollar per acre. "To help the settlers," as the Fort Frances Museum Permanent Exhibit states, "the government shipped in, by steamboat, loads of cows, horses, sheeps, and pigs." By the 1890s, Fort Frances was "a thriving farming community," with many new homes and businesses.

Forestry operations also accelerated, with sawmills operating along Rainy River and at Lake of the Woods. Agriculture and forestry were seen as interdependent economic engines:

As the lumbermen removed the trees, they were helping to clear the land. Settlers could then turn this land into new farmland. The farmers would then be able to supply the lumber camps with food, and ... add to their income by working as lumberjacks during the winters. (FF Museum Permanent Exhibit 2006/07)

Several gold mines also opened in the region. The first "colonization road" was constructed in 1885, connecting farmers and lumberjacks to Fort Frances (see figure 1.2).[8] By 1891, there were 7,000 whites and 2,800 Indians in the Rainy River District, a significant change from two decades earlier when Indigenous peoples had been the majority (Drache 1983).

As the settler population grew, the Anishinaabe were devastated by smallpox epidemics in the 1880s and early 1900s and by the 1918/19 influenza pandemic. Meanwhile, government policy towards Indigenous peoples had become increasingly coercive and paternalistic. Contrary to the spirit of a treaty (as understood by the Anishinaabe), the 1876 Indian Act designated Indigenous peoples as "wards of the state" and unilaterally distinguished "status" from "non-status" Indians, thereby

Figure 1.2 Colonization Road, Fort Frances, Ontario. Many towns in northwestern Ontario, including Fort Frances, have a Colonization Road – a visible reminder of a pivotal historical and ongoing process. Photo courtesy of the author.

determining who was eligible for treaty rights and other state benefits.[9] For example, it denied Indian status to First Nation women who married non-status men and to First Nation persons who attended university or voted in Canadian elections.[10]

The federal government also imposed a band council system,[11] undermining traditional governments, and assumed the right to veto band legislation and depose Indian chiefs. As "free land" was being granted to white settlers, Indigenous peoples were increasingly driven off their lands and restricted to reserves (Daschuk 2013). Under the pass system,[12] established in 1885 (but inconsistently enforced), Indigenous people were forbidden to leave and non-Indigenous people forbidden to enter Indian reserves without permission of the local Indian agent.[13] Indigenous ceremonies were banned, and children began to be abducted and placed in residential schools (for detailed reviews, see Miller 1996; Milloy 1999; Royal Commission on Aboriginal Peoples [RCAP] 1996; Truth and Reconciliation Commission [TRC] 2015).[14]

In the Rainy River District, these and other government regulations, and the ongoing appropriation and destruction of Indigenous harvesting areas, were associated with substantial declines in Indigenous peoples' political, economic, and social position and overall well-being. During treaty negotiations, Simon Dawson had promised to assist in the selection of reserves (both wild lands and farm lots) that would have "minerals and timber capable of providing revenue to swell Native coffers" (Chute and Knight 2006, 116). However, Ottawa passed an order-in-council in 1874 that no reserves should include "any lands known to the Commissioners to be mineral lands." When gold was discovered on the Wauzhushk Onigum (Rat Portage) reserve near Kenora in 1886, over half a million dollars in gold was mined, and the local Anishinaabe received none of it.

Nevertheless, seven reserves were selected along Rainy River, representing 9 per cent of the fertile clay plain, including riverfront villages and fishing stations (Waisberg, Lovisek, and Holzkamm 1996). Additional reserves were set aside north of Fort Frances, on Rainy Lake, and at various locations east.

By this time, the local fur trade had virtually ended. As treaty negotiators and government officials had encouraged, some Anishinaabe turned more to farming. The Anishinaabe had long sold agricultural produce, including corn, potatoes, pumpkins, onions, and carrots, to fur traders. In the first decade after the treaty, farming output increased. Reports by Inspector McColl in the early 1880s observed "decided advancement" and increased cultivation, especially among the Rainy River and Rainy Lake bands. In 1884, he said, "The industry and perseverance of these Indians are most remarkable" (quoted in Waisberg and Holzkamm 1993, 184) and noted their prime location for supplying timber companies.

In 1881, however, the federal government prohibited the sale of Indian produce to non-Indian consumers (without written permission of the Indian agent), to white farmers' benefit. Additional barriers to agricultural development on reserves included lack of training and inadequate equipment, despite many complaints to government that these were treaty promises. Lacking any response, the Anishinaabe of the Rainy River District ceased commercial farming. Between 1886 and 1900, cultivation on the Fort Frances agency reserves fell from 186 acres to 13.5 acres. Instead, the Anishinaabe relied more heavily again on hunting, fishing, and gathering, and sometimes found employment in lumber camps and gold mines, on the CPR, and as fishing guides and domestic servants.

The new resource-extraction industries quickly took their toll on Indigenous peoples and their lands and waters. Although the "lumber business breathed new life into the economy of Fort Frances ... virtually

the entire shoreline of Rainy Lake, as well as land along the streams leading to it on both sides of the border, was logged over" (McQuarrie 2003,
35–6). Magnificent old-growth white pines (used for ship-building)
were nearly extinct.

Flooding from navigation and power dams caused further problems. A petition from the Grand Council in 1892 charged that flooding
of their wild rice crops by a dam at the outlet of Lake of the Woods
was "the principal cause of our starving in winter" (quoted in Waisberg
and Holzkamm 1998, 15). Believing that the treaty had promised
non-interference in Anishinaabe harvesting practices, they added, "We
have kept our part of the Treaty, is it not hard that the government
should not keep theirs?"

In 1909–10, another dam was completed at Koochiching Falls, supplying hydroelectric power to the towns of Fort Frances and International Falls and their big new pulp and paper mills. Yet it also raised
water levels by about eight feet, causing extensive damage:

> Flooding destroyed Ojibwa houses, gardens, hay and rice fields, cemeter-
> ies, and eroded shorelines around Rainy Lake and up the Seine River ...
> Effluent from the mill degraded sturgeon spawning grounds on Rainy
> River and adversely affected drinking water quality. (Lovisek, Waisberg,
> and Holzkamm 1995, 7)

Although the Fort Frances Indian agent dismissed the complaints of
Rainy Lake chiefs as "a few crotchety kickers," every chief and coun-
cillor in the Fort Frances area sent petitions about the flood damage.
Homes were destroyed and families forced to relocate. Wild rice beds
and cultivated gardens were ruined, raising fears of starvation. As one
Rainy Lake chief expressed:

> At Hay Marsh Bay ... we are prohibited to fish without license in our re-
> serve [and our] Rice crop, Hay marsh, Musk Rats, were all flooded by the
> backing up of the [Fort Frances] dam. We have been deprived of all our
> best of privileges and our Indian agent is our greatest enemy ... who does
> his best in working against us in curtailing our rights. (quoted in Lovisek,
> Waisberg, and Holzkamm 1995, 9–10)

Meanwhile, the spiritually, socially, and economically significant sturgeon stock was virtually exhausted by "government encouragement
of large-scale non-Native commercial fisheries" (Waisberg and Holzkamm 1998, 9). Between 1895 and 1899, over one million pounds of
sturgeon was harvested, primarily by non-Native commercial fishers,

sometimes only for the caviar, leading to the species' near extinction; "a resource managed by traditional means on a sustained yield basis [for centuries] was appropriated and destroyed within two decades" (10).

"The Indian Uprising That Wasn't"

Despite the shifting balance of power and the negative impacts of colonial settlement on Indigenous peoples, the sense of group positions in the Rainy River District remained somewhat unsettled at the turn of the twentieth century. A curious incident, described in local history books as "The Last Indian Menace" (Emo 1978) and "The Indian Uprising That Wasn't" (McQuarrie 2003), helps illustrate the point.

In June 1900, "wild rumours" circulated that the Boundary Waters Ojibwa were planning a revolt (Emo 1978, 298). According to settler gossip, Indigenous residents blamed settlers for recent forest fires and threatened to burn down their homes. Ah-na-ma-ay-ka-bou, a medicine man from Leech Lake, Minnesota (192 kilometres southwest of Fort Frances), reportedly had received messages from the Great Spirit that the Anishinaabe should terminate relations with whites and return to traditional ways; he also prophesied a "great storm" that would wipe out the settlers and sent messengers to the Rainy River District to share the news (McQuarrie 2003, 47). On 28 June the Rainy Lake Herald reported:

> Considerable excitement was caused this week by the strange actions of the Indians in this district, who were leaving their reserves and gathering in large numbers ... There was so much talk of an Indian rebellion that Reeve Thompson, Fort Frances, called a meeting to discuss the matter. (quoted in Drache 1983, 82)

Members of the Manitou Rapids, Little Fork, Rainy Lake, and Seine River reserves all assembled north of Fort Frances, on the banks of Rainy Lake. Other Anishinaabe simultaneously assembled at Big Grassy, on Lake of the Woods. When Mrs Johnson, a "pioneer" on the US side of Rainy River, saw thirty canoes filled with Indigenous people in what appeared to be war paint, she was terrified (Thompson 1979, 8). Mr Wheeler, a white neighbour married to an Anishinaabe woman, told her that "the Sioux were trying to stir up our Chippewa Indians and have called a big pow-wow on the lake" (8). He advised her to give them whatever they wanted and "don't show fear or disgust." When the Indigenous people stopped in her store, "they all paid [for bread and supplies] and there was no marauding" (8).

Meanwhile, many settlers were so frightened that they fled to Rat Portage (now Kenora). Others hid in root cellars with their guns. The Rainy River Valley was "almost deserted by women and children" (Drache 1983, 83). The Minnesota National Guard was called to International Falls with ten thousand rounds of ammunition, guards were stationed in Fort Frances, and preparations were made to send back-up troops from Winnipeg. Indigenous singing and drumming could be heard for miles.

Yet there was "little or no evidence" of the rumoured uprising (McQuarrie 2003, 47). In July, the mayor of Rat Portage and an Indian agent met with the Anishinaabe at Big Grassy. They found about 450 people gathered, "none of whom had any thoughts or intentions of harming anyone. In fact, they expressed great indignation over such reports" (47). Soon after, the gatherings ended, and the Anishinaabe, placing white flags on their canoes, paddled home. According to local history books, "Life in the district quickly returned to normal" (47).

What is especially curious about this incident is that the same local history books (and oral histories) generally describe friendly relations in the Rainy River District. Although some settler families had little interaction with Indigenous people, others said "Indians were a major factor in their social life" (Drache 1983, 84). In the late nineteenth and early twentieth centuries, some Indigenous and settler people hunted and did business together, Indigenous and non-Indigenous children played together, and Indigenous people sometimes worked for settlers (as midwives, guides, lumberjacks, etc.). Intermarriage was relatively common. But even some whites who had such contact with Indigenous people believed the rumours of an imminent uprising and fled. Most settlers were likely aware of the recent "Indian wars" to the south[15] and exposed to media propaganda about "savage" Indians resisting "progress."[16] Moreover,

> The pioneers realized that the Indians did have reason to resent the white man's presence as the settlers along the Rainy River and the lake were squatters on Indian land which had never [been] ceded ... ancient Indian burial grounds along the river were being overrun by settlement. Sacred graves had been tampered with and even destroyed. (Thompson 1979, 8)

These observations suggest that, despite often having friendly relations with local Indigenous people, white settlers also had a deep-seated fear that perhaps the benefits they had accrued from colonization were not secure, that they were not naturally entitled to resources and privileges (including the Indigenous land they now occupied) but also had treaty obligations, and that Indigenous people were not so happy with the arrangement.

Overall, the rumoured uprising might be seen as an early test of whites' sense of superior group position, after the balance of power had begun to swing. Yet the perceived threat did not materialize. The "scare" was over as quickly as it started, whites and Indians returned to their "places," and colonial policies and practices were only further entrenched in the coming years.

Nevertheless, the rumoured uprising did set the tone of local Indigenous-settler relations for decades. As we will see in subsequent chapters, there is still a curious blend of intermixing and congeniality with mistrust and miscommunication, which sometimes escalates to the point of threatened open conflict but usually dissipates just as promptly.

Settler Booms, Indigenous Struggles

For most white settlers, the early twentieth century was "a time of growth and prosperity" (McQuarrie 2003, 72). Rainy River District was "booming. Logging continued at a rapid pace ... Settlers were taking up the last ... available agricultural lands" (55). The Canadian National rail line, from Thunder Bay to Winnipeg via Fort Frances, was completed in 1901, bringing more settlers and easing the shipment of lumber, mining resources, and agricultural equipment. The Town of Fort Frances was incorporated in 1903, but already had a municipal government, school, church, general stores, hotels, two sawmills, and more than a thousand residents.

The Shevlin-Clarke Lumber Company opened additional sawmills in 1911 and 1913, "the largest ... at the time," eventually employing over seven hundred men and producing eight hundred thousand board feet of lumber per day (FF Museum Permanent Exhibit 2006/07). Meanwhile, timber baron E.W. Backus, who had financed the construction of the Fort Frances dam, opened two large pulp and paper mills, one in International Falls in 1910 and another across the river in Fort Frances in 1914.

The 1905 power agreement to supply hydroelectricity to the mills also provided Fort Frances with four thousand horsepower per year at no more than fourteen dollars per horsepower, in perpetuity, in exchange for land and water-power rights. This agreement has long provided residents with "the lowest power rates in the province" (*Fort Frances Times* 2006).

Meanwhile, the Rainy River and Kenora districts "produced over half of Ontario's gold from 1890 to 1910" (FF Museum Permanent Exhibit

2006/07). In the 1920s, massive gold reserves were discovered north of Red Lake, sparking "the biggest gold rush since Klondike." Another major discovery after the First World War was the iron deposit at Steep Rock Lake, near Atikokan, where one hundred billion gallons of lake water was drained and a river diverted to enable open-pit mining.

In 1909, the Town of Fort Frances also leased a valuable lakefront property on the Agency One reserve, between Fort Frances and the Couchiching First Nation, from the federal government on behalf of four "Rainy Lake bands" (Couchiching, Mitaanjigamiing, Naicatchewenin, and Nigigoonsiminikaaning).[17] Although it had long been a summer gathering and ceremonial site of the Anishinaabe, the town called it Pither's Point Park (after the local Indian agent who had built a home there).[18] With its natural sand beach and oak trees, it quickly became a hub of town social life, including picnics, swimming, camping, concerts, dancing, and athletic competitions. Many residents also enjoyed the Rainy Lake Golf and Country Club, adjacent to the park. However, the lease arrangements were controversial. The town had hoped the park would be sold or given to them rather than leased. The First Nations disagreed among themselves who was authorized to sign the lease, since Agency One had been used by the Rainy River, Seine River, and other bands as well. Moreover, the terms of the ninety-nine-year lease (thirty-five dollars per acre) were never updated for inflation (see chapter 3).

Meanwhile, as the remaining free grants and homesteads were taken up, some settlers complained that the Indian reserves were too large, "tying up some of the best agricultural and timber lands," and that more should be opened to settlers (McQuarrie 2003, 60). The Ontario government agreed that Treaty No. 3 was "overly generous" and "routinely asserted that the reservations [were] larger than required, and had an unfair effect on White settlement" (Waisberg, Lovisek, and Holzkamm 1996, 342). In the interim, a pivotal court case, St. Catherine's Milling and Lumber Co. v. The Queen, had gone in Ontario's favour, to the detriment of Indigenous and treaty rights.[19]

Technically, the case, filed in 1884, was about the right to issue timber licences on crown land. The federal government, which had issued a permit to the lumber company, claimed the right based on its constitutional authority (in the 1867 British North America [BNA] Act) over "Indians and Lands Reserved for Indians," and on Treaty No. 3, which, it argued, had transferred land title to it. Ontario claimed the right based on the 1867 BNA Act, which gave provinces jurisdiction over lands and natural resources. Although Ontario was not party to Treaty No. 3 and provincial boundaries were disputed with Manitoba and

Minnesota (the land in question had been part of Rupert's Land), Ontario asserted provincial ownership, denied Indian title, and assumed the right to confirm or deny reserves. The Anishinaabe complained that they were "neither consulted nor brought to the witness stand," but were ignored (Dickason 2006, 259).

Oliver Mowat, then premier of Ontario, argued that "there is no Indian title in law or in equity" (ibid.). Against all evidence, the Anishinaabe were described in court as an "inferior race ... in an inferior state of civilization," "heathens and barbarians," and "rude red men," with "no government and no organization, and cannot be regarded as a nation capable of holding lands" (260). The Ontario court, "strongly influenced by the racial considerations raised in Ontario's depositions" (Waisberg, Lovisek, and Holzkamm 1996, 342), agreed. Chancellor Boyd ruled that the Anishinaabe did not have "proprietary title to the soil, nor any claim thereto as to interfere with ... colonization" (quoted in Dickason 2006, 259). His decision was upheld through three appeals, with the final one by the Judicial Committee of the Privy Council in 1888.[20] One year later, the Canada (Ontario Boundary) Act decreed that most of Treaty No. 3 territory was in Ontario. The implications of this decision were profound. As the European imperialist and social Darwinist era peaked, the racist rhetoric of "whites" over and against "Indians" prevailed.[21]

As Leo Waisberg and colleagues (1996, 343) document, Ontario, as a condition for confirming the Treaty No. 3 reserves, "demanded federal concessions and Indian removals." This included "elimination of all but one reserve on the fertile Rainy River plain, 'cancellation' of the Anishinaabe reserve within Quetico Provincial Park, provincial retention of water areas and hydro powers, and payment of federal money [to the province]" (344). The provincial treasurer, in 1905, called the Anishinaabe "an incubus [i.e., sexually violent demon] upon the territory" and portrayed the appropriation of Indigenous lands as "a civilized remedy" (339). The federal minister of Indian affairs agreed that "the interests of the people [i.e., settlers] must come first, and if it becomes a question between the Indians and the whites, the interests of the whites will have to be provided for" (344). Thus, when white settlers in the Rainy River District clamoured for more land, including a former mayor of Fort Frances, who lobbied government officials to "open up" more reserves, six of the Rainy River bands were relocated:

> By threats of removal without payment, Ojibwa were forced to abandon their villages and relocate to Manitou Rapids. Over 43,000 acres of reserve lands, the most arable in the region, were taken. The seven Rainy River bands lost 89% of their land. (345)

Meanwhile, the Sturgeon Lake Band to the east was formally "extinguished." When Quetico Park, a 1.18-million-acre wilderness preserve, was created in 1909, it fully encompassed the Sturgeon Lake Indian Reserve 24C. The following year, while Quetico was advertised as a world-class tourist destination, park rangers expelled Anishinaabe families "at gun point":

> Traplines and cabins were destroyed. Random shootings of "poachers" occurred. The Ojibwa were completely removed from part of their homeland, while rangers planted gardens, built houses, and dined on wild fare. (347)

Moreover, "there was no legal surrender ... the band was not consulted ... [and] compensation or replacement lands were not offered" (347). Ironically, given Quetico's purported aim of creating a refuge free from human impacts, intensive logging began in it around 1918; there were five lumber camps in the area, and "even the timber rights to Lac La Croix First Nation went on the auction block" (Peruniak 2000, 79).

Restrictive provincial game laws also were enforced. Despite treaty promises to protect Indigenous harvesting practices, hunting and fishing off reserve without a licence was criminalized, and Anishinaabe were arrested. In 1916, Pierre Hunter of Lac Seul was convicted of possession of moose meat, imprisoned for thirty days in Port Arthur, and then released to walk home (more than three hundred kilometres). "Afraid to kill game, he died after four weeks travel" (Waisberg, Lovisek, and Holzkamm 1996, 348).

Treaty No. 3 chiefs routinely petitioned Indian agents and other government officials about these and other broken treaty promises. Delegations of Fort Frances chiefs in 1909 and 1912 asked for "understanding" and "fair play":

> We don't want to be stopped and Game Inspectors cutting our lines and taking our nets it is in our Treaty Papers and you are not right to take our privilages [sic] away ... Are your words or the words of the Great White Queen, our Mother, to be as smoke? (Waisberg, Lovisek, and Holzkamm 1996, 347)

Yet, by and large, the Anishinaabe were ignored. Ontario's "Indian removal policy" was justified by "provincial rights" and racist ideology, and ultimately served to enrich the province and many settlers, at Indigenous peoples' expense.

After the First World War, when both Indigenous and non-Indigenous residents enlisted at high rates in the Canadian Armed Forces,

Indigenous peoples almost disappear from local history books, which focus more on the development of settler towns and communities.[22] Perhaps, by this time, white residents' political and economic dominance was more secure. Reserve lands were diminished and the pass system limited interaction. For many settlers, Indigenous neighbours became an afterthought. As Ralph Paulsen (2015) of Nestor Falls (ninety-four kilometres northwest of Fort Frances, population 692) explained:

> I don't think my family ever held ill will towards our First Nation neighbours. We didn't have any feelings about them at all. They were them and we were us.

In 1920, Indian residential school attendance became mandatory for all Indigenous children. Some Anishinaabe parents fought with and were arrested by the RCMP officers who tried to kidnap their children. Other families hid in the bush. Multiple generations were subject to this system of cultural genocide, which disrupted identities, families, and communities, inhibited the transmission of languages and cultural practices, and left many survivors alienated from both settler and Indigenous societies (TRC 2015). At the borders of Fort Frances and Couchiching First Nation, St. Margaret's Residential School operated from 1906 to 1974 (see chapter 9). Residential schools also existed in Kenora and Sioux Lookout. In addition to their traumatic intergenerational effects on Indigenous peoples (Bombay, Matheson, and Anisman 2014), residential schools ripped apart Indigenous and settler residents. As told by Bertha Davis Moore, an older white resident of Chapple (fifty-eight kilometres northwest of Fort Frances, population 741):

> I used to play with the little Indian children who often frequented our home and I would walk ... to the Manitou Reserve to play with a little girl that I loved. Her name was Victoria ... [She] was sent away to boarding school. I have never seen or heard of her since. I often wonder what became of Victoria. Does she remember me? (Clink 1997, 80)

Even when residential schools began to be phased out and many First Nations children attended day schools in town, the "Sixties Scoop" wreaked havoc on Indigenous communities and families.[23] In the Rainy River District, hundreds of Indigenous children were apprehended by the Children's Aid Society, on grounds that their parents (many of whom had been abused in residential school and had therefore never had the opportunity to learn proper parenting skills) were unfit to parent.[24] Rather than being kept with kin, these children were often adopted out to white families, sometimes in distant regions, and forbidden contact with their birth families. These practices began to change only with the creation of the local First Nations–controlled Weechi-it-te-win Family Services in 1982.[25]

In the 1950s and 1960s, without Indigenous consent, burial mounds were excavated at Point Park, Long Sault Rapids, and Oak Grove Camp (north of Rainy River), the latter of which was described by the Royal Ontario Museum's assistant curator as "the most spectacular in Canada" (Thompson 1979, 160). Although some Indigenous residents continued to work as fishing guides and lumberjacks, and there were always individuals who excelled despite the odds, most Anishinaabe were excluded from "good jobs" in town, opportunities to practise traditional livelihoods were increasingly limited, and health and well-being suffered.

Otherwise, the Rainy River District continued to grow and thrive. Although the forestry sector faced setbacks during the Great Depression, including temporary shutdowns at the Fort Frances mill, resource industries rebounded after the Second World War. Between 1947 and 1949, pulp and paper production tripled in northern Ontario (Bray and Epp 1984). Meanwhile, large-scale labour strikes in the late 1930s had resulted in union recognition, higher wages, benefits, and pensions for most white forestry workers. Although some Indigenous war veterans were hired at the Fort Frances mill (which reportedly had a "jobs for veterans" policy), Indigenous forestry workers were mostly employed in the less well paid and less secure bush camp and wood drive processes. Moreover, the experiences of Indigenous veterans were not always positive. According to an older First Nations man I interviewed, who had served in the Canadian army during the Second World War:

> When I was in the military, I was treated better over in Europe than ... in my own country. And I tended to think, "Hey, I should've stayed there." I know some of my fellow Native Canadian soldiers [did].

Many returning Indigenous soldiers were also denied government benefits that non-Indigenous veterans took for granted.

Although the Fort Frances mill flourished in the postwar period, the J.A. Mathieu sawmill on Couchiching First Nation (which had employed some band members) shut in 1951, leaving contaminated soil to this day. In the 1960s, a pulp and paper mill in Dryden dumped toxic sludge into the English-Wabigoon river system, resulting in (ongoing) mercury poisoning in the Grassy Narrows and Whitedog First Nations communities, in the north of Treaty No. 3. This poisoning effectively demolished the traditional fishing economy, eliminated a food staple, and created persisting health problems, from birth defects to neurological disorders (Willow 2012).

The Second World War also boosted regional mining, with mineral production in Ontario doubling between 1945 and 1951 (Bray and Epp 1984) and staying strong until the 1970s. But, as with forestry, most of the jobs and revenue went to whites. Immigration, especially from eastern and southern Europe, increased as well, and the population of Fort Frances reached a record high of 9,947 in 1971. Many Anishinaabe people also moved into town, renewing the higher historic levels of interaction and intermarriage.

With the opening of major new highways, including Highway 71 to Kenora and Highway 11 via the Noden Causeway to Thunder Bay in 1936 and 1965, respectively, tourism increased, and cottages and cabins were built across the Rainy River District. Locals and visitors alike enjoyed going "up the lakes" in summer. According to some residents, the highway connections were a mixed blessing for First Nations, however, as they reportedly encouraged assimilation but also provided job opportunities and access to the goods and services of larger towns. The Kenora highway project also bulldozed Onigaming First Nation gravesites, and local First Nations were not compensated for highway right-of-ways (see chapter 10).

During this same period, new technology pushed many Indigenous people out of work. As Howard Hampton, the long-serving local member of provincial Parliament (MPP) from 1987 to 2011 and former leader of the Ontario New Democratic Party, explained:

> One [issue that] has always brought people together is ... dependence on the natural environment ... The first voyageurs and fur traders ... could never have survived here without working hand-in-glove with the First Nations ... The logging industry ... relied upon the First Nations, because all of the wood moved by water [and] the people who understood the water routes were the First Nations. (interview with author, 10 November 2008)

However, he said, the shift to transporting logs by train or truck "eliminated all kinds of jobs that were [held] by First Nations" due to government regulations and credentialing processes. Wealthy tourists with sonar devices no longer hired First Nations guides "to show [them] where to fish and ... avoid the reefs." While new businesses opened in town, First Nations had difficulty securing financing for economic development because of the legal status of reserve lands.

Even today, despite treaty promises of a school on every reserve, most First Nations in the Rainy River District bus their children to schools in Fort Frances or other townships; those that do have schools receive two to three thousand dollars less funding per pupil. First Nations child welfare agencies also receive between 22 and 34 per cent less funding than their provincial counterparts (Murphy 2016). Couchiching First Nation pays three times the rate for water and sewer services as the Town of Fort Frances. As elsewhere in Canada, Indigenous residents have higher than average rates of chronic illnesses (heart disease, diabetes) and psychological distress (Newton-Taylor and Larion 2009). They are more highly represented in the Fort Frances and Kenora jails and more often the victims of crime and violence. Reflecting a wider ongoing Canadian problem (RCMP 2014), several local Indigenous women have been murdered or have gone missing in recent decades. At the political level, First Nations band councils are highly regulated and restricted by Indigenous and Northern Affairs Canada (INAC), while Indigenous laws and policies (such as the Treaty No. 3 resource law or Grassy Narrows First Nation's declaration against clear-cutting) are routinely ignored. There has never been an Anishinaabe mayor or councillor in Fort Frances, despite Indigenous people now comprising nearly 17 per cent of the town's population (22 per cent of the district population).

In short, like elsewhere in Canada, historical and ongoing processes of colonization have created a racialized social structure wherein settler-Canadians (especially whites) have long enjoyed advantages over Indigenous peoples – often at the latter's expense – in terms of access to and control of lands, jobs, money, education, political power, safety/violence, and health outcomes.[26] For more than a century, this inequitable racial structure has supported whites' sense of group superiority and entitlement.

Turning Tides: Indigenous Resurgence, Settler Uncertainty, and (Renewed) Group Threat

Since the 1970s, and especially since the turn of the twenty-first century, Indigenous communities in the Rainy River District have enjoyed a remarkable resurgence and new opportunities, while local settlers have faced economic decline and growing uncertainty. This changing context has precipitated an ongoing (and very much unsettled) shift in power dynamics, challenging group positions and enhancing settlers' perceptions of group threat.

The Anishinaabe have always protested treaty violations and resisted colonial impositions. With the new balance of power in the late nineteenth and early twentieth centuries, however, most of their concerns were ignored. In 1924, Treaty No. 3 First Nations retained a Kenora lawyer to show that "their Treaty Rights have been violated and gross injustice done them for the past forty years" (Waisberg and Holzkamm 1998, 16). In response, Canada amended the Indian Act in 1927 to prevent First Nations from hiring legal counsel; the Kenora lawyer was told that pursuing the case "could result in criminal conviction" (16). At this point, the Grand Council Treaty No. 3 was reactivated and formalized to provide a "national voice" regarding treaty rights and interests. In 1941, Grand Chief John McGinnis petitioned Canada as follows:

> Queen Victoria promised to love the Indians just as she loved the white people ... The promise has grown less every year. What us Indians lived as for a living, the white man is taking these away from us now ... Our old people and children look as if they would starve ... We have given many complaints to the Indian Agent [and he has sent] our complaints to Ottawa and we never get an answer. (quoted in Waisberg and Holzkamm 1998, 19)

Meanwhile, political organizations representing Indigenous peoples across Canada, such as the North American Indian Brotherhood (precursor to the Assembly of First Nations), also formed. Under pressure, Ottawa revised some of the most coercive aspects of the Indian Act in 1951, such as the ban on spiritual practices and ceremonies.

In another turning point, the federal government's 1969 White Paper proposed abolishing the Indian Act, Indian status, and all associated rights and benefits. When First Nations across Canada protested, condemning the proposal as a "thinly disguised policy of extermination" (Cardinal 1969, 1) and emphasizing that treaties are historic, moral, and legal obligations, the government retracted its proposal. Within Treaty No. 3, the Ojibway Warrior Society's armed occupation of Anicinabe Park in Kenora in 1974 sent a strong message that there would be serious consequences to the violation of Indigenous and treaty rights; as group position theory would predict, it also sparked a vicious racist backlash (see chapter 10).

Fort Frances residents compared their local situation favourably to both Kenora and the United States (where the American Indian Movement [AIM] was in full swing). Although Indigenous residents still faced subtle and overt racism (see chapter 4), and although many sympathized with AIM and the Anicinabe Park warriors, no such protest occurred in the Rainy River District; local relations were generally peaceful and cooperative. However, the chief of Couchiching First Nation did threaten a road blockade over the town's refusal to extend water and sewer services to the reserve. When the lease on the Rainy Lake Golf and Country Club expired in 1977, the land reverted to the Agency One bands and the golf course eventually shut, generating on-going resentment by many whites.[27] At the same time, intense discussions over the Point Park lease began: "The bands felt that the $35 lease was no longer reasonable and wanted it raised," while the town sought ownership "but the bands and Indian Affairs rejected the idea" (Mc-Quarrie 2003, 149) (see chapter 3).

On a national level, "aboriginal and treaty rights" were "recognized and affirmed" in Canada's 1982 Constitution Act. The 1997 Delgamuukw decision upheld the notion of Aboriginal title, while the 1999 Marshall decision lent more support to Indigenous harvesting rights.[28] Such decisions have helped realign (though have not equalized) the legal playing field.[29]

In this new legal and political environment, dozens of land claims were filed in the Rainy River District (and hundreds across Canada). The first local land claim settlement – concerning Mitaanjigamiing First Nation's forced relocation (see below) – was reached in 1990, after the community's well-researched case garnered media attention and the government was accused of "constructive dismissal." The same year, the Quebec municipality of Oka approved a golf course and luxury condominiums on Mohawk burial grounds, triggering the Oka Crisis, or Kanehsatake Resistance.[30] Big Grassy (Mishkosiimiiniiziibing) First Nation in the northwest of the Rainy River District blockaded a bridge in solidarity and to draw attention to their own land claims (see chapter 10). Subsequent direct actions occurred at Ipperwash, Burnt Church, Gustafsen Lake, Grassy Narrows, and many other communities across the country, but never in Fort Frances.[31]

In 2005, Rainy River First Nations (RRFN) (forty kilometres west of Fort Frances) signed the then largest land claim settlement in Ontario. As compensation for lands taken from them in 1914–15 to make way for white settlers, the community received seventy-one million dollars with which to purchase up to forty-six thousand acres of land. It also regained control over sacred sites and management of the local sturgeon stock, which has been revived, thanks to RRFN's efforts (see chapter 3).

Meanwhile, the Indigenous population has been booming and the white population declining. Between 1971 and 2006, the overall Rainy River District population decreased by 16.3 per cent and that of Fort Frances dropped by 18.5 per cent (Statistics Canada 2007). Between 1996 and 2006 alone, however, the district Indigenous population increased by 51 per cent (from 3,040 to 4,615); First Nations and Métis people now constituted nearly 22 per cent of district residents.[32]

These population shifts are indicative of further changes in the local political economy:

> Declining employment opportunities in forestry and agriculture are un-leashing a spiral of interconnected effects: youth out-migration, retail fading from main streets, a shrinking tax base reducing municipal capacity to update services and infrastructure, while new policies (e.g. new standards for water and fire management) increase fiscal pressures and add momentum to the current crisis. (Ortiz-Guerrero 2010, 48)

The regional mining sector began to wane in the 1970s, with some highly industry-dependent towns (such as Atikokan) suffering massive job losses. Many family farms have shuttered due to competition from agribusiness, an aging farming population, and youth out-migration. Between 1931 and 1981, the number of farms in northern Ontario dropped from 16,757 to 3,715 (Bray and Epp 1984). Local businesses have also struggled due to competition from big box retailers (such as Walmart and Canadian Tire in Fort Frances) and a rise in online consumers. Schools and hospitals have been amalgamated and centralized. Meanwhile, CN rail passenger service and bus service from Fort Frances to Thunder Bay and Winnipeg were cancelled (in the 1970s and early 2000s, respectively), increasing geographic isolation, especially for those who relied on public transportation.

Above all, the forestry sector – the backbone of the local economy – has struggled, with dozens of mill closures and thousands of layoffs since the early 2000s (Ontario Forestry Coalition 2007). Thousands more had jobs dependent on forestry, whether hauling logs to the mill or providing support services. Yet Indigenous people have not been affected nearly as much as whites. At the Fort Frances pulp and paper mill, the town's largest employer as of 2008, less than 2 per cent of the seven-hundred-plus employees identified as Indigenous.[33] During my fieldwork in 2007–9, the Fort Frances mill was temporarily spared the fate of its neighbours in Atikokan, Ignace, and Kenora. But in 2014 it too was indefinitely shut.[34]

These conditions have generated a perfect storm for the regional economy (Ortiz-Guerrero 2010). If there is an economic bright spot, it is among the Indigenous communities, who are opening new businesses (including an eighteen-hole golf course, restaurants, engineering and consulting services, a furniture-making business, a historical interpretive centre, and eco-tourism), entering into profitable agreements with mining companies, and regaining some control over natural resource management. Now more than a generation removed from the residential school era, and with the support of at least symbolic recognition through government and church apologies, the Indian Residential School Settlement Agreement, and work done by the Truth and Reconciliation Commission of Canada (see chapter 9), local Indigenous communities are undertaking their own healing and cultural revitalization initiatives: reviving their languages and traditional governments, rebuilding their institutions, and asserting their identities and rights (see chapter 10). Indigenous youth are increasingly graduating from high school, attending university or college, and returning to the district to support their communities.

As group position theory would predict, the conditions are ripe for the historically dominant white settlers to perceive a (realistic and symbolic) threat to their group position: declining economic security and population loss for them, and population growth, material gains, and a cultural renaissance among the long marginalized Indigenous peoples.

The Role and Position of the Métis

To understand the history of group relations in the region, it is also important to consider the Métis. Although I have described group positioning in terms of "Indigenous" and "settler," these are not monolithic groups, as different individuals and communities have different experiences, resources, and opportunities, and relationships vary. In the Rainy River District, since the fur trade era, there have been *three* salient groups: First Nations (primarily Anishinaabe), settlers (primarily whites), and Métis (offspring of mixed marriages who formed their own distinct communities).

The Métis originated in two major streams. First, French voyageurs from the early eighteenth to the mid-nineteenth centuries sometimes married Anishinaabe women. Not only were there no white women in Rupert's Land at the time, but intermarriages solidified trading partnerships, and Anishinaabe women often taught European traders vital local knowledge and skills. Their mixed children usually lived among the First Nations, largely assimilating to their culture, but also bringing outside influences such as Roman Catholicism, and often working in the fur trade or as interpreters, guides, or clerks. By the early 1800s, many "half-breed" families clustered around the Rainy Lake trading posts, and a unique sense of Métis identity emerged (Botsford 2013).[35]

Meanwhile, the Red River Métis in Manitoba, mainly descendants of Scottish fur traders and Cree or Ojibwa women, developed their own large settlements and thought of themselves "as neither European, nor First Nation, but as a distinct and separate people" (Botsford 2013, 2). They farmed, hunted buffalo, and developed their own customs and Michif language. After the Red River Resistance in 1870, when the federal government sent military troops to quash Louis Riel's provisional government, many Métis families who had lost land and homes fled west, but others came east to the Rainy River District, settling in towns like Fort Frances. At least one white soldier from the Wolseley expedition (George C. Allan) also returned to the district and married a Métis woman. Since this time, Métis residents of the Rainy River District have continued to intermarry with Anishinaabe, with settlers, and among themselves.

When asked about intergroup bridges in my interviews, many residents cited the long history of intermarriage and the prominence of local Métis, which they said had created bonds between Indigenous and white residents and helped limit conflict and violence (see chapter 7). Yet the situation is complex. Although many mixed families live in Fort Frances, Indigenous/white remains the primary dividing line for many residents.

In the late nineteenth century, the federal and provincial governments refused to recognize a distinct Métis community, only allowing identification on the census, for example, as "Indian" or "white." Overt anti-Indian racism was common. Thus, some Métis, especially the Red River stream (Allan, Calder, McLeod, Tucker), "went underground ... no longer admitted their mixed heritage," and tried to blend in with European settlers in town (Botsford 2013, 13). Many thought this would protect them and their children from both interpersonal and institutional racism. Others, especially the French "half-breed" stream (Bruyere, Jourdain, Mainville, Morrisseau), joined the First Nations on newly created reserves. During treaty negotiations in 1873 several Métis played important roles as translators and note-takers, including Joseph Nolin, who was hired by the Anishinaabe and whose notes inform the Paypom Treaty; George McPherson, who was hired by Morris; and Nicholas Chatelaine, who was described by a government official in 1889 as having "great influence [and] inducing the Indians to make a Treaty with the Government in 1873" (Botsford 2013, 39).

In this context, local Anishinaabe chiefs, including Mawedopenais, felt that if their Métis relatives chose to live with them and participate in their communities, they should enjoy the same treaty rights and obligations. They therefore worked with Métis leaders to lobby the federal government to include people of mixed descent who lived among the First Nations as treaty beneficiaries. In 1875, a "half-breed adhesion" was signed – the only such adhesion to any treaty in Canada.

Given this unique history, it is unsurprising that my research showed Métis residents often viewed themselves as a bridge between First Nations and settlers. Every Métis interviewee had close friends and family members in both groups, and they often found themselves playing "peacekeeper" (see chapter 7). A fair-skinned Métis woman explained:

> Couchiching is a Métis community, just as much as Fort Frances. It was two Métis communities growing up side by side, yet one got the prejudice and the other one didn't, which is a really interesting comparison because it's not the blood, it's not the roots ... it's not even the cards that have been dealt; it's the cards that were chosen ... Because in the 1870s, we were given the choice to be white or Indian. We weren't given the choice to be Métis ... My ancestors chose to be white and other people chose to be Indian. And I've had many benefits because of it, but I've also [experienced] many prejudices ... And it doesn't matter which community I'm in, I'm the defender of the other one.

These comments also suggest underlying tensions. As described by interviewees, people of mixed descent who "chose to be Indian" were permitted by Chief Migiziis of the Little Eagle Band and Chief Gobe of the Mitaanjigamiing (Stanjikoming) Band to share their reserves at what is now Couchiching First Nation. Soon after, the federal government imposed the band council system, and the "half-breed" population outgrew the original Anishinaabe bands. Conflicts over leadership arose. Members of the Little Eagle Band who felt that their way of life was not respected by the "half-breeds" broke away to form their own community to the north. Meanwhile, the local Indian agent relocated the Mitaanjigamiing Band to another reserve that became an island after hydro-dam flooding in the early twentieth century (the basis of the 1990 land claim settlement). By 1908, when the land surrender (for lease) was taken at Point Park, the "half-breeds" were politically dominant at Couchiching. Even as recently as the 1960s, Couchiching band members said, there were near-daily fistfights between descendants of the half-breeds and the Little Eagle Band.

Meanwhile, half-breed residents who "chose to live as white" often downplayed their Indigenous ancestry and distanced themselves from their more stigmatized relatives who lived as "Indians" on reserve. Some of the former rose to prominent positions in town, owning businesses and integrating with the "whites."

Since the 1970s, dramatic changes have occurred among the Métis, consistent with the trends outlined above for First Nations. The 1982 Constitution Act recognized the Métis as a distinct people with

Aboriginal rights. The 2003 Powley decision extended (limited) harvesting rights to the Métis.[36] The Métis Nation of Ontario (MNO), whose president (as of this writing) is from Fort Frances, now provides many programs and services (including education and training, economic development, healing and wellness). In this context, and with the growing Indigenous rights movements across Canada and globally, more and more residents of mixed descent who previously identified as white have traced their ancestry and applied for Métis status.[37]

Securing Métis status was a source of pride for many Rainy River District residents – it was often described as "coming home" and experienced as the freedom to be who they are and to have their "true" identity recognized. Consistent with group position theory, however, it also enhanced tensions with both whites and First Nations and within Métis communities over who should be eligible for which rights and privileges. On one hand, individuals who had always identified as Indigenous were sometimes reluctant to recognize others who appeared to be applying for Métis status (or Indian status through Bill C-31) for opportunistic reasons and who, due to federal rules, had come to enjoy similar rights without experiencing the same barriers.[38] While some agreed that people of mixed descent who could trace their ancestry to distinct Métis communities (or whose ancestors had lost Indian status by marrying out) should be entitled to Aboriginal rights, they worried that the government had not expanded the available pot of resources to keep pace with Indigenous-identity population growth. Meanwhile, many whites felt angry and betrayed by friends and neighbours who had once identified as white and distanced themselves from "Indians," but who then claimed Métis or Indian status when it was financially or otherwise beneficial. Alternatively, one white municipal leader described the Métis as "integrated fully" and "hard-working, tax-paying citizens who have pitched in to help ... and yet don't ask for appreciation in return" – an implicit contrast with stereotypes of "Indians" that perhaps enables whites to view themselves as non-racist and yet maintain a sense of superiority vis-à-vis First Nations (a form of subtyping; see chapter 7). As some interviewees suggested, one thing the Canadian government does very well is "divide and conquer."

In short, the history of intermarriage and the distinct role of the Métis in the Rainy River District have long constituted a bridge between First Nations and settlers and perhaps reduced violent conflict. The inequalities in the district are somewhat less than in many parts of Canada. But recent shifts in the political and legal environment, including the ongoing Métis resurgence (as part of a wider Indigenous resurgence), have exposed and exacerbated tensions within and between all three communities, raising perceptions of group threat and posing further challenges to the sense of group positions.

Given the complexities outlined in this chapter, and the marked shifts in power and positions over time, I began to enquire how Indigenous and non-Indigenous residents of the Rainy River District understood their relationships. What did they perceive as the greatest boundaries and bridges? How were group positions and structural inequities being sustained or challenged in daily interaction? And what might be the most promising ways forward? These questions are the focus of subsequent chapters.

Chapter Two

Perceiving Group Relations, Constructing Group Positions: "It's Okay as Long as the Indians Know Their Place!"

Friday night at the Legion ... As midnight approaches, everyone in our clique is half-drunk and merry, Harry the First Nations bartender is wiping tables and taking drink orders, and an older Métis man belts out a raw karaoke rendition of "American Pie." Polishing his pool cue, George, a tall brawny man of unknown descent, asks about my research. I tell him I am studying Aboriginal–non-Aboriginal relations in the Rainy River District: the "boundaries" that divide and the "bridges" that bring people together. "Oh!" he exclaims, eyes bulging. "That is the question!"

Field notes, January 2008

As George said, *the* question for many locals continues to be the state of Indigenous-settler relations. This chapter examines how Indigenous and white residents perceived and evaluated intergroup relations and how their perceptions reflected and reinforced their sense of group positions. As Blumer (1958, 6) suggests, these perceptions are rooted in the history of group interactions, but also filtered through cultural frames, or interpretive lenses, which are shaped by current political and material conditions, media representations, and public discourses. Thus, although individual beliefs and feelings vary, there are often common images of the positional arrangement of groups, and shared ideas about where each group belongs, which help constitute and reproduce (and sometimes challenge) structural inequities.

The analyses below are based primarily on responses to the interview question "In general, how would you describe the relationship between Aboriginal and non-Aboriginal communities in the Rainy River District today?" Despite important variations in residents' perceptions, several theoretically significant patterns emerged.

First, although residents most often described Indigenous-settler relations in mixed terms ("good and bad," "up and down"), there was a
striking difference in emphasis between groups: white residents were
more likely to describe relations in positive terms ("good," "cooperative,"
"integrated"), whereas Indigenous residents – especially First Nations –
were more critical, often using terms like "strained," "conflicted," "two-
faced," and "hostile." Such a pattern might be expected in a situation of
entrenched inequality where the dominant group has long protected its
privileges, at least in part by downplaying and avoiding conflict (Gaventa
1980; Jackman 1994), but the historically marginalized group has begun
to publicly assert its rights and interests in transforming the status quo.

Second, it became clear that Indigenous-settler relations, and residents' perceptions of them, were increasingly in flux. As large-scale political, economic, and demographic shifts – including the collapse of the
forestry sector and the healing and growth of Indigenous communities –
and a series of local racialized incidents – beginning with the video
incident, but continuing with tensions over an ongoing land dispute at
Point Park (see chapters 3 and 7), backlash to the proposed relocation of
an Anishinaabe child welfare facility (see chapter 5), and, most recently,
the Idle No More movement (see chapter 10) – disrupted the apparent
stability and threatened the long-standing balance of power, residents'
descriptions became increasingly mixed and nuanced.

In such a dynamic context, group position theory is especially useful
for understanding intergroup relations (Bobo 1999). Under more stable
conditions of structural inequality, settlers might perceive relations as
"good" or "fair" and even express warmth towards Indigenous individuals, but as settlers' sense of superiority is challenged, and conflict
becomes more open, the dominant sentiment tends to shift to fear or
resentment (about potential loss of resources and status) or at least am-
bivalence (about the disconnect between personal feelings of closeness
and divergent group interests). These patterns are evident in the data
analysed below.

Analytic Approach

To construct a sense of group position, one must first have an idea of
where "we" stand in relation to "them," or more generally the nature
of intergroup relations. To begin to examine the local sense of group
positions, I asked all 160 interviewees to describe the relationship between Indigenous and non-Indigenous communities in the Rainy River
District.[1] I then coded their responses by emotional valence. Some
interviewees used multiple descriptors that fit multiple evaluative

Table 2.1 Predominant Descriptions of Indigenous-Settler Relations among Subgroups of Interviewees

| Interviewees | Predominant description of Indigenous-settler relations | | | | |
	Positive	Negative	Mixed[1]	Neutral[2]	Total
All	53 (31.2%)	34 (20.0%)	77 (45.3%)	6 (3.6%)	170 (100%)
Non-Indigenous	31 (38.8%)	11 (13.8%)	36 (45.0%)	2 (2.5%)	80 (100%)
First Nations	16 (21.6%)	19 (25.7%)	35 (47.3%)	4 (5.4%)	74 (100%)
Métis	6 (37.5%)	4 (25.0%)	6 (37.5%)	0	16 (100%)
Indigenous	22 (24.4%)	23 (25.6%)	41 (45.6%)	4 (4.4%)	90 (100%)
February–July 2008[3]	13 (24.5%)	13 (24.5%)	24 (45.3%)	2 (3.8%)	52 (100%)
August–December 2008[4]	38 (41.8%)	15 (16.5%)	34 (37.4%)	4 (4.4%)	91 (100%)
Summer 2009[5]	2 (7.4%)	6 (22.2%)	19 (70.4%)	0	27 (100%)

[1] Includes residents who gave both positive and negative descriptions in relatively equal proportions and those who explicitly used terms such as "mixed" or "depends."
[2] Includes residents who declined to take a clear position on the state of Indigenous-settler relations or who emphasized such terms as "normal" or "same as elsewhere."
[3] Includes all interviews conducted within six months of the video incident. Twenty (38%) interviewees were white. Only five described relations in predominantly positive terms.
[4] Forty-nine (54%) interviewees were white. More than half described relations in predominantly positive terms.
[5] Includes all interviews conducted during my follow-up fieldwork in 2009. Eleven (41%) interviewees were white. Only one described relations in predominantly positive terms.

categories. However, I also categorized each interviewee's overall response as predominantly positive, predominantly negative, mixed, or neutral (see table 2.1).[2] While the modal description (45 per cent) was mixed, there were significant differences between groups – with Indigenous and white residents frequently offering different reasons for their evaluations, and white residents being more positive overall – and over time, in conjunction with local racialized incidents. Closer analysis reveals how Indigenous and white residents' divergent perceptions reflected and reinforced their respective senses of group position.

Residents' Perceptions of Intergroup Relations

Positive Descriptions

When they were asked to describe Indigenous-settler relations in the Rainy River District, residents' single most common response was "good." This term, or a close variation, was explicitly used by forty interviewees. More colourful but less common "positive" descriptors included "accepting," "close-knit," "cooperative," "equal," "familial," "harmonious," "healthy," "polite," and "respectful." Altogether, 130 interviewees (76.5 per cent) used at least one positive term or phrase to describe local intergroup relations. For fifty-three residents (31 per cent), this was the predominant description. What did they mean?

First, many interviewees, especially whites, were cheerful about the high degree of "integration" that they perceived, with terms such as "integrated" or "intermingled" used by twenty-seven interviewees.[3] Nine participants referred to the history of intermarriage between Indigenous peoples and settlers in the Rainy River District, believing that "pretty much everyone is related." Moreover, five whites and one older man who had recently acquired Indian status through Bill C-31[4] described Couchiching First Nation as an "extension" or "suburb" of Fort Frances and nearby Rainy River First Nations as an extension or suburb of Emo (thirty-four kilometres west, population 1,000). For example, a white woman in her thirties thought relationships were "great" because "we have a reserve *right in town* ... you're going to the same grocery store, same schools." Given this physical proximity, a white man in his fifties said "pretty well every family I know" is "mixed" because "any families that have been here for a while [have] intermarriages." In his view, this indicated "fairly good" relations.

Some Indigenous residents agreed. A middle-aged Anishinaabe man called it "a good relationship" because "there is *a lot* of Native blood in Fort Frances." An Anishinaabe woman in her eighties who lived on reserve said she had "a lot of friends that are non-Natives" and she had not been "hurt" by white people "since the boarding school."

On first glance, then, relations appeared "harmonious," and group positioning was difficult to discern. Yet in a settler colonial context, (claims about) a high degree of assimilation and the incorporation of Indigenous people into town can take on different meanings; they may signal the erasure of Indigenous presence and cultural distinctiveness, and domination by the Euro-Canadian majority. Indeed, some Anishinaabe described relations as problematic for precisely the *same* reason: they worried that their people had been too assimilated and were losing their language, traditions, communities, and lands.

Nevertheless, many residents, including some Indigenous, compared contemporary local conditions favourably to other times and places. Thirty-seven interviewees described Indigenous-settler relations in the Rainy River District as "better than elsewhere," and thirty-five said they were "improving." In the former case, many made invidious comparisons to Kenora (a slightly larger mill town 220 kilometres northwest),

Sioux Lookout (a slightly smaller service town 286 kilometres north-east), Caledonia (a small town in southern Ontario where Indigenous protestors occupied a proposed housing development site on contested land), and other hot spots of racial tension. For example, a middle-aged Anishinaabe man said, "There's a world of difference in attitudes" between Fort Frances and Kenora, both towns where he had lived. A First Nations woman in her twenties agreed: "It's not like ... northern communities [where] Aboriginal people don't really intermingle." In the Rainy River District, she said, "everybody lives so closely together ... and there is a lot of Aboriginal people that live in Fort [so] their relationship is pretty good."

Similarly, a Métis man in his thirties who lived in Fort Frances believed that "in this district, everyone lives in harmony ... we go to school together, we work together, we play together," whereas "in southern Ontario" relations were "worse." He was glad "the big disputes" in Caledonia, for example, had not reached Fort Frances, and although he conceded that such conflicts might develop "if there was that style of leadership," he said, "it's different up here ... there's less people ... and more familiarity amongst everybody, whereas down there if you don't know somebody, it's quite easy to just dislike them." For this interviewee, local relations were better because they seemed more integrated and there was less open conflict. As some Anishinaabe emphasized, however, absence of conflict does not necessarily mean better or more just relations; it might mean acquiescence to the structural inequities of settler colonialism.

Yet a common view held – especially among settlers – was that "getting along" and "assimilating" are signs of progress. For a white man in his thirties who lived in Fort Frances, "it's infinitely better than Kenora" where he grew up.[5] Although there were still "issues" in the district, "certain groups ... do a better job. Like, I think Manitou [Rainy River First Nations], they seem to be on track" – by which he meant high employment rates and manicured lawns.

When asked to explain the widely perceived differences from other towns in the region, interviewees often pointed to the larger homeless/street populations with a reputation for public intoxication in Sioux Lookout and Kenora, both of which act as service centres for more remote northern "fly-in" communities;[6] the presence of this subpopulation (and its relative absence from Fort Frances), they said, affected residents' perceptions of Indigenous people.[7] For a Native woman in her sixties, "it's better here [in Fort Frances] than Sioux Lookout [where] the Native people [are] sitting around park benches and ... drinking ... they're *not* from there. They're from way up north. They just fly in ... from the reserves." In contrast, the physical proximity of Couchiching First Nation to Fort Frances (and of Rainy River First Nations to Emo) and the relatively high intermarriage rate helps account for the local sense of close-knit, familial relations – at least among those whose families have resided in the Rainy River District for generations.[8] For instance, a First Nations man in his fifties said relations in Kenora were "bad news," whereas in Fort Frances, "I've got fifteen hundred relatives in one little town, and you're all through the same ... economy and social system. [Our] clan is very big here ... it's doing very well, and that's not going to change."

Interviewees, especially whites, were also more likely to say that relations had been improving over time, rather than stable or worsening. They compared the current situation favourably with the more overt racism of the past and believed that increasing interaction across generations can only have positive effects. For example, a middle-aged white woman who lived in town felt "the relationship now is ... much better ... than when I first moved here twenty-five years ago" because "there's a lot more integration." Within her family, she said, "My son is married to an Aboriginal woman [who] is terrific and I think the world of her. And, of course, my grandchildren now have Native blood."

These perceptions were shared by some Indigenous interviewees. For an Anishinaabe Elder who lived on reserve, "there's been a lot of good changes," including better communication. He personally had "a lot of [non-Aboriginal] friends" and was often invited to "functions planned by non-Aboriginal people," to say an opening prayer, for instance. Likewise, a teenager of mixed descent said, "the majority of [his] friends," including his "best friend," were white, and "race is not an issue there."

In sum, the vast majority of interviewees (76.5 per cent) described local intergroup relations in somewhat positive terms. They were optimistic about the high degree of interaction between Indigenous and non-Indigenous residents, the prevalence of intermarriage, and the sense that relations were improving or, in any case, "better than elsewhere."

Negative Descriptions

Despite these hopeful descriptions, negative portrayals of local intergroup relations were almost as pervasive – even more so among Indigenous residents. While not discounting their (often) close personal ties with some settlers, Indigenous interviewees were more likely to describe intergroup relations in negative rather than positive terms.

The words "conflict" or "division" (or close variations such as "conflicted" or "divided") were used by 25 interviewees, while "tensions" or "issues" were cited by 29. Some residents employed more colourful variants such as "animosity," "hostility," "resentment," and "crap." Altogether, 111 interviewees (65 per cent) used at least one negative term or phrase to describe intergroup relations, and for 34 residents (20 per cent), this was the predominant description. What did they mean?

In many cases, they were referring to competition for scarce resources such as money, jobs, and land. Some whites expressed resentment over the perceived unfairness of their "hard-earned tax dollars" being used to fund reparations, treaty rights, and social benefits for Indigenous peoples. For example, when asked to describe the state of Indigenous-settler relations in the Rainy River District, a white farmer in his thirties paused for several seconds before stating: "in a word: animosity." He explained that he opposed the seventy-one-million-dollar Rainy River First Nations land claim settlement, which enabled the First Nations to acquire up to forty-six thousand acres of land as compensation for land appropriation and forced relocation in 1914–15.[9] From his perspective:

> First Nations folk shouldn't be placed above [settlers] in rights ... You're taking land out of production that settlers have used [and] put into production. So, I think "animosity" is ... a very good word to represent what local farmers feel towards First Nations.

For this interviewee, Indigenous-settler relations are an "us versus them," zero-sum competition. Rather than focusing on personal friendships with Indigenous neighbours, he emphasized the perception that First Nations, *as a group*, have been benefiting – from land claim settlements and "huge chunks of money" – at whites' expense. He believed this to be unfair because, in his view, "settlers" built this country, with "sweat and blood." "Whether the original allocation [of reserve lands to RRFN] was proper or not," his reaction to land claims was "animosity."

Dozens of white interviewees expressed similar views, often drawing on stereotypes about Indigenous peoples' alleged sense of entitlement or "abuse" of "privileges." According to a middle-aged white woman who lived in Fort Frances, small-town residents must "pull their weight." Although there is support for "accessing social benefits" when there is unemployment, she said, "if it's consistent and it's abused, then we have a problem ... how are we going to pay for this? How are we going to help these people?" For this interviewee, intergroup relations were poor because First Nations were not "pulling their weight," thereby placing a burden on "responsible" white citizens who merely wanted to "help." Her comments implicitly *positioned* settlers above Indigenous peoples in both socio-economic and moral terms. Other interviewees expressed a similar sense of group position, but from a morally ambivalent standpoint. For example, after acknowledging "a holdover of misunderstanding or intolerance," a white mill manager said settlers' attitudes towards Indigenous people were "slowly changing," but "I think people still struggle with the ... cost or implication of trying to right two hundred years of wrongs." In other words, some settlers recognized that they and their ancestors had benefited at Indigenous peoples' expense, but were reluctant to pay the "cost" of rectifying injustice – to give up their (own unearned) resources and privileges.

When Indigenous interviewees described relations in negative terms, they were sometimes referring to the same resource-based conflicts, but from an opposite perspective. According to an older Métis man who lived near Fort Frances, Indigenous-settler relations were characterized by "conflict." Chuckling, he suggested speaking with his neighbour, a well-off white farmer: "He'll tell you *all* about it ... He don't think we should get anything. He likes to say, 'The white man is paying for everything!'" From an Indigenous viewpoint, the reality is the reverse: many settlers feel entitled to Indigenous land and resources and fail to acknowledge how treaties have enabled them to live on and benefit from Anishinaabe territory. For instance, a First Nations man in his fifties said he was sick of the "crude" stereotype that

> Indians get everything free. They don't pay taxes and get education and health care. And my quick response is always, "Well, just give me my land back. That's fine, I'll give up the rights, but ... the rights that you have, where you live, are worth something. And you don't have the right to be there until I've agreed to that."

Many Indigenous interviewees also described relations as "divided" or "strained" by virtue of recent personal experiences with racial discrimination, highly publicized incidents such as the "powwow video" (see Introduction), and persisting structural inequities in economic opportunity. One Anishinaabe man in his twenties said that unlike Winnipeg where he grew up, in Fort Frances there was "a lot of discrimination against Native people." When he moved to Fort Frances High School, for example, "certain teachers" routinely engaged in "racist" behaviour. He recounted an incident when a First Nation parent physically confronted a teacher who had called his daughter "a spoiled little

Native kid who gets everything she wants ... because we don't have to pay for *anything*, they say." In addition to such personal encounters with discrimination, many interviewees cited the long-standing exclusion of First Nation people from well-paid jobs at the mill and other local businesses, as well as systemic racism in health care, education, criminal justice, and other sectors (see chapters 1 and 4). Clearly, Indigenous residents' experiences with their white neighbours were not as positive or inclusive as many whites presumed.

Still other interviewees – Indigenous and white – described the relationship in general as one of mistrust, fear, and misunderstanding. A white teacher in town said relations were "better before the [video] incident" and now "there isn't a whole lot of *trust*." He had since been accused of discrimination and had become so "cautious" when "dealing with ... First Nation kids" that he always made sure to have another adult present. He further speculated that negative attitudes were fuelled by in-group gossip: "they [Indigenous people] are definitely talking about 'the white person,' just as we're talking about them." A middle-aged Anishinaabe woman who lived in town similarly described relations as "strained" and "conflictual." Although there were "exceptions," she was haunted by what one white resident said at a community forum after the video incident: "I don't feel comfortable coming to your community." Moreover, she said, she used to assume that because of their "close proximity to First Nations that everybody in Fort Frances had been to a powwow or knew they could go." However, when she was dating a white man the previous summer and suggested attending a powwow,

> he goes, "Well, am I allowed on the First Nation?" I said, "What?! ... Why wouldn't you be?" Then he says, "Cause I'm not Native" ... That just *totally* blew my mind ... He had a lot of fear, even though he was with me ... like, will somebody confront him if they see him there? And so, it's still very much [that] we don't understand ... each other.

Thus, although many Indigenous and white residents had close personal ties, there was a pervasive sense of "us versus them" at the *group* level. As implied by some of the above quotations, several residents also believed that local intergroup relations were worse than elsewhere (six) or worsening over time (nine). According to the then local MPP Howard Hampton, relations had been worsening due to external technological forces and government policies that had driven a wedge between communities and fostered economic competition. In his view, local relations were generally positive and more cooperative than in most of Canada, all residents had common interests in good jobs, schools, and health care, and there were many examples of Indigenous and non-Indigenous people working together across the district (see chapter 6). However, "as the resource economy [was] pulled apart," tensions had emerged. "Whereas before, you had Aboriginal and non-Aboriginal people working side by side, driving wood to the mill," environmental regulations that required transport by train or truck rather than the river "eliminated all kinds of jobs that were [held] by First Nations." After the Second World War, "the policy of the paper mill was 'jobs for veterans'":

> There was no distinction made between "Are you an Aboriginal soldier returning or a non-Aboriginal soldier returning?" You're a soldier returning and ... you've got a job. That history [of economic interdependence] has been so strong. But now, as First Nations have lost jobs in forestry [and] tourism ... the original model of cooperative effort and a common process and purpose has been replaced by competition ... I would say there are more potential points of friction between First Nations and non–First Nations now than there ever were. (interview with the author, 10 November 2008)

Mixed Descriptions

Significantly, MPP Hampton noted that although economic competition and tensions had risen between Indigenous and settler communities, there was also a strong history of economic interdependence and interfamilial ties that, to date, may have helped prevent the underlying conflicts from escalating into physical violence. Indeed, when asked to describe local intergroup relations, nearly half of all interviewees (45 per cent) gave "mixed" descriptions that simultaneously conveyed positive and negative dimensions. Some cited instances of conflict or discrimination while balancing them with stories of intergroup friendship, cooperation, or positive changes in racial attitudes over time. A middle-aged white resident described relations as "mixed" because he personally had Indigenous friends and family members and treated them "the same as I'd treat anybody. But I do know there's attitudes out there that 'they get this' and 'they get that' ... you hear it all the time." Like many residents, this interviewee perceived widespread anti-Indigenous prejudice, but tried to distance himself from it. Granted, the colour-blind ideology he espoused can also bolster whites' sense of group position and reinforce structural inequities, as it fails to recognize Indigenous sovereignty, treaty rights, or cultural diversity (see chapter 4). His point, though, was that the overall state of relations was mixed because there were both cross-group friendships and inter-marriages and pervasive stereotypes. A local First Nation chief agreed, saying there was "good and bad" in all groups and thus relations depended on the individuals involved: some "interact[ed] ... admirably" whereas others were "adversarial."

Other interviewees alluded to fluctuations in Indigenous-settler relations, describing them as "up and down" or "one step forward, one step back." An older white man said Indigenous-settler relations in Canada started off "better than in the United States" because "for a long time, all the peoples worked together here for survival." But then there were (unspecified) "situations where things didn't go well," and today "you get people with different opinions ... and a lot of it centres down to who's getting the money." Ultimately, he suggested, First Nations were "getting the money" at settlers' expense, and although this was not always the case, and some compensation for historical injustices was due, he thought the pendulum had swung too far. A white man in his twenties thought relations had been "improving, but because of recent issues with the mining and the logging [conflicts over land rights and use] and the different racial issues [including the video incident]," tensions had returned. Similarly, a middle-aged First Nation woman said the relationship had improved, "but you still see racism." She predicted:

> You may see more [racism] in the next few years when the issue of Point Park comes up ... I think there's some tension over it right now because you have people [on affluent nearby streets] that have sold their houses. [They originally] bought into it thinking "that is the prime land where I'm going to spend the rest of my life, something that I'm going to hand down to my children."

Residents' perceptions of Indigenous-settler relations were thus shaped not only by personal experience, but also by broader shifts in the political economy and specific local incidents that had become racialized, forcing residents to take sides.

In fact, some interviewees, especially Indigenous residents, carefully distinguished between the "surface" appearance of racial harmony and "deeper" racial tensions, or between the relative congeniality at an interpersonal level and the conflict and competing interests at an intergroup (or "political") level. Such distinctions were explicitly made by twenty-five interviewees. For example, a young Anishinaabe man not from the district originally described locals as "two-faced." His Anishinaabe girlfriend agreed:

They'll be nice to each other ... but once they're at home [in] their own little groups, then they'll talk about how – there's *us* sittin' over here and there's *them* sittin' over there, and they'll talk about us and we'll talk about them. Everybody's two-faced like that ... Two-faced friends.

In other words, despite collegial public relations, there was a strong sense of *group positions* apparent in private in-group discussions.

This perceived division between the interpersonal and the political, or between the public and the private – a distinction that will take on greater significance in chapter 7 – was brought out in more detail in a conversation between an older Indigenous couple on a First Nation reserve. Although they personally had many white friends, the husband described local relations as "strained" because "the way I see some of the people treated ... there's got to be a bit of tension there." His (lighter-skinned) wife initially said she did not "feel that." He clarified: "*Not personally.* I know most of the people in Fort Frances. We don't have a problem. But I think ... a lot of [Indigenous people] do." He then told multiple stories of structural inequality and systemic discrimination, which his wife confirmed. For example, at the Fort Frances mill, which used to employ more than one thousand people, "we have *two* people from this community working there. The plant in Barwick [forty-five kilometres west of town], we don't have any. We watch *millions* of dollars cross through the community, but [see] absolutely no benefit." In another case,

[there was] a business in the district ... in big trouble financially. We was looking to invest money in a business. As a community ... we thought it would be good to get into that because we use a lot of their products ... So, we ... sent down a rep, a non-Indian, to make this offer. He come back sheepishly and ... he put down his head and said, "I'm almost ashamed to say it: He don't want any 'f-ing Indian partners' in his business."

For these reasons, the couple concluded that although they personally got along with Indigenous and non-Indigenous neighbours alike, at an intergroup level relations were "strained" and racism was a barrier.

Many Indigenous residents drew similar conclusions. Although they often had white friends and family members, they also perceived widespread discrimination and political conflict. As a middle-aged Anishinaabe woman who lived in town said:

On the surface it appears to be cooperative [but] it's really insidious. And it's ... not as blatant as in ... Kenora ... [In] Fort Frances, by all appearances, it's like, "Oh, we live in this rosy little world" ... and unless you're a First Nations person, or you're in a position to be working with First Nations people, you don't see it.

For example, she said, if an Indigenous and a non-Indigenous person walk into a store, the store clerk's eyes will be on the Indigenous person "to see what they might be taking." Moreover, some landlords "don't want to rent" to Indigenous people:

We even ... had somebody phone, who quite obviously by her voice was a First Nations person ... and ask for an apartment, and she was told it was taken. I called back. The apartment was available.

For another Anishinaabe woman, "it's a really good positive relationship ... on a first-person basis," but on "the political level, like once you get to the mayor and council of Fort Frances and [the First Nations] chiefs and councils, there's a certain level of ignorance that just drives me nuts." She was frustrated that "major issues," such as the Point Park land dispute, were not discussed "openly." Instead, "all we're doing is supporting lawyers' retirements" and exacerbating intergroup tensions. Referring to the video incident, a middle-aged Métis man who lived in Fort Frances admitted that even though he had "worked on the rez [reserve]," he had his "head in a pink cloud" and "thought things were a lot better here than they were." After seeing the video and discussing it with First Nations people, he "started realizing" that racism "is a problem here and it's always been here, but it's beneath the surface. It's hidden. Whereas in Kenora, at least it's in your face."

Some whites similarly described a surface-level tolerance and close personal friendships, but persistent underlying tensions. For example, a white millwright in his thirties whose best friend was Indigenous laughed nervously before admitting there were "issues" and that most residents were "tolerant ... as long as it doesn't get too close to home ... it's the same argument people will make about the gay community or something: people can do whatever they want. Just don't bring it in my house." As Blumer (1958, 5) says, a sense of superior group position may include "the claim to certain areas of intimacy and privacy," and although exceptions are made for selected individuals, minority "intrusion" into such areas is often experienced as threatening.

Meanwhile, in comments predicted by theories of white privilege – in which whiteness is equated with normality and an inability or unwillingness to "see" inequality (see, e.g., Lewis 2004; McKinney 2005) – a white woman in her thirties said she "just took for granted that it's a normal relationship" because "in high school, everyone just seemed so equal. It could have been my own tainted world bubble, but I thought everyone was treated ... good." Later, she dated "a Native fellow" who lived on reserve, and when she attended "a couple powwows with him," she "noticed a bit of a strange relationship." In those situations, she "felt uncomfortable" because "I would stand out like a sore thumb." This experience of being "one of the few white folk" at an Indigenous cultural event she did not fully understand helped her appreciate "what feeling like a minority was [like]." More recently, she said, she thought relations had improved, and was "shocked" by the "YouTube video": "that's when I realized there must be something still in the air that I'm unaware of."

As these stories suggest, many residents had friendly, cooperative relations with at least some members of the "other" group, but there were often limits, persisting forms of inequality and discrimination, and long-standing political conflicts (such as land disputes) that created deep-seated, yet rarely spoken, intergroup tensions. Some residents, especially whites, also reported living in a "bubble" until a crisis forced them to confront deeper issues that were already all too palpable for many Indigenous people.

Beyond this "appearance versus reality" theme, some residents also perceived differences across generations. While eight interviewees thought Indigenous-settler relations were better among younger than older people, at least six had the opposite perception. A self-described "half-breed" in his sixties who lived on reserve believed "the relationship between that society and ours" had improved with each generation "because ... a lot of them intermarried." A teenager of mixed descent agreed "racism is mainly in the older generations." However, a white woman in her fifties expressed the reverse view:

> Things have changed so much. When I look at the generations younger than me, there is so much *division* between the communities. When I was a child ... Kooch [Couchiching First Nation] was like a second village. It's a whole different world now.

Apart from changes over time in intergroup relations, twelve residents emphasized variations across the district, depending on the reserve and town or municipality in question (and the individuals within them). For example, a middle-aged Anishinaabe woman perceived that many whites in Nestor Falls resented Indigenous hunting and fishing rights because tourism is white residents' "livelihood; that's where they get their money from – and [by] welcoming the tourists [who don't always] respect the [Indigenous] people or the land." Although resentment over such rights also existed in Fort Frances, she thought people there were generally "more open." Meanwhile, an older white man described how relationships differed for each reserve in the district. In his view, Couchiching First Nation was "basically integrated into town" and many of its members worked in Fort Frances. Rainy River First Nations was likewise "a suburb" of Emo. Other First Nations, he said, were "more traditional" and "maybe not as integrated," and still others were "in between." These comments illustrate an awareness of the diversity within and between Indigenous communities. However, he also made the settler colonial assumption that "integrated" reserves were a model to which others should aspire, noting that "traditional" reserves had lots of "improving" to do and were places "you went only when you *had* to."

Overall, residents described Indigenous-settler relations in the Rainy River District in a range of complex and sometimes contradictory ways. Given the uniqueness of individual experiences, variations across the district and over time, and the common perception that Fort Frances in general was "cliquish" (a term used by nine interviewees), it is possible that some residents' social worlds were highly integrated across group lines and perhaps experienced as colour-blind, whereas other social worlds were highly segregated or conflictual. Perhaps the majority of residents simultaneously encountered positive intergroup interactions and prejudice and discrimination. Whatever the reality of their individual experiences, their *perceptions* of intergroup relations, of where "we" stand in relation to "them," helped to constitute their sense of group positions, thereby reproducing (and sometimes challenging) the structural inequities associated with settler colonialism.

Between-Group and Over-Time Comparisons

Despite the overall variations outlined above, closer analysis of the interview data revealed two clear and theoretically significant patterns. First, white interviewees were nearly three times more likely to describe intergroup relations in predominantly positive rather than negative terms, whereas Indigenous interviewees (especially First Nations) were nearly three times more likely to describe relations in mixed or negative rather than positive terms (see table 2.1).[10] Such a difference might be expected in a situation of entrenched inequality where the dominant group has long maintained its historically rooted material privileges, at least in part by avoiding open conflict, and where the subordinate group increasingly is publicly asserting its desire for change (Jackman 1994). Although many Indigenous residents reported having close white friends (and family members), they were also frustrated by ongoing systemic and interpersonal racism, treaty violations, and the Canadian state's persisting colonial grip on their communities, which many of their white neighbours appeared not to understand or appreciate. If anything, settlers increasingly viewed themselves as victims of "reverse racism." At a time when Aboriginal and treaty rights had been entrenched in the Constitution Act (1982) and the federal government, as of June 2008, had formally apologized for the Indian residential school system, settler Canadians, especially white residents in regions like northwestern Ontario, faced rising economic insecurity and population stagnation – conditions likely to exacerbate perceived "group threat" (Blalock 1967; Wilson 1999). Thus, although many white residents tried to remain upbeat amid this turning of the tides, some of their positive descriptions were tempered by defensiveness and others were downright hostile.

The second clear pattern was that Indigenous-settler relations – and residents' perceptions of them – were in flux. The video incident was the first "wake-up call" for many, especially whites. When I first arrived in Fort Frances, before I conducted any formal interviews, residents often told me informally that Indigenous and non-Indigenous people got along well; one long-time white resident said he did not understand what I meant by a "relationship between communities," since, in his mind, they were all part of the *same* community (Field notes, August 2007). When the video incident struck, many changed their tune; in the first few months, interviewees were far more likely to describe intergroup relations in mixed or negative terms. Between February and July 2008, the modal response (45 per cent) was mixed and less than one-quarter of interviewees described relations in predominantly positive terms (see table 2.1).[11] As the video incident faded from public attention, residents (including Anishinaabe) were once again more optimistic. Between August and December 2008, the modal response (42 per cent) was positive and only a small minority (16.5 per cent) described relations in predominantly negative terms.

When I returned in the summer of 2009 to conduct follow-up research, local conditions had shifted yet again. In the interim (January to May 2009), tensions surrounding the Point Park land claim had reached a head, with local First Nations threatening a road blockade and Fort Frances town council digging in its heels. Then tensions quickly subsided after the parties agreed to an indefinite lease extension as the case proceeded in court (see chapter 7). Meanwhile, a new controversy was brewing over an Anishinaabe child welfare agency's proposal to relocate its group home facility to the neighbouring Township of Alberton and the distribution of an anonymous flyer suggesting that this "non-secure Native detention centre" would "threaten community safety" (see chapter 5). Not surprisingly, the proportion of "negative" and (especially) "mixed" descriptions of Indigenous-settler relations increased in this last set of interviews (see table 2.1).[12] Only two interviewees (both settler politicians) described relations in predominantly positive terms, while six (22 per cent) described relations negatively and nineteen (70 per cent) gave mixed assessments. Ten of these last twenty-seven interviews were follow-ups with individuals directly involved in Alberton. Four of them described relations in decidedly more negative terms, and none had become more positive.

Moreover, upon my return in 2009, three earlier interviewees spontaneously told me that they had changed their views. A Métis man said he had been too optimistic that group relations had improved over time; recent events had led him to believe that racial discrimination was just as prevalent now as it was thirty-five years ago – just "more hidden." Meanwhile, a white millwright who had been temporarily laid off confessed that he had "held back" in his first interview; he expressed, in a second interview, openly harsh criticisms of Indigenous leaders, antipathy towards treaty rights, and negative stereotypes of Indigenous people. A few months later, a young man of mixed heritage contacted me to say that he had changed his mind as well. He had once endorsed "laissez-faire" views, described group relations as generally "good," and did not think racism affected him, but in his second interview, after expanding his historical education and contemplating recent developments, he expressed more pride in his Anishinaabe heritage, staunchly defended treaty rights, and believed that racism was a persisting problem. In short, as events unfolded both locally (video incident, Point Park land dispute, Alberton group home controversy) and nationally (residential school apology, ongoing land and resource disputes), some residents altered their conceptions of Indigenous-settler relations – and, in a few cases, reframed their own identities and interests – precisely as expected by group position theory.

In one of my first interviews in the spring of 2008, a middle-aged Métis man who had grown up in Kenora but now lived in Fort Frances provided a possible explanation for these trends. In a manner consistent with group position theory, he articulated how the shifting balance of power was starting to threaten the historically dominant white population:

The general population anywhere doesn't like it when the minority starts asserting themselves ... Everything was fine in Kenora when [Indigenous people] got off the sidewalk and went to their own restaurant, but after the incident at [Anicinabe] Park in 1974 ... where militancy was shown in Canada for the first time ... it was a huge wake-up call ... There were suddenly Indian uprisings that had never happened before. Things have been very tense ever since [in Kenora] because [Indigenous] people started saying, "We don't like getting off the sidewalk, we don't like having to go to specific restaurants, we're not going to tip our hat ... We're as good as anybody else and we want to at least be equal." And it's been tension ever since ... And I think here – same thing. The general populations are uncomfortable because somebody is starting to assert themselves and they're going to be even more uncomfortable when you know that, really, they [Indigenous people] are right ... When you take the moral high ground, it's hard to fight you ... because the bottom line is they [settlers] know they're wrong.

Similar themes were echoed in subsequent interviews and interactions with Indigenous and white residents alike, but especially during my follow-up research in 2009. Like the Métis man above, several interviewees suggested, at least implicitly, that Indigenous peoples' recent gains and more openly expressed aspirations were perceived as threatening whites' position, thereby generating an adverse reaction. When asked to describe local intergroup relations, a middle-aged Anishinaabe man said:

It's okay as long as the Indians know their place! So, don't try and argue that you've got unique rights or position in Canada, you know? Sometimes I'd just like to reverse the positions and make all the white people Indians, and vice versa, and then see what they'd be doing about giving up all their legal and constitutional rights! (Emphasis added)

As Blumer (1958, 4–5) says, "a given race is all right in 'its place,'" but perceived "challenge[s] to power and privilege" will elicit backlash. In this case, local whites tolerated Indigenous peoples until they questioned the status quo or asserted Indigenous and treaty rights.

Lending further support to this view, a middle-aged white woman said relations generally were "good" because "there's a lot of interaction," but

it did seem ... there was an underlying tension as the Pither's Point Park issue was coming up, that it could almost become adversarial. It was both sides kind of getting into positioning or something [nervous laughter]. That's probably the first time that I've felt, "Whoa!" ... like "Could it be an Oka? Could it be a barricade?" (Emphasis added)

While some Anishinaabe were inspired by the Oka Crisis, or Kanehsa-take Resistance (see chapter 10), some settlers worried that local land disputes could also get to that point.

Another white woman admitted, "I think a lot of [white] people are afraid of losing their place." When asked what she meant, she said that locally

> the job situation is terrible [and] not everybody can afford to ... further their education. The Native people do get a lot more ... the education is ba-sically there for them if they want it ... And then ... you drive through the reserves and the homes are pretty gorgeous, but ... at one time ... the white people had the fancy houses and the Natives were living in a one-room shack.

Although some of these claims are dubious,[13] the *perception* that Natives are gaining at whites' expense, or that group positions are changing, certainly helps explain intergroup tensions.

Elaborating on these dynamics, a white woman in her sixties, dis-cussing the Alberton and Point Park disputes, drew an analogy to the Jim Crow era in the US Deep South:

> I think it's this whole idea that "our niggers were well behaved until the Northerners ... started inciting them" ... So, it's like, yes, *as long as we're here and you're there [placing one hand a foot above the other] everything is fine, but now something is upsetting the equilibrium,* and that's what was happening in the South ... The equilibrium was getting upset because things were not staying in the places that, um, they had been. (Emphasis added)

As group position theory suggests, when the equilibrium gets upset, dominant groups, such as white settlers, are more likely to express prejudice and employ predictable tactics to maintain their position (see chapter 5).

Within-Group Differences

Beyond these overall trends, it is important to note that the responses of Indigenous and non-Indigenous interviewees also varied with de-mographic and social characteristics (including age, gender, and ed-ucation) and due to individual experiences. Although a detailed within-group analysis is beyond the scope of this chapter, a few trends are worth highlighting.

First, there was a distinct difference in the perspectives of white and Indigenous community leaders (elected officials, church leaders, school board administrators, senior forestry managers, First Nation chiefs, and Métis Nation of Ontario representatives). White leaders were two and a half times more likely to describe relations in positive rather than mixed terms, and none described relations in predominantly negative terms. In contrast, Indigenous leaders were three times more likely to describe relations in mixed or negative rather than positive terms. This polarization of views is important because, as Blumer (1958) and Bobo and Tuan (2006) suggest, community leaders have disproportionate influence in shaping public opinion and thereby the sense of group positions. In this case, most white leaders (regardless of political stripe) – as well as two Métis leaders and one First Nation person who held a leadership role in the public school system – portrayed the status quo in a positive light, implying that "radical" change was neither necessary nor desirable because most residents "get along" and, apart from "a few bad apples," racism was "a thing of the past" (at least locally). In contrast, most Indigenous leaders expressed deep frustrations over persisting socio-economic inequalities, never-ending land disputes, and lack of recognition for their unique identities, sovereignty, and rights (both locally and nationally). In other words, while most Indigenous leaders sought to alter the prevailing group positions, most white leaders suggested that local relations were fine as is.

Indigenous interviewees who described relations in mixed and especially negative terms also tended to be younger and more highly educated than those who described relations in positive terms. This trend might reflect a generational shift in willingness to discuss and confront racism/colonialism, as well as greater awareness of historical and political context among those with a post-secondary education. Curiously, white interviewees who described relations in mixed and especially negative terms tended to be somewhat older. They were also more likely to have a university or college degree, less likely to be employed full time, more likely to depend for employment on economically fragile industries (such as forestry or small-scale agriculture), and somewhat less likely to have been born and raised in the region. These findings suggest that local economic uncertainty was influencing residents' perceptions of Indigenous-settler relations: as economic insecurity rose, so did perceived group threat, leading some – such as the young white farmer quoted above who resented the RRFN land claim settlement – to perceive relations as increasingly antagonistic. These findings also indicate that well-educated residents who had spent significant time outside the region (and thus who may have had more points of comparison) tended to perceive more conflict or tension locally than those who had never lived elsewhere.

Conclusion

As some perceptive interviewees noted, the relationship between Indigenous and non-Indigenous communities in the Rainy River District – however valid the other descriptions in this chapter – was shifting overall: from one of relatively stable paternalistic relations where "everyone gets along" provided that "Indians know their place," to one where Indigenous people increasingly were publicly asserting their identities and rights, challenging racism and colonialism, and often winning court battles and land claim settlements, and where the historically dominant white-settler majority increasingly felt threatened by Indigenous peoples' gains and aspirations. Within this region generally, white residents had long held a sense of superior group position and believed that their relationship with Indigenous people was "pretty good." Given the history of intermarriage, friendship, and cooperation, many Anishinaabe and Métis residents agreed. Nevertheless, the shifting balance of power – including the increasingly precarious position of settlers dependent on resource-extraction industries and the political and cultural resurgence of Indigenous nations – had exposed underlying tensions and heightened divisions, leading some to reassess their very conception of intergroup relations.

The next few chapters will examine more directly the perceived sources of tension or division as well as the bridges that held local Indigenous and settler communities together, even as the "equilibrium" shifted beneath their feet.

Chapter Three

Boundary Work and Group Positioning: How Perceptions of Boundaries Reproduce and Challenge Settler Colonial Relations

"See that?" Tom says, pointing through the cracked windshield, as we bump along the icy road in a rusty old pick-up truck. The peeling yellow-painted words jut out from the rotting wooden sign: "No Trespassing – Indian Reserve."

"You know what we do to white people here?" he says. "Scalp 'em."

He and Sam laugh heartily. Repressing a pang of fear, I laugh along with them. I have no choice but to trust my new friends – sandwiched, as I am, between these two large, proud Anishinaabe men.

"Where'd that sign come from?" I ask.

"Government."

Sam explains that we are now entering the old reserve; the entire First Nation community was relocated after a smallpox epidemic decades ago when the Canadian government not only forbade Native people to leave the reserve without permission of the Indian agent but also forbade non-Natives to enter.

Field notes, March 2008

This anecdote reveals at least two important boundaries: one marked by the "No Trespassing" sign, a remnant of Canadian legislation that physically separated Indigenous and settler peoples, and the other by the fear and mistrust that I, as a white person, momentarily experienced (and struggled to overcome), perhaps due to immersion in a society with pervasive anti-Indigenous stereotypes. Moreover, the anecdote shows how Tom and Sam actively used these boundaries to joke with and test me and, at least situationally, shift power relations.

This chapter investigates the relationship between such "boundary work" and group positioning. Specifically, I examine how Indigenous and white residents of the Rainy River District perceive and evaluate intergroup boundaries and how their perceptions reflect and reinforce their respective senses of group position. Drawing primarily on interview data, I identify fifteen distinct categories of boundaries, or perceived sources of division. A central conflict in how Indigenous and non-Indigenous residents tend to *frame* boundaries is then highlighted: whereas many whites view treaties, land claims, and self-government as boundaries to better relations, many Anishinaabe and Métis say the "real" boundary is lack of understanding and respect for their histories, rights, and worldviews. These conflicting ways of framing boundaries serve, respectively, to legitimize and challenge the structural inequities associated with settler colonialism. The dominant white frame *positions* whites as inherently entitled to their current resources and privileges and threatened by such "boundaries" as Indigenous sovereignty and treaties, which require settlers to take responsibility and share power. It also rationalizes material boundaries, such as higher poverty rates among Indigenous families, via the construction of moral boundaries, or stereotypes about Indigenous peoples' alleged moral failings. In contrast, the dominant Indigenous frame challenges their presumed inferiority and articulates an alternative vision of group relations that asserts cultural and political boundaries – including distinct identities, beliefs, and governance systems – as positive goods and inherent rights, while also seeking to overcome the boundaries of poverty, racism, and (wilful) ignorance.

Boundary Work and Group Positioning

In general, boundaries are "lines that include and define some people, groups and things while excluding others" (Lamont 2001, 15341). There is a long tradition of empirical research on group boundaries, much of it inspired by the work of anthropologist Fredrik Barth (1969). Social scientists have distinguished various dimensions of boundaries, including type (symbolic versus material), salience, permeability, durability, and so on (Lamont and Molnar 2002). They have also theorized the relationship between boundary construction and power dynamics (Wimmer 2008). In this chapter, I take an inductive approach, looking at how interviewees understand boundaries and assessing how their perceptions of boundaries relate to group positioning.[1]

Although few scholars have explicitly studied boundary work in Indigenous-settler relations, earlier ethnographies have described similar processes. As discussed in the Introduction, Braroe (1975, 186–7) found an almost complete separation of "Indian and white" social, spatial, and moral worlds in a small Prairie community in the early 1970s, where very few Indians lived in town, they were not involved in community organizations, and they were "tacitly forbidden" access to restaurants, parks, and hotels (42). Conversely, "whites [were] seldom present on the reserve" (61). On rare occasions when they did interact, there was a logic of "mutual exploitation," and each group behaved in ways that reinforced their image of the other as "morally inferior" (186).

Nearly two decades later, in Thunder Bay, Dunk (1991) observed similar dynamics, but added the "third element" of working-class whites' class subordination (130). In this case, "The Indian [was] perceived as an inferior other against whom [working class male] whites define[d] themselves" (103). Yet working-class whites also defined themselves against "the perceived dominant power bloc," or upper-class whites in big southern cities. Indians were thought to receive special treatment from these elites and were the object of both "derision" and "envy." Although working-class whites did not benefit from colonization as much as urban elites, they were motivated to maintain their socio-economic status over Indians *and* their sense of moral superiority over both Indians and elites, a dynamic that appears in my data as well.

Conversely, Basso (1979) examined Western Apaches' joking imitations of Anglo-Americans, arguing that "in all Indian cultures 'the Whiteman' serves as a conspicuous vehicle for conceptions that define and characterize what 'the Indian' is not." Indigenous people respond to centuries of colonial oppression by using the symbolic resources of language and humour to maintain self-worth. Similarly, Vasquez and Wetzel (2009, 1557) showed how Mexican Americans and Potawatomi Indians "challenge contemporary institutional racism through elaborating symbolic boundaries and articulating moral discourses. By emphasizing authentic traditions – conceived of as values, roots, and cultural toolkits – these historically and currently marginalized groups distinguish themselves from the American mainstream," and thereby uphold their dignity.

Despite these insights, none of these scholars explicitly addressed how boundary work relates to group positioning (or wider colonial structures). In group position theory, individuals must first identify with a group and form an image of their group and its relationship to other groups. This implies a symbolic boundary between "us" and "them." However, us/them distinctions alone are insufficient for prejudice, which also depends on a hierarchical positioning of groups – a feeling that "we" are superior and "they" are inferior, a sense of entitlement to resources and privileges, and a perception of threat from marginalized group members who challenge one's prerogatives (Blumer

1958; Bobo 1999). Prejudice is a "defensive reaction" to perceived group threat, including challenges to power/control, economic competition, and perceived moral affronts.

In the language of boundary work, I suggest that whether us/them distinctions translate into a sense of superior group position depends on how boundaries are framed, that is, actors' conceptions of which boundaries exist, which should exist, and what they mean. These boundary-framing processes, in turn, are shaped by historically endowed resources, available cultural repertoires, and the latent balance of power.

Residents' Conceptions of Boundaries: Overall Trends

To examine how residents conceived of intergroup boundaries, I asked all 160 interviewees "What do you think are the biggest boundaries between Aboriginal and non-Aboriginal people today? In other words, what (if any) are the key sources of division?"[2]

In response, Rainy River District residents described hundreds of unique boundaries or sources of division.[3] To make the results more manageable, I condensed their responses into fifteen conceptually distinct but empirically overlapping categories. These included (from most to least frequently mentioned by interviewees):

- Treaty rights and ignorance of or disrespect for treaty rights
- Historical events/processes/experiences and ignorance of or disrespect for history
- Canadian government laws, policies, and (in)actions
- Racism, stereotypes, and "reverse racism"
- Cultural differences (i.e., identities, languages, customs) and ignorance of or disrespect for cultural diversity
- Land disputes and ignorance of or disrespect for land rights
- Indigenous self-government and ignorance of or disrespect for Indigenous sovereignty
- Alleged Indigenous moral deficits
- Alleged white moral deficits
- Different ways of thinking, or "deep" cultural differences (i.e., value conflicts)
- Reserve system and/or spatial segregation
- Policies and (in)actions of non-government organizations (i.e., religion, media, business)
- Mistrust
- Social segregation, or lack of meaningful intergroup contact
- Political avoidance, or unwillingness to openly discuss the "real" issues

In the next section, I compare and contrast how Indigenous and white residents framed seven of the most salient boundaries. My analysis shows how their perceptions reflected and reinforced their respective senses of group position. The boundary of racism will be analysed more closely in chapter 4.

Indigenous and White Perspectives on Boundaries: Comparative Analysis

To what extent did Indigenous and non-Indigenous residents agree on the boundaries (or sources of division) between their communities? As table 3.1 shows, many residents concurred that the salient boundaries revolved around history, treaties, land and other resources, Canadian government laws and policies, Indigenous self-government, and (perceived) cultural and moral differences. At a group level, however, the similarities ended there.

Indigenous and white interviewees tended to frame these boundaries in divergent ways that reflected and reinforced their respective senses of group position. Many whites viewed treaties, land claims, self-government, and cultural differences as boundaries to be overcome or erased; they also constructed moral boundaries (against Indigenous people) to defend and justify their privileges, thereby legitimating structural inequalities and their own sense of superiority. In contrast, Indigenous residents tended to conceive of boundaries in terms of ignorance of or disrespect for their histories, rights, and worldviews. They asserted distinct identities and rights as positive boundaries and sought to eliminate political and material boundaries that inhibited their self-determination and well-being. These different ways of thinking about boundaries constitute a source of division in themselves.

History and Ignorance of or Disrespect for History

History was implicated in many of the boundaries cited by residents. A majority of both Indigenous and white interviewees directly discussed historical processes, events, experiences, or legacies when asked about the boundaries between Indigenous and non-Indigenous peoples. As Furniss (1999) emphasizes in her study of Indigenous-settler relations in Williams Lake, BC, however, the ways in which these groups think about history, and the meanings they attribute to it, differ.[4]

On one hand, some Anishinaabe and Métis residents emphasized the historical and ongoing impacts of settler colonialism. For Mashkawegaabo (Al Hunter), the fundamental problem is "Colonization, man! It's imperialism," which has included residential schools, language

Table 3.1 Percentage of Indigenous and White Interviewees Who Discussed Selected Boundaries

Category of boundaries	% of Indigenous interviewees who discussed it	% of white interviewees who discussed it	Total number of interviewees who discussed it
1. Treaty rights	50.0	64.1	91
Ignorance of or disrespect for treaties	45.1	19.2	52
2. Historical events/processes	53.7	52.6	85
Ignorance of or disrespect for history	48.8	20.5	56
Residential schools	17.1	7.7	20
3. Laws, policies, (in)actions of Canadian governments	43.9	46.2	72
Reserve system	9.8	21.8	25
Indian Act	12.2	2.6	12
4. Racism and reverse racism	57.3	30.8	71
Racism	41.5	16.7	47
Reverse racism	18.3	24.4	34
5. Cultural differences	41.5	42.3	67
Ignorance of or disrespect for cultural differences	31.7	19.2	41
Ways of thinking/value conflict ("deep" culture)	25.6	15.4	33
6. Land disputes	30.5	46.2	61
Ignorance of or disrespect for Indigenous land rights	24.4	7.7	26
7. Self-gov't/sovereignty	30.5	25.6	45
Ignorance of or disrespect for Indigenous sovereignty	19.5	1.3	17
8. Moral distinctions			
Indigenous deficit	18.3	33.3	41
White deficit	30.5	11.5	34

assimilation, land theft, and unilateral rule-making by Canadian governments. Although First Nations "are doing their best to survive within that system," he said, "it's killing us." Indigenous peoples, therefore, "need to revive our own government systems." As Mashkawegaabo suggests, colonization involves *erasing* boundaries – in this case, the unique identities, cultures, languages, political, economic, and spiritual systems of Indigenous peoples – and replacing them with those of the colonizer (Veracini 2010; Wolfe 2006). The process of resistance, therefore, entails *asserting* boundaries through reviving Indigenous governments and exercising cultural and political autonomy.

Mashkawegaabo further explained that the doctrine of discovery that European settlers imported to the Americas has always shaped (consciously or not) the attitudes and policies of settler Canadians and their governments (for critical analyses of this and related doctrines, see Borrows 2010; Mackey 2016; Newcomb 2008; Williams 2012). In his words:

> The bottom line is that the attitude that the newcomers brought to this land was already manifested in Europe hundreds of years [earlier] and that's based on religious doctrine that "Wherever we go, we have a right to take whatever is there. And it doesn't matter if anybody is living there; they'll be treated as if they're not people."

He described how a set of fifteenth-century papal decrees is "entrenched in Canadian and US law," and thereby affects how governments treat Indigenous peoples: "That's why you have the interests of corporations superseding those of treaty nations." In short, he said, the biggest boundary is the "superiority complex," rooted in religious doctrine, that Europeans brought to the "New World" and used – and continue to use – to justify colonialism.

While most interviewees did not explicitly name "colonization," let alone papal decrees, many Indigenous residents did describe how they or their parents or grandparents were directly affected by the residential school system and other historical injustices. They further asserted that settlers' lack of awareness or appreciation of this history constitutes a boundary between communities.[5] A middle-aged First Nation woman who lived in town said residential schools were "just the tip of the iceberg":

> People ... aren't informed and they don't care to be informed ... That's what breeds racism ... People aren't aware that my dad couldn't vote, [or] get a mortgage, that my uncle fought a war but [was denied access to veterans' benefits] ... that you weren't allowed to leave the reserve without permission of an Indian agent.

For her, then, ignorance of history is a key divider, and the education system is "responsible" because "they need to teach the proper history" and its ongoing effects.

Although many white interviewees also cited history as a boundary, they tended to frame it differently – in ways that bolstered their sense of group superiority and entitlement. Specifically, many whites felt unfairly blamed and forced to pay for their "ancestors' mistakes." In their view, the "real" boundary is Indigenous peoples' refusal to "let go" of the past and "move on." According to three white residents whom I interviewed together:

> JIM [middle-aged white man]: I'm thinking that it's their [Indigenous peoples'] history. We're still paying the price for the ancestors, instead of just letting go and moving on ...
>
> SUE [middle-aged white woman]: Why do they [Indigenous peoples] have special privileges and we [settlers] don't?
>
> JIM: Yeah, why do they get tax-free –
>
> SUE: Everybody should be equal.
>
> JIM: We have to work. Why don't they?
>
> CHARLIE [older white man]: Why don't they have to pay taxes? ... when they fill up their vehicles, they get twenty-eight dollars worth of gas for twenty dollars ...
>
> JIM: Again, we're paying for past history. When does that stop? When do we all just blend in like one?
>
> CHARLIE: Well, it's just like that big thing on TV about ... residential schools. These guys all got money ...

Clearly, these white residents positioned themselves as disadvantaged and unfairly treated relative to Indigenous peoples, who were perceived as enjoying undeserved tax breaks and monetary payments. Absent historical context, such attitudes might seem warranted. However, the information omitted is just as important as that provided. For instance, these residents ignore the fact that First Nation families are three times more likely than settler Canadian families to be (economically) poor, despite treaty-based tax exemptions. They also ignore (and perhaps do not know) why such treaty rights exist and how, via treaties, settlers too came to enjoy "special privileges" such as living in Canada with their own laws and governments. Playing the victim enables white settlers to defend such (unacknowledged) privileges without "paying the price" and thereby uphold their sense of moral superiority.

To give another example, an older white businessman said, "people are getting tired of paying and when does it end?" Raising his voice, he added: "we gotta get over it and let everybody get on with their life and not use excuses." Similarly, a white woman in her sixties said her "forefathers did the right thing" in signing treaties with "the Natives":

> They thought "innocent people" and tried to protect them. But they have put into place [legislation whereby First Nations] can't make any decisions on their own, and I think that's unfair to them. But I also see another side

where they like to live in the history. You know, if someone did something four centuries ago that I'm not aware of ... you have to let the history go. If you want to be a partner ... in job creation and business creation ... you have to get into this century and not rely on "Well, this thing happened to us." A lot of things happened to a lot of people.

While the former interviewee expressed overt hostility, the latter was more paternalistic. However, both accused Indigenous peoples of creating a boundary by dwelling on or demanding reparations for historical injustices. This laissez-faire stance protects whites' existing material privileges and portrays Indigenous peoples as morally inferior.

A few Indigenous residents agreed that everyone would be better off leaving the past behind and starting anew from a blank state, as Canadian citizens with the same rights and responsibilities. According to a fair-skinned Métis man in his twenties, "both sides need to spend more time facing forward than looking back." Although "horrible stuff" happened "a hundred years ago," he said, it is time to "move forward" and "fix the problems that you have now." Revealing his own identification with Canada, he added, "*They* [First Nations] lost land. Well, *we*'ve been giving it back. Let's drop the issue ... 'cause that's gonna cause resentment." Thus, it seems, some Indigenous people endorsed the dominant white frame.

Meanwhile, some whites acknowledged their ignorance about the history of Indigenous-settler relations and said they wished they had learned more in school. The few white interviewees who reported having changed their views attributed great importance to learning the "real" history outside the classroom, including a middle-aged white man who said:

A lot of people don't understand the history ... I do. I did all the research on my [Métis] wife's genealogy ... I read all the Manitoba history ... I studied Treaty No. 3 ... But the vast majority of people just don't understand the background. That's probably one of the biggest barriers. It's the same as the French-English thing; they don't understand that when this country was formed, that's what we agreed to.

Many of the pictures from my photovoice project with Indigenous and settler residents also depicted historical boundaries, including colonial policies and practices, residential schools, and the "whitewashing" of Canadian history. One reflective white participant (Dorothy, age fifty-nine) presented a "found" picture of her grandparents along with a caption describing how their opportunity to escape poverty in Europe and build a better life in Canada tragically came "at the expense" of Indigenous peoples. She hoped that greater historical consciousness would spark changes in contemporary policies and attitudes.[6] In her words:

> My Mennonite ancestors ... lived in enclosed "colonies" in the Ukraine and ... my mother's family ... became landless after a few generations since their plot could no longer be divided among the sons into a size that could support a family. My mother's grandparents and parents immigrated to Saskatchewan in 1899 to homestead land that was wrested from Cree and Assiniboine and Métis people fourteen years earlier, after the destruction of ... Métis and allied Aboriginal forces ... and the hanging of Louis Riel and eight Aboriginal leaders. The Canadian government probably did not mention these bloody facts when recruiting pacifist homesteaders. My mother's family got an opportunity to escape poverty ... but *at the expense of a whole way of life and survival of another group of people. This unjust history feels like a great barrier to right relations.* I don't know the full way through, but one interim step ... would surely be to make sure there is ample land available for the growing Aboriginal population. (Emphasis added)

In short, Indigenous and white residents both described history as a source of intergroup division, but they tended to frame the problem in ways that supported their respective senses of group position. For many whites, history is a "burden" (Furniss 1999), forcing them to pay for ancestors' mistakes. They often blame Indigenous people for not relinquishing the past and accepting their place in Canada, for not acquiescing to colonialism. For many Anishinaabe and Métis, in contrast, the "real" boundary is settler Canadians' (wilful) ignorance of how historical forces have not only harmed them (through land appropriation, intergenerational trauma, and forced assimilation), but also created the framework of rights and responsibilities (i.e., treaties) that give the Canadian state its legitimacy. If truly honoured and respected, these treaties could, in their eyes, potentially save our relationships with one another and Mother Earth.

Canadian Government Laws, Policies, and (In)actions

A number of historical boundaries also involve laws, policies, and practices of the Canadian government, many of which still exist today. Both Indigenous and white interviewees directly stated that governments have created intergroup divisions – sometimes, ironically, by trying to erase boundaries via assimilation policies. Again, however, they tended to refer to different types of policies or frame them differently. Many Indigenous residents (and some settlers) described the ongoing impacts of residential schools, the pass system, and federal legislation such as the 1876 Indian Act, which unilaterally distinguished status from non-status Indians. This latter legislation (still in effect, in slightly modified form) is critical to any discussion of intergroup boundaries, because in it the federal government unilaterally defines who is an Indian and thus is eligible for treaty rights and various state benefits (see chapter 1). As the more powerful party (in terms of material resources, means of violence, and so on), the government has the capacity to enforce its definitions, whether or not Indigenous peoples agree.

Other Indigenous interviewees criticized the bureaucratic inertia and the "maze" they must navigate to accomplish basic tasks with government. A local First Nation chief described Indigenous and Northern Affairs Canada as "a cancer that feeds on itself ... they continue to grow and grow at our expense" – evidenced by reports showing that one-third of the funding earmarked for First Nations pays the salaries of bureaucrats in Ottawa (e.g., AFN 2004). Moreover, there are restrictions on how the rest is spent: "We get a hundred per cent of the criticism from the taxpayer, but we don't get a hundred per cent of the tax dollar [budgeted for First Nations]." One Anishinaabe photovoice participant creatively expressed a similar dilemma with the photo and caption presented in figure 3.1.

Many Indigenous interviewees also considered funding inequities to be a boundary. For example, as of writing, in Ontario on-reserve schools still receive two to three thousand dollars less funding per capita than off-reserve schools (Blackstock 2011). Child welfare agencies on reserve receive 22 to 34 per cent less funding than their provincial counterparts (Murphy 2016), a situation that the Canadian Human Rights Tribunal (2016) has deemed systemic discrimination. Several residents also pointed to higher food prices in the north, which disproportionately affect Indigenous people and could be alleviated by better government subsidies.

Although some non-Indigenous residents agreed that funding inequities and federal laws like the Indian Act are boundaries that systematically disadvantage Indigenous peoples, white interviewees were far more likely to say the "real" boundary is the "preferential treatment" that Indigenous peoples allegedly receive from federal and provincial governments. Like working-class whites in Dunk's (1991) Thunder Bay study, they saw themselves as losing out in a competition for state resources. Some also criticized the reserve system for separating First

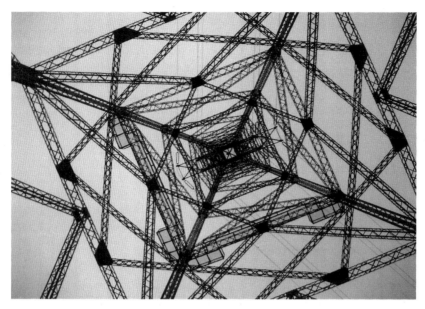

Figure 3.1 The Maze. "This picture was taken laying on the ground, looking up at the hydro tower. To me, as an Anishinaabe person living and working in Treaty No. 3, it represents the maze that we still have to jump through as First Nations just to get the simplest things accomplished, things taken for granted by the mainstream." – Naa-Gaabiinegee-zhig, Anishinaabe man, age fifty-three. Photo courtesy of Naa-Gaabiinegee-zhig.

Nations from "mainstream" Canada, thereby creating a hard, physical boundary. According to a retired white businessman, the reserve system

> keep[s] them separated from ... society and gaining meaningful employment ... how the hell do you get a job when you're a hundred miles from nowhere? There's nothing for them to do. It's no wonder that they snort gas and are on drugs, and crime is probably about the only thing that there's an opportunity for. *So, I think when [the government] formed reserves and made a boundary ... that they did wrong.* (Emphasis added)

For this interviewee, the main boundary is the reserve system, which separates First Nations from "society" and creates stereotypical social problems. In his view, reserves should be abolished, and Indigenous people should assimilate.

The settler colonial desire for assimilation, and for the abolition of an Indigenous land base, conveniently ignores that, in Treaty No. 3 at least, reserves were created as a condition of the treaty that allowed for non-Indigenous Canadian settlement (see chapter 1). Further, while some Anishinaabe also criticize the reserve system, particularly for inadequate land allocations and restrictive land use policies, they reject the idea of abandoning their homelands and assimilating into settler society. For many, the reserve represents home and community, a refuge from an often hostile "mainstream" society.

As chapter 2 emphasizes, some whites feel there has been "a total switch-around" whereby government policy now favours Indigenous interests and disadvantages white people. According to a white male trucker:

> The biggest boundary is the government catering to 'em and givin' in. We [white people] do what they do, we wind up in [jail]. They [Indigenous people] do it, it's all right ... Like the land fights. We buy our land and pay for it for the rest of our life ... they got the land, and that's it. They don't pay taxes. They don't pay nothin' ... It's unfair now for the white people and it's the government's fault. They're puttin' a wall between us.

Echoing the laissez-faire discourse in the previous section, such interviewees advocated *erasing* "boundaries" such as treaty rights and tax exemptions, a colour-blind approach that reinforces structural inequities, advances colonization, and protects whites' sense of group position.

Similarly, when asked about boundaries, a municipal representative in Fort Frances discussed the ongoing land dispute at Point Park (see more below):

> *We* didn't make the mistakes. The [provincial and federal] government made the mistakes. But we have to pay for their mistakes. Because we have to put in our budget every year a tremendous amount of money for legal costs in order to fight ... a problem we didn't create ... Now, I don't know how *they* [First Nations] get their funding for that, but every time we go to the table, there's a lawyer from Canada, there's a lawyer from Ontario, and we have our lawyer that we're paying. But Canada and Ontario isn't fighting to help us. And that's where the resentment comes in ... the governments are creating that issue by the unfairness. Yes, we might have done things wrong over the last fifty or seventy-five years, but [*pause*] – it's *tipping*. You've got to find that level ground. (Emphasis added)

Like the trucker above, this municipal leader acknowledges historical "mistakes" but refuses to pay the cost. He suggests that the equilibrium is shifting, that the balance of power is "tipping" in Indigenous peoples' favour, *at whites' expense* – and, he says, it is the government's fault. Yet the fact remains that Indigenous people today, including those living off reserve, are more likely than non-Indigenous Canadians to live in (economic) poverty, less likely to graduate from high school or find meaningful employment, and more likely to commit suicide, suffer chronic health conditions, and die prematurely. Their ability to exercise self-determination on their lands is constrained because settler governments and corporations routinely ignore Indigenous laws and policies. To suggest that the current playing field is "level" or even "unfair" for whites is to assume that whites, as a group, are inherently superior and deserving of their existing (and long-standing) political, economic, health, and other advantages.

In short, many Indigenous and white interviewees agreed that government policies and (in)actions have created "boundaries" between their communities. However, the specific policies and (in)actions they cited, and the meanings attributed to them, tended to differ in ways that supported their respective senses of group position: whereas many whites opposed compensatory policies as undeserved "handouts" and advocated abolishing reserves (or Indigenous land title), many Anishinaabe and Métis complained about persistent underfunding, unilateral legislation, and paternalistic governments that presume to define their "Indianness."

Treaty Rights and Ignorance of or Disrespect for Treaties

Closely related to history and state laws and policies are the treaties that govern Indigenous-settler relations in much of Canada. Although treaties are also a potential bridge (see chapter 6), treaty rights and ignorance of or disrespect for treaties was the single most frequently cited boundary in my interviews. Many white interviewees believed that treaties per se are a divider because they treat groups differently and, they claim, provide "special privileges" to Indigenous peoples. From an Anishinaabe perspective, however, treaties represent a partnership between nations, an agreement to share the land and its resources equitably, "in perpetuity." The "real" boundary, in their view, is the widespread lack of understanding that "we are all treaty people" with ongoing rights and responsibilities to one another. These divergent ways of thinking about treaties reflect and reinforce respective senses of group position.

On one hand, many whites assume that "we are all Canadian" and therefore "should be treated the same." They reject the notion of treaties as a sustainable foundation for society. As former prime minister Pierre Elliott Trudeau stated in 1969:

> It's inconceivable ... that in a given society one section of the society have a treaty with the other section of the society. We must all be equal under the laws and we must not sign treaties amongst ourselves. (Quoted in Miller 2000, 329)

Similar arguments are espoused today by some academics (Flanagan 2000; Widdowson and Howard 2008), who dismiss Indigenous self-understandings that they are distinct nations who entered treaties with *another society*. A more moderate version of this argument acknowledges the legal validity of treaties, but interprets them narrowly in terms of the specific written contract signed by both parties. For example, if Canada's written text of Treaty No. 3 states that the crown should "within the territory ceded, pay to each Indian person the sum of five dollars per head yearly" and provide "two hoes" and "one spade ... for every family actually cultivating," then, some argue, this is precisely what First Nations should receive – nothing more and nothing less – *in exchange for* the agreement to "cede, release, surrender and yield up to the Government of the Dominion of Canada for Her Majesty the Queen and Her successors forever, all their rights, titles and privileges whatsoever, to the lands" covered by the treaty – in this case, fifty-five thousand square miles.

While some white interviewees opposed the principle of treaties ("equality means treating people the same"), most were more concerned about the vast quantities of "free" (and implicitly undeserved) money perceived to be flowing to Indigenous peoples – in the form of treaty-based tax exemptions, post-secondary education funding, and other social benefits. For example, a white resident in his fifties said the main source of division is "all the regular stuff," by which he meant common stereotypes that "Indians don't pay taxes" and that "there's a different set of laws for them." Similarly, an older white farmer said he opposed Indigenous peoples' "special rights": "I feel that my children, my grandchildren, should be treated the same as them." When asked what he meant by "special rights," he said:

> Well, practically everything! If you get a treaty card, a band number, you know, you don't have to pay taxes.[7] ... I don't like paying taxes, but I have to pay taxes! Well, okay, if I pay taxes, I'm entitled to ... special rights. If

they don't pay taxes, well, then, I guess they better forfeit all those nice social services!

From an Indigenous perspective, this view ignores that the agreement made between the crown and the Anishinaabe when Canada expanded into Treaty No. 3 territory specified that the land would be shared *in exchange* for selected "services." Taxation was never part of these discussions and is not mentioned in any version of the treaty. Thus, most Anishinaabe argue that they never agreed to be taxed by Canada. As a sovereign nation, they should not have to pay taxes to another nation – just as Canadians do not pay American taxes, and vice versa.

Many non-Indigenous residents see it differently. A middle-aged white woman complained about the "disparity" whereby two nurses could be working side-by-side "and one's Native ... and doesn't pay any taxes, and the other [non-Native] one does, right?"[8] Meanwhile, she claimed, "all the privileges" that Indigenous people have access to, such as health care, are "funded through *our* taxes. So, I think ... people resent that." A white man in his twenties agreed: "there's always been an unease in our area" over such issues. For example, he said, "I have some Native friends and ... they had all their schooling paid for," whereas "I have to work my butt off just to pay for schooling and then I'm stuck with a twenty-five-thousand-dollar loan." Likewise, an older white man said "a lot of non-Native people" were "annoyed" that First Nations people could "take a gill net, set it in the lake, and catch all the fish they want," whereas non-Natives had a "limit."[9] For these residents, then, the main source of tension is the alleged "privileges" (including health care, education, and harvesting rights) that Indigenous peoples enjoy due to the treaties and their distinct legal status. They ignore, however, that most Indigenous people *do* pay taxes ("their" privileges are not all funded through "our" taxes) and that settlers also get something in return: the right to live in Canada with their own laws and governments, and the abundant wealth and infrastructure generated from resource extraction on Indigenous and treaty lands.[10]

For most Indigenous interviewees, treaties are the foundation of our relationships with each other and of the Canadian state. If Canada fails to honour its treaties with the First Nations, it has no legitimacy – from an Indigenous or international legal perspective – to govern its presumed land base (see Asch 2002, 2014; Borrows 2010).[11] Moreover, a treaty is not simply a written contract; it is a sacred agreement to share the land in "peace and friendship," to recognize one another's distinctness and to share our gifts as needed (Craft 2013; Mainville 2007; Mills 2017). From this perspective, it is "the spirit and intent" of treaties – not the (often problematic) literal written word – that must be honoured (see chapter 1). If, for example, the treaty refers to a "medicine chest," this should be interpreted liberally to mean equitable access to public health care services. If the treaty promises "to maintain schools for instruction ... whenever the Indians of the reserve shall desire it," in the twenty-first century this should extend to post-secondary schooling.[12] Some Indigenous interviewees added that if settler-Canadians envy Indigenous peoples' treaty rights so much, perhaps they should lobby their own government for the same rights. For example, why don't Canadians receive free or subsidized post-secondary education? Why do Canadians have so many hunting and fishing restrictions? Do they not know how to conserve resources without government regulation?

Further, some interviewees emphasized, Indigenous peoples do not "get everything free": acquiring treaty rights meant giving settlers access to their land. Moreover, post-secondary funding for Indigenous students is limited, and there are strict rules governing its use. Dozens of First Nation communities do not have functioning schools or clean running water, and federally hired contractors have repeatedly built reserve housing in poor locations with low-quality materials (see, e.g., Frideres 2011; Palmater 2015; Vowel 2016). Many Indigenous people view these problems as ongoing treaty violations; if anything, it is settler Canadians who have been getting the "free ride."

As one Anishinaabe man quoted in the previous chapter said, First Nations' treaty rights were *in exchange* for sharing the land: "the rights that you have, where you live, are worth something. And you don't have the right to be there until I've agreed to that." Chief Gary Allen of Nigigoonsiminikaaning First Nation elaborated: Treaty No. 3 "allowed for the settlement of non-Indigenous people in this area," but the federal government, and by extension settler-Canadians, acquired "fiduciary responsibilities." Moreover, the Anishinaabe never "signed away their rights to the resources," including water, minerals, and timber; this is a central point in ongoing legal battles. Until residents on all sides better understand their treaty rights and responsibilities, therefore, conflict will persist.

Mashkawegaabo (Al Hunter) further challenged the dominant settler lens in a way that transforms the sense of group positions and highlights the agency of Indigenous peoples:

> Treaties are a grant of rights given *from* Indians ... not a grant of rights given *to* Indians ... Entrenched in the treaties are rights of passage, occupation, [and] use. But Native people also reserved rights to hunt, gather, fish, occupy; their own rights of passage, their economic, political, and

spiritual interests are all maintained in those treaties. And that's what people have to understand. You didn't come here and say, "Oh, we're gonna give you free schooling." No. The Indian people foresaw genera- tions ahead because of the ceremonies they conducted and said, "What our children are gonna need is a clause in this treaty that says, 'Yes, we will agree to your living here, but, *in return*, you have to agree that from this day forward ... our kids will not have to pay for their education, will not have to pay for their health care ... '" It's a contract ... Indian people knew what they were doing. And it's misunderstood now because of this superiority complex that [white] people have, that they had before they came here.

Indeed, a few non-Indigenous interviewees acknowledged that most settlers have limited understanding of treaties and that this – rather than the treaty itself – creates a boundary. For example, a white man in his sixties not originally from the region said, "There's an enormous amount of ignorance about the treaties ... white folks have been getting a good deal for over a hundred years, and they need to understand what a treaty is: it's an agreement, a covenant."

Local First Nations have worked hard to educate their neighbours about treaties. In spring 2008, for example, Naicatchewenin First Na- tion organized a free, public conference entitled "Recapturing Our Anishinaabe Spirit," parts of which were attended by local MPP How- ard Hampton, future MP John Rafferty, and dozens of Indigenous and non-Indigenous children from Crossroads Public School, twenty-two kilometres west of Fort Frances. On the advice of Naicatchewenin El- ders, an entire afternoon was devoted to Aboriginal and treaty rights. But, I observed, the topic also surfaced throughout the four-day confer- ence and at many other events organized by Indigenous communities throughout the region.

In August 2008, the local First Nations hosted a (separate) four-day National Treaties No. 1 to 11 Gathering, inviting speakers from the eleven numbered treaty territories across Central and Western Canada to share stories, educate the public, and build momentum for a national treaty rights movement. Although the event was free, open to the pub- lic, and well advertised, I counted only a few white residents in attend- ance. Nevertheless, even if more settlers could be persuaded to attend such events, the extent to which such educational opportunities can alter perceptions – and indeed the sense of group positions – remains to be seen. If the deeper problem is an imbalance of power and settlers' desire to protect their resources and privileges, then education alone may be insufficient (see chapter 8).

In sum, the single most frequently cited boundary in my interviews was the treaty relationship between Indigenous and non-Indigenous peoples – a unique type of boundary that has not been discussed in previous research on "boundary work." For most white interviewees, the problem was treaty rights per se. They viewed treaties as a historic relic that should be interpreted narrowly, if retained at all, and that give an unfair advantage to Indigenous peoples; in their view, treaties should be abolished and replaced with the same laws for all Canadians, including Indigenous peoples. Although this solution might seem fair in the abstract, in a settler colonial context it amounts to land theft and genocide (destruction of a people, as a people). For most Anishinaabe and Métis (and a minority of settlers), treaties are essential to fair and equitable relations between nations, a sacred bond. To be legitimate, they say, the Canadian state and its citizens must honour their original covenant with the First Nations, for "we are all treaty people."

Land Disputes and Ignorance of or Disrespect for Land Rights

As of this writing, every First Nation community in the Rainy River District is involved in at least one land claim relating to alleged historical or ongoing injustices, such as improper reserve allocations, the flooding of reserve lands, and other treaty violations. Across Canada, more than eight hundred land claims have been launched, and few have been settled. Not surprisingly, then, large numbers of white and Indigenous interviewees viewed land disputes as a major source of division. Many whites perceived land claims as boundaries that generate uncertainty about property ownership, potential loss of tax revenue (if lands are converted into non-taxable reserves), and potentially disruptive protests. In contrast, many Indigenous interviewees said they were trying to protect their treaty lands for future generations, with minimal disruption to non-Indigenous neighbours; the boundary for them is the resistance and misunderstandings from both governments and ordinary settler-Canadians.

Coming from the dominant white perspective, a resident in his sixties said: "it's just like 'pay, pay, pay, pay, pay.' Where do we come to an end on this? Like ... all these land rights ... They'd have the whole of Canada, you get the feeling, if they had their way!" Similarly, a white man in his thirties worried:

My house ... in Fort Frances is on their land, according to them. And that bothers me because ... I live here, I pay my taxes, I work really hard. You may have been the first people in this area, but you know what? Things change. The world changes. We can't live in the past all the time. And

Figure 3.2 Boom and Bust. "This is an abandoned mine ... Each day, I sit on our reserve and count the trucks that go by filled with resources taken from Treaty No. 3 land. Not one single penny of those resources taken from our land goes to us. This not only violates the treaty but makes us beggars in our own land." – Naa-Gaabiinegee-zhig, Anishinaabe man, age fifty-three. Photo courtesy of Naa-Gaabiinegee-zhig.

> that's the part that I don't know if I'll ever get over ... the fishing rights, that doesn't bother me. The monthly checks, that doesn't bother me. But ... the land claim stuff, that's really starting to bother me.

Such laissez-faire views plainly protect settlers' interests in the land and other resources. Land claims generate resentment by disrupting settlers' sense of security and entitlement and thereby threatening their group position.

In contrast, an Anishinaabe man in his fifties framed the problem this way:

> One [boundary] is that they [settler-Canadians] reject the idea that we *are* First Peoples [and] that we have unique rights and relationships with the Crown, as a result ... They don't acknowledge or accept that the *land* rights of First Nations are *legal* rights. In fact, the Supreme Court of Canada didn't until recently.

Perhaps the most prominent local case – and the largest land claim settlement in Ontario at the time – was that of Rainy River First Nations (RRFN).[13] This land claim was launched in 1983, accepted for negotiations in 1994, and finally settled in 2005 in an agreement signed by the First Nations and the federal and provincial governments.[14] As compensation for lands taken from them in 1914–15 when six communities were forcibly relocated to make way for white farmers,[15] the First Nations received seventy-one million dollars with which to purchase up to forty-six thousand acres of land. To protect the money for future generations, much of it was put into an independently managed community trust. Fifteen thousand acres of Crown land were selected upfront and the remaining thirty-one thousand acres may be purchased from private landholders, on a willing buyer/willing seller basis, over the next four decades. No settlers have been forced to move (nor would this ever happen in a land claim settlement under Canadian law). Rather, if settlers one day wish to sell their property, the First Nation (if interested) may purchase it at fair market value. In addition, RRFN quickly purchased some land from struggling local farmers[16] and leased it back to them so they could continue to practise their livelihoods. While some interviewees, including some white farmers, viewed this as a "win-win" situation and cited the RRFN case as a "model" settlement that fairly accommodates everyone, others – especially municipal officials – complained that they were not consulted or party to the agreement, and feared that they might be forced to provide services to reserves without the necessary tax base.

A white male photovoice participant wrote the following caption to accompany a photo of the then RRFN chief signing the settlement agreement:

> The Rainy River First Nations land claim settlement was viewed by many as just and fair and long overdue. Others have been distrustful of the process and fearful of the outcome. It is ironic that those on whose behalf the land was wrongfully taken are distrustful of those who would right that wrong. The land claim settlement resulted from a willingness to negotiate rather than litigate.

However, most white interviewees were not so optimistic. According to a middle-aged white woman in Fort Frances, non-Indigenous residents were feeling "intimidated" by RRFN's "land acquisition" efforts. She thought the First Nation should "work with the municipalities that they're purchasing their land in," and if they had discussed it with them in advance, "there'd probably be less friction." An older white farmer had deeper concerns:

They wanted to be compensated for the land they lost and the resources that come off the land ... and I was all for that. Okay, there you are, you're paid off. [*taps table*] But ... they got this *big* land claim settlement, they got this block of money; now, *what* the hell are they doing? ... They're out *buying up* more land and creating more reserves, which I think, in this modern day and age, it's a *disgrace!* [*pounds table harder*] Who the hell is going to pick the slack up [in municipal taxes]? The remaining property owners! They're just sticking more burden on the people that's left. Maybe we better give *all* of the goddamn land to the Indians and let them run it!

Clearly, the RRFN land claim settlement struck a nerve with some white residents. The older farmer not only viewed it as a "burden" on taxpayers, but as "damaging to the country." Returning land to Indigenous peoples is a boundary for whites because it threatens whites' sense of entitlement to the land (Mackey 2016) and, ultimately, their sense of group position.

From an Indigenous perspective, in contrast, such settlements are merely restoring equity. According to an Anishinaabe man who was involved in the land claim settlement:

The point is that ... Rainy River [First Nations] were supposed to have this forty-six thousand acres of land forever, as part of the original treaty ... So, the municipalities in the area have actually had a tax holiday for one hundred years. [Moreover,] this is a constitutional obligation, a treaty obligation, and now a settlement agreement obligation to provide land out of the band's *own* territory to keep forever. And as they said in Delgamuukw,[17] every square inch of northwestern Ontario was owned in legal title by Indians ... But most non-Indian people still don't understand or accept that.

As for claims that municipalities were not consulted, RRFN representatives countered that "consultations were extensive," "municipal meetings [were] held throughout the district," "all kinds of ... information [was] made available publicly," and it was "front-page" news "for years." Further, the municipalities would not suffer greater tax burdens because RRFN promised to negotiate service agreements to compensate for lost revenue. Ultimately, however, some white residents distrusted these promises and felt they were "losing out" in a zero-sum game.

The second major local land dispute discussed as a boundary was that of Pither's Point Park – a highly valued 162-acre lakefront property leased to the Town of Fort Frances by the federal government on behalf of the Agency One bands (Couchiching, Mitaanjigamiing, Naicatchewenin, and Nigigoonsiminikaaning First Nations) for ninety-nine years (see chapter 1). As the lease approached expiry (1 May 2009), this was perhaps the biggest source of tension in local Indigenous-settler relations. The original land claim was filed in 1998 by the four First Nations against the federal government for breach of fiduciary duty;[18] the land in question had been leased to the town for thirty-five dollars per year, a rate never updated for inflation. The First Nations argued that, upon expiration of the lease, the land should revert to them, although they might be willing to renegotiate a lease with the town at fair market value. The town intervened, claiming that it should own the land because it had maintained the property for ninety-nine years and because the Province of Ontario, in 1908, passed an order-in-council granting the federal government "permission" to bestow the land to the town as a municipal park. Under the Constitution, the federal government has authority over "Indians and lands reserved for Indians," but provinces have authority over crown lands and natural resources – an authority that, according to the Supreme Court, must be "reconciled" with Aboriginal and treaty rights – creating ongoing jurisdictional disputes.

From the perspective of a white municipal official:

> They surrendered that [land] to the federal government ... to sell on their behalf ... The [First Nations] are making a claim ... of mismanagement of the land. "You were supposed to sell that on our behalf and you never [did] – we want this much money ... in restitution. *Plus*, we want the land back ... " Our [Town of Fort Frances] approach is ... "Absolutely, you [federal government] were supposed to sell it. Pay them." We don't necessarily believe the land should go with it. [*laughs*] ... But the park area ... It's been one hundred years ... we've maintained that as a park for the enjoyment of *everybody* ... First Nations, townsfolk, visitors ... We've spent *significant* money in that regard ... And *Ontario's intent* [in 1908] was to provide an area there for the town, not to be leased, to be *given* to the town ... That means *forever*. (Emphasis added)

In this interviewee's mind, the town is entitled to the park, because the province promised it (at a time when the province assumed the legal right to confirm or deny reserve lands; see chapter 1) and because the town has managed the land for "everybody" (implying that the First Nations are unwilling or unable to do so, if not downright selfish for "want[ing] the land back"). The town's particular interests are framed as universal, a stance that protects the town's "property" and settlers' assumed morality, thereby bolstering their sense of group position.

Although most white residents were unaware of the legal details of the case and not overly concerned about who *owned* the park, many felt strongly that public access should be retained and feared that if the land were returned to the First Nations it would not be maintained or settlers would be forbidden access. For a white woman in her thirties:

> I think the biggest boundary in this area is ... over Pither's Point – because now the contract's coming up ... so what happens to the land? ... Are the Aboriginal people going to take advantage [and] start charging us a toll to come on the beach? You know, a lot of stigma ... goes with Aboriginal people ... Are they going to wreck the land or is it just going to become nothing ... after it's been built up to be something?

When asked about the park, many residents became nostalgic, sharing fond memories of childhood picnics, swimming, bicycling, barbecues, and Canada Day celebrations. Many wanted to enjoy the same activities with their children.

For Anishinaabe, the Point has similar meanings, but is also a historical gathering place and a sacred burial ground used by Indigenous peoples for centuries (see chapter 1). Their roots go deeper. Although Indigenous interviewees strongly believed that the First Nations should be recognized as the rightful owners (or stewards) of the land, many also agreed that it should continue to be used as a park for everyone's benefit. According to a First Nation woman in her twenties, the ongoing "battle" over this land was a major source of intergroup division. In her words:

> Maybe they [First Nations] could take back the ownership, but still let everybody use it [because] the Point [is] a really big part to this community ... I wouldn't want ... to take that away from everybody. And how would that make us [First Nations] look? [*half-laughs*] It would make us look ... hateful, like we really don't want to contribute ... And I think it would cause more problems and bring out a lot more racism in a lot of people.

This interviewee intuitively linked the land dispute to potential racist backlash, especially if the First Nations insisted on changing land use. As group position theory (Blumer 1958; Bobo 1999) predicts, when dominant groups feel that their rights or privileges are threatened, they will lash out with prejudice.

Further, although most Anishinaabe interviewees agreed the land should remain a park, the "real" boundary, they said, was the lack of recognition that they are the rightful owners/stewards and should have the final word. As a middle-aged Anishinaabe man put it, the disagreement was not so much over how to use the land, but rather the town's unwillingness to relinquish control:

> [The town] want to continue to portray that they're in *control* [so] then our issue does become with the town, because it's them saying, "it was ours for ninety-nine years and we want to maintain it." And ... that is *so* wrong. I tell [my co-workers], "I'm gonna go camping." And one of these days I will. Because that is *our* land; it's not *theirs* ... I got no problem with it being a park ... I go there with my family ... If people want to continue to use it, go ahead. But you know what? It's *ours*.

In short, residents tended to frame land disputes – like treaty rights – in ways that supported their respective senses of group position. Whites, as a group, struggled to maintain control (and tax revenue), whereas Indigenous peoples, as a group, sought to regain control but also achieve recognition of their land and treaty rights. Although tensions had risen and fallen in the ongoing Point Park case, with some Anishinaabe threatening actions such as road blockades and some whites fearing such escalations, the dominant response observed among both white and Indigenous residents was to *avoid* publicly discussing the issue (for more details, see chapter 7).

Indigenous Self-Government and Ignorance of or Disrespect for Indigenous Sovereignty

While Indigenous-settler conflicts often revolve around land, struggles for control extend beyond the land itself. As Cree leader Harold Cardinal (1969, 13) asserted, First Nations are not just "red tiles" in the "Canadian mosaic"; they are sovereign, self-determining nations. Most Indigenous people agree that in signing treaties, they never relinquished political autonomy. Moreover, Canada's Constitution Act (1982) recognizes self-government as an inherent Aboriginal right, and the United Nations Declaration on the Rights of Indigenous Peoples (2007) includes the right to self-determination. Precisely what this means is subject to ongoing debate. In this context, when asked about intergroup boundaries, some Indigenous and settler interviewees directly discussed Indigenous sovereignty and self-government. Whereas most whites framed self-government as a "problem" that reinforces us/them distinctions and prevents "integration," most Indigenous – and two white – interviewees explicitly framed it as a *positive* boundary that should be respected and, if anything, strengthened, to restore collective freedom.

Figure 3.3 Fly the Flags. "I love these flags that hang in our [high school] atrium. The only thing I dislike is that if I requested a flag of the Netherlands to be displayed it would be rejected. Either every flag of every nation should be displayed if asked or only the Canadian flag that represents us all should be displayed." More than a year later, this participant contacted me to say they had changed their mind and would like to revise their caption. In their words: "I now believe that each First Nation is its own sovereign nation. I hold Canadian citizenship, but also band membership. Each of these flags represents a nation entirely separate from Canada, and it is very important that this is recognized." – Native Canadian, age sixteen. Photo courtesy of the caption speaker.

Some Anishinaabe proudly discussed recent measures taken by the Grand Council Treaty No. 3 (the traditional government of the twenty-eight First Nations in Treaty No. 3) to create and enforce their own laws. Perhaps most well-known is the Resource Law (*Manito Aki Inakonigaawin*) that requires resource extraction companies to consult with local First Nations, obtain their informed consent, follow Anishinaabe principles and values (including environmental standards), and negotiate agreements about job creation and revenue sharing, *before* working on their traditional lands.[19] Others spoke generally of the need to revive traditional ceremonies and consensus-based decision-making rather than follow the Indian Act and the state-imposed band council system.

One Native man in his sixties said he was "bothered" by ignorant comments such as "The laws of the land apply to you too!" and "Why do you think you're special?" He tried to educate his white neighbours that "before anybody came from Europe ... there was people here and they had their [own] laws." For Mashkawegaabo (Al Hunter):

> [We need] to go back to our own system of governance that is based upon natural law and spirituality and ceremonies ... Some people say, "You can't go back to the wigwam." But that's not it ... It all has to do with the *mind* ... And the stronger we make our spiritual ways and bring back the bedrock of who we are as Anishinaabe, Cree, Mi'kmaq, Haudenosaunee ... that's the strength that we had before the newcomers were here [and] that's why we're still here – because the political, military and economic might of the governments of the day, then and now, could never overpower the spiritual resilience ... of Native peoples. We have to understand where *our* strength lies. And once we accept that and believe that, we will never be defeated.

Every First Nation chief interviewed said self-government was a goal, even if logistical challenges first had to be overcome. According to one chief, "before the Europeans came here, we governed ourselves ... through our traditional ways [and] values." His community therefore was seeking to revitalize its laws and govern itself: "That's always been our goal." Still other Anishinaabe emphasized the need to (re)create their own citizenship rules, highlighting the unfairness of the federal government's unilaterally defining status Indians and hence who is eligible for treaty rights and state benefits. As sovereign nations, they said, First Nations should define their *own* membership criteria.[20]

While a few white interviewees supported Indigenous sovereignty and the right to develop their own laws and policies, far more described it as a *negative* boundary and source of conflict. Some objected on principle: "Can't we all just be Canadian?" These respondents assumed that "they" (Indigenous peoples) should submit to "our" (presumably superior) Canadian laws and institutions. Others said they would tolerate self-government *only if* First Nations were cut off from all federal funding, thereby abrogating the treaties. Yet the most common concern was that self-government (like the reserve system) would distance Indigenous peoples from settler-Canadians and thereby prevent integration and mutual understanding. They accused Indigenous people of creating boundaries by "self-segregating." For example, a middle-aged white man said:

> I think culturally some of them see themselves very distinctly as a separate people, and ... want to be separate. It doesn't strike me as being

particularly Canadian ... I don't think it's going to build the cultural bridge that we need ... Now, if you're a First Nation and you're three hundred miles from the nearest non-Aboriginal community and you want to have your own school, that makes sense ... But for Couchiching to ... say, "We gotta have our own school ... because we're a First Nation" ... it's not going to build a bridge ... it's not going to get us to understand each other ... And your kids will come out of grade 12 and be completely separate from ours and then we'll be saying, "Why can't they integrate?"

For this interviewee, integrated schools made practical sense, especially in a small-town setting where Indigenous and non-Indigenous people live side by side. Still, he assumed that Indigenous children should attend settler-Canadian schools, and not vice versa, and resented that many Anishinaabe do not identify as Canadian. An older white man put it more bluntly:

The thing that bothers me is [that] white people and Native people [are] treated differently ... that's going to lead to problems. In fact, all over the world, you see the different nationalities, different religions – and that's where the problem is ... We are breeding separatism ... I feel that if we owe the First Nations people something, we pay the debt and go forward as equals. This is *not* happening ... I can remember my father, when I was young, saying that the way Canada's headed, we're heading for civil war. And I thought, "Well, he's older." Well, now I'm older, but now I can see what he meant.

Further to rejecting Indigenous sovereignty today, some white interviewees denied that First Nations ever were "nations." Against both historical evidence (Asch 2002, 2014; Cornell 1988) and the Canadian Constitution, they argued that Indigenous peoples had no right to self-government. One white man in his sixties, for example, said he rejected the term "First Nation" because "there wasn't really ever a *nation* here ... as far as what *I* learned in history, they were more like ... groups of people surviving in their own little clusters where they could eke out a living." Accepting his decades-old history lessons at face value, he wondered if the term "First Nation" was "invented ... to make it sound better" and suggested it is a tool to persuade "people who don't know history," especially urban Canadians, to think in a way that unfairly advantages Indigenous peoples. As various scholars (Alfred 2005, 2009; Tuck and Yang 2012; Wolfe 2006) have shown, the racialization of Indigenous peoples and the denial of their independent nationhood is a stock tool of settler colonialism. Echoing Ontario's arguments in the

1888 St. Catherine's Milling court case that denied Indigenous rights (see chapter 1), this interviewee suggested that Indigenous peoples were never as civilized as Europeans and that the discourse of nationhood is a contemporary ploy.[21] Like working-class whites in Dunk's (1991) Thunder Bay study, he also expressed alienation from southern city-dwellers, perceiving them as dupes for sympathizing with Indigenous causes but ignoring white northerners' struggles.

Yet even white residents who accepted the principle of Indigenous nationhood and self-government often expressed concerns about how it might play out in practice. One municipal leader wanted "a clearer picture of how this Resource Law applies ... Like if a mining company wants to explore a piece of land, what do they have to do? Who do they have to deal with?" He worried that mining companies would have to acquire permits from both First Nations and the Ontario Ministry of Natural Resources, which would "duplicate efforts" and potentially result in "lost opportunities for Ontario."

In sum, although less commonly cited as a "boundary" than treaties, land claims, history, or Canadian laws and policies, Indigenous sovereignty or self-determination was extremely important for a substantial minority of interviewees. In discussing it, some Anishinaabe became so passionate that they said they would die for the cause. Conversely, some whites felt so threatened by the prospects that they viewed "civil war"[22] as a realistic possibility. For whites, rejecting Indigenous self-government and erasing political-national boundaries bolstered their sense of superior group position by privileging Canadian laws and institutions with which they identified. For Anishinaabe and Métis nationalists, exercising sovereignty and asserting their own laws, policies, and membership codes would not only challenge the dominant white frame, but also be essential for restoring respectful, equitable nation-to-nation relationships.

Cultural Differences and Ignorance of or Disrespect for Cultural Diversity

In addition to conflicts over land and material resources, treaties, self-government, and historical and contemporary state policies and practices, many interviewees described (perceived) cultural differences – including language barriers, communication styles, spiritual practices, and other norms or customs – as intergroup boundaries. However, whites were twice as likely as Indigenous interviewees to describe cultural differences per se as sources of division, whereas Anishinaabe and Métis were more likely to describe ignorance of or disrespect for their

Figure 3.4 Language Is Healing. "Although I have lost parts of my culture, I know I am Anishinaabekwe and I still speak Anishinaabemowin. Maintaining my language has helped me to heal and be proud of who I am." – Anishinaabe woman, age 44. Photo courtesy of the caption speaker.

cultures and traditions as the problem; indeed, some Indigenous residents described their distinct cultural identities as *positive* boundaries that should be respected.

On one hand, many whites said they accepted or tolerated cultural differences. Some even embraced multiculturalism as a defining feature of Canadian identity, averring that cultural differences "enrich us" and that "we just need to learn different people's cultures" to improve intergroup relations. For some residents, the biggest boundary was "ignorance of the cultures." According to one, "Powwows have always fascinated me. Who are we to be condescending? ... I think [the boundary] is arrogance ... and intolerance of anything that's different."

Indeed, similar numbers of whites admitted that they did not understand Indigenous cultures or viewed them as inferior or as a symbolic threat (Stephan and Stephan 2000). For example, a middle-aged white man said the greatest barrier was that "culturally, non-Aboriginals do not understand Aboriginals," including "what motivates them." Indigenous peoples' behaviour, in his view, often "seems kinda foreign ... and so, you start to paint the stereotype ... based on what you heard as a kid or saw on TV or read in a book." Given this perceived foreignness and lack of understanding, some residents advocated one-way "integration" into mainstream Canadian society. A white woman in her sixties insisted:

> It's a *culture* thing ... When we [settler-Canadians] say there's a meeting at 10 o'clock, there's a meeting at 10 o'clock. When Natives say there's a meeting at 10 o'clock ... you can count on them not getting there on time ... And in this fast-moving world ... you've gotta show up for work on time and ... stay there ... They talk about wanting to be there, but their *culture* sometimes interferes with it ... You know, if you're asking us to let you in ... *you need to work under these parameters and this is how you do it*. And I want them to do that ... But they have a bit of trouble ... and they need to get some drive ... You know how *we* [settlers] have those days where we don't feel like going to work, *but we do, don't we*, 'cause we know that's [what] you have to do; you have to continue on. And *they* just sometimes – they rest on their laurels. (Emphasis added)

Although claiming it "isn't a criticism," here this interviewee frames the problem in a paternalistic way. She wants Indigenous people to assimilate, as settler colonial theory would predict, but doubts that they can because they allegedly lack "drive" and "rest on their laurels." This, she thinks, is "the biggest" boundary, a stance that bolsters her sense of group superiority. Like several other interviewees, she also tried to connect with me, as a fellow white person, to distinguish how "we" are different from, and implicitly better than, "them."

Still other residents felt that both groups could learn from one another and that the ideal culture would be a hybrid. For instance, a middle-aged white man said white people tend to "get all fired up about stuff" and are very "structured," whereas Indigenous people "have a more laid-back approach." In his mind:

> We should take a little bit from them and they can take a little bit from us ... I see it all the time. They'll joke about it with us ... "We're on Native time" ... there is differences like that. The things that we value ... are not necessarily [their values]. Theirs is more family oriented and spending time and laughter [whereas] we're a little more geared up.

One of the two non-white, non-Indigenous interviewees also framed cultural differences as a boundary, but emphasized that this is only a problem insofar as "mainstream Canadians" do not understand or respect

Indigenous culture and therefore become frustrated or have difficulty interacting with Indigenous people. In his view, Anishinaabe culture is "diametrically opposite to Anglo-Saxon ways": rather than being "competitive" and individualistic, he said, Indigenous people "like to work together collectively ... that's how they've survived." For example, "they kill a deer, they share it ... whereas a mainstream Canadian kills a deer, they just put it in the freezer and think about themselves." Echoing comments above, he added, "misunderstandings" often arise over "the concept of time":

> I can just see those white people from Toronto coming here for a meeting [at] ten o'clock and these guys arrive at eleven on Indian standard time. That can be very frustrating ... because their time is money, as they say in Toronto. Over here, they just lean back, and when people get there is when they'll start the meeting. One can easily get frustrated if you don't understand the culture, if you're not patient, if you don't know their ways.[23]

A few Indigenous residents (like many whites) agreed that Indigenous peoples' lack of integration into "white culture" is a boundary. According to an older Native man who proudly called himself an "apple" (red on the outside, white on the inside):

> [If] all the ... Native communities around here had the same access to white culture – International Falls, Fort Frances – I don't think there'd be the same barriers ... The people from Lac La Croix look at Fort Frances and think, "Why should I be working nine to five every day when I can fish in a boat and do whatever?"

Unlike Couchiching, which he likened to a suburb of Fort Frances, Lac La Croix First Nation is nearly two hundred kilometres southeast of town and did not have road access until the late 1960s. Thus, he suggested, the boundaries are thicker.

However, most Indigenous interviewees did not frame cultural differences in such terms. They (and a minority of settlers) asserted that while cultural differences may constitute boundaries, they, like nationhood and self-government, are "good" boundaries – essential to identity and well-being – and should be preserved. In their view, it is possible and desirable for multiple cultures to coexist; cultural differences are only problematic when they are not understood or respected. For instance, an Anishinaabe Elder and residential school survivor told a story about a non-Indigenous preacher who knocked on his door while he was cleaning his pipes and feathers. He invited her in. She claimed it was "wrong" for him to use these sacred items. He explained:

"No," I says. "For you, it might not be good. But for me ... that's my way of connecting to my spirituality ... It helps me realize who I am. I'm proud of who I am, but not boastful ... I respect other peoples' ways ... You's have your ways, I have mine ... You can't make me who you are and I can't make you who I am."

When asked about boundaries, several Indigenous interviewees described experiencing cultural discrimination. For example, a First Nation woman recalled going into town one night with a friend who had a "Native drawing on the back of her jacket." When they approached the Mohawk gas station/convenience store, a young white man who was hanging out with about twenty peers "turns around and he said, 'You know what? We know you're Indian. You don't have to *display* it.'" Far from accepting cultural diversity, this white youth appeared threatened by the mere display of an Indigenous symbol (while ironically shopping at the *Mohawk* store) and lashed out angrily, nearly resulting in a physical fight, according to the interviewee. A middle-aged Métis woman also shared the following story of discrimination:

> My son is nine years old ... [At school] he wrote his Indian name on the back of his project. They were doing group work. And this little girl *erased* his name. So, he had a sulky face, and the teacher says to him, "What's wrong with you? Why do you look so sad?" He says, "Because so-and-so took my Indian name off ... and it hurt me because I don't like anybody shaming my name." And the teacher says, "Well, get over it ... because your Canadian name is [Canadian name]. At school, you are [Canadian name]." [This was] 2008. He came home [and said], "I need to be [Anishinaabe name] over there, Mom. I really need to be [Anishinaabe name]." What my son was saying was very powerful; he felt so disconnected at school that he *needed* to have his Anishinaabe name just to keep him going ... So, identity is very important, and it was totally disregarded.

The interviewee and her husband demanded a meeting with the teacher and principal who, after much discussion, eventually agreed to address their son by his Anishinaabe name. In their view, the problem is not cultural differences, but rather the lack of respect for Indigenous cultures, including ongoing attempts to *erase* Indigenous identities.

Finally, a few Anishinaabe interviewees alluded to Canada's official multiculturalism policy and criticized the hypocrisy of a state that welcomes ethnic groups from around the globe, yet fails to fulfil its own stated values in its treatment of Indigenous peoples. For instance, a

First Nation woman described attending a "big conference in Ottawa [with] one other Indian man ... the rest were non-Native":

> They were writing policies for Canada on heritage. I listened for a day and a half. And then they said to me, "What do you think?" ... I said, "If we're going to talk about heritage ... if you could just add ... a couple words ... that 'there was heritage and culture here when we arrived,' *that* would make us feel – or make me feel – included ... I am Anishinaabekwe. That's who I am. I am *not* Canadian. But if you put in that one sentence ... I would just be happy ... with that." What did they do? Nothing.

Although the policymakers agreed these were "wonderful ideas," she did not find her ideas represented in the final document, so she "walked out" and concluded that "this country's not ready to be ... inclusive."

In short, many whites framed cultural differences as boundaries to be overcome and expressed a settler colonial desire for Indigenous peoples to assimilate to the dominant culture. Yet they also questioned Indigenous peoples' ability to assimilate – a stance that reflects and reinforces whites' sense of group superiority and entitlement. Many Indigenous residents, in contrast, did not identify as Canadian and viewed their Anishinaabe or Métis identities and cultures as positive boundaries that should be valued, maintained, and strengthened. The real source of division, they said, is settlers' ignorance of and disrespect for cultural diversity.

Alleged "Moral Deficits"

Implicit in many of the quotations in this chapter – and indeed in this book – are allegations that the other group, or some of its members, or perhaps even one's own group, are *morally* flawed in some way. As Lamont (2000) asserts, all humans construct moral boundaries to distinguish themselves from others and thereby uphold their self-worth. Like political, cultural, and other boundaries, moral boundaries are not necessarily drawn along strictly racial lines. At the group level, however, they often have racial implications. For example, if someone looks down on "lazy people" and then attributes higher poverty rates among Indigenous families to laziness, she is implying that Indigenous people are more likely to be lazy and hence less morally worthy. This conclusion not only justifies the material boundary of economic inequality (from which whites collectively benefit) but also reinforces whites' sense of group superiority.

When asked about intergroup boundaries, at least twenty-six white and fifteen Indigenous interviewees explicitly referred to the alleged moral failings of Indigenous people. Some endorsed stereotypes that Indigenous people lack ambition, are too demanding, are overly sensitive to racism, cannot manage money, or live in the past. Others discussed the problems of addictions, family breakdown, and welfare dependence, which, when not historically or structurally contextualized, can constitute victim-blaming.[24] In each case, the implication was that Indigenous people are lacking in some valued quality, and that whites are morally superior. Such claims were evident in many of the interviews referenced throughout this chapter, such as the woman who claimed that Indigenous people lack "drive," "rest on their laurels" and, unlike "us," are unable to keep pace with this "fast-moving world," or the pervasive suggestions that Indigenous people would rather have "special privileges" handed to them, at whites' expense, than work for a paycheque. To provide one further example, a middle-aged millwright alleged:

> The reason there's this alcoholism and drug thing and suicide thing is, well, they don't *want* to leave [the reserve] to better themselves ... they still get the money [government funding] and the people that are running the band are usually well off and then everybody else is [*pause*] poverty ... there is a lot of jealousy and corruption [and] embezzling.

Although he admitted he could not "prove" these allegations, he blamed the poverty and social problems on reserves on the presumed moral shortcomings of First Nation people (not wanting "to better themselves"). The nature and extent of racial prejudice, and its relation to the sense of group position, will be examined in more detail in chapter 4. The point here is that when asked about intergroup boundaries, many whites emphasized the alleged moral deficits of Indigenous peoples.

In contrast, some Indigenous residents (and a few settlers) said that white racism and the moral deficits of "mainstream" Canadians helped explain the poverty, lack of opportunity, and other problems that Indigenous peoples disproportionately faced. When asked about boundaries, at least twenty-five Indigenous and nine white interviewees used terms that suggest white moral failings, including "arrogance," "greed," "selfishness," and (wilful) "ignorance." While some emphasized that these are human characteristics, not unique to any race, they also tended to suggest that, *at a group level*, settler-Canadians follow a different and, in some respects, inferior value system. In their view, if "traditional" Anishinaabe ways of thinking and living were understood, respected, and practised more widely (by people of *all* backgrounds), we could solve many social problems and salvage our relationships with one another and Mother Earth. Naa-Gaabiinegee-zhig (Calvin Morrisseau) explained that before colonization, Indigenous people

> had everything ... all the game that you need to live ... all the resources ... a sense of spirituality ... a sense of family. There's a system in place in which you will never starve ... I'm going to teach you because you're my brother. We're equal. Your survival is just as important to me as mine ... And then all of a sudden ... some guy comes along and says, "Hey, that's all wrong! What are you doing? What are you worrying about him for? Worry about yourself ... Acquire goods ... Become rich ... " *So ... all your values have to realign.* And then you try to do that, but there's nothin' but barren ground. There's [no opportunity to] acquire the riches and goods that everybody else has. So, you become a failure. You think yourself less than ... you don't succeed at anything that *they* think you should be succeeding at. (Emphasis added)

The main reason for not succeeding, he said, is structural: "equality of opportunity" is a myth. "The laws which impact our community are different. You can't own property [on reserve]," which discourages business investment. So, "how are you supposed to compete?" Yet, even if these structural barriers could be removed, he added:

> [Competition is] not our great *value.* We value things like sharing, love, compassion, understanding. It's not "look out for number one." I think that's [why] we have difficulties in the outside world. [Plus] the outside world just doesn't care.

In short, Naa-Gaabiinegee-zhig juxtaposed the pre-colonized Anishinaabe value system with that of Euro-Canadian settlers, expressing a strong preference for the former. He lamented how colonization has fostered an inferiority complex among many Indigenous people, which, together with persisting structural barriers in an apathetic "outside world," explains their current predicament. To overcome these boundaries, he said, "sharing, love, compassion, understanding," and other traditional principles must be revived and practised.

An Anishinaabe man in his thirties likewise suggested that the biggest boundary is the contrast between traditional Anishinaabe and Euro-Canadian ways of thinking:

> Native people used hunting and harvesting as a way to *survive.* And the European way of thinking was to *acquire.* [For them,] it wasn't out of *respect;* it was out of *prestige* – like, "Look at me! I got a big shiny car!" ... That's

how they evaluated their social status ... If you don't have a car, then you're obviously in the lower class. *But the Anishinaabe people didn't think that way.* I think that's why if you allow [white people] to hunt, then they'll hunt and hunt until there's nothing left ... Because they don't see it as a way of life ... they see a deer as a trophy on their wall, [whereas Anishinaabe] look at it as six months of food and maybe moccasins out of the hide and medicines out of other areas.

He then provided a personal case in point:

People always ask me "Why don't you work? You're a [smart] person. You can get any job you want ... " But ... it's not about making money – for me, anyways. *A lot of people consider themselves wealthy if they have lots of money. But I proudly say, "In the terms that people understand it today, I guess you can call me a bum."* I don't have no income. I have no job ... in the [mainstream conception of] social status, I would be at the bottom of the totem pole. But the way I live ... I got a beautiful home ... a vehicle ... an awesome family ... we always have food in our fridge ... That's pretty good for a guy who doesn't work![25] [*laughs*] ... *So, it's a different way of thinking.* (Emphasis added)

In a fine example of "normative inversion" (Wimmer 2008), here this interviewee takes pride in being "a bum," and in being at the bottom of the Canadian status hierarchy because he does not work nine to five in the mainstream economy. Yet, in his Anishinaabe way of thinking, he is happy and healthy; he lives by his traditions, in harmony with Creation, and provides for his family.

At a "deep" cultural level (basic ways of thinking, belief and value systems), both Anishinaabe men drew sharp moral boundaries – emphasizing their Indigenous "values, roots, and cultural toolkits" (Vasquez and Wetzel 2009) – in ways that upheld their dignity and challenged settlers' sense of superiority. In doing so, however, they did not seek to reverse group positions. Rather, they presented an alternative model for group relations – a vision of the good society based on "love, compassion, understanding" and "respect" rather than "competition," selfishness, greed, and arrogance – leaving the door open for all humans (not just Indigenous peoples) to join.

Conclusion

Despite tremendous variation in residents' conceptions of boundaries (both within and between groups), a salient pattern at the group level was that whites tended to frame boundaries in ways that bolstered their

Figure 3.5 Clear-Cut. "This is one of many clear-cuts in northwestern Ontario. For me, the way we view the land is different. Within our society, most of us believe that the Earth is our Mother. We never take anything from the land without replacing it or making an offering. Forestry and mining companies have raped the land. They came here with machines, destroyed the wild rice, and sold it for profit. When an Anishinaabe person goes out in the traditional way, with a canoe and a stick, there is an automatic re-seeding." – Naa-Gaabiinegee-zhig, Anishinaabe man, age fifty-three. Photo courtesy of Naa-Gaabiinegee-zhig.

sense of group superiority and defended structural inequities, whereas Anishinaabe and Métis residents tended to frame boundaries in ways that challenged their presumed inferiority and articulated alternative ways of relating to one another.

Overall, these findings support the argument (of some residents themselves) that *different ways of thinking about intergroup relations are a boundary in themselves.* In other words, the divergent conceptions of which boundaries exist – and which *should* exist – constitute a basic source of conflict. Such disputed boundaries in the context of the colonial history outlined in chapter 1 and in the absence of sufficient bridges (see chapter 6) inevitably leads to distrust and division. Yet it should not be inferred from this that every member of a given racial, ethnic, or national group thinks the same way. Boundaries inhere in cultural frames, or worldviews, and in alternative ways of being in the world, not in skin or blood.

Nevertheless, at the group level, such dominant perspectives on boundaries as those articulated by white and Indigenous interviewees in this study help constitute respective senses of group position. The dominant white frame defends material inequalities, such as higher poverty rates among Indigenous families, by attributing them to Indigenous peoples' alleged moral deficits. It also seeks to *erase* or *deny* the political boundary of Indigenous self-government and to *eliminate* or *minimize* the social responsibilities stemming from treaties. In other words, it envisions a society in which "we are all Canadian," but where most whites are, at least implicitly, *above* most Indigenous people in status and entitled to Indigenous lands and resources.

The dominant Indigenous frame, by contrast, supports an alternative vision of group relations that validates Indigenous peoples' unique identities, honours treaties, and respects Indigenous self-determination, but also enables social inclusion. It positions First Nations and Métis peoples as *distinct from but as beside* (rather than above or beneath) their treaty partners, the non-Indigenous Canadians. It thereby challenges the settler colonial system and seeks to reconfigure both symbolic and material boundaries.

Chapter Four

Racism, Prejudice, and Discrimination: Group Positioning in Everyday Attitudes and Behaviours

During an interview with a retired white Fort Frances businessman (hereafter, Roger), who was initially diplomatic, refusing to take a firm position on any issue, I asked, "Have you ever talked to your kids about Native people?"[1] His wife (hereafter, Sally), who had been shuffling in and out of the room and had begun putting on her shoes at the front door, suddenly exclaimed, laughing: "Oh God, I better get out of here!"

ROGER: Sure, we have, yeah.
JEFF: What are some of the things you've told them?
R: Um, probably –
SALLY: That Indians are *bad*! We've had some *dealings*.
[*Roger's face turns beat red; raises palm towards Sally.*]
R: Okay, [Sally], that's enough!
[*Roger looks back at me; laughs nervously.*]
S: Well, he asked the right question. No, they – Natives – are the ones who are prejudiced! When you see a [job] ad in the paper ... and it says "white people need not apply."
J: That's like an affirmative action thing?
R: Yeah, I guess ...
S: No, we've had –
R: We've had some dealings and ... our son lives with a Native lady. And –
S [*interrupting*]: And she's a *bitch*!
R: She flaunts it. She flaunts her Native heritage big time.
S: That's right, and she broke up, she – his kids won't even go there anymore and she's really mean to them. And we're not – *I'm not a big Indian person* ...
R: [We have] some good Indian friends though, really nice –
S: But the majority ... are what they can get and ... *gimme gimme gimme*! They're the ones that are prejudiced. And the Métis ... are the *worst*!

That's another of my pet peeves are the Métis who when we grew up,
they wouldn't even *acknowledge* that they were Native ... but now that
they're getting everything, yeah, now they and their kids get paid to go
to school ... That's the big bug-a-boo of this whole Native thing ... And all
our criminals around here is Natives.

R: Eighty per cent.

s: Because we had our garage broken into and –

R [*interrupting*]: Anyway, you've heard it from [Sally]; you've heard it
from me ... when the kids were growing up, did we ever tell them to be
prejudiced against Natives? No.

s: No.

R: But, like –

s: Now? Yes!

R: Now, [*clears throat*] I think, in some, some of those areas, yes.

This exchange is striking for many reasons. In addition to blowing
her husband's cover, the irate Sally refers to several of the perceived
boundaries described in chapter 3 (including treaty rights and cultural differences) and numerous anti-Indigenous stereotypes. She and
her husband explicitly draw moral boundaries against "bad" Indians
who "flaunt" their heritage or seek greater resources. They characterize most Indigenous people as greedy criminals who enjoy undeserved privileges at taxpayers' expense. To counter the perceived threat, Sally
even admits teaching her children "to be prejudiced against Natives."

While such overt admissions of prejudice are rare, it is important to remember that some settlers still think and feel this way in
twenty-first-century Canada. Such attitudes are sometimes expressed
openly on Facebook, Twitter, and newspaper comment pages. More
widespread, however, are the subtler, more insidious expressions of a
sense of superior group position and justifications for racial inequity.
Many white residents denied that racism was a problem and insisted
that "everyone gets along," often pointing to Indigenous friends and
family members as evidence; the couple quoted above mentioned
"some good Indian friends." Yet a majority of whites *also* endorsed beliefs and attitudes that would uphold white-settler power and privilege. Conversely, Indigenous residents reported experiencing very high
levels of interpersonal discrimination, in addition to the historical traumas and ongoing structural inequities outlined in earlier chapters.

The mechanisms accounting for the (paradoxical) coexistence of
positive intergroup contact, including intermarriage and friendship,
with racism, will be the focus of chapter 7. Here, I simply provide evidence that prejudice and discrimination were alive and well in the

Rainy River District, evident in both the attitudes of whites and the numerous cases of unfair and demeaning treatment reported by Indigenous residents.

The Nature of Prejudice and Discrimination

According to classical psychological models, *(old-fashioned) prejudice* may be defined as overt categorical hostility, or "antipathy based upon a faulty and inflexible generalization" (Allport 1954, 9). From this perspective, the root problem is irrational individual beliefs and feelings that have been learned through socialization and that may be corrected through intergroup contact and education.

As Blumer (1958) argued, however, this conceptualization of prejudice is sociologically insufficient: beyond negative stereotypes and attitudes, prejudice involves a *sense of superior group position*, a normative belief in in-group superiority. In this case, prejudice entails identification with and attachment to the in-group (Euro-Canadians), but does not require negative affect towards the entire outgroup (Indigenous peoples). The essential features are a sense of entitlement to resources and privileges, and a perceived threat from Indigenous people who challenge these prerogatives. As suggested in a 2015 *Maclean's* feature story on racism in Winnipeg, prejudice is largely born of fear "that Indians are getting something you don't have" (Macdonald 2015).

According to Blumer (1958, 6), the sense of group position is not primarily a result of "direct personal [interracial] experience," but is shaped by historical, political, and economic forces (such as colonization), media discourse around "big events" (such as large-scale protests), and "a running process in which the dominant racial group is led to define and redefine the subordinate racial group." As we will see in chapter 7, contact may reduce whites' negative feelings towards Indigenous peoples without altering whites' sense of superior group position. This is important because a sense of superior group position is a constituent element of racial ideologies, such as laissez-faire racism, that defend and justify structural inequities (Bobo 1999) and uphold the settler colonial system.

This chapter shows that a majority of white interviewees, including some with close Indigenous friends and family members, displayed a sense of entitlement to their resources and privileges, viewed racial inequalities as natural or justified, and opposed concrete measures to recognize Indigenous rights or rectify injustices. While often tinged with resentment, such views were sometimes expressed with paternalism, including a warm disposition towards Indigenous individuals, but with an assumption that "we" know what is best for "them." As Bobo (1999) hypothesizes, such paternalism may be more prevalent on a day-to-day basis, as the dominant group seeks to stabilize its power and privileges by avoiding conflict (Jackman 1994), whereas competitive threat is more pronounced during periods of crisis or challenge. What both have in common is that they serve to reinforce whites' sense of group superiority and justify existing structural inequities.

At the same time, most Indigenous residents reported frequent experiences with racial discrimination or inferior and demeaning treatment in daily interactions. Such experiences ranged from overt instances of violence and slurs to the more common but subtle "micro-aggressions" (Sue 2010), including insults and slights of ambiguous intent but distressing consequences. Although discriminatory acts might not always be driven by a desire to bolster group position, they are often experienced as a reminder of one's "place" in the settler colonial order, as a denial of one's dignity or self-worth as an Indigenous person.

Perceptions of Racism and "Reverse Racism"

As discussed in chapter 2, many residents – especially whites – described local intergroup relations in positive terms, accurately noting that Indigenous and non-Indigenous residents often lived side by side; worked, played, and went to school together; and sometimes intermarried. However, many residents – especially Anishinaabe – *also* described contemporary racism, or related processes such as stereotypes, prejudice, and discrimination, as a salient boundary or source of division (see chapter 3).

In nearly half the cases where interviewees described racism as a boundary, they were explicitly referring to *systemic* racism – government policies and practices, such as the Indian Act, that systematically disadvantage Indigenous peoples. Some whites also claimed to be the victims of "reverse discrimination," including the couple quoted above who viewed employment equity policies (which seek to rectify the under-representation of Indigenous peoples in selected occupations) as unfair to white people. The remaining cases, as well as most of those who also discussed systemic racism against Indigenous peoples, referred to various forms of *interpersonal* racism, including stereotypical remarks that impugn a group's moral character ("lazy," "drunken," "welfare-dependent") and negative attitudes (hostility, paternalism) and behaviours (exclusion, violence).

For example, an Anishinaabe teenager said she was "having a really tough time" in high school because "[the teacher] does not like

Indians." Indigenous students were reportedly "singled out," assigned to the back of the room, and discouraged from taking advanced academic courses. Meanwhile, a local First Nation chief declared that many whites have stereotypes of "the no-good, lazy Indian," but most Indigenous people are hard workers who are denied employment opportunities because of racism. According to an older Métis man, "The white man will discriminate against the Native for *any* reason whatsoever." For instance, when he was telling a wealthy white neighbour about Métis hunting rights, the neighbour allegedly retorted, "You bastards don't have the right to do nothin'! We give you everything you want!" These comments again reflect the profound ignorance of many settler Canadians regarding the nature and origins of Indigenous and treaty rights (see chapter 3).

Nearly half the Indigenous interviewees who discussed racism as a boundary acknowledged that Indigenous people themselves are not exempt from prejudice. For example, a First Nations woman in her twenties said:

> I think it's ... ignorance ... or ... not *wanting* to understand or respect the other ... Not all white people are like that, but ... there are some that just don't want to respect the Natives or [their] culture. Or, vice versa ... there are Natives that are racist against white people and don't want to ... try to step in their shoes.[2]

Some whites agreed that a major boundary is white racism against Indigenous peoples. A white man in his twenties admitted, "there always seems to be Native jokes," which "might influence some racial negativity."[3] However, whites were more likely to claim that the "real" problem is "reverse racism," or Indigenous people's alleged oversensitivity to racism. A few whites shared stories of being accused of prejudice, insisting that it was not their intention. According to a white female restaurant manager:

> Native, umm, customers tend to use a prejudice thing more so than we [settlers] would ... and this has happened to me quite a few times ... where, say, the dining room's full and ... I'd say, "I'm completely full right now. If you want to wait in the lobby ... or come back later," but [then they'd] say, "What, are you prejudiced against us?" ... I'm like, "Really? Are you kidding me?" Because it's 2008 and we live in a [seemingly integrated] town.

In her view, Indigenous people too often use racism as an "excuse" for not getting their way.

Contrary to stereotypes about "playing the race card," however, I observed that most Indigenous people undertake a complex process of observation, self-reflection, testing, and analysis before labelling a person or incident "racist." Dozens of interviewees reported cases of possible discrimination but lingering uncertainty about the underlying cause, and they often gave their white neighbours the benefit of the doubt. For example, a First Nations man recalled:

> There used to be a store in town [and] when the [white] patrons bought something they'd get their items and then exchange the money. Well, whenever I bought something, they always made sure I put my money on the counter first; it was like they didn't want to touch your hand; and then he'd give me [my groceries]. Now, that's kind of left to interpretation because I never asked him why he did it.

An older white woman married to a First Nations man offered a different perspective. After describing her initial challenges in being accepted on the reserve where they live, she said she came to understand why some Indigenous people are wary of whites:

> Look at the way *they* were treated! You know, taken away from your parents, not allowed to speak your language ... the only culture you knew, they wouldn't allow you to practise it ... They were [also] taken advantage of by a lot of business people, and I experienced that ... You could see it. Being on the other side of the fence, them [business people] not knowing that I was from [the reserve], they treated me differently.

For example, she described being served first in restaurants and observing colder, slower service towards Indigenous customers: "It's like they were saying, 'I don't want you here.'" Moreover, she personally had been called an "Indian lover" by white people in town, although she said this epithet was "not as prevalent as it used to be."

In short, racism – at least as understood by most residents, in terms of overt stereotypes, derogatory name-calling, and intentional discrimination – although perhaps not as widespread as in the past, was still a significant boundary for many Indigenous residents.

Some residents also perceived "reverse racism." Granted, some Indigenous people do have negative beliefs or attitudes towards white people (and other groups), mainly because of how they and their ancestors have been treated by settlers. However, the consequences of such prejudice are not the same because settlers (especially white people) hold structural power in Canada; whites have long been the beneficiaries, and Indigenous peoples the targets, of systemic racism; and whites continue to be advantaged on an array of political, economic, social, and health outcomes (for more detailed arguments along these lines, see Bonilla-Silva 2010; Feagin 2010; Henry and Tator 2006). Moreover, even when the focus is restricted to interpersonal discrimination, Indigenous residents were far more likely to have experienced it (see below). Claiming (falsely) that anti-white discrimination is at least as pervasive enables whites to maintain a sense of group superiority, by implying that Indigenous people should not use racism as an "excuse" for poverty or social problems because white people have faced difficulties too and apparently "gotten over" them.

Evidence of Group Position Prejudice and Laissez-Faire Racism

Beyond these general perceptions, my interviews, surveys, and ethnographic field notes on daily interactions over an eighteen-month period provide strong evidence that interpersonal racism remains widespread in the Rainy River District. Although few interviewees (less than 5 per cent) expressed old-fashioned prejudice (such as the categorical belief that "Indians are bad!"), a majority endorsed laissez-faire racist views. In addition to denying that racism still existed (or was still a barrier), they blamed Indigenous peoples' (economic) poverty on Indigenous people themselves, rejected policies designed to improve Indigenous living conditions, and resented those who fought for or exercised Indigenous and treaty rights.

When asked why Indigenous families are three times more likely to be poor (according to Statistics Canada's low-income cut-off), at least half the white interviewees emphasized alleged cultural deficits or individualistic stereotypical explanations such as laziness, alcoholism, or welfare dependence.[4] In contrast, 88 per cent of Indigenous interviewees included structural (blocked opportunities) or historical (intergenerational trauma) factors as essential parts of their explanations.[5] As Bobo and colleagues (1997) explain, victim-blaming attributions are one aspect of laissez-faire racism; if Indigenous people themselves are responsible for their plight, then settler-Canadians, and existing policies and practices, need not change.

After the prime minister formally apologized for the Indian residential school system in 2008, I asked interviewees how they felt about it. While most agreed an apology was necessary, whites tended to see it as a final act of "closure," whereas Anishinaabe and Métis saw it as one step in an ongoing "healing journey" that required follow-up action. In chapter 9, I will examine Indigenous and settler responses to the

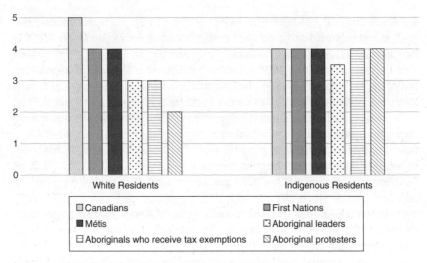

Figure 4.1 White and Indigenous Respondents' Median Ratings of Selected Groups on a Feeling Thermometer from 1 ("strongly negative") to 5 ("strongly positive"), N = 112.

apology more closely. My point here is that rejecting concrete actions to rectify historical and ongoing injustices is another sign of laissez-faire racism (Bobo et al. 1997).

Moreover, when asked to rate groups and individuals on a feeling thermometer, whites expressed clear signs of group position prejudice (see figure 4.1). On a one-to-five scale, from "strongly negative" to "strongly positive," whites gave Canadians a median rating of five; First Nations and Métis a four; four well-known (national and local) Indigenous leaders a three; Indigenous people who receive tax exemptions a three; and Indigenous protesters a two. Clearly, Indigenous people who challenge the power structure – political leaders, treaty rights asserters, and especially protesters – are devalued relative to the dominant group, Canadians.[6]

These attitudes were echoed in dozens of expressions of group superiority/entitlement and fear/threat throughout my research. White residents routinely framed intergroup relations as an "us versus them" zero-sum competition, suggesting that "they" are a threat to "our" resources and way of life, that they are to blame for their social problems, and that "we" know what's best for "them." Such views serve to justify inequities and inaction, thereby protecting the settler colonial system.

For example, when asked to explain the higher poverty rates among Indigenous families, one white resident said:

> Just no ambition. They have their kids, there's a cheque comin' in every week, whether it's GST, welfare, whatever it is, and they're out gun-bootin' it up ... they give the kids a bag of chips and a bottle of pop and "good-bye!" ... They're probably their own worst enemy ... you can give 'em a brand new house and they'll have it wrecked in three years.

Although this interviewee was married to an Indigenous woman, he blamed Indigenous people for their poverty, combining stereotypes about laziness and irresponsibility with the conviction that nothing can be done to improve their living conditions.

In another case, while chatting with my white working-class neighbour Ron over beer one day, as we watched his girlfriend's Indigenous children play, he told me that he was "colour-blind," quickly adding: "If he's an asshole, he's an asshole. If he's a good guy, bring him along." The problem, he said, is that we need to "leave the past behind ... Why should they [Indigenous people] have separate rules for fishin' and huntin'? That's not fair ... Why should they have reserves? ... This is one country ... We need one law." Indeed, a majority of white interviewees endorsed such views: "we are all Canadian," so the "same laws" should apply to everyone. After a while, however, Ron added, "I don't care how much research you do, you'll never get rid of [racism]. You can be friends ... live with them and love them. But ... white will always trust white, Native will always trust Native" (Field notes, March 2008).

This comment clearly undermines his claims to colour-blindness. Yet even if Ron was completely consistent in his creed, it would still be problematic. On the surface, it may sound egalitarian; but in a settler colonial context, colour-blind ideology represents a rejection of Indigenous sovereignty, treaties, and cultural distinctiveness; an avoidance of responsibility for historically rooted structural inequities; and an ongoing sense of superiority and entitlement to, for example, impose "one" set of Canadian laws. It is thus a form of laissez-faire racism.

Still other whites displayed an overbearing posture that assumed Indigenous peoples are incapable of managing their own affairs. Such paternalism was often expressed subtly, perhaps unintentionally, through use of a high-pitched tone and facial expressions connoting pity, and language equating Indigenous people with property or dependents. Several white women, including some with close Indigenous friends, did this repeatedly. Many other residents, including some Métis, referred condescendingly to "our Indians," whom they said are better off than remote northern First Nations. While material prosperity may be somewhat higher on nearby reserves, the language of "our Indians" and the belief that proximity to a "mainstream" town is necessary for well-being presupposes settler supremacy.

Two distinctions should be made here. First, although prejudice was often directed at status and treaty Indians, who have unique rights and benefits (including tax exemptions and harvesting rights), many white interviewees also resented Métis and non-status Indians who had sought expanded rights. The logic is similar: Indigenous people who asserted their rights or had sought more power and resources were perceived as threatening. Second, some white residents expressed different attitudes towards Indigenous people living on- and off-reserve; these opinions tended to surface during discussions about the Indigenous-white poverty gap. Many whites recognized that remote northern reserves have limited job opportunities (a structural barrier). However, they often blamed Indigenous people for not moving south and assimilating, with a seeming lack of appreciation for how Indigenous identities are tied to the land. Many whites also assumed that Anishinaabe and Métis people living in town or on nearby reserves were at least as well off as whites; when told that urban Indigenous people were still more likely to be poor, they attributed this to "laziness" or cultural deficits, overlooking the effects of labour market discrimination, educational barriers, and historical trauma, among other factors.[7]

Evidence of Racial Discrimination

Echoing the views of many white residents, in a 2008 interview a local municipal leader claimed, "I don't think racism exists in this area." My discrimination survey,[8] however, suggests that racism not only existed but thrived. As table 4.1 shows, among respondents, 92 per cent of First Nations and 62 per cent of Métis (versus 40 per cent of settlers) reported personal experiences with racial discrimination in at least one setting ($N = 142$). Seventy-three per cent of Anishinaabe and 38 per cent of Métis (versus 19 per cent of settlers) reported multiple experiences in multiple settings. The median number of reported cases was 11.5 for First Nations, 3 for Métis, and 0 for whites.[9]

Indigenous interviewees' experiences with discrimination ranged from subtle and covert – including fearful or mistrusting glances and

Table 4.1 Survey Results on the Experiences of Discrimination Scale

	First Nations	Métis	Non-Indigenous
Number of interviewees	60	13	69
Total number of incidents discussed	204	24	160
Reports at least one experience of discrimination in at least one setting (%)	92	62	40
Reports at least one experience of discrimination in multiple settings (%)	80	46	25
Reports multiple experiences of discrimination in multiple settings (%)	73	38	19
Settings where discrimination was experienced (in order of prevalence) (%)	At school (78) On the street or in a public setting (68) Getting service at a restaurant, store, or hotel (63) At work (45) From the police or in the courts (45) Getting hired or getting a job (42) Getting medical care (42) Getting housing (33) Getting credit, bank loans, or a mortgage (23)	On the street or in a public setting (46) At school (38) Getting service at a restaurant, store, or hotel (38) From the police or in the courts (31) At work (23) Getting hired or getting a job (23) Getting medical care (23) Getting housing (15) Getting credit, bank loans, or a mortgage (15)	At work (28) On the street or in a public setting (18) At school (14) Getting hired or getting a job (14) Getting service at a restaurant, store, or hotel (2.8) From the police or in the courts (2.8) Getting medical care (1.4) Getting housing (1.4) Getting credit, bank loans, or a mortgage (0)

backhanded compliments such as "There aren't many Natives like you!" – to obvious and overt – such as strangers shouting racial epithets in the street, or physical and sexual assaults – and everything in between – denial of jobs for which the applicant was qualified, denial of apartments or hotel rooms even when they were available, rude or slow service, being followed in stores, being talked down to, being misdiagnosed by doctors, having one's abilities doubted, having one's Indian status questioned, and so on. In addition, some mentioned frequent negative media coverage, prejudicial comments on social media, and local coffee shop banter about "drunken Indians" exploiting the system and wasting tax dollars (banter that I also frequently heard). The common thread in all these instances is *disrespect*: an assault on the dignity and self-worth of Indigenous people, both personally and collectively.

Several caveats should be noted regarding settler reports of having experienced "reverse discrimination." In nearly half of these cases, the respondent's group historically was racialized as non-white (e.g., Italian or Ukrainian), and the perpetrator of discrimination was white. The remaining cases mainly referred to the perceived unfairness of treaty rights or employment equity policies. Only a few whites reported being personally discriminated against by Indigenous people (such as being bullied in school), while just as many conceded that they may have *benefited* from systemic racism.

In contrast, most Indigenous interviewees offered concrete, vivid accounts. After completing the survey, Simon, a First Nations man in his thirties, shared this experience:

> My first week in high school, I tried out for the Muskies [hockey] team ... One of the coaches was the [subject] teacher, and I was in his class ... And I still remember today, it's almost haunting, you know, he [took attendance] and after each [name] he'd look up and [the students would] say, "I'm here." But when he got to my name, he didn't look up. He just kept on reading ... And I [raised my hand] – but he moved on; he didn't care if I was there or not. And everyone just went "*Woo*, a Goulet!"[10] ... So, I confronted him about it [later]. I said, "Mr. [X], why wouldn't you look at me?" And he said, "Well, because you're Indian." And he said it straight up, just like that ... And then he continued ... I said, "Wait a minute, Mr. [X] ... " And then he says, "Simon, shut up. I wanna talk to you outside class right now." *So we go outside and he grabbed me by the collar, threw me up against the locker, and he says, "Listen here, you fuckin' Indian: You're not makin' my hockey team and you're not passing my class"* ... And I – I – I – honestly, I buckled. I didn't know what to do. He went back inside. I did not return to class. Ever since, I have never passed a [subject] class. And I loved

[subject] ... But I dropped out of school because of it ... I went home and cried ... I quit playing hockey ... *And I hid my identity for some time after that. I'd be like, "No, I'm not Indian. Why are you asking me that?" I used to shy away from [it] because of what happened.* (Emphasis added)

This is one of more than two hundred stories of discrimination reported in my interviews. Simon is keenly aware of the ongoing consequences of such negative treatment; the experience led him to drop out of school and quit playing hockey, but also to deny his Indigenous ancestry and pretend that he was white, to look down on Indigenous peoples, and then to blame himself for his internalized racism and denial. Although Simon's story is shocking, it is not the most extreme.

On a wider scale, 78 per cent of First Nations interviewees reported being discriminated against at school, the single most common setting. Also common were reports of discrimination in a restaurant, store, or hotel, from 63 per cent of First Nations and 38 per cent of Métis respondents. One woman in her thirties, who said she was often mistaken for Italian, but who had mixed Anishinaabe-Irish background, said that how she was treated would "depen[d] [on] where I go and who I'm with":

If I'm with my boyfriend who *looks* really Native, then, yeah, we sometimes get discriminated [against] and told that there's no rooms at hotels and then we find out there really is [a room available]. So that's a bummer ... we're sent away a lot to the more scruffier places. We don't get problems at the cheaper hotels though – well, except the Pinetree.[11] [*laughter*]

Unfortunately, discrimination is not unique to the Pinetree Inn. In the northern Ontario hotel industry, it appears to be systemic. A white woman in her fifties who used to work at another motel in Fort Frances said her supervisor once sent a memo warning staff *not* to rent rooms to Natives. When she did, she was reprimanded. As a result, she quit and changed professions.

In addition to hearing such stories, I witnessed discrimination first-hand at another hotel in a demographically similar mill town two hundred kilometres northeast of Fort Frances. In 2008, my partner Lisa organized a conference in Dryden, Ontario. After picking up two guest speakers from the local airport, we returned to the hotel. Although the desk clerk, a fair-skinned white man in his twenties, checked in the two of us and an older white male speaker routinely, he threatened to deny a room to a visibly Indigenous female speaker (who had darker skin, straight black hair, and colourful beaded earrings) unless she produced a credit card for a "security deposit." It was only when Lisa intervened, reminding the clerk that he had not asked the rest of us for a security deposit, that he reluctantly backed down and gave her the room key (Field notes, June 2008).

Granted, many hotels have a standard policy of asking for a credit card for "incidentals." What is noteworthy in this case is that the three white guests were not asked but the one Indigenous guest was – by the same desk clerk. More generally, in northern Ontario it is well known that many First Nations people do not have credit cards. Whether intended to exclude Indigenous people or not, such policies have a systemically discriminatory effect. Moreover, even when Indigenous people are offered a room and able to provide a security deposit, many complain of being regularly lodged in the run-down "Indian section" in many hotels. This was a recurrent theme in my interviews and fieldwork.

To provide one further example, a middle-aged Métis woman who lived on reserve shared her frustrations with the inflammatory, anti-treaty remarks of some white neighbours. She frequently heard comments such as:

> "When I buy a car, I got to pay all the taxes. Those damn Indians ... don't have to pay tax on their vehicle, and that's not fair!" [And,] "What is this about residential school? Why should *my* tax pay [for reparations] for *their* residential school [experience]? That happened a long time ago. They shouldn't get that ... They're always whining and crying."

She also told a personal account about how when her status Indian husband went net fishing to feed his family and his father "who was too sick to fish," a white fisherman said to him, "You fuckin' Indians with your nets. You're taking all the fish from this lake." Meanwhile, she noted, the white fisherman was "on the boundaries of the reserve to fish." Such comments clearly illustrate the "us versus them" mentality and the deep-seated resentment that some settlers express towards Indigenous peoples. Indigenous and treaty rights and compensation for historical injustices are particular sources of grievance, perhaps because they threaten whites' sense of group superiority and entitlement.

Conclusion

Although intergroup marriage and friendship were found to be relatively common in the Rainy River District (a point discussed in more detail in chapter 7), and many Indigenous and non-Indigenous residents did "get along," prejudice and discrimination were also widespread.

A majority of white interviewees displayed at least an implicit assumption of group superiority, a sense of entitlement to their resources and privileges, and a perception of threat specifically from Indigenous people who challenged the power structure. Even whites with close Indigenous friends or family members often blamed Indigenous people for their poverty and social problems and opposed concrete policies or actions to rectify injustices. Meanwhile, more than 90 per cent of Anishinaabe interviewees reported personal experiences with racial discrimination, including what some described as near daily micro-aggressions.

These findings confirm the views of many Indigenous residents that racism was still a significant barrier. Indigenous residents were generally more aware of structural inequities and power dynamics (including in personal interactions), whereas many whites were either oblivious or perhaps wilfully ignorant (a sign of white privilege). Although old-fashioned prejudice was rare, laissez-faire and paternalistic attitudes predominated among whites. And so long as systemic racism and colonialism persist, many settlers will be motivated to maintain their power, resources, and status.

In the next chapter, I examine some of the more deliberate strategies whereby Indigenous residents tried to transform group relations and white residents tried to defend their privileges in a specific case where the status quo was challenged. In chapter 7, I will turn to the question of how contact and prejudice coexisted in the area, identifying some of the taken-for-granted mechanisms that enabled whites to maintain their sense of superior group position and justifications for racial inequity amid frequent positive interaction with Indigenous peoples.

Chapter Five

The Alberton Group Home Controversy: "I Have Native Friends, but This Is Going Too Far"*

In the past three chapters, we have seen how the sense of group positions is expressed in formal interviews and informal conversations about Indigenous-settler relations. We now turn to the question of how group positioning plays out in face-to-face "encounters"[1] between Indigenous and non-Indigenous residents. How do whites defend, and First Nations and Métis people challenge, their presumed "places" in the settler colonial order? What strategies do Euro-Canadian settlers and Indigenous peoples use to negotiate their positions in situations that (potentially) threaten the status quo?

In this case, the proposed relocation of an Anishinaabe child welfare facility – the Weechi-it-te-win Family Services Training and Learning Centre – to the predominantly white rural township of Alberton (directly west of Fort Frances) provoked heated backlash and boundary-maintenance mechanisms. Before rejecting the proposal on "planning" grounds, white residents and municipal councillors used delaying tactics, searched for race-neutral justifications, offered unsolicited advice, created new rules, and censured perceived traitors. The Anishinaabe agency (and its few white allies), guided by traditional decision-making practices, initially tried to provide neutral information, stay positive, and emphasize common interests. When these tactics failed, they considered mobilizing their national political and media contacts before forgoing the opportunity to appeal to an independent tribunal.

This chapter analyses how the conflict unfolded and why white residents succeeded in blocking the land purchase. It shows how the entrenched laissez-faire attitudes of a critical mass of whites, as well as the practical constraints of small-town living, limit the choice and

---

*An earlier version of this chapter was published as an article in *Ethnic and Racial Studies* (Denis 2012).

Figure 5.1 Opportunity or Threat? "In the summer of 2009, Weechi-it-te-win Family Services proposed to purchase the above property in Alberton Township for its Training and Learning Centre (TLC). Rather than seeing it as an opportunity for healing and social and economic development, many residents viewed the TLC as a 'threat' to their 'way of life.' The TLC proposal was blocked when Alberton Council rejected a rezoning application." – Gene, non-Indigenous man, age sixty-eight. Photo courtesy of Gene.

effectiveness of strategies for change. Until settler-Canadians learn to reframe their interests as aligned with Indigenous neighbours, they will use a predictable set of tactics and justifications to uphold their sense of group position and protect their privileges.

Background and Setting

It's hot, sticky, and standing-room only at the Alberton municipal office where hundreds of angry white residents crowd inside for a raucous public meeting on the proposed relocation of the Weechi-it-te-win Family Services Training and Learning Centre to this small rural township. I expect opposition, but am unprepared for what one witness later calls the "lynch mob mentality." As resident after resident condemns the proposal, questioning

the competence and trustworthiness of Weechi-it-te-win staff, and raising concerns about their safety, taxes, and property values, and even the
well-being of Anishinaabe children, I feel transported into the US Deep
South of decades past, like a scene from *To Kill a Mockingbird*. The publicly
expressed resentment, mixed with subtle and not-so-subtle racial innuendo,
catches me off guard, despite having lived in the district for over a year
and hearing all manner of racial attitudes in private interviews ... After the
meeting, in the parking lot, a white woman says to her white neighbours,
"I have Native friends, but this is going too far!" (Field notes, 24 June 2009)

This woman's statement expresses the profound sense of *threat* experienced by the historically dominant white population struggling
to maintain its sense of superior group position (Blumer 1955, 1958).
As Herbert Blumer theorized in post–World War Two America, prejudice does not stem from a lack of intergroup friendships, but from
a historically developed sense of group superiority; it is a "defensive
reaction" triggered when the dominant group's sense of entitlement
to resources and privileges appears threatened by subordinate group
gains or aspirations.

> The dominant group construes the crossing of the line, or preparations to
> cross the line, as threats to its status, its power, and its livelihood. It thus
> develops fears, apprehensions, resentments, angers, and bitterness, which
> become fused into a general feeling of prejudice. (Blumer 1955, 13)

How does this relate to the statement "I have Native friends, but this is
going too far"?

As described in chapter 1, white Canadians have long enjoyed political, economic, educational, and health advantages over Indigenous
peoples, as a result of colonization. In this case, the Township of Alberton was established in 1891 on prime agricultural land, directly west of
Fort Frances. Soon afterwards, members of Little Forks Indian Reserve
10, on the southwestern border of Alberton, were forcibly relocated to
make way for white farmers, and local Indigenous children began to
be taken to residential schools. While white residents benefited from
opportunities in forestry, mining, and agriculture on traditional Anishinaabe lands, the First Nations were reeling from treaty violations,
coercive assimilation policies, and social exclusion (Waisberg and Holzkamm 1993; Waisberg, Lovisek, and Holzkamm 1996).

As of the 2006 Census, 93 per cent of Alberton's 958 residents identified as white/Euro-Canadian, and 7 per cent as Aboriginal (Statistics Canada 2007). Alberton residents had higher incomes and less

unemployment than local Indigenous peoples or average Canadians. The township motto – "Country Livin' and Lovin' It" – reflects residents' pride in their "quiet, peaceful" rural abode. The big blue sign on Highway 11/71 declares it a World Health Organization–recognized "Safe Community." Anything that might diminish these privileges could be seen as a threat to group position.

Since the turn of the twenty-first century, white residents of the Rainy River District, Alberton included, have faced rising economic insecurity (due to the collapse of forestry and agricultural sectors) and declining population.[2] Meanwhile, the local Indigenous population is growing, healing from historical traumas, and regaining land and resources through major land claim settlements (see chapters 1, 3, and 10). Thus, the conditions are ripe for the historically dominant whites to perceive a threat to their group position.

Given this context, in the fall of 2008, Weechi-it-te-win Family Services (WFS) – an Anishinaabe child welfare agency servicing ten First Nation communities – began searching for a new home for its Training and Learning Centre (TLC), a provincially licenced facility offering culturally based education, life-skills training, and clinical services to children in foster care.[3] For over twenty years, it had been leasing property east of Fort Frances, but there were problems with the site – including unsafe drinking water, a steep cliff, and low-hanging hydro wires – and the lease was expiring. The Anishinaabe agency also wished to *own* property to facilitate long-term planning and "leave a legacy of land for our children."[4]

So, when a picturesque 162-acre lot became available in Alberton, WFS sought to purchase it.[5] To comply with municipal bylaws, the property first had to be rezoned: a formal application had to be submitted, a public meeting held, and a vote taken by council.[6] The process was expected to be routine. It was anything but.

Two weeks before the meeting, an anonymous flyer appeared in every Alberton mailbox. In big bold letters, it warned residents that if they did not attend the 24 June 2009 meeting and speak out against it, a "NON-SECURE NATIVE DETENTION CENTRE" would enter the community and threaten their safety.

A WFS staff member, whom I had met through earlier fieldwork, contacted me about it. She was palpably nervous. Yet given the local political avoidance norm, the tendency to avoid public discussions of politically controversial issues (see chapter 7), we both expected that few residents would even attend the meeting. We were wrong.

On 24 June, after WFS representatives carefully described their programs and plans in the allotted ten minutes, nearly two hundred angry

ATTENTION

Are you aware that **WEECH-IT-TE-WIN**
is attempting to purchase the former Chuck
Arpin residence located on Hwy. 11/71.
They intend on opening a
**NON-SECURE NATIVE DETENTION
CENTRE/GROUP HOME.**

If you **don't** attend this meeting, or make a
written submission opposing this proposed
zoning by-law amendment. You will have a
**NON-SECURE NATIVE DETENTION
CENTRE/GROUP HOME
IN YOUR COMMUNITY**

Meeting Date: Wednesday, June 24, 2009
Meeting Time: 7:00 p.m.
Meeting Place: Alberton Municipal Office

PLEASE! HELP KEEP OUR COMMUNITY SAFE

Figure 5.2 Anonymous Flyer (scanned copy). Scan courtesy of the author.

Alberton residents (representing more than half the households in the township) overflowed council chambers and spent three hours lambasting the proposal. They claimed it was part of an alleged Native conspiracy to buy up the land and convert it into a giant reserve, stating that it would "change the whole face of the neighbourhood," be a "threat to our present lifestyle," reduce public safety, increase taxes, decrease property values, and violate their "sense of security and privacy."[7]

After the meeting, WFS representatives said they felt "bruised and battered"; some were in tears at the perceived racist onslaught. Yet when I approached a township councillor for an interview, he told me that Indigenous and white people here have "good relations"; "we're all friends, eh?" It's just that sometimes Indigenous people "use" allegations of racism as a tool. "It's like a tennis game," the councillor said. "They try to win a few points here and there."

To reiterate, prejudice is not defined by an absence of intergroup friendships; it is a defensive reaction to perceived group threat. As the councillor suggested, what was really going on – at least in some minds – was a battle for group position: the historically dominant whites were struggling to maintain resources and status in the face of rising economic uncertainty for them and the recent gains for Indigenous peoples who aspired to control more land. Thus, when WFS proposed to purchase property in Alberton, many residents perceived it as a "threat" (a "NON-SECURE NATIVE DETENTION CENTRE"). Likewise, when residents opposed the group home, they were, in effect, defending the status quo and preventing WFS from, in its eyes, improving the life-chances of Anishinaabe children.

Past Research on Antiracist Strategies, Group Positioning Tactics, and Framing

A growing body of research on responding to racism examines how stigmatized groups (attempt to) transform the *meanings* associated with their group (Lamont and Mizrachi 2012). In Lamont's (2009, 151) terms, destigmatization strategies are ways of "challenging stereotypes that feed and justify discriminatory behaviour and rebutting the notion of [group] inferiority." They include the expansion or contraction of "symbolic boundaries" between "us" and "them" (157), a "normative inversion" in which "the category of the excluded and despised comes to designate a chosen people who are morally, physically, and culturally superior to the dominant group" (Wimmer 2008, 988), and various forms of "social creativity," such as comparing groups on alternative dimensions (Tajfel and Turner 2001).[8]

In the settler colonial context, Indigenous peoples often draw upon their "values, roots, and cultural toolkits" (Vasquez and Wetzel 2009, 1557) – including their language and sense of humour (Basso 1979) – to distinguish themselves from settler society and thereby uphold their dignity. Indigenous peoples in northwestern Ontario (Treaty No. 3 territory) engage in similar processes, from reclaiming their Anishinaabe names and languages to reviving formerly banned customs and ceremonies[9] to priding themselves on their commitment to the Seven Grandfather Teachings.[10] In doing so, they promote *both* social inclusion *and* respect for cultural diversity, Indigenous sovereignty, and treaties. For example, Anishinaabe Elders explain how the medicine wheel (a circle with red, white, black, and yellow quadrants) teaches that all peoples have a place in the circle of life; they are distinct but connected and give the circle balance; removing one or painting them all white would disrupt the balance. Thus, each nation has equal worth but also a right to autonomy and difference.

This dual emphasis on inclusion and differentiation is also, in part, a response to the dual pressures Indigenous peoples face – both boundary imposition and forced assimilation, as epitomized by residential schools.[11] The message Indigenous peoples historically received from whites was: "You must be like us, but you can never be like us." Consequently, they fight two battles: one, to demonstrate their equal worth and be accepted in mainstream society; the other, to practise self-determination, exercise their rights, and sustain their unique identities.[12]

A complementary approach to studying intergroup encounters investigates the *tactics* that historically dominant and marginalized groups use to negotiate their positions in situations that threaten the status quo.[13] Given social competition over scarce resources (Nagel 1995b; Tajfel and Turner 2001), how do groups (attempt to) defend or alter their relative positions on salient dimensions of inequality, such as land ownership/control?

Sociologists working in other contexts offer clues on what to expect. John Gaventa (1980) has documented numerous strategies that the (relatively) powerful and powerless use to test or shift the balance of power. Although criticized for intimations of "false consciousness" (i.e., the suggestion that the targets of oppression do not know what is in their own interests), his study of quiescence and rebellion in an Appalachian mining community provides helpful tools for analysing group-positioning tactics. He describes how the powerful inhibit challenges to the existing order through the use of force; the threat of sanctions; the invocation of existing norms, rules, or precedents; the creation of new rules or barriers; and the use of discrediting labels such as "radical" or "troublemaker." Over time, the historically marginalized group may internalize a sense of powerlessness, anticipate defeat, and fear reprisal, thereby preventing them from pursuing their (self-defined) interests even when they have a chance to alter the status quo.

In another classic work, James C. Scott (1990, 198) shows how subordinate groups frequently do resist domination, even if "offstage" or in "disguised" form. He distinguishes openly declared acts, such as protests, petitions, and public assertions of worth by gesture, speech, or dress, from "everyday forms of resistance," such as poaching, squatting, foot-dragging, gossip, rumour, euphemism, and world-upside-down imagery. In contexts where racism is politically incorrect, such as twenty-first-century Canada, the rhetoric of racism itself may be used to discredit dominant groups and thereby gain at least a moral victory.

The widely used concept of *framing* (Benford and Snow 2000; Goffman 1974) helps bridge these approaches. As interpretive lenses for organizing experience and guiding action, frames enable us to make sense of situations and define our identities and interests. They also may be used strategically, to try to change others' opinions or behaviours. Thus, white and Indigenous residents may frame their encounters in ways that bolster their respective senses of group position. In contemporary North America, whites often use abstract liberalism and personal responsibility frames to justify racial inequality in seemingly race-neutral ways (Bonilla-Silva 2010). Such laissez-faire attitudes enable them to defend their resources and privileges and avoid taking action to rectify inequities. By contrast, I suggest, Indigenous peoples – both in responding to settlers and in drawing on their own cultural traditions – tend to frame their interests in more inclusive, communal terms; rather than seeking to reverse group positions, they aim to restore balance to the circle of life.

Analytic Approach

According to Blumer (1958, 5), "Race prejudice should be studied as the collective process through which a sense of group position is formed." This process is both historical (as outlined in chapter 1) and interpretive, as group members make sense of their identities and relationships by drawing on the cultural tools at their disposal (see chapters 2, 3, and 4). It is also an ongoing social process that potentially occurs whenever groups interact, but especially during rare "big events," such as the video incident (see Introduction) or the Point Park land dispute (see chapters 3 and 7):

> The happening that seems momentous, that touches deep sentiments, that seems to raise fundamental questions about relations, and that awakens strong feelings of identification with one's racial group is the kind of event that is central in the formation of the racial image. (Blumer 1958, 6)

The Alberton group home controversy is another such event that provides an opportunity to examine how group positions are maintained and contested – the situational mechanisms of reproduction and transformation that Blumer and his adherents leave unspecified.

By analysing eight hours of audio recordings and field notes from four public meetings (24 June, 8 and 29 July, and 12 August 2009) concerning the rezoning issue, as well as selected public documents and a dozen interviews with key informants, including Alberton councillors and residents and WFS representatives and their allies, I document the salient strategies and tactics that white and Indigenous residents used to defend and challenge their group positions.

Defending and Challenging Group Positions

In situations that threaten the status quo, how do historically dominant and subordinate groups negotiate their positions? Although the details will vary across local contexts, this case reveals two distinct sets of strategies and tactics. On one hand, white residents and their elected councillors tried to exclude the group home by using delay tactics, searching for race-neutral justifications, offering unsolicited advice, denying racial motives, playing the victim, creating new rules, and censuring "traitors." The Anishinaabe agency and its few white allies – guided by traditional decision-making ceremonies – initially tried to provide neutral information, stay positive, and emphasize common interests. When these tactics failed, they considered mobilizing their national political and media contacts, before foregoing the opportunity to appeal to an independent tribunal, the Ontario Municipal Board (OMB).[14] This section describes how the conflict played out and illuminates why Weechi-it-te-win avoided a more confrontational approach.

Dominant Group Tactics: Alberton Council and Residents

When under threat, a common first line of defence for historically dominant groups – in this case, white residents and their elected councillors – is to delay making a decision for as long as possible in hopes that the challenger will relent. As one councillor said:

> We might as well take it right to the furthest distance down the road before we make our decision because by the time August comes around and we put some information together, we can [probably beat] this, you know?

After the first meeting, I asked the reeve (small-town mayor) which of the residents' many concerns were legitimate reasons to deny the rezoning application. "None," he replied. Under the Ontario Planning Act and the Canadian Charter of Rights and Freedoms, there was no "legitimate excuse." Although many wished to stop Weechi-it-te-win in its tracks (a vote by hand on 24 June showed that only two of nearly two hundred residents openly supported the proposal), council realized that without a legally defensible reason, a "no" decision could be overturned by the OMB (upon appeal). How, then, could white residents exclude the Anishinaabe facility without looking like "bad guys"?

First, they searched for race-neutral justifications: they claimed that the group home would reduce public safety, decrease property values, increase taxes, create traffic jams, strain the water system, and so on. Although proffered with conviction, none of these rationalizations withstood scrutiny. As one WFS supporter put it, "It was like make-up reasons – when you went over all those reasons, they were just made-up reasons because nobody wanted to say why they really didn't want it there."

A detailed analysis of all these justifications is beyond the scope of this chapter. But let us briefly consider the two most frequently cited: perceived safety and financial risks. After the distribution of the anonymous flyer and rumours about a case in Edmonton, Alberta (a city of over one million people seventeen hundred kilometres west), where two youth reportedly had escaped from a First Nations group home and murdered a white couple, many residents believed there was a high chance that WFS clients would endanger them and their children. Yet even after it was clearly explained at the first meeting that this was not the same type of facility as in Edmonton, that it was not a jail or detention centre, that there were separate "secure" facilities for violent criminals and sex offenders, and that in twenty-five years of operation the most serious incident perpetrated by "runaway" youth from the TLC had been a few overturned picnic benches and broken windows at the Sunny Cove Bible Camp (the costs of which WFS repaid), some residents still feared for their lives. Others shifted attention to the safety of WFS *clients*, claiming that their real concern was that an Indigenous child might run away and get hit by a car.

Meanwhile, a majority of residents were deeply concerned about the impact of the facility on their property values and taxes. The assertion that property values would decline was not supported by the Municipal Property Assessment Corporation in a letter read aloud at the first meeting. Moreover, although the property in question would be taken out of the municipal tax base, WFS had offered to enter a service agreement with the township that would more than compensate for lost revenue. After each concern was discussed and discredited, the general pattern was for residents to return to an earlier concern and repeat the same line of questioning or suggest that WFS representatives were incompetent or untrustworthy.

In raising these objections, of course, not all residents were personally motivated by racism. From a short-term individualistic perspective, the perceived safety or financial risks might have outweighed the benefits. However, residents' concerns were often expressed with racial over-tones ("you people"), associated with stereotypes (such as Indigenous youths' purported criminality),[15] highly exaggerated (some feared they would be murdered in their beds), and resistant to contrary evidence or assurances from Weechi-it-te-win (derided privately in some circles as "We-cheat-to-win"). As Allport (1954, 14) said, where prejudice is involved, "the belief system has a way of slithering around to justify the more permanent attitude."

For example, some white residents assumed the facility was tax-exempt because it was Indigenous-run.[16] The WFS lawyer clari-fied that it was tax-exempt because it was a non-profit. Many retorted that they still opposed the facility because it was "an additional cost to the taxpayer." The Métis lawyer replied that WFS was "not looking for a free ride" and "would find ways to make that [potential loss of tax revenue] up to the municipality." Some residents said they did not believe him. Others began searching for alternative reasons to deny the application. In an era of "colour-blind racism," whites tend to explain their opposition to initiatives to improve the life chances of Indigenous peoples and other racialized minorities in terms of "anything but race" (Bonilla-Silva 2010, 62). Yet when the discussion later returned to taxes, it spiralled into a broader lament about the perceived unfairness of Ab-original and treaty rights. As the reeve stated, these were not legitimate grounds to deny the rezoning request.

While searching for race-neutral justifications, the dominant group may buttress its sense of group position by offering unsolicited advice to "help" the other in a way that does not affect it personally. Such "false generosity" (Freire 1970) positions whites in the superior role of knowing what is best for Indigenous peoples. In this case, residents tried to convince WFS to "stay on reserve" so that its clients could be closer to their "culture," which would help them to "heal" – a crafty form of "boundary policing" (Wimmer 2008) that uses Indigenous peo-ples' own ideas against them and tries to convince them to change their conception of their own interests.[17]

To the extent that the dominant group's lack of "legitimate excuses" is transparent or the marginalized group challenges them, as WFS did, the former will react with both denial and increasing force, including new legal barriers and sanctions directed not only at the challenger, but also at traitors within its own group (i.e., whites who support Indige-nous struggles). As Jackman (1994) suggests, overt coercion only be-comes necessary when the ideological system for sustaining the status quo (i.e., paternalistic racism) breaks down.

When, after two hours of repetitive questioning and false accusations, the WFS lawyer suggested that the Anishinaabe agency was being discriminated against, residents staunchly denied it: "It's not a Native thing"; "It has nothing to do with whether it's Aboriginal"; "I am not a racist, but ... "[18] To admit that one's opposition was in any way linked to prejudice would be to cede the moral high ground in an era when racism is no longer socially acceptable.[19]

If residents did concede that the issue was racialized, it usually was to suggest that they, as taxpayers, were on the receiving end of "reverse discrimination." Just like whites in Bobo and Tuan's (2006) study of a Chippewa fishing rights dispute, Alberton residents portrayed themselves as *victims* who must "roll over" to Indigenous peoples' demands and pay more taxes as First Nations reacquire land and threaten their "security."[20]

Meanwhile, council realized that if WFS purchased another property that was already zoned appropriately, it could establish a group home without the municipality's vetting.[21] To prevent the Anishinaabe agency from "sneakin' in the back door," therefore, council passed an interim control bylaw, which prohibited group homes in "rural residential" zones for up to two years.

The official reason for the interim control bylaw was to "conduct a study to determine ... whether or not the group home use can be legally eliminated from the Zoning By-Law." The interim bylaw was passed on 8 July, after council had turned to other business and everyone except the author, a local newspaper reporter, and one other resident had left the meeting. Councillors then debated whether passing the bylaw was "in bad faith" and apparently convinced themselves that they were acting in "the township interests." As that conversation went:

COUNCILLOR 1: Well, I just don't want [*pause*] – sneakin' in the back door.
MUNICIPAL OFFICIAL: Yeah.
[*Long pause*]
COUNCILLOR 2: We need to stop them from finding a loophole –
COUNCILLOR 3: Yeah, well, they're probably looking right now for somewhere else.
COUNCILLOR 2: Oh, they are.
COUNCILLOR 3: And they'll jump right in [*chuckles*].
COUNCILLOR 2: We already got the *threat* on that.
COUNCILLOR 3: Yeah, but would it be good of us [*pause*] – would we be acting in "bad faith" if we passed an interim bylaw right now?
COUNCILLOR 4: Well, why are we passing it for?
COUNCILLOR 3: Well, so they don't find a loophole.
COUNCILLOR 1: We need to –

COUNCILLOR 3: But we also need time to, uh –

COUNCILLOR 1: We need to evaluate this.

MUNICIPAL OFFICIAL: That's the purpose of an interim control bylaw is to *stop* something from happening because there is a loophole in there right now.

COUNCILLOR 1: Mm-hmm. It's like, "Hold on a minute; put the brakes on" …

MUNICIPAL OFFICIAL: It is a drastic measure. There's *no* question it's a drastic measure. But it's meant to protect until you can get a grasp on what to do. [*pause*]

COUNCILLOR 1: *We gotta protect the township interests.* (Emphasis added)

While council created these new rules and barriers, some residents resorted to bullying. At each meeting, they intimidated and interrogated WFS staff, interrupted them repeatedly, and questioned their competence. A petition with sixty-eight signatures opposing the TLC as "detrimental to our region" was submitted. Several residents suggested that the Training and Learning Centre lacked "qualified" teachers. One demanded "an unbiased report on its curriculum, operational strengths and areas of improvement or recommendations for change." Another vowed to use "any means necessary to protect [his] family" if Weechi-it-te-win moved to Alberton.

Sanctions and threats also were aimed at fellow whites who broke ranks and supported WFS – a classic tactic for ensuring in-group conformity (Elias and Scotson 1965; Gaventa 1980). As Blumer (1958, 5) says, the sense of group position is "a norm and imperative … a fundamental kind of group affiliation"; to deny it is to risk "self-alienation and [social] ostracism." Thus, the family who proposed to sell their property to the Anishinaabe agency became subject to rumours and exclusion by neighbours. They reported a drop in sales at their local business. And the township clerk's car tires were slashed, an incident that some interpreted as a warning to toe the line.

Ultimately, when council could no longer delay its decision, it bowed to public pressure and denied the application.[22] Although the reeve had said there was no "legitimate excuse," residents threatened to vote councillors out of power if they failed to do their bidding.

Subordinate Group Tactics: Weechi-it-te-win and Allies

Historically marginalized groups use their own set of tactics to advance their positions in encounters with dominant groups. Reviving and practising traditions is one way that Indigenous peoples "draw positive distinctions from the dominant culture" and reinvest their groups with "a pride and dignity that they are not normally accorded" (Vasquez and Wetzel 2009, 1569). In this case, WFS used traditional ceremonies – formerly banned by the Canadian government – to guide its decision-making. For example, senior staff and board members attended a "shaking tent ceremony" to obtain advice from a shaman who would communicate with the spirit world.

Before the first meeting, WFS was aware of the flyer and other rumours, which one staff member privately called "small-town racism masked as 'community safety.'" However, drawing on ceremonial messages and other "cultural teachings," they decided to give residents the benefit of the doubt. They hoped that the brewing backlash was the work of a few extremists and that if residents were given accurate information, their fears would be quelled.

Thus, Weechi-it-te-win researched the NIMBY ("Not in my backyard") syndrome; consulted legal professionals, Elders, and allies; and focused on providing "neutral" information, staying positive, and emphasizing common interests. They consciously avoided "the 'R' word" and adversarial approaches, and instead underscored their mandate and proposed use of the land, how local businesses could benefit, and how supporting the health and education of Indigenous children would lead to a healthier, more productive society. Even when confronted with racial epithets at the first meeting, an Anishinaabe board member "tried to look at it in a good way ... tried to put [herself] in their place." After long internal discussions and further ceremonies (including a sweat lodge for healing), WFS resolved to continue pursuing the property, believing that "common sense" would prevail.

The Anishinaabe agency's framing of the issue contrasted sharply with that of most white residents. Rather than viewing it as an "us versus them" situation, they tried to show that, from a long-term collective perspective, everyone gains from supporting programs like the TLC. As one of Weechi-it-te-win's few white supporters put it:

> In this economic downturn with many for-sale signs ... with little real estate moving, we are fortunate to have a buyer ... who ... wants to develop the property. Empty houses and barns are not good economically or safety-wise ... New people, more people spending money for goods and services ... is *good* for the local economy ... I see there will be cultural teachings as part of the school curriculum. It may be that we as neighbours could attend at selected times to enrich our knowledge. In return we could share our particular skills and specialties with the centre. Any time we can contribute to the development of young people, any young people, we and the township as a whole become healthier long into the future.

Such positive messages about common economic and social benefits and investments in the future were grossly overshadowed by fear-mongering, financial worries, mistrust, and suspicion at the township meetings. As one WFS representative later concluded, the goal of many white residents was "pre-set: 'Let's not let this Native agency into our community.'"

After the first meeting, Weechi-it-te-win also debated using its national political and media contacts to more directly pressure council. They decided against this. The fact that they did not mobilize these networks more extensively may be seen by some as a strategic error. But rather than shame their neighbours, they preferred to seek local solutions, if possible. From a practical standpoint, if WFS did relocate to Alberton, they would have to work with the township and its residents for many years. It therefore made sense, in this small-town setting, to try to stay on good terms and resolve issues locally.

In late July 2009, I attended a meeting where WFS representatives met with the Fort Frances Diversity Committee, which had formed in the wake of the video incident (described in the Introduction) with a mandate to "celebrate diversity by actively practicing and promoting dignity, respect and inclusiveness."[23] Although WFS expected the committee to offer a public statement of support, instead committee members engaged in many of the same processes as Alberton residents. Local white community leaders offered unsolicited advice on how to be more successful next time, such as educating the community about its programs, avoiding acronyms, and contacting white allies. After listening patiently for nearly an hour, a WFS representative said she was offended by "the suggestion that we didn't already think about this" and challenged the committee to "put your name out there in support of us." Then the familiar pattern of delaying and searching for excuses began, with such comments as: "This committee doesn't just deal with race issues ... We're just getting started ... I don't know what we can do ... I don't know if we really have any authority ... Is our voice any more than one in the wilderness?" When one committee member said she was willing to write a letter supporting WFS, another interjected that *all* members would have to "agree on the wording," which "could take time because people are away for the summer." By September, of course, it would be too late.

Nevertheless, the long-serving, well-respected local MPP Howard Hampton did speak at the third meeting in Alberton, praising Weechi-it-te-win as "an outstanding organization" and suggesting that partnerships with First Nations are the way of the future:

> When I look at where the world is going and the kinds of co-operative relationships that we will *have* to form with First Nation communities, this

[proposal] is absolutely something that I think the municipality should support ... Given that we're going to see many more First Nation organizations, some involved in economic development, some involved in education, and some involved in activities like this, I think it would be advantageous for the municipality to say, "We're willing to work with organizations like Weechi-it-te-win."

Although Hampton's eloquent speech appeared to change the reeve's mind ("The more you look at it, the better it looks!" he quipped), WFS did not ask him to speak at this meeting, and it was too little, too late. Likewise, it was not until after the rezoning application had been rejected that WFS sought media support. In September 2009, the Aboriginal Peoples Television Network ran a national news story suggesting that the public outcry had been driven largely by racism.[24]

At this point, WFS had one last option: it could appeal the decision to an independent tribunal, the Ontario Municipal Board, as it was then called.[25] Given that the reeve had said, on record, that there was no "legitimate excuse" for denying the rezoning application and that the decision probably would be overturned by the OMB, the Anishinaabe agency had a good chance of winning an appeal. Yet it let the deadline pass.

Why would Weechi-it-te-win forego this option, thereby allowing residents to succeed in blocking the land purchase? According to WFS's official statement on 15 September 2009:

This decision was primarily based on the time and expense of the appeal process, but also on the fact that, even if the appeal was successful, there were other issues which would need to be addressed with the assistance of Alberton Township. Given the attitudes demonstrated by ... Council and some of its citizens to date, Weechi-it-te-win was concerned that further roadblocks to the TLC relocation ... might arise. Weechi-it-te-win is deeply disappointed that Alberton chose to view the relocation ... as *a threat to their way of life*, rather than embracing it as *an opportunity* to do something exciting with a well-respected child welfare organization ... We continue to hope that Alberton reconsiders its position. In the meantime, Weechi-it-te-win remains committed to finding a suitable location for the TLC that meets the needs of its children. (Emphasis added)

This situation can be likened to the Appalachian mining case that Gaventa (1980) analysed: the decision *not* to appeal reflects both "anticipated defeat" and "fear of reprisal." However, it also reflects a pragmatic reassessment of options. Indigenous peoples in the Rainy River District have learned – from this experience, past OMB decisions (such as a 2001 ruling against the nearby Couchiching First Nation) and court cases, repeated violations of Indigenous and treaty rights (such as the UN-recognized right to free, prior, and informed consent), and frequent use of military/police force to subdue Indigenous protests (from the Red River Resistance to Oka and beyond) – that if they challenge white settler society, the latter will fight them every step of the way. In this case, WFS expected "further roadblocks" and a long costly legal battle. Some feared for their children's safety. According to one board member:

> It was kind of scary for us ... I thought, what could I say to these people? Or what *should* I say? ... I had so many thoughts running in my head. And I started to feel angry and [*pause*] a bit scared – not only for myself, but for our people.

Thus, Weechi-it-te-win prioritized the practical need to quickly find a safe home for its clients over the urge to fight this particular battle. Although the Alberton property was "ideal for what [they] needed," and some WFS staff wanted to "go through with it all the way," the organization had to be "realistic" given provincial funding cuts and local feedback. It therefore chose to maintain its present position, temporarily renew its lease at the old (if less than ideal) site, and wait for a better option, in a community that would understand "we are all in it together" and view its presence as an "opportunity," not a "threat."

Conclusion

In their study of a treaty rights dispute in 1990s Wisconsin, Bobo and Tuan (2006, 172) showed how white opposition to Chippewa fishing rights was driven by "a feeling of group deprivation" rooted in "whites' fear of losing ... status and power." Similar processes are repeatedly observed in northwestern Ontario. The Alberton case shows how even something as seemingly minor as the attempted purchase of a small plot of land for an Indigenous youth centre can trigger a deep sense of group threat among many settlers.

This chapter has identified a set of interpretive and behavioural strategies that white and Indigenous residents use to defend or advance their positions in such situations. Although the details will vary across contexts, similar patterns may be observable in other encounters between historically dominant and marginalized groups. In this case, most whites framed their interests in short-term personal/familial terms, whereas the Anishinaabe and their allies emphasized long-term collective interests. These conflicting approaches are rooted in the latent balance of power and long-standing cultural traditions.

While highlighting common interests sometimes may help "bridge the racial divide" (Wilson, 1999), it failed to resonate with most Alberton residents. The dominant white frame here suggests that there is little to gain from an Indigenous group home as a neighbour and at least some risk. From this perspective, "they" (Natives) are placing a "burden" on "us" (whites). That is the lens through which most white residents view the world, a lens that has crystallized under conditions of economic uncertainty and that reinforces whites' sense of group superiority. Although WFS tried to frame the group home proposal as a "win-win," many settlers appeared to have already made up their minds and tried to rationalize their opposition, regardless of the evidence. It would require not only sustained emphasis on common interests, but also a shift in how most white residents perceive their interests, for them to see that "we are all in it together" and that supporting Indigenous children today will benefit everyone in the long run.

Another lesson concerns the Anishinaabe agency's reluctance to utilize more confrontational political/legal strategies. In this respect, WFS's response resembles that of the Appalachian coal miners, whose apparent quiescence Gaventa (1980) attributed to their historically developed sense of powerlessness. Despite possessing the formal right of appeal, marginalized groups may decline to use it, particularly in small-town contexts where they are outnumbered and success can come with a price (including time, money, and resentment from neighbours). As one Anishinaabe woman cautioned, however, in drawing an analogy to Oka, withdrawing from a battle does not necessarily mean abandoning the wider struggle (see chapter 10).

As it stands, deeply entrenched laissez-faire frames and small-town dynamics limit the choice and effectiveness of strategies for change. The desire of many whites to protect their group position remains a barrier. This observation reiterates the need to transform the meanings associated with Indigenous peoples in settler-Canadians' minds, so that one day both symbolic recognition and material justice (including access to land) will be forthcoming.

Two caveats should be noted. First, neither "settler" nor "Indigenous" is a homogenous group. Although most Alberton residents opposed the TLC, one white couple openly supported it and dozens kept silent. While many Indigenous people were disturbed by the "racist" backlash, a minority sympathized with settlers' concerns. More-assimilated Indigenous people may not have used traditional ceremonies, and some WFS staff wished to appeal to the OMB, believing that if the decision could be reversed and the group home established, residents' fears would dissipate.[26] Nevertheless, the predominant frames and tactics varied substantially between groups.

Second, opponents of the Anishinaabe facility were not necessarily all personally motivated by racism. Some residents appeared genuinely concerned about potential changes to their quality of life. Some also said they would oppose a group home for white children. Further, councillors' decision to deny the rezoning application may have been influenced more by re-election chances than by a desire to exclude Weechi-it-te-win; in their eyes, they acted democratically to protect "the township interests." Nevertheless, the racial overtones in public speeches, the racial slurs uttered in private, the emotional intensity of the opposition, and the frequent digressions into broader "Indigenous issues" (such as the perceived unfairness of treaty rights) suggest that the Alberton rezoning controversy was not just a case of NIMBYism; for many, it was also about where each group – Indigenous and white – stands in the settler colonial order. Even those who thought only about their *personal* interests (such as property values) indirectly reinforced the status quo and protected their *group* position; by forbidding rezoning, they effectively forced WFS to renew its lease at the problematic old site, rather than enabling it to acquire its "ideal" property. Such short-term individualistic framing often facilitates decisions that bolster systemic racial inequities, even in an era of "truth and reconciliation."

Addendum

Although Weechi-it-te-win chose not to appeal the rezoning decision, an older white couple (Ms Friesen and Mr Stoltzfus) – both active members of the Right Relations Circle – did appeal the interim control by-law, which prohibited group homes in rural residential zones for up to two years so that the township could "conduct a study to determine ... whether or not the group home use can be legally eliminated from the Zoning By-Law." The fact that these white individuals not only disagreed with the dominant interpretation of fellow white residents, but actively challenged the township through a quasi-judicial process seems difficult to reconcile with group position theory. If the controversy was ultimately about group positions, as I have argued, then why would any member of a historically dominant group forego their "superior" position and side with the marginalized in trying to alter the status quo? While a complete answer requires more systematic analysis, this case offers preliminary clues.

When asked why they chose to appeal, as private citizens, Ms Friesen and Mr Stoltzfus said it was partly to pave the way for WFS and the current property owners (while they still had the opportunity to appeal) and partly out of their own desire for social justice. In their words:

> The council has hidden behind land use planning phrases, to the detriment of real land use planning for economic and social development. Further, they have undermined the township's future economic and social development under pressure from some vocal residents who came to the meetings with pre-set prejudicial judgements. This was clearly a misuse of their authority.[27]

In addition to their abiding sense of justice, principled reasons to take a stand, and the belief that it was in the township's long-term interests to support WFS, certain demographic and social characteristics might predispose individuals like Ms Friesen and Mr Stoltzfus to make such interpretations and take such (antiracist) actions. As relative outsiders not originally from the region, who had spent most of their adult lives abroad as peace activists, who both had university degrees in the humanities or social sciences, who were not dependent on the economically fragile forestry sector, and who had a rare sense of conviction, courage, and patience, they had less to lose by fighting on principle. Although this couple, like the family who proposed to sell their property to WFS, did face subtle forms of exclusion and stigmatization from some neighbours (such as interruptions, mocking, and angry glares at public meetings), they also received private praise from others (including a few long-time white residents) for standing up for their beliefs. Moreover, they earned the deep respect of local First Nations for their "bravery"; an Anishinaabe friend gifted Ms Friesen with an eagle feather and a star blanket and fondly called her a "white-haired warrior," while Mr Stoltzfus received an honorary feather "for his work in the district" upon his passing in March 2010.

The township, meanwhile, reacted predictably. First, it filed a motion to dismiss the appeal "on the basis that there are no valid land use planning grounds to support the appeal." The initial meeting with an OMB officer to determine whether the appeal should be heard was scheduled for 9 November 2009, but was postponed due to "incompatible technology for videoconferencing." A new date was set. However, when the meeting started in March 2010, the township's lawyer

claimed he had not received some of the appellants' documents.[28] After
another delay, the meeting finally transpired on 20 April 2010 – after the
deadline for a WFS appeal had lapsed, meaning there was no longer a
realistic "threat" of an Indigenous-run group home being established
in Alberton.

During the hearing, Ms Friesen argued that the township had passed
the bylaw not for purposes of "land use planning," but rather "to exclude a specific party from using property in a manner which was
otherwise permitted under the current zoning bylaw." The Alberton
lawyer countered that the township had followed all necessary legal
procedures, and that Ms Friesen's argument was "not grounded in
land use planning objections." Moreover, the township clerk had, in
the intervening period, written a ten-page planning report clarifying
allowable group home uses and conditions under the zoning by-law
and recommending amendments to the official plan. Since this was the
stated purpose of the interim control bylaw, the latter would expire in
July 2010, and it would be impossible to schedule a full board hearing
before that date. Thus, the OMB officer dismissed the appeal because
she had to "look at it from a procedural point of view." However, she
concluded her written decision:

> That does not mean that the issues raised by Ms. Friesen and the partici-
> pants are not valid, merely that there is no planning expertise that sets out
> valid land use planning grounds to support the appeal, as currently con-
> stituted. In this regard the Board urges the Township to consider carefully
> the objections and submissions of Ms. Friesen and the participants as their
> concerns are real.[29]

Thus, although the appeal was defeated on procedural grounds,
Ms Friesen, WFS, and their Indigenous and non-Indigenous supporters
won a moral victory. Moreover, the OMB required Alberton to revise its
development plan under the OMB's watch.

In short, Alberton residents provisionally protected their material
privileges, but group positions are not etched in stone. In April 2011,
Weechi-it-te-win purchased a new property for its Training and Learning Centre in La Vallee, a small rural township west of Alberton where
rezoning was unnecessary. Although some white residents there also
tried to block the purchase by pooling their resources and attempting
to outbid WFS, the purchase was finalized, and the new facility opened
in 2013.

Chapter Six

Bridge Work: Beyond Group Positioning?

To this point, we have seen how the sense of group positions is rooted in history, entrenched in local and state institutions, and reproduced through everyday perceptions, attitudes, and interactions. What, if anything, can (or should) be done to overcome these divisions between Indigenous and settler peoples?

The concept of bridges was not part of Blumer's original formulation of group position theory. Nor for that matter were boundaries. To have a sense of group position, though, clearly requires drawing a boundary between "us" and "them." Throughout my research, therefore, my first question for Rainy River District residents was, how do they think about boundaries? To provide balance, I also asked about bridges. In principle, bridges represent a connection between two distinct entities, without necessarily erasing their distinctness. They are an apt metaphor for promoting connection, dialogue, and interdependence, but not necessarily assimilation. One may wonder, however, whether bridges can break down the sense of group positions or whether group positioning inhibits the formation of bridges.

When I asked residents about boundaries and bridges, there was more consensus about what brings Indigenous and non-Indigenous people together than about what divides them. The most frequently cited bridges were: shared participation in local institutions, such as school, church, sports and recreation; opportunities to learn about Indigenous cultures; shared beliefs and values; education and communication; the physical proximity of Indigenous and settler communities; their shared history and economic interdependence; shared health and environmental concerns; and their ability to work together in a crisis. A few residents mentioned the potential of collective action, including antiracist and anticolonial activism. In the wake of the federal government's 2008 residential school apology, many agreed that apologies and reparations are necessary steps towards healing.

Nevertheless, some people's bridges are others' boundaries, and white and Indigenous residents tended to frame bridges in ways that bolstered their respective senses of group position. In this chapter, I will show that white residents tended to conceptualize bridges in ways that upheld their sense of group superiority and entitlement, whereas Indigenous residents conceptualized bridges in ways that sought to transform group positions.

Conceptualizing Bridges across Boundaries

Like boundaries, the concept of bridges is widely used in the social sciences. Again, however, we need to think critically about how to define and apply it in the context of Indigenous-settler relations. Network analysts distinguish between "bridging" and "bonding" social capital (Putnam 2000). Social psychologists have examined multiple bases of interpersonal friendship, including homophily ("birds of a feather flock together"), complementarity ("opposites attract"), and physical proximity (which provides the opportunity for interaction) (McPherson, Smith-Lovin, and Cook 2001). Hundreds of quantitative studies support the notion that intergroup contact *per se* reduces stereotyping and prejudice (Pettigrew and Tropp 2006). Nevertheless, numerous cases of war and genocide suggest that neither geographic closeness nor histories of cooperation inevitably prevent intergroup violence (on the potential and limitations of contact, see chapter 7).

Another view on bridges may be found in the growing literature on alliance-building and solidarity work between Indigenous and settler peoples (Davis 2010; Grossman 2017; Lawrence and Dua 2005; Wallace 2013), and between visible minorities and whites (Srivastava 2006; Warren 2010), including activities aimed at combating racism and colonialism. As Margaret (2010, 8–9) concluded from a review of this literature, however, "there is not a simple checklist" for constructing effective alliances; the process of becoming an "ally" is complex and ongoing, and "issues need to be worked through [in] the specific circumstance(s) and relationship(s)." Moreover, Indigenous-settler coalitions can be "a microcosm of colonial relationships" and "a site of pain," but also "a site of learning and transformation" (Davis and Shpuniarsky 2010, 336).

From a radically different perspective, some academics conceive of bridges in terms of the assimilation or integration of Indigenous peoples into Canadian society (Flanagan 2000; Widdowson and Howard 2008). Although some settlers might consider such processes "bridges," most Indigenous scholars see them as highly destructive of Indigenous nations (Coulthard 2014; Simpson 2014). Rather than seeking recognition via assimilation (which may create bridges at the expense of unique identities, ways of life, and political control), they advocate for self-determination and "a politics of refusal" to submit to settler colonialism. Although not ruling out intergroup interaction, they promote the maintenance and revitalization of traditional Indigenous values and principles and a critical stance on "mainstream" norms and institutions.

My aim here is not to evaluate these different theories, but to investigate how Rainy River District residents themselves conceived of bridges and how their conceptions related to their sense of group position. My premise is that bridges do not necessarily eliminate boundaries; rather, they often provide a linkage between two or more distinct entities – in this case, Indigenous and settler communities. The question is: what materials compose these bridges? Just as physical bridges require concrete, construction workers, engineering plans, and other ingredients, so do intergroup bridges require appropriate resources. What are those ingredients and how do they support or challenge the sense of group positions?

Residents' Conceptions of Bridges: Overall Trends

After enquiring about boundaries, I asked all 160 interviewees, "What do you think are the biggest bridges between Aboriginal and non-Aboriginal people today? In other words, what (if anything) brings people together or enables them to cooperate?"

In response, Rainy River District residents described hundreds of unique bridges or sources of cooperation.[1] To make the results more manageable, I condensed their responses into thirteen conceptually distinct but empirically overlapping categories. From most to least frequently mentioned by interviewees, these were:

- Shared participation in local institutions, such as schools, churches, and volunteer groups
- Cultural opportunities and Indigenous peoples' openness to sharing their culture through events like powwows and fish fries
- Shared interests in sports and recreation, hunting and fishing, music and the arts
- Shared cultural frames or repertoires, including beliefs or phrases like "we're all in it together" or "people are people"
- Physical proximity and contact/exposure
- Communication and/or education

- Individual characteristics, such as open-mindedness, empathy, and acceptance
- Indigenous people's willingness to assimilate into "mainstream" society
- Economic interdependence
- Shared history, including multiple generations of intermarriage and the large local Métis community
- Local crises, including the video incident
- Shared health and environmental concerns
- Antiracist activism

As with the boundaries examined in chapter 3, many of the bridges cited by interviewees have close parallels in the academic literature. Numerous studies have addressed the roles of proximity, contact, education, personality traits, and, to a lesser extent, local institutions, cultural repertoires, and antiracist activism in moderating racial attitudes and fostering more equitable intergroup relations. However, the content and meaning of some of these bridges appear to be unique to the Indigenous-settler context. Indigenous residents in particular mobilized distinct cultural resources, such as the belief that "we are all treaty people," in attempts to forge bridges with their non-Indigenous neighbours. References to shared healing concerns and the historical buffering role of the local Métis were also quite distinct.

In the next section, I compare and contrast how Indigenous and white residents framed selected bridges, showing how their perceptions reflected and reinforced their respective senses of group position.

Indigenous and White Perspectives on Bridges: Comparative Analysis

Indigenous and settler interviewees were more likely to concur about bridges than about boundaries. As table 6.1 shows, substantial numbers agreed that shared participation in local institutions, cultural opportunities, selected personal characteristics, and other such bridges facilitated cooperation or helped to bring Indigenous and non-Indigenous people together in mutually beneficial relationships. Smaller numbers of interviewees (especially the Indigenous) also mentioned the communities' shared history of working together, the impact of local crises in forging stronger bonds, shared health and environmental concerns, and antiracist activism.

Table 6.1 Percentage of Indigenous and White Interviewees Who Discussed Selected
Bridges

Category of bridge	% of Indigenous interviewees who discussed it	% of white interviewees who discussed it	Total number of interviewees who discussed it
1. Shared participation in local institutions	37.8	44.9	66
2. Cultural opportunities and openness to sharing	37.8	33.3	57
3. Sports and recreation or other leisure activities	30.5	38.5	55
4. Shared cultural frames or repertoires	35.4	32.1	54
5. Physical proximity and contact/exposure	24.4	39.7	51
6. Communication and/or education	37.8	25.6	51
7. Individual characteristics	36.6	24.4	49
8. Indigenous people's willingness to assimilate	4.9	28.2	26
9. Economic interdependence	12.2	17.9	24
10. Shared history	18.3	7.7	21
11. Local crises	14.6	7.7	18
12. Shared health and environmental concerns	14.6	6.4	17
13. Antiracist activism	9.8	9.0	15

Nevertheless, closer analysis revealed three troublesome patterns. First, many white residents conceived of bridges in terms of Indigenous people's willingness to assimilate, whereas Anishinaabe and Métis residents were more likely to emphasize opportunities to learn about Indigenous cultures and collective responsibilities as well as individual traits such as respect for diversity. Second, some peoples' bridges were others' boundaries. While some residents viewed religion or treaties, for example, as promising ways to bring Indigenous and non-Indigenous people together, others viewed these same institutions as major sources of division. Third, Indigenous and white residents often attributed different meanings to the same bridges. For instance, both used common phrases such as "we're all in it together" or "we're all human" to actively illustrate a bridge. Yet whites often inferred from

Figure 6.1 Children Are Our Future. "As the song reminds us, 'children are
our future.' The revival of the Métis and North American Indian traditions
is promoting pride of culture in the young. I believe that in conjunction with
growing social tolerance this next generation will coexist in peace such as we
haven't seen since the eighteenth century." – Paul, Métis man, age fifty-six. Photo
courtesy of Paul, taken at the Naicatchewenin First Nation 2008 summer powwow.

such tropes that we should "treat everyone the same," whereas Indigenous peoples inferred that we should respect each other's diversity and
autonomy. The common thread was that many whites framed bridges
in ways that bolstered their sense of group superiority, whereas Anishinaabe and Métis residents were more likely to present alternative
visions that challenged whites' sense of group position. Below, I draw
selectively on interview, ethnographic, and photovoice data to illustrate these three patterns.

Assimilation versus Accommodation

In his classic ethnography of Indian-white relations in a Canadian plains community, Braroe (1975, 131) described "a general unwillingness on the part of Indians to reveal cultural differences that would call attention to their Indianness, which they know is disparaged by whites and hinders interaction." Cree names and religious beliefs and practices – "things they themselves feel to be characteristically and essentially Indian" – were deliberately concealed from whites in the interests of protecting Cree dignity.

In the four decades since Braroe's research, social norms have shifted. In the Rainy River District, at least, I observed that Indigenous culture is no longer concealed but often openly expressed in such diverse forms as "Native Pride" baseball caps, moccasins worn in public, dream catchers hanging in car windshields, language revitalization camps, and public use of the Anishinaabemowin language. Many Indigenous interviewees described a transformation in their own lives, from feeling ashamed of and trying to "cover" their "Indianness" to being proud of their heritage and practising their traditions, a transformation that they often linked to improved health, sobriety, and self-esteem (see Chandler and Lalonde 1998). In one of my first interviews, a First Nations man told the intimate story of how he received his Anishinaabe name. In my eighteen months in the district, I was invited to powwows, fish fries, sweat lodge ceremonies, and other cultural gatherings, including a family reunion. Whenever I asked about their traditions or customs, most Anishinaabe and Métis residents seemed happy to teach me. Further, cultural events were often advertised in local newspapers and radio stations as free and open to the public. Local public schools also had taken steps to be more inclusive of and show respect for Indigenous identities and traditions, inviting Elders into classrooms, taking students on field trips to First Nations communities, and so on (see chapter 8). Rather than "retreating" from mainstream society (Braroe 1975), many Indigenous peoples are actively engaging with it, sharing their knowledge and practices, and increasingly finding ways to combine, or coexist in, "both worlds."

Thirty-one Indigenous and twenty-six non-Indigenous interviewees explicitly described such opportunities to learn about and experience Indigenous cultures as a bridge. Many also credited the local Anishinaabe and Métis for their openness around sharing their knowledge and traditions. For instance, at the time of my fieldwork, every First Nation community in the district held at least one annual powwow, described most simply as "a celebration of life." These free public events provided exposure to traditional music, dancing, and regalia, and a chance to meet and interact with Indigenous people on Indigenous turf. An older white man, originally from the United States, called powwows "an enormous bridging opportunity" and praised the local First Nations for their "openness to invite white folks to participate." An older white woman, born and raised in the region, similarly stated: "When the Native community hosts powwows, everyone has the opportunity to go ... I've gone to some, and they're a wonderful [way] for all groups to come together." A middle-aged Métis woman reminded me that this was not always possible due to Canadian laws that banned Indigenous ceremonies for much of the twentieth century. But, she said, in "being allowed to dance, in '69, getting our regalia out, and not being charged with a [criminal] offence ... when we had more rights, that's when the bridges started happening." Similarly reflecting on these changes, an older Anishinaabe woman said that "powwows help" because they enhance "cultural awareness," and that children of all backgrounds are "anxious to learn."

In addition to powwows, some interviewees described other cultural "bridge work" being done by local Indigenous communities. For example, a middle-aged white woman in town said:

> Manitou [Rainy River First Nations] has their annual fish fry ... They invite everybody. They're very welcoming. There's a lot of intermarriage ... They maintain a cultural base. And I think there's lots to learn from people if they're willing to share.

An Anishinaabe woman in town described the "cultural week" at Naicatchewenin First Nation in spring 2008 as a "bridge" because "they invited the schools ... and different people to come in and learn about the Aboriginal culture." A white man in his twenties confirmed how he had learned from and developed closer relationships with Indigenous people through such opportunities:

> For me, personally, it was just being open to ... trying new things ... Getting involved at the local [United Native] Friendship Centre was one of the biggest ... I met a bunch of friends through there and eventually did the Native drumming ... Just sitting there and listening to an Elder speak and then giving you a ceremonial blanket; it's pretty cool ... the average white person would probably think we don't understand what their culture is, but if we don't understand it, how can we be persecuting it or how can we be saying something bad against it if we haven't experienced it?

A few interviewees also mentioned cultural events organized by non-Indigenous residents, including a travelling Indian residential school exhibit hosted by the Fort Frances Museum in the summer of 2008 (shortly after the federal government apology) and a Heritage Day event celebrating Métis culture organized by then member of Parliament Ken Boshcoff. They also remembered the now-defunct "Culturama," an annual event that used to showcase foods, music, and other traditions of the various ethnic groups in the Rainy River District.

One limitation to such cultural bridges, however, is that many settlers do not partake in the opportunities afforded by Indigenous peoples. For example, a white man in his thirties admitted:

> I know the Manitou fish fry is extremely popular. Tons of people go to that. But, beyond that, there's still just so much [*pause*] division. I don't know why. Like, if Emo [a primarily white town] was having ... the Emo Fair, we would go to that. If Kooch [Couchiching First Nation] was having a powwow, we probably wouldn't go to that ... I would just assume that it's, you know, a Native event and it's just Natives that go to it, even though they probably would be more than welcoming to non-Natives.

A further limitation is that while such cultural events could potentially alleviate some of the ignorance or misunderstandings around cultural differences (an important boundary discussed in chapter 3), it is difficult to see how attending powwows or fish fries alone could address deeper conflicts around treaties, land rights, or Indigenous sovereignty. Further, feel-good celebrations of cultural diversity that gloss over Indigenous peoples' unique relationships with Canada, including processes of colonization, risk obfuscating the issue – avoiding difficult discussions about socio-economic inequality, racism, and land theft in favour of a vague, unthreatening "diversity discourse" (Bell and Hartmann 2008).[2] Moreover, as discussed in chapter 3, some whites appear *threatened* by open cultural displays; one Native woman recalled how her friend was confronted by white youth and told, "We know you're Indian. You don't have to *display* it."

Although many whites said they were open to learning about Indigenous cultures and considered respect for diversity to be a bridge, a substantial minority of whites framed bridges in terms of Indigenous people's willingness to assimilate – both culturally and politically/ legally – into "mainstream" society. Such a framing supports whites' sense of superior group position by suggesting that Indigenous peoples must accommodate settlers (and not vice versa). For instance, a young white farmer said, "the Ministry of Indian Affairs was designed for assimilation," and although "they're trying to push away from that now," he thought "the only true way to be Canadian is to assimilate." An older white man in town agreed that "the government of the day should try to integrate them," and that the greatest bridge would be Indigenous people choosing to forsake their "heritage" and "move into *our* society." If that did not happen, he foresaw "more conflict ... because the young people I don't think are as tolerant as the older people," especially when it comes to tax exemptions and post-secondary education funding. A middle-aged white woman similarly accused Indigenous people of self-segregation and described "integration" as a bridge:

> Whenever you put a wall around yourself or isolate in a group, you identify yourself as different ... It's like a club ... I think that's very dangerous ... just by having that group, you don't allow things to come in [or] go out. So ... that framework needs to change. And you can do that with a lot more integration.

As settler colonial theory would predict, these interviewees believed that Indigenous people should conform to the (presumed superior) settler Canadian norms and practices. They did not consider the need for whites to learn about or accommodate Indigenous norms and practices, nor did they acknowledge Indigenous peoples' willingness to share. Moreover, they tended to blend discussions of the perceived need for cultural integration with that of the desire for *formal legal* equality, that is, abolition of treaties and the separate legal status of Indigenous peoples, a stance that inhibits *substantive* equality and thereby protects whites' sense of group superiority.

To provide one further example, an older white farmer explicitly described bridges in terms of "access to the white population" and Indigenous peoples' willingness to assimilate:

> When I was a kid ... you'd be sort of *ashamed* to admit that you had any Native blood ... today, that has changed ... I don't know what per cent of Native blood you need to get one of those [status] cards that gives you these [tax] exemptions, but it's – it's an honour! ... that sort of rubs me the wrong way. And there is a per cent of people that ... have Native blood [but] don't believe that's the right way to go. And they want to be like a *Canadian*. They want to pay their way. But I think, in recent years, there's been less of those, and I've been shocked by the number of people ... that have a treaty card. But, every now and then, somebody really impresses me: they're Native and they say, "No way, I don't want any special rights. I want to be treated the same as everybody else."

In short, this individual rejected Indigenous sovereignty and treaties, and the open expression of Indigenous identities and cultures "rub[bed] [him] the wrong way." For him, bridges are created by Native people who reject their "status" and "want to be treated the same as everyone else."

Although not all white residents thought this way – as table 6.1 shows, they were more likely to describe bridges in terms of opportunities to learn about Indigenous cultures – the underlying conflict seemed to revolve around who should accommodate whom. Some white (and a few Indigenous) interviewees insisted that Indigenous people must assimilate to "mainstream" culture and abandon their "special rights," an argument that, as explained in chapter 4, amounts to laissez-faire racism. In contrast, many Indigenous (and some white) interviewees emphasized the need to learn about and respect cultural diversity, often pointing to local cultural opportunities as a bridge – though, interestingly, still one where the onus is largely put on Indigenous peoples to share their knowledge and traditions.

Adding to the divergence in perceptions, Indigenous residents were far more likely than whites to describe treaties as a (potential) bridge and to emphasize the notion of mutual or shared responsibilities towards the earth and one another. For instance, an Anishinaabe man said:

> Everybody is a treaty person ... When [your] ancestors came to this continent, they signed a treaty. It's a legally binding contract to share the resources. But ever since signing that contract, the government has done everything in their power *not* to honour [it], to try and dismiss it and allow a different system to evolve.

In his view, treaties bind Indigenous and settler communities together and create rights and responsibilities for each. If Treaty No. 3 were honoured, he said, both parties would benefit.

Indigenous interviewees were also more likely to emphasize individual characteristics, such as empathy, understanding, patience, and self-reflection, which they believed facilitate cooperation and respect. While some suggested that these are innate dispositions, others were optimistic that individuals can change and develop such traits over time, given nurturing environments. For instance, a First Nations woman in her fifties said that bridges are created by "people who accept me without putting any definitions on me, [who] just treat you like you're a person." A white municipal politician emphasized the importance of trust: "If you're honest and you nurture the relationship, then it's a good relationship. If you go in there with bad faith, then there's always that doubt." Perhaps most commonly, interviewees highlighted the need for open minds and hearts. For an Anishinaabe woman in her thirties, the key was "wanting to learn and being open to learning ... It's ultimately your choice [to] see what kind of bridges you can form." Still others named individuals who exemplified such traits. For example, a middle-aged First Nations man described his white colleague, Hugh, as having

> a good heart ... he's very gentle and committed to his work ... what he does, he does very well ... he's done some stuff for our community ... we've made contributions to his [initiatives in town]. That's gonna change things ... And we *do* have to work together.

In short, my interviews revealed common ground between some white and Indigenous residents around the need for mutual accommodation and the kinds of individual characteristics that facilitate cooperation. However, I also found that a substantial number of whites continued to advocate one-way assimilation, reflecting and reinforcing their sense of group superiority, whereas Indigenous residents were far more likely to describe treaties – and shared social and environmental responsibilities – as a bridge.

A Boundary for Some, a Bridge for Others

Not only did Indigenous and white residents tend to emphasize different bridges, but some people's bridges were others' boundaries. While some Indigenous residents agreed that assimilating into mainstream society could be a "bridge," they usually said it was detrimental to their nation and therefore also a source of division. For example, an Anishinaabe man who lived on reserve and practised many of his traditions, while working full time and taking online university courses, said:

> Couchiching is ... different [from many First Nations] because it's so close to town; a lot of people do work in town. But, by the same token, we've probably suffered the most in terms of assimilation ... I think something like 0.5 per cent of our people speak the language fluently. That's going to be a goner [soon] and the sad reality is that nobody really cares.[3]

Although many white residents described integration, assimilation, or blending into a common "Canadian" identity as a bridge, the vast majority of Indigenous interviewees rejected such a vision. They regarded it not as a "bridge," but as a "sad reality" that their communities have "suffered" due to their physical proximity to Fort Frances and historical experiences with residential schooling and other settler colonial policies. From the perspective of national and cultural group survival, they said, some bridges are better left unbuilt.

Figure 6.2 Boundary or Bridge? "Our Lady of Lourdes Roman Catholic Church on Couchiching First Nation: a boundary for some, a bridge for others." – Naa-Gaabiinegee-zhig, Anishinaabe man, age fifty-three. Photo courtesy of Naa-Gaabiinegee-zhig.

To give another example, one prominent local institution described by some as a bridge was the Catholic Church. From 1906 to 1974, the Missionary Oblates of Mary Immaculate operated St. Margaret's Residential School at the borders of Fort Frances and Couchiching First Nation. At the time of my interviews, dozens of Couchiching band members still attended church and identified as Catholic. Indeed, some attended both Our Lady of Lourdes Church on reserve and St. Mary's Church in town; some whites also attended both services. At least two intermarried couples I interviewed initially met through local church functions. In total, 30 per cent of Indigenous and 40 per cent of non-Indigenous interviewees identified as Catholic.[4]

According to a self-described "half-breed" who was interviewed in Our Lady of Lourdes Church basement:

This is a Native parish. In the old days, it was ... filled with people from Couchiching because this was a Roman Catholic community ... but a big section ... was Indian [residential] school kids ... Today, about 75 per cent of the people that are in this church, nine o'clock on Sunday, is from Saint Mary's parish, which is a white parish in Fort Frances, and Saint Thomas parish, which is a white parish in International Falls, Minnesota. They come here [and] how many have I heard say, "I *love* that church!"? ... A lot of them come here because they like the location on the lake. They also like the church itself, how simple it is ... And we're all there [together].

A non-Indigenous church official in town was equally optimistic. Although he admitted that "undesirable things [had] happened [in] the past," he described the church as "a great bridge-builder":

Blaming something or someone is not gonna make things better ... Sometimes you have to let go of the past and keep moving on ... The church has great respect for the Native communities and ... we've done some wonderful things in the diocese for them.

From a critical perspective, these comments echo the laissez-faire racist discourse discussed in previous chapters. Here, he calls on Indigenous people to "let go of the past" and refuses to take responsibility for the church's role in colonization. Instead, he says the church does "wonderful things" *for* Indigenous people, a paternalistic view that reinforces settlers' sense of group superiority. On the other hand, a middle-aged Métis woman who lived in town and was married to a white man said the Catholic Church was "the only place" where she had not experienced racial discrimination, because church attendees

try to treat everyone equally. There's no, "Oh, because you have this much money [or] because you're this nationality, you're different from this person." Like the Catholic Women's League, the ladies are not like that.

Although Christianity has brought some Indigenous and non-Indigenous people together in cooperative, mutually beneficial relationships, and although those who reported attending church services sometimes experienced them as "colour-blind," other Indigenous residents refused to step foot in a church because of the physical, sexual, emotional, and spiritual violence that church policies and members inflicted on them and their ancestors. For instance, one interviewee described how his mother would physically shake every time they drove past St. Margaret's due to her experiences in residential school. As Mashkawegabo (Al Hunter) said (see chapter 3), the doctrine of discovery that was used to justify the theft of Indigenous lands and the assumption of crown sovereignty is rooted in Vatican decrees. While some Indigenous residents had found ways to combine traditional spirituality with Christian teachings, emphasizing the positive messages and commonalities of each (including lessons about love, community, and forgiveness), others regarded an unquestioning faith in Christianity as incompatible with Indigenous worldviews and as a sign of (internalized) colonization. According to one Anishinaabe man, the church "create[d] confusion, hence dissension and disagreement within the [First Nations]" and "most of the older generation is still very Catholic" and "not willing to rock the boat." Thus, although the Catholic Church is a bridge for some, it – and organized religion generally – is a major source of division for others.[5]

To provide one further example, several interviewees described shared interests in hunting and fishing as a bridge. As discussed in chapter 3, however, there is great controversy over the interpretation and perceived unfairness or "abuse" of Indigenous harvesting rights. One middle-aged white man said his annual fall "hunting party [includes] four Natives ... and we have a pretty good time, drinkin' and huntin'. There's no racial [issue] there!" However, for a white man in his thirties, the situation was more complex:

> My [First Nations] brother-in-law is one of my best friends. He's my hunting partner. I can't shoot his moose ... I know those rules and that's fine ... But it gets tricky ... because we get the whole, "Oh, you got a freezer full and your brother-in-law shot it." Well, no, that's not the way it happens. But if that's what people need to think ... I don't care. I know how my freezer gets full. And the way it works, my brother-in-law and my sister, myself and my dad all hunt together.

In this case, hunting is a bridge for the interviewee and his brother-in-law, but also a source of conflict with other whites who have misconceptions about how harvesting rights work and who assume that they are being "abused." In some cases, hunting and fishing bridges also extend beyond international borders. According to an Anishinaabe woman:

> There's a group of black guys from the States that always come, maybe like the last ten years ... they went to MNR [the Ontario Ministry of Natural Resources] and said ... they wanted to ... go hunting, so they recommended [a lake]. But [the MNR officials] said, "Go there, that's a really good spot, but watch out for those people from Stanjikoming!" [*laughter*] And we didn't know this ... but [then] the guys [from Stanjikoming] became friends with these black guys and they went hunting together ... that's how [we found out].

Thus, for Rainy River District residents, hunting and fishing were shared activities that, like church attendance, reportedly brought many Indigenous and non-Indigenous people together in positive, mutually supportive relationships. However, they also remained sites of conflict and tension, and residents tended to interpret and experience them in ways that reflected and reinforced their respective senses of group position.

Divergent Interpretations of the Same Bridges

When asked about the bridges between Indigenous and non-Indigenous communities, some residents said they shared a common culture or values that outweighed their differences. Others used common cultural repertoires – phrases, metaphors, or stories – to illustrate a bridge or to suggest that if certain beliefs (such as "we're all human") were more widely held or acted upon, intergroup relations would improve. While often describing the same bridges on the surface, Indigenous and white residents sometimes attributed divergent meanings to them or drew contrary implications, echoing the pattern discussed above, whereby some whites promote assimilation into Euro-Canadian society whereas the Anishinaabe and Métis are more likely to advocate respect for their unique cultures, sovereignty, and treaty rights.

Some interviewees explicitly stated that Indigenous and settler peoples in the Rainy River District already shared a common culture. However, their understanding of what this culture entailed sometimes differed. If we consider the following two responses, it is clear that the white and Anishinaabe interviewees agreed that "a good education, good jobs, safe communities, good health care" and "environmental protection" were important values shared by many residents. However, the former also perceived and promoted integration into a common "Canadian" culture, whereas the latter emphasized the common interests of First Nations and farmers and identified the nation-to-nation treaty as the ultimate bridge. According to a middle-aged white woman who lived in town:

> The bridges are that we share a country ... a common interest, and, to a large extent, we share a culture ... Those Facebook pages that were found [with the powwow video] was because they [Indigenous and non-Indigenous youth] are both on Facebook ... First Nations people aren't back in the woods hunting and trapping.[6] They're on the Internet and at the high school wearing Roxy and Billabong sweatshirts ... So, we're sharing ... a common culture and a common understanding of being Canadian ... there's great hope and promise in that ... [We also have] common interests in terms of popular entertainment [and] wanting to have a strong economy, wanting our kids to have a good education, good jobs, safe

Figure 6.3 Ice Fishing. When I first discussed photovoice with J.R. (the professional photographer who helped facilitate the project), he responded: "I know what my picture would be: fishing." When asked why, he explained that it could be both a boundary and a bridge. Although fishing is enjoyed by Indigenous and non-Indigenous residents alike, a common interest that brings them together, it is also a source of tension because many non-Indigenous people do not understand or respect Indigenous peoples' harvesting rights. Photo of the author, in which he has just caught a crappie on Lost Lake, taken by J.R. Shebagegit in March 2008.

communities, good health care ... I think if you go to Couchiching or ... Fort Frances and ... ask, "What do you want for your children?" they're going to want the same things.

Indeed, the conclusion that most Indigenous and non-Indigenous people in Canada have similar aspirations – a good education, fulfilling career, loving family – was largely supported by the Urban Aboriginal

Peoples' Survey of over 2,500 Aboriginal and 2,500 non-Aboriginal people living in eleven large Canadian cities in 2009 (Environics 2010). However, the assumption of "a common understanding of being Canadian" is questionable, as many First Nations people do not even identify as Canadian (see below).

Despite agreeing on some of the shared interests and values, Mashkawegaabo (Al Hunter) provided a different, more locally rooted, and explicitly anticapitalist, anticolonial take on what "shared culture" means:

> Here in the Rainy River District ... farmers and Indians have so much in common. We're natural allies. Because [we share] a rural culture. The same forces that are threatening the farming community today are ... threatening the Indian community: gentrification; multinational business over family farms; agri-business versus agriculture ... Our interests are intertwined ... So, if people really want to preserve what we have left and make it better and leave something for [future generations], then ... swallow your pride and ... stand up for treaty rights. Because treaty rights are the last bastion of environmental protection, not only for Native people but for the tourist camps, for the farmers, for the sports fishermen ... And if [settlers] don't stand with the Indian people, and if Indian people don't support the farmers and ... the fishing and tourism community, then the multinationals [and] the government ... are gonna take over and you're not gonna have fuck all ... What are you gonna say to your grandchildren someday who say, "Why didn't you do something before they poisoned the last fish ... before they opened that mine ... before they took all the trees?" How are you gonna answer that question? ... it doesn't matter whether you're brown, white, or anything else: Do you want to protect this land? Do you want to protect these waters? That's all it comes down to; that's all that's gonna matter.

Members of each group also used phrases such as "we're all in it together" or "there's good and bad in every race" to directly *illustrate* a bridge. Others referred to our "common humanity" or (potentially) shared "belief in the common good." According to an older white man, "You gotta look at them as a person, not as [a race]. Turn 'em inside out, and they're all the same." A First Nations woman in her fifties likewise said she "raised [her] kids to believe" that skin colour "doesn't matter" because "we're all the same underneath." For a younger white man who said he had "many" Indigenous friends, "it's not a matter of looking at the person as a Native ... if you treat people as people, you can develop friendships." As Lamont (2000) has shown in other societal contexts, such cultural repertoires are often used as antiracist strategies, to demonstrate that no group is inherently superior or inferior. Such repertoires perform similar work in the Indigenous-settler Canadian context: no "race" is inherently better, all have human dignity, and there is good and bad in all groups. However, white and Indigenous interviewees sometimes used these sayings to different ends or drew different implications. For example, some whites inferred that because people are "the same underneath," everyone should be treated the same – meaning there is no need for treaties, Indigenous self-government, or reparations. Such colour-blind views ignore existing structural inequities and serve to protect the status quo, including whites' resources and status.

In contrast, many Indigenous residents inferred that because we are all human, we should respect each other's autonomy and differences – including treaty rights, sovereignty, and cultures – while also working together for our common interests. As a middle-aged Métis man put it, "We come from the same Creator. We have different cultural identities, but in order to survive we have to [cooperate]." Similarly, a young Anishinaabe man, quoting Chief Seattle, said:

> "It's a web of life." What we do ... to others, we do to ourselves. [We must] keep our sovereignty [and] who we are as very self-evident and central ... But we all are in the same boat ... These schools we have to share, these streets, these jobs.

Meanwhile, at least half a dozen whites – but no Anishinaabe interviewees – explicitly described our (presumed) shared Canadian identity as a bridge. Many others alluded to the idea that "we are all Canadian," suggesting that Indigenous people should stop emphasizing cultural differences, forsake their Indigenous and treaty rights, and "integrate." For example, one white man in his thirties said his hope for the future was "that there isn't a 'Native' and a 'non-Native' community." He recalled working at a sawmill with Indigenous and white co-workers in 1999:

> There was four [First Nations] guys [who] worked the same schedule as us [white guys]. We all fished together, golfed together, didn't care who was dark and who was white ... Well, gettin' towards the end of December, we were talkin' about the whole "Year 2000" thing and this one fella ... went out and bought himself a ... tax-free snow machine. Whatever. You're entitled to it ... you live on the reserve ... Somebody piped up and said, "You know what? Year 2000: No more. We are *all* Canadians. We're not blacks, we're not whites, we're not Natives" ... Well, the [Native] fella, he stood

up and made this big speech about how his people were persecuted and this is what they deserve ... and [said], "I have to travel because there's no work in my community and ... I wanna live on my traditional land." And us four [white] guys said, "You know what? What you just said is us too. We don't wanna leave [our town]. We all wanna live here just as bad as you." And ... it's not like this was a sixty-year-old guy that lived through some bad stuff. He's the same age as me, went to high school in Dryden, played hockey, had all the same opportunities and then some that I did. And ... when the guy said *we should all be the same,* I thought, "I like that idea ... whatever race, colour, nationality you are, *if you're in Canada, you're a Canadian."* (Emphasis added)

Such a powerful invitation to shared citizenship and formal legal equality in some contexts may be considered antiracist and inclusive. In a settler colonial context, however, it is also a form of colour-blind or laissez-faire racism that (consciously or not) seeks to expunge Indigenous nationhood and facilitate assimilation to an inequitable social structure.[7] Although the interviewee, having grown up in the district, might have had much in common with his Indigenous friends and might have wanted "to live here just as bad" as them, this does not erase the fact that his opportunity to live there was a result of settler colonial systems, policies, and practices that displaced – and continue to displace – Indigenous peoples from their homelands; nor would it give him any moral right to impose Canadian laws, norms, or identities on Indigenous peoples. For that matter, since he lived in Treaty No. 3 territory, on traditional Anishinaabe lands, one might ask, why were he and his co-workers not adhering to Anishinaabe laws, beliefs, and customs?

Indeed, nearly half the First Nations interviewees did not identify as Canadian. In their view, their ancestors never "gave away" their sovereignty by signing treaties; they entered into a nation-to-nation *partnership.* Even Indigenous interviewees who identified as Canadian often defended their unique legal status, treaties, and right to cultural difference – a stance that challenges the notion that "if you're in Canada, you're [just] a Canadian," and should be treated "the same," regardless of context.

Moreover, when asked about intergroup bridges, Indigenous interviewees used several unique cultural references. For example, some referred to the Seven Grandfather Teachings[8] or the medicine wheel,[9] or drew analogies to the natural environment (see figure 6.4), to highlight the values of *both* cultural diversity *and* social inclusion. According to Mashkawegaabo (Al Hunter):

Figure 6.4 Pebble Beach. "The variety of shapes, sizes, and colours of the 'grandfathers in waiting'[10] on this unique Lake Superior beach reminds me that people also come with differences, but still may coexist peacefully together." – Paul, Métis man, age fifty-six. Photo courtesy of Paul.

People just have to decide what they want in life. Do you want just homogeneity? Look around you here [in the forest where we sit]: there's red willow, balsam, poplar, spruce, ash, plants. They're all living together ... The world is not just made up of one species of tree ... We're all in this together ... Just observe the natural world, and hopefully that will change people's attitudes.

In short, although white and Indigenous interviewees often used similar cultural repertoires to illustrate intergroup bridges, they sometimes used them to different ends; whereas many whites used such phrases and metaphors to bolster their sense of group position and call for the abolition of Indigenous and treaty rights, many Indigenous residents used them to promote an alternative vision of group relations premised on equity and respect for diversity.

To provide one further example of the divergent meanings that Indigenous and white residents attributed to the same bridges, consider what they meant by "economic interdependence." Several Indigenous interviewees suggested that it was in settlers' interests to work with them on economic development projects; Indigenous residents' economic power – as workers and consumers – was only increasing and if settlers did not invest in these opportunities, they were "shooting themselves in the foot."[11] In other words, as Indigenous peoples continue to heal and revitalize their own institutions, they may be more willing and able to boycott "mainstream" schools, stores, and other facilities and create their own instead, especially if they continue to encounter racism in settler society.[12] Most interviewees added, however, that they would rather work with their non-Indigenous neighbours in mutually beneficial partnerships, seeking "win-win" solutions whenever possible.

For example, multiple Indigenous residents pointed to a 2006 study by Pwi-Di-Goo-Zing-Ne-Yaa-Zhing Advisory Services, which estimated that the local First Nations contributed $62 million (and rising) to the $530 million district economy (Ortiz-Guerrero 2010, 52). A self-described "half-breed" noted that some white residents "boycotted" Heron Landing, an eighteen-hole golf course owned and operated by Couchiching First Nation on reserve land (which some whites saw as a competitive threat to the Kitchen Creek golf course west of town), "even though they want us to buy in their stores!" He added, "[Imagine] what the effect would be on the town if the Indian people started doing things for themselves." An older Anishinaabe man put it this way:

> We need one another ... to live a decent life ... For example, we need their material, like what we see here [*taps table*]. We need their food because we don't just live off the land anymore ... clothing, too ... Everything that we use, we buy from their stores. But they need us, too, Fort Frances: if we were to quit shopping here ... it would affect ... a lot of businesses ... Safeway... Canadian Tire ... Wal-Mart ...

Likewise, a middle-aged Anishinaabe man said that, with the fast-growing Indigenous population, it is to white residents' "benefit to cooperate, to collaborate, to be partners; if they want to maintain the status quo ... they're gonna be left in the dust."

Although some white residents were reluctant to partner with First Nations, and many complained about the "special privileges" that status Indians allegedly receive from government (see chapter 3), others recognized Indigenous peoples' contributions to the local economy and were willing to collaborate on business initiatives. An older Emo resident, for example, said Rainy River First Nations (RRFN) was "good for the economy" because "they do all their shopping here ... They bought material for fifty houses this year and everybody knows that." Moreover, the RRFN land claim settlement "drove the price of land *up* a little bit." Likewise, a white businessman in Fort Frances acknowledged: "We have *excellent* customers that are Natives ... they're very good for the economy 'cause they buy lots." Others praised a joint initiative between the Rainy River Future Development Corporation and the local First Nations to bring broadband and cell phone towers to the district. With the phase-out of coal-fired power plants in Ontario (completed in 2014), Mayor Brown of Atikokan saw potential for partnerships with Seine River First Nation to help "keep the plant going by using wood and biomass," which would create jobs for Natives and settlers alike.

More generally, white interviewees were more likely to emphasize the communities' (perceived) mutual dependence on forestry as a bridge. According to a recent retiree from the Fort Frances pulp and paper mill, not only was the mill always the largest single employer of white families, but "a significant portion of Métis people" also worked there, and "on the woodlands side,[13] we always had a lot of Métis and Status Indians ... probably up to 20 per cent of the workforce at times." Reflecting on the ongoing "decay" in the forestry sector in northwestern Ontario, a senior manager at the mill (in 2008) said:

> We're going to try and make sure that we can create an environment where we can keep this mill, which means *this town*, sustained ... I [tell] employees, "It's AbitibiBowater's mill, but you've got to think about it as *your* mill because you've got a lot more at stake here than anybody else ... *if the mill goes down, you can stay here, but ... there won't be a big supermarket, there won't be this and there won't be that, and there won't be any cultural activity ...* So, if you enjoy living in the town the way it is today, we better hope that we can keep the mill going." (Emphasis added)

In fact, however, Indigenous residents were far less dependent on forestry and far less affected by the downturn in that sector. As in Lithman's (1984) study of a Manitoban reserve community, as of 2008/09 some First Nations had temporary trucking contracts (hauling logs to the mill), but very few had high-paid unionized jobs in the mill itself.[14] Some Anishinaabe interviewees also highlighted the environmental devastation caused by clear-cut logging, open-pit mining, and other resource-extraction activities, and thus cautioned fellow Indigenous people to think carefully about "partnering" with such industries. As one said:

> If Abitibi went under, or if the OSB mill in Barwick went under, it would have virtually no effect on us ... because there are no Native people, or very few, employed in that industry ... It would affect [Rainy River First Nations] because [of] a business deal with Ainsworth [the mill in Barwick]. But that's it. Economically, First Nations contribute over sixty million dollrs a year to this district. If it wasn't for the First Nations, this place would be [*pause*] Appalachia ... If we bought into that "become part of our industry" [rhetoric], that to me would be our downfall.

Although this interviewee was wary of partnering with resource-extraction companies, he still saw economic interdependence in a broader sense as one of the greatest (potential) bridges between Indigenous and settler communities. In his words, "our fates are intertwined."[15]

Conclusion

Overall, Rainy River District residents readily described numerous institutions, ideas, activities, and interests that brought Indigenous and non-Indigenous people together in positive, mutually beneficial relationships. However, many of these bridges did not in themselves counteract the group positioning processes and structural inequities outlined in previous chapters. Indeed, Indigenous and white residents tended to think about bridges in ways that reflected and reinforced their respective senses of group position.

Despite the relative consensus about some sources of cooperation, white residents were more likely to emphasize bridges that would require Indigenous people to assimilate to settler society, whereas Indigenous residents were more likely to highlight opportunities for settlers to learn about Indigenous history and culture. Many Anishinaabe and Métis residents also discussed the need for mutual accommodation, as well as personal characteristics (humility, empathy, etc.) that disposed some individuals to seek more just and equitable relationships.

Moreover, some institutions (such as the Catholic Church) and activities (such as hunting and fishing) were considered bridges by some residents but boundaries by others. Many whites viewed shared Canadian citizenship as a potential bridge, whereas many Anishinaabe did not identify as Canadian and were more likely to emphasize nation-to-nation treaties and Indigenous cultural teachings as a way of bridging (but not homogenizing) the various nations in Canada. Still other Indigenous residents cautioned against an exclusive focus on "bridges," asserting that "real peace and harmony" in the long run will require (hopefully non-violent) conflict in the short run.

Finally, even when Indigenous and white interviewees named the same bridges, they often meant different things. Referencing our "common humanity" as a bridge, for example, whites often inferred that we should "treat everyone the same," whereas Indigenous residents emphasized the values of autonomy and respect for diversity.

In short, these divergent ways of framing bridges represent another barrier to overcoming the dominant sense of group position and the persisting structural inequities that are rooted in settler colonialism. Nevertheless, the interpretive lenses in question do not follow rigid group lines; in the thoughtful responses of many interviewees emerged the seeds of an alternative social order, one that strives to transcend "us versus them" thinking while maintaining respect for the dignity, diversity, and sovereignty of each group. In the next set of chapters, I will assess the benefits and limitations of some of the most frequently discussed bridges, both in my interviews and in the academic literature: contact, education, apologies, and collective action.

Chapter Seven

A Tenuous Balance: How Contact and Prejudice Coexist[*]

The best way to have an understanding is to get together with people, sit down and talk.

White school board administrator

Getting to know people and seeing that they're *not* what you thought they were ... that they have the same ideas as you, the same dreams ... that's probably the best [bridge].

Retired First Nations man

As these residents suggest, one commonly proposed remedy to racism is intergroup contact: if people get to know each other, everything will be okay. But soon after arriving in Fort Frances, I noticed a paradox: widespread intergroup marriage and friendship, and extensive interaction in local organizations and public spaces, coexisted with pervasive prejudice and discrimination. This situation appeared to violate the contact hypothesis (Allport 1954; Pettigrew and Tropp 2006), one of the bedrocks of social psychology. How was this possible?

This chapter shows that although contact is associated with less old-fashioned prejudice, such as the crass belief that "Indians are bad" (see chapter 4), it does not necessarily eliminate whites' sense of superior group position or the structural inequities that it supports. I found that even white individuals with close Indigenous friends or spouses often expressed laissez-faire racism; they would blame Indigenous people for their poverty and other social problems, oppose policies designed to rectify injustices or improve Indigenous peoples' living

---

[*] An earlier version of this chapter was published as an article in *American Sociological Review* (Denis 2015).

conditions, and resent Indigenous people who exercised treaty rights or sought substantive equality.

As detailed below, three mutually reinforcing social processes – subtyping, ideology-based homophily, and political avoidance – interacted to sustain whites' sense of group superiority and justifications for racial inequity. Specifically, Indigenous people who violated stereotypes were seen as "good Indians," exceptions who proved the rule, while those who endorsed self-blaming explanations for poverty appeared to validate laissez-faire views. Above all, residents tended to avoid controversial discussions, treating racism as the "elephant in the room." These phenomena were facilitated by historical and ongoing colonial policies and practices and by small-town dynamics, which together maintained congenial daily interactions despite the stark inequities in power and resources.

Contact, Prejudice, and Intervening Mechanisms

To understand the limited role of contact in improving intergroup relations, it is important to distinguish old-fashioned prejudice, or negative affect towards Indigenous peoples, from the sense of group positions that undergirds racist ideologies and structures. As Bobo and Hutchings (1996, 954) write, "the classical prejudice model [including contact theory] does not expect expressed feelings of competitive threat to differ sharply from other expressions of prejudice." Group position theory does not make this assumption (Blumer 1958). Yet only a few studies (Durrheim and Dixon 2005; Jackman and Crane 1986) have demonstrated that contact may reduce old-fashioned prejudice while leaving the sense of group positions intact.[1] Here, I extend this finding to a new context and explicate some of the social processes that generate it.

One such process is *subtyping*: individuals who disconfirm stereotypes are viewed as exceptions that prove the rule. According to the subcategorization model of intergroup contact (Brown and Hewstone 2005; Hewstone and Brown 1986), if outgroup members are perceived only as discrete individuals and not as group representatives, the effects of contact may fail to generalize (Wilder 1984). My research confirms this prediction, but emphasizes that subtyping is not just an internal cognitive bias. Rather, it is a routine social practice whereby dominant group members justify the status quo and their own sense of superiority and entitlement. The sociological question is, how does this process work and what does it mean in the context at hand? The answer lies, in part, in habitual use of shared cultural images that cast the "typical" Indigenous person as a threat to social order (e.g., those who protest for "special rights" or exploit welfare) (RCAP 1996). Conversely, Indigenous

186 Canada at a Crossroads

individuals who conform to dominant norms and values and downplay their Indian status may be accepted by whites but considered atypical.

Indeed, one basis for subtyping is *ideology-based homophily*, the tendency to befriend others with similar (racial) ideologies, regardless of their "race." Because contemporary racism does not require categorical rejection of an entire outgroup, but rather thinking and acting in ways that reinforce structural inequities, whites may befriend Indigenous individuals who appear to share their racial views and then subtype them as "good Indians," thereby maintaining a sense of superior *group* position. The perceived attitude similarity may result from some Indigenous people endorsing laissez-faire ideology – a form of internalized racism (Pyke 2010) historically promoted by Canada's assimilationist policies – or covering their "Indianness" (Braroe 1975) to cope with racism. When Indigenous people (appear to) share the dominant racial ideology, it validates whites' sense of group position and perhaps even carries more weight because of the messenger. Thus, ideology-based homophily is both a basis for subtyping and a potentially independent means of maintaining and justifying racist views.

Subtyping and ideology-based homophily are also reinforced by a *political avoidance norm*, whereby public discussions of racism and colonization are taboo. In small-town Ontario, just as in civic groups in the United States (Eliasoph 1999, 498), "a bond of shared civic etiquette" puts "race-talk" in the category of "topics to be avoided by polite people." Avoiding race-talk, as opposed to contact with racialized others, is central to contemporary racism (Bonilla-Silva 2010; Feagin 2010; McKinney 2005; Wingfield and Feagin 2010). In addition to code words being used in place of racial terminology, sensitive topics (such as residential schools or treaty violations) are conspicuously absent from public discussion. If such issues are avoided, then the learning, perspective-taking, and motivations to combat injustice that otherwise might result from contact fail to transpire. Whites can remain ignorant about racism and colonialism despite daily interaction with Indigenous neighbours, and may assume ideological similarity and subtype their "good Indian" friends. Yet the apparent harmony may be a "thin veneer" (Winship 2004) that cracks when the avoidance norm is breached and underlying contradictions are exposed.

Perceptions of Intergroup Contact

When asked about intergroup bridges, or sources of cooperation, many Rainy River District residents – but especially whites – emphasized that local Indigenous and non-Indigenous communities have interacted closely for decades, resulting in widespread inter-marriage, long-lasting friendships, and relative harmony (see chap-ters 1, 2, and 6). Consistent with the contact hypothesis, they often described how long-term contact could improve intergroup attitudes and behaviours by enhancing familiarity with and understanding of one another. For instance, an older white woman described how she "grew up ... next door to a Native family," and they "never looked at each other any different. We were just kids." Similarly, a white man in his forties said:

> When you grow up with them and you get a bond between you, it's pretty hard to break. Like, we been good friends for years ... My daughter spends a lot of time in Seine River, on the reserve, [and] nobody bothers her ... she's just part of them.

Residents who had come from other rural and northern areas were sometimes astonished by local interaction patterns. According to a thirty-something white woman and her mother, who had moved from Manitoba, intergroup relations were better in Fort Frances:

> WOMAN: ... because Couchiching is so close and [many Native people] work in town.
> MOTHER: And they're so intermarried here – so different from where I was raised where ... if you even *looked* at a Native boy sideways, you were [seen as deviant]. It was odd. But here, you're so intermarried. I don't think there's too many families that *don't* have some connection through marriage.
> WOMAN: I even feel odd saying "them" and "us" and "white" and "Native." We're just one big town.

Although such views were less common among Indigenous inter-viewees, several First Nations and Métis residents discussed the ben-efits of long-term interaction, and some intermarried couples talked about how contact had gradually softened their relatives' prejudice. One older Native man who lived in town said the "best" bridge was "getting to know people and seeing that they're *not* what you thought they were ... that they have the same ideas as you, the same dreams." His white wife of more than forty years agreed. Her own mother was reportedly an outspoken bigot, but on her deathbed, while being cared for by her daughter and Native son-in-law, she ceased making racist remarks: by "the look in her eye," they said they could tell she had changed her mind.

Likewise, a younger First Nations man who was married to a white woman and lived on reserve said:

> I know my [white] wife had a heck of a time when we first were going out. Her father was pretty much right-wing PC [Progressive Conservative] 'cause his father was PC ... And to this day, she still says, "My grandfather would roll in his grave," knowing that she married a Native ... My father-in-law, when I would ... visit, I'd go in one driveway, he'd come out the other. He wasn't too accepting ... But I guess once ... we were engaged, he didn't have a choice. But now, I think, for the most part, it's opened his eyes as to the person I am ... And his view, from what he knew of Natives, was going to a reserve, burned out cars, garbage on the driveways, just terrible. [But when] he came to our community, he said "Holy shit, this is totally different!" Like, there, everybody takes care of their yards, keeps their houses clean.

Such stories illustrate how contact can transform attitudes by disproving stereotypes. By showing his father-in-law that he was "different," this young man was able to develop "a pretty good relationship," so that, by the time of our interview in 2008, he said, "I call him 'Dad,' call her 'Mum.'" As will be shown below, however, some whites may rationalize individual exceptions without overturning their sense of group position.

Increasingly, positive Indigenous-white relationships are facilitated by shared participation in local institutions, such as schools, churches, some workplaces, and sports and recreation. The benefits and limitations of education for mitigating racism will be analysed in chapter 8, but it is worth noting here that many residents described the local school system as a bridge because it is often where Indigenous and non-Indigenous children meet, interact, recognize their common humanity, and sometimes develop lasting friendships.

In the district, a common interest in ice hockey was particularly perceived as a bridge. As a white woman in her thirties shared, "Sports brings us together. Go down to the arena any night [and] you will see people from all communities there." Indeed, at local Junior A hockey games, I often observed Indigenous and non-Indigenous children sitting together, chatting, sharing snacks, and high-fiving their Indigenous and non-Indigenous hockey-playing heroes as they headed to the dressing room. Just as several Indigenous interviewees described a local history of mixing through sports and recreation, Mayor Roy Avis also recalled playing "hockey as a young fellow" and how First Nations children from St. Margaret's Residential School "were part of our hockey league ... they'd come and play in town and we'd play out there ... It was great ... I always thought there was a good rapport." A school board administrator further explained:

> People's differences ... are eroded when you're suddenly working together for a common goal ... when they're on opposing teams, sometimes they just don't see eye to eye and there's conflict ... But you can take people who have been in conflict and suddenly trade them and they're on the same team; it's amazing how the differences disappear.

Several interviewees described music and arts in similar ways. For an Anishinaabe woman in her thirties:

> Music and arts are awesome bridges because you can say so much in such a gentle way and ... have the essence of how you're feeling be understood [whereas] language is more challenging to be perceived accurately through ... And when the kids are involved in athletics, or the band, or drama, you stop thinking about ... "she's this and he's that." You just think, "We gotta do drama."

A middle-aged Métis woman who lived in town added:

> I went to that "Singing for Supper" [Christmas charity concert] with Tom Jackson [a Métis singer] out at Couchiching Rec Complex, and that was really nice ... it was geared towards kids ... and there was Native, non-Native, Métis people, all there together ... I think that's a bridge.

Indeed, while living in Fort Frances, I often experienced the bridging power of music directly – tapping my foot to the beat of a beloved rock song at the Rendez-Vous hotel bar or at the Oshki Aa-yaa'aag Mino Bimaadiziiwin (Good Life for Young People) annual benefit concert and making eye contact with an Indigenous or non-Indigenous stranger doing the same thing.

Perhaps the most promising bridges are those that involve working together towards a common interest or goal without threatening the unique identities of Anishinaabe, Métis, or non-Indigenous Canadians. For example, the Healthy Living Food Box Program is a joint initiative of the Northwestern Health Unit (Ontario government agency), Sunset Country Métis (local Métis association), and Gizhewaadiziiwin Health Access Centre (managed by the local First Nations). It brings together dozens of Indigenous and non-Indigenous volunteers each month to sort healthy and (mostly) locally grown fruits and vegetables into colourful "food boxes" to be sold at affordable rates to local Indigenous

Figure 7.1 Halloween Rock. "Centre-Line is a local rock band with Native and non-Native members. In this picture, the band performs at a local bar for a mixed-race crowd on Halloween night." – Middle-aged Native Canadian man. Photo courtesy of the caption speaker.

and non-Indigenous residents. A Métis organizer described the origins and goals of the program:

> We started in November '06 with 40 boxes and we've hit as high as 860 ... and now we've rounded off around 600. [The goal is to promote] healthy eating throughout the district for everyone ... no matter what your income ... It's very much volunteer-driven ... We're also trying to get more of the local farmers [involved] ... the reserves order [food boxes] and a lot of the clients are either First Nation or Métis ... a good quarter, at least.

In the summer of 2009, I volunteered for the Healthy Living Food Box Program. After a hard day's work sorting fruit into baskets and carrying food to elderly clients' cars, I reflected in my field notes on the bridging potential and health benefits of this innovative program:

> On paper, I can't think of a better bridge. The Healthy Living Food Box Program is run in partnership by Aboriginal and non-Aboriginal

organizations and involves both Aboriginal and non-Aboriginal volunteers and clients. Of the 25–30 volunteers today, about 1/3 were Aboriginal. There is time for unstructured socializing, which helps build social ties and a sense of community. The program also provides clients with healthy fruits and vegetables at reduced cost. It's open to everyone, regardless of race, income, or residence. Many clients have friendly chats with the staff and volunteers while picking up their boxes. There is a strong community spirit, and I felt proud to be part of it today. (Field notes, July 2009)

The Paradoxical Coexistence of Contact and Prejudice

By any reasonable measure, there is widespread intergroup contact in Fort Frances. In addition to mixing and mingling at school, on sports teams, and in other domains, there is a long history of intermarriage and friendship, dating back to the fur trade. Several residents had recently discovered Indigenous ancestors in their family trees. Among married or common law interviewees, roughly one in five whites had an Indigenous partner,[2] and even more had children who were dating or married to Indigenous persons. Meanwhile, 42 per cent of Anishinaabe and 67 per cent of Métis interviewees had a white partner.[3] Intergroup friendships were also common. When asked about the racial/ethnic background of their five best friends, 50 per cent of white interviewees cited at least one Indigenous friend, and 76 per cent of Anishinaabe and 100 per cent of Métis cited at least one white friend.[4] Many interviewees also discussed their children's cross-group friendships, including such intimate activities as sleepovers.

Nevertheless, I found that prejudice, discrimination, and more subtle discourses and practices that perpetuate racial inequities and settler colonial structures were prevalent. As discussed in earlier chapters, a majority of white residents expressed at least an implicit sense of group superiority and entitlement, and perceived Indigenous people who challenge the status quo as threatening. Laissez-faire, paternalistic, and colour-blind ideologies were also widespread. In chapter 5, I illustrated how white residents in Alberton used deliberate strategies, such as creating new rules, playing the victim, intimidation, and coercion, to maintain their "way of life" and exclude an Anishinaabe group home. Yet racist attitudes, behaviours, and interaction patterns were also observed within institutions and activities that many residents described as bridges, including within the local school system. These experiences included low expectations and inferior treatment by some teachers and bullying and exclusion by fellow students, and were amplified by the systemic problems of misrepresentation, denigration, and neglect of

Indigenous histories, cultures, and knowledges in school curricula (see chapter 8).

Although playing sports and cheering on professional sports teams and home-grown hockey heroes (such as Duncan Keith of the 2010 Olympic gold medal–winning Canadian men's hockey team) was a common interest of many residents, racism was also common in sports. Some local sports leagues pitted "reserve teams" *against* "town teams," rather than mixing players together, thereby potentially exacerbating conflict. Yet even mixed sports teams had their issues. The infamous video incident (see Introduction) involved a distortion of pre-game rituals of the Fort Frances High School girls' hockey team. While Indigenous teammates reportedly had suggested listening to powwow music to pump themselves up before games, the video girls' frequent interaction with these teammates apparently did not prevent them from engaging in offensive behaviour.

Moreover, some whites who had played on mixed teams expressed some of the most overt prejudice in interviews. An older couple living on reserve reflected on the dynamics of racism in hockey. According to the wife:

> At one time, the Native kids did not play [on the high school hockey team] ... Indian kids were often snubbed ... in our kids' day, they did [play]. We didn't take any of that shit ... 'Cause there was a lot of us there to stand behind them. And ... they had the biggest turnout that year ... of Native [fans]. With just three Native kids on [the team], the whole arena was packed.

In 1989, the Fort Frances High School boys' hockey team had three players from Rainy River First Nations and at least two Indigenous players from town, and they won the All-Ontario Championships. Nevertheless, the husband added, when their son played, they often heard white parents shouting at Native players: "'Scalp the buggers!' 'Kill 'em!'" When asked if they still heard such comments, they said it was not as prevalent, but "you [still] see it out there. I was watching my grandson playing hockey [at] eight years old ... I can't believe the parents ... calling the *kids* names!"

Similar dynamics were observed at popular local music festivals and at the Royal Canadian Legion, where my partner Lisa and I spent several Friday nights drinking, dancing, and singing karaoke songs with Indigenous and non-Indigenous neighbours. On one occasion, several white residents ridiculed a young developmentally delayed First Nation man's singing. A middle-aged white woman exclaimed, "I don't think he can read!" to which another replied, "Maybe he's drunk," and a third added, sarcastically, "I think he's singing in Ojibwa." I debated whether to intervene but opted, as an ethnographer, to observe how the scene "naturally" un-folded. I felt sick as the white onlookers snickered and then clapped and howled obnoxiously when the song was over. A young white man then ripped the songbook from the First Nation man's hands, saying, "You can't read anyway." Later, Lisa confronted this same white man for telling "racist jokes" about Indigenous people. He claimed he wasn't being racist; he just didn't know any jokes about white people (Field notes, June 2008).

Beyond school, sports, and popular culture, I found that even the Healthy Living Food Box Program was not immune to occasional be-haviours and remarks that reinforced systemic racial inequities. As I described in my field notes in July 2009:

> During a lull in action, a Métis female organizer suggested that next time we should play traditional Métis fiddle music on the stereo while distrib-uting the food. "Great idea!" exclaimed a white female volunteer. "Or we could just play normal music," said a young Métis man, who then quickly glanced at me with a worried expression as if sensing he had said some-thing wrong.

While this exchange might seem trivial, the young man's assumption that Indigenous music is somehow "abnormal" and less desirable sub-tly reinforced the existing colonial structure; settlers and their cultural products, by contrast, were assumed to be normal and superior. The fact that he was Métis reveals how deeply such assumptions have been engrained. Yet his follow-up glance at me, knowing that I was a researcher studying Indigenous-settler relations, also suggested an awareness of the implications of his reflex-like statement and perhaps even shame or guilt for the way it was expressed.

In short, shared participation in local institutions had formed and likely will continue to form durable bridges in the Rainy River District. Yet wider settler colonial structures and racist ideologies continued to infringe on the interactions and thought patterns operating within these institutions, even if in sometimes subtle and not fully recognized ways.

Perhaps there is a simple explanation: the 50 per cent of white in-dividuals who had intimate contact with Indigenous people may not have been the prejudiced ones. In fact, although no white interviewees with close Indigenous friends or spouses expressed old-fashioned prej-udice, at least half retained a sense of superior group position. For this subgroup of twenty-eight whites, median ratings on the feeling ther-mometer – with which I assessed attitudes towards Canadian, First Na-tions and Métis people, and various subgroups, as described in chapter 4 – were virtually unchanged.[5] A majority also expressed at least some

aspects of laissez-faire racism, blaming Indigenous people for their social problems and rejecting follow-up action on the residential school
apology (see table 7.1).

As suggested above, some residents intuited a connection between
contact and prejudice. According to one Anishinaabe man, whites
"who've had relationships [with Indigenous people], long- and short-
term, familial and non-familial ... are more enlightened and understand
that we're in this together." Confirming this view, the only white millworker who presented himself as "antiracist" was married to a Métis
woman and cited her influence in changing his views.

Conversely, the white resident who claimed that Indigenous people
are more often poor because they have "no ambition" and are "their own
worst enemy" (see chapter 4) was married to an Indigenous woman.
Many other white interviewees with close Indigenous friends or relatives
endorsed colour-blind views, claiming to be egalitarian, but rejecting Indigenous sovereignty and treaties and avoiding responsibility for rectifying structural inequities. Their prejudice was most clearly expressed as
resentment towards Indigenous people perceived as "getting out of place"
(Blumer 1958, 6), such as those who protested or exercised their rights.

The case of Frankie, a white blue-collar worker in his sixties, perhaps
best exemplifies how contact, under the right conditions, might reduce
whites' negative feelings towards Natives *without* eliminating whites'
sense of group position. Frankie personally attributed his changing attitudes to ongoing exposure to Indigenous people in Alcoholics Anonymous (AA) meetings:

> Some of those stories [about residential schools] are just unbelievable ... I've
> been in AA and these people start to spill their guts ... people will say stuff
> there that they'd never say anywhere else ... It's just mind-boggling.

When asked if his views had changed as a result of these interactions,
he responded, "Absolutely ... Before they were just drunken Indians,
right? Now, they're my friends." Elaborating on *how* this change occurred, he said:

> Just by getting to know them as people ... like, if you and I hung out for a
> while, if you come and hung out in my world or I went and hung out in
> your world ... we'd either become friends [or] acquaintances or you'd just
> kind of wander off ... And I think that's it. A lot of it is just exposure.

This case seems to confirm the contact hypothesis, just as Allport described it: ongoing contact, under conditions such as those fostered

Table 7.1 Selected Attitudes and Characteristics of Non-Indigenous Interviewees with and without Close Indigenous Friends

Characteristic/variable	Non-Indigenous interviewees	White interviewees with close Indigenous friends
Number of interviewees	78	N/A[1]
Number of survey respondents	56	28
% male	55	46
Median age in years	53	51.5
Marital status		
% married or common law	77	79
% with Indigenous partner (among married or common law interviewees)	18[2]	25
Friendships		
% with at least one close Indigenous friend	50	100
% with at least one close white friend	100	100
Median ratings on feeling thermometer (from 1, "strongly negative," to 5, "strongly positive")		
Canadians	5	5
First Nations	4	4
Métis	4	4
Indigenous political leaders	3	3.5
Indigenous people who receive tax exemptions	3	3
Indigenous protesters	2	2
Main explanation for Indigenous-white poverty gap		
% emphasizing historical and/or structural factors	26	25
% emphasizing cultural inferiority/victim-blaming	50	50
% saying equally both or other	24	25
Main reaction to residential school apology		
% saying "move on"	55	46
% saying governments and/or churches should take follow-up actions	36	46
% other	9	7

[1] Not available/unknown.
[2] In another 9% of cases, the partner was described as "Canadian" (Indigenous background unclear).

at AA meetings – face to face, equal status in the setting, shared experience of working towards common goals, and an open supportive environment – *is* associated with less old-fashioned prejudice, at the individual level.

Nevertheless, despite moderating his views and making Indigenous friends, Frankie continued to oppose policies designed to alleviate structural inequities and insisted that residential school survivors should "move on." He further believed that Indigenous people are more likely to be poor because they are "lazy" and that Indigenous protesters are "criminals against Canada" who "oughta be in jail." Although he empathized with Indigenous individuals who had experienced trauma, and even had Indigenous friends and extended family members, like many residents, he still expressed a sense of superior group position as a white Canadian.

Similarly, many whites on mixed hockey teams retained group position prejudice. On successful teams, at least, contact conditions were optimal – face to face, equal status in the setting, goal interdependence, and coaches who promoted cooperation. Many white players befriended Indigenous teammates, whom they praised for their hockey skills and to whom they surely would pass the puck to win. Yet while these individuals were unlikely to express overt categorical anti-Indigenous hostility, many still opposed treaty rights and compensation for historical injustices; some even told racist jokes in the locker room. Thus, the positive effects of contact were often limited to specific individuals or situations.

A closer analysis of the white residents who had Indigenous friends suggests that contact can coexist with a range of intergroup attitudes, including paternalistic, antagonistic, laissez-faire, and antiracist ones. Many residents were inconsistent in expressing their views, and attitudes did not always match behaviours. Although a minority of white interviewees (15–20 per cent) supported Indigenous rights or spoke out against racism,[6] just as many appeared confused or transitional, and more than half of those with Indigenous friends or relatives expressed racist views.[7] Although contact may reduce old-fashioned prejudice, it alone does not eliminate group positioning or the ideological frameworks that sustain settler colonialism. In the next section, I show how the three mutually reinforcing social processes of subtyping, ideology-based homophily, and political avoidance enabled many whites to maintain a sense of group superiority and justifications for racial inequity, despite extensive and often intimate contact with Indigenous people.

Social Processes Maintaining Group Position Prejudice

Subtyping: "He's Not Your Ordinary, Everyday First Nations Person"

One way that whites reconciled their relationships with their views was through the social-cognitive process of subtyping, where individuals who violate stereotypes are construed as exceptions that prove the rule: "My best friend is Native, but he's not your typical Native!" "We have good Indians in this town!" Such rationalizations were common (expressed spontaneously by 25 per cent of whites with close Indigenous friends) and worked to reinforce group position prejudice.

Among the many cases of subtyping in my data, an older, white, working-class couple, building on and affirming one another's views, as discourse analysts (Durrheim and Dixon 2005) would expect, described the husband's First Nations fishing partner as one such exception:

> HUSBAND: He's not your ordinary, everyday First Nations person. He's a graduate forest technician and he worked ... along with us ... in the bush ... He's a forward-thinking person.
> WIFE: He's always inventing things.
> HUSBAND: And he tried his best to improve the lot of the people on his reserve and he was shunned – I think partly because he was doing too much good!

Similarly, a younger white man described his "responsible" Indigenous co-worker as an exception – a rationalization that enabled him to maintain the laissez-faire racist view that Indigenous people in general are more likely to be (economically) poor due to cultural inferiority and an unwillingness to assimilate to settler-Canadian norms:

> Until they are integrated into our society, they're not going to make any money and they're not going to get ahead. They're going to live in poverty. I also think it's very accepted amongst Natives to live like that ... I worked with a guy that lived on a reserve. He was very responsible with money and family and that kind of stuff, and he was ostracized heavily by his community for doing that. He'd ... sod his lawn ... and other people in the community have torn it up with trucks and four-wheelers 'cause he's "trying to be better than them" ... He'd put new siding on [his house], go away for a weekend, come back, and it's all ripped off and his windows are smashed. And they called him "Macintosh" because he was red on the outside but white on the inside.

In Bonilla-Silva's (2010) terms, such personal "testimonies" serve to justify structural inequities and exempt settlers from responsibility for change, but also, in their minds, from prejudice (since they recognize exceptions like "Macintosh").

On another occasion, a retired white man – after learning my research topic over coffee – turned to his retired Native friend and said, "There aren't many Natives like you, you know? A lot of 'em think they can run a business and next thing you know they run it into the ground." The Native man (the only one in the room) lowered his eyes, shifted in his seat, mumbled something about education, and changed the subject (Field notes, June 2009).

Some Indigenous interviewees also alluded to subtyping and being offended by it. A few even suggested that it is a rhetorical tool to justify racism (Bonilla-Silva 2010; Jackman and Crane 1986). Consider this exchange between two middle-aged First Nations men, a middle-aged First Nations woman, and a younger Métis woman whom I interviewed together in their shared office on a local reserve:

> FN1 (*First Nations man*): There are very subtle forms of racism ... I don't think you're gonna run into too many non-Native people [today] saying, "Oh, well, the dirty Indians."
> FN2 (*First Nations man*): Mm-hmm.
> FN1: Or "the drunken Indian." Okay? But you are going to hear "Well, one of my best friends –," you know, that patronizing bullshit?
> FN3 (*First Nations woman*): Yeah!
> FN1: And you know what? *That's* racism!
> FN3: Yeah.
> FN2: At its worst.
> JEFF: What do you mean by that, "One of my best friends"? [*pause*] Like, they'll say, "One of my best friends is Native, *but* ... "?
> FN1: Yeah! Or "You're one of the good ones."
> FN3: "You're not like the rest of them."
> JEFF: Okay, I've heard that ...
> FN2: Or a token Indian, eh?
> M1 (*Métis woman*): "I'm not racist, my best friend is Native!" [*laughter*]

Indeed, a local white farmer, in a separate interview, agreed:

> Everybody probably has Indian friends and acquaintances and they make exceptions [but] maybe that's part of racism, to say, "I'm not a racist because I like this person" ... It sort of *proves* I'm not a racist? "I've got friends who are Indian! I can't be racist!"

Given these remarks, one might wonder whether the cross-group friendships claimed by white interviewees were reciprocated. Were some whites just saying their "best friend is Native" in order to sound progressive or avoid being seen as racist? Although I cannot rule out this explanation in some cases because I do not have truly dyadic data, I do know from both formal interviews and informal interactions with many of the "best friends" listed that the feelings often were mutual – even in cases where the white friend had laissez-faire or paternalistic views.

Naa-Gaabiinegee-zhig, a traditional man who once denied his Anishinaabe heritage, provided further insight into how this process works:

> Years ago, when I got my first job at the mill, [my white co-workers] would say, "Yeah, but you're a good Indian. You got a job." And, as a young man, I remember saying, "Yeah, that's pretty good of me. That makes me feel real good." [But I later realized] that the way approval is given Aboriginal people, whether it's in a government program or anything else, is your willingness and your capacity to assimilate is really how you gain approval. If you don't assimilate, then there's no approval process.

As these examples suggest, subtyping is a largely taken-for-granted social practice that some white residents enacted when thinking and talking about their Indigenous friends. While rejecting absolute racial categorizations, this process draws on shared images of what constitutes a "typical" or "bad" Indian. By viewing characteristics like being forward thinking, educated, entrepreneurial, responsible, and trustworthy, and "doing good" as fundamentally "un-Indian," whites preserved the negative connotations of the larger "Indian" category and upheld their sense of *group* superiority. Perhaps most striking was that, while many whites viewed Indigenous protesters as "bad Indians," local Indigenous residents (at least "assimilated" ones with jobs) were seen as "good Indians" because, as one Anishinaabe interviewee put it, they "know their place." For instance, they did not block the highways – at least not at the time of my interviews (but see chapter 10).

Ideology-Based Homophily: "She Calls Me an Apple"

As Naa-Gaabiinegee-zhig suggested, subtyping is often based on (perceived) assimilation. Indigenous persons who conform to dominant norms and values and do not openly challenge the settler colonial structure may be socially accepted, whereas those who protest are seen as a threat. Thus, I found that although racial segregation in friendship networks persisted, as indicated by the 50 per cent of whites who did not have close Indigenous friends and the 24 per cent of Anishinaabe who did not have close white friends, ideology-based homophily – befriending others with similar racial ideologies, regardless of their "race" – was also widespread and reinforced residents' biases.

Just as whites expressed diverse racial views, so did Indigenous people. Although most First Nations and Métis residents defended Indigenous and treaty rights, a minority (10–15 per cent) endorsed colour-blindness. And while many were revitalizing their cultures, others were indifferent to tradition. Some with mixed backgrounds or lighter skin tried to pass as white or cover their "Indianness" (Braroe 1975); others literally wore their identity, from beaded moccasins to "Native Pride" baseball caps. Although Indigenous Pride has been resurgent since the 1960s (Nagel 1995a), some individuals still carried the scars of internalized racism, which was engraved through residential schools or other traumatic experiences, and was revealed in stereotypes that some expressed about their own people, including self-blaming explanations for poverty and a tendency to buy into laissez-faire ideology. Such individuals often embraced and were embraced by whites, who both subtyped them (as "good Indians") and saw them as validating their prejudice (because "if my Native friend says it, it *must* be true!").

In one exchange between a Native man and his white wife of thirty-five years, the husband proclaimed, "She calls me an apple." Grinning, his wife concurred, "He's kind of red on the outside, white on the inside," partly because although he "doesn't wear a watch" he is always on time, whereas, according to the husband, "A lot of Native people don't carry a time-clock" and are always late. Although the term "Macintosh" was used as an insult in the earlier story about the younger Native man allegedly "ostracized" by his community, in this case the older Native man considered "apple" a term of endearment; he and his wife were proud that he had "more white traits" than "Native traits." As the interview proceeded, moreover, both husband and wife expressed and supported one another's laissez-faire views, calling unemployed Indigenous people "lazy" and dismissing the need for follow-up action on the residential school apology.

Ideological affinity also appeared between two middle-aged female co-workers (one Native, the other white and married to a Native man), whom I interviewed in their shared office at a local Indigenous organization. Explaining racial tensions in the district, they said:

NATIVE WOMAN: I think what happens is everybody is so close, and *they* [whites] must see like *we* [status Indians] don't have to pay taxes, right? *We* can hunt wherever, whenever ... I'm sure that ... blows a lot of steam towards the racism.

WHITE WOMAN: Well, I don't know if this is racism, but *I* have a problem with some of that ... like when these fish are spawning and these people are ... taking all these fish.

NATIVE WOMAN: And it's Native people doing it!

WHITE WOMAN: And they're killing off the species and they think it's okay![8]

NATIVE WOMAN [*laughing*]: Yeah ... And then you hear a lot of it on the news ... *I know I'm Native, but* there's a lot of Native people out there that complain about nothin' for nothin'. And you can imagine how *that* gets to people.

WHITE WOMAN: Like I said, they bring it on themselves. (Emphasis added)

As in the previous case, the white resident's laissez-faire racist views were co-constructed, elaborated, and validated by the Native friend, who was simultaneously portrayed – and indeed portrayed herself ("I know I'm Native, but ... ") – as an exception. In this way, ideology-based homophily – perhaps facilitated by internalized racism among some Indigenous people – enables contact, even between spouses and equal-status co-workers, to coexist with group position prejudice. As one young Anishinaabe woman put it, intergroup bridges are often strongest among individuals who have been most thoroughly colonized.

Of course, Indigenous and white residents who identified as antiracist or pro–Indigenous rights also tended to associate with each other. When the Right Relations Circle, a small group of Anishinaabe, Métis, and white residents who joined together to promote "just and equitable" relations, organized the first ever local antiracism walk in March 2008 – attracting nearly two hundred Indigenous and one hundred non-Indigenous participants – new friendships formed. A First Nations woman in her sixties who had lived abroad for years told me that she had "met some wonderful people," including a retired white woman whom she now met regularly for tea. As I observed, she also began attending Right Relations Circle meetings, leading to further friendships with non-Indigenous neighbours who shared a common commitment to racial justice and reconciliation.

To some extent, ideology-based homophily may derive from status characteristics other than race, such as education, occupation, or gender (McPherson, Smith-Lovin, and Cook 2001). Nevertheless, interviewees often perceived ideology as a bridging force. At least three inter-married couples said "common values" helped bring them together. Similarly, when asked about their Indigenous friends, whites often mentioned a shared worldview. Among white interviewees who expressed laissez-faire racism, ideology-based homophily almost always coincided with subtyping. For example, a white millworker in his thirties described his best friend, a similar-aged First Nation man, as "the kind of guy I ... respect" because he "graduated from high school ... got married, had a kid ... busted his ass ... bettered himself ... and now he's working full-time in a gold mine." Furthermore, "he has a real problem with the Natives that abuse the system ... maybe because he had the same opportunities and took advantage of some of them."

As Hewstone and Brown (1986, 6) note, economically successful "token" minorities may be seen as "proof that [minorities] in general are *not* oppressed or discriminated against, but are just 'too lazy.'" Applying this to the context at hand, by viewing some Indigenous individuals as exceptions, whites can continue blaming Indigenous people in general for Indigenous poverty, opposing compensation for historical injustices, and resenting those who refuse to assimilate. Moreover, when Indigenous friends or spokespersons endorse the dominant ideology and disparage fellow Indigenous people, it not only bolsters their status as "good Indians," but also upholds whites' sense of group superiority (validation straight from an Indian him/herself).

Political Avoidance: "We've Never Ever Talked about It. And We Don't Want to Talk about It"

Perhaps more surprising is the degree to which Indigenous and white residents who disagreed on fundamental issues still tended to live, work, and play together without much open conflict. This was facilitated by a widely shared norm of separating the interpersonal from the systemic, such that daily interactions were typically congenial, but political and economic tensions – the material bases of group position prejudice – had festered for years.[9]

As shown in chapters 3 and 6, Indigenous and white residents often framed boundaries and bridges in conflicting ways. Yet the lack of public discussion concerning these issues might have been the biggest barrier of all. As some interviewees noted, there had never been an open and respectful discussion between Indigenous and non-Indigenous residents about implementing Treaty No. 3, sharing the land and resources, or healing from historical trauma and building a more equitable and sustainable society. This local "culture of political avoidance" (Eliasoph 1999) enabled both the persistence of laissez-faire racism and friendly, cooperative intergroup relations.

Bob, a middle-aged white man whose family had settled in Fort Frances generations ago, and who had many Indigenous friends and relatives, articulated this principle well:

> The way I look at it, you've got the formal structures: organizational and political. And those are ... very rigid. First Nations have their own aspirations,

their own agendas ... Underneath ... there's all this intermarriage. You've got friends and family, they're all First Nations, non-First Nations ... My daycare lady for my kids ... she's [Indigenous]. Well, I don't know how you reconcile that. Usually we just let the politics roll ... We keep our lives separate ... Politics has got nothing to do with the guys on my [hockey] team. It's got nothing to do with the family ... When we have Christmas dinner, [my Indigenous relatives] and I don't talk about the politics ... we'll be in a [business] meeting, and that's what they've gotta do, but after the meeting, we're family, you know?

Like many other residents, Bob consciously tried to separate the "system," where political and economic conflict is rife and laissez-faire racism prevails among whites, from the "lifeworld" of family, friends, sports, and entertainment (Habermas 1984). This powerful norm of political avoidance discourages open discussion of racism and colonialism and helps maintain the appearance (or front-stage reality) of racial harmony, despite continuing structural inequities.[10]

Whites were particularly likely to follow this norm, perhaps out of perceived interest in maintaining the status quo. When I first began my research, no one spoke publicly of racism. Many Indigenous residents wished to speak about it privately. Some whites denied there was a problem: "If you want to see racism, go to Kenora." Others expressed prejudice "backstage" (e.g., at all-white dinner parties), but were guarded in public.

This avoidance norm played out at both personal and political levels. For example, one Métis woman described her husband, a white schoolteacher, as "prejudiced against Natives." When asked how their marriage was possible given her proud heritage, she said he saw her as "different" (subtyping) and they had "agree[d] to disagree" about politics (meaning that neither race- nor ideology-based homophily operated in this case). Although she had encouraged her husband to be interviewed, she said he "refused. He doesn't want to talk about it. I told him 'Jeff needs to hear your views to get a true picture of how people feel.' But he just said no."[11]

Meanwhile, a former municipal politician, who endorsed laissez-faire views, described how he avoided "political" issues when interacting with Native friends in order to keep the peace:

Some of my best friends are Natives, but we don't – you know, we kid each other, but we don't go into the details. We just don't. And when it comes to the government ... you say lots of things in camera, but you don't say it [in public]. (Emphasis added)

Even the local (now retired) MPP, Howard Hampton, who routinely supported Indigenous rights in the legislature, consciously tried to avoid "divisive" racial issues when at home in Fort Frances. "As a practical politician," he said, he had to "set aside the law school courses in Aboriginal and treaty rights" and "find common ground." Especially during elections, he "emphasize[d] the things that bring people together," such as shared interests in good jobs and health care. Perhaps this is one reason he held office for twenty-four straight years (1987–2011).

Some Indigenous residents also avoided such conversations or altered their behaviour in public, which might have led whites to perceive exaggerated ideological similarity. For instance, an older white millwright recalled asking a First Nations friend about his initiatives "to promote ... job opportunities on the reserve" and receiving only "a vague answer" because he "doesn't talk too much about that sort of thing."

During an interview with an Anishinaabe man who argued passionately for Indigenous sovereignty, two balding white men entered the coffee shop. They cheerfully greeted him, and he half-smiled and waved back. He then faced me directly, pulled his chair closer, and continued at a lower volume. I soon discovered that the white men were local municipal leaders with vastly different political ideologies from his. Publicly, however, the three were on a friendly first-name basis. This interviewee later explained that although Fort Frances whites compared themselves favourably with "places like Kenora" (where he used to live):

> [Fort Frances] isn't immune to [racism]. And I think the fundamental issue has always been that *we've never ever talked about it. And we don't want to talk about it. We don't.* (Emphasis added).

In general, by not talking about racism, residents maintained a balance whereby prejudice and discrimination could coexist with daily positive intergroup contact.

A Tenuous Balance: Repeated Crises and the Rush to Restore Order

The problem is that such a "balance" is tenuous, and normally unspoken tensions can boil over at any moment – as they did during the rumoured Indian uprising of 1900 (see chapter 1) and during the 2008 video incident.

As described in the Introduction, the "powwow video" provoked heated conflict among residents, with most whites denying or minimizing the racial implications, and most Anishinaabe and Métis viewing it as a sign of ongoing racism. The Right Relations Circle organized a public forum and antiracism walk (*"Biimosetaa*: Walking Together to Overcome Racism"). Letters to the editor flooded the local newspaper. Friends and spouses argued bitterly.

Of the six girls and their families, only one parent agreed to an interview. She said her daughter had become estranged from Indigenous friends and struggled to finish the school year (but notably remained best friends with an Indigenous girl). Three Indigenous parents described how their daughters ended friendships with "the video girls." A woman of mixed descent said her husband, a "full-blooded Native," became upset when she downplayed the video, telling her that she would never understand because she is a "mutt" (derogatory name for Métis). She left him, temporarily, because of this incident.

Within a few weeks, however, the "balance" was restored. Virtually every interviewee agreed that the healing ceremony organized by local Anishinaabe Elders was an appropriate response. However, it also inadvertently made racism seem, once again, taboo for public discussion. Traditionally, after a healing ceremony has concluded, it is considered rude to discuss the offence that necessitated it. When debates continued in the media, an Anishinaabe Elder wrote the local newspaper, saying the girls had been forgiven and asking residents to "move on." While it would have been unfair to scapegoat the girls, the promising public dialogue on the broader issues of racism and colonialism also ground to a halt. In a later interview, another Elder said that, in retrospect, perhaps they had rushed the healing process and should have taken the opportunity to continue discussing the root problems.

Over the following year, a similar process of *avoidance-panic-avoidance* unfolded with respect to the ongoing dispute between the Town of Fort Frances, the federal and provincial governments, and the Agency One bands over Point Park (see chapters 1 and 3). In my first eighteen months in Fort Frances, there was virtually no public discussion about the land claim. It was only in the spring of 2009 that some movement began, and the underlying tensions, which had been bottled up, threatened to boil over again.

Apparently unbeknownst to many residents, discussions had proceeded behind closed doors for years. As a former municipal councillor said, town council generally only spoke of it "in camera." Between July 2007 and December 2008 there was only one *Fort Frances Times* article specifically about the land claim. In August 2008, a large gathering of First Nations leaders and activists from across Canada was held at Point Park on the subject of treaties, and this land dispute was discussed. Although the gathering was open to everyone, and publicly advertised as such, only a handful of whites attended.[12]

Figure 7.2 Biimosetaa – Walking Together to Overcome Racism. Crises have the capacity to bring communities together or tear them apart. The "video incident" of February 2008 did both for Rainy River District residents. Amid the physical confrontations and polarization of arguments, Anishinaabe Elders said it was an opportunity for learning and change. On 21 March, the United Nations' International Day for the Elimination of Racial Discrimination, nearly three hundred Indigenous and non-Indigenous residents participated in "Biimosetaa – Walking Together to Overcome Racism." Photo courtesy of the author.

After becoming aware of the land claim, a few months into my field-work, I asked interviewees about their hopes and expectations for the land. Many became apprehensive and some were visibly upset, but few knew any of the details. They felt kept in the dark by authorities and admitted that their opinions might be based on misinformation. As a white millwright in his thirties put it: "Nobody wants to talk about it and I don't even know ... if [the lease has] come up or when it's due."

As detailed in my field notes, at the September 2008 Right Relations Circle meeting, a few members (only one of whom was born and raised in Fort Frances) raised the issue and suggested hosting a public forum in which each party would be invited to clarify its position and residents could obtain accurate information. Yet the proposal was abruptly rejected by other Right Relations Circle members, both Indigenous and white, and all from families who had lived in the region for generations. One Anishinaabe member – an otherwise staunch advocate for Indigenous rights – suggested "steering clear" of the issue because "to take one side or the other in the long run would only serve to undermine the integrity of the [Right Relations] group." Instead, he suggested doing "a media campaign designed to bring positive messages," since this would be "seen as something positive and non-political." This emphasis on staying "neutral" was echoed by a Métis man and several white women with deep roots in the region. Other group members remained silent, and the initiative was dropped.

It was only in February 2009 that public discussion began, and then only with significant resistance. On 18 February the First Nations chiefs broke the ice by sending an open letter to the town offering to extend the lease on Point Park at fair market value in order to keep discussions going and avoid chaos when the lease expired on 1 May. Two weeks later (3 March) the mayor, on behalf of town council, mailed a letter to every Fort Frances household stating that the town was prepared to offer "gratuitous monies" to purchase the land, "only so as to avoid costly litigation," and claiming that the dispute was "commenced by them [the Agency One bands]." Shortly afterwards, the popular local radio station B93 FM hosted a call-in show on the topic. Many white residents expressed hostility towards the Agency One bands, confusion and fear over what might happen when the lease expired, and a desire to either "take the playground equipment and run" (as one put it) or keep pursuing ownership, even if it meant a costly legal battle.

According to one First Nations chief, the radio show so disturbed members of his community that some advised him to cease negotiating with the town. At the same time, town authorities became more entrenched in their position, as indicated by this email from a municipal official upon my enquiry as to how residents were responding to the mayor's letter:

People have been very thankful for the communique [and] very surprised by the Town's significant interest regarding the land. I think people just assumed the land reverted to Agency One following the lease expiration. The fact that the land was always intended to be for municipal park purposes and the supporting Order in Council confirms this. *The land was surrendered for sale as were all the lands in the region.* The park portion was to be set aside for the municipality and the province did not intend for the federal government to affix a lease to the area or charge any monies for it. (Emphasis added)

Meanwhile, a local non-status Indian in his twenties who was making a documentary film about his journey to understand his Indigenous identity resurrected the idea of a public forum with the goal being "to inform, educate and give a voice to community members on the issues surrounding Agency No. 1 land and Pither's Point Park." Despite advertising it as a "positive," "peaceful" event where he would give an "unbiased presentation based on historical and legal fact" and then open the floor for discussion, he had difficulty booking space because local organizations refused to host it. He was called a "shit disturber," even though he said he was trying to prevent violence by clarifying the facts, and a police officer reportedly tried to dissuade him, claiming that Native gangs from Winnipeg would hijack the event. The meeting ultimately was held on 1 April and attended by about fifty residents. After two hours of heated debate, where white and Indigenous residents expressed sharply divided views, many stayed afterwards for tea and cake.

Nevertheless, tensions continued to rise in the streets. Municipal officials now publicly denied the First Nations' claims to the land, while Anishinaabe warriors increasingly discussed the possibility of blocking roads and occupying the park on 1 May. Some white residents began to worry that the sort of violent conflict – witnessed in Kenora, Oka, Caledonia, and elsewhere – they had so prided themselves on avoiding was perhaps imminent.

Two weeks later, the Right Relations Circle finally hosted its own community forum. At that meeting, a long-time Métis resident expressed the following frustrations:

Everybody knew it was coming, but nobody was talking about it, right? [Background voices: Absolutely. Yeah.] Now, all of a sudden, people are talking about it. I didn't know until about three months ago ... that the town was spending my tax money every year to keep some lawyers ... looking into this issue and possibly litigating. I mean why was that a big secret? ... they weren't telling anybody, and it's been going [on for] years ... They should have been having community consultations with the people here, as well as with the people on the different First Nations, saying: "This is coming up. What are we going to do about it?" But it seems to be a big secret, even now, what's happening in negotiations – and whether there are any. Maybe there aren't! (Emphasis added)

Likewise frustrated, an older white man stated:

> Just like [an Anishinaabe Elder] said, they [municipal and First Nations leaders] just have to get their act together and agree to meet ... and settle it ... We go to school with one another. We work with one another. We play with one another. We do everything with one another around here. And, you know, they used to call it "coexistence." Now, they might call it fighting. [*nervous laughter*] Or jealousy of whatever, eh?

That same day, the town and Agency One announced a one-year lease extension, at no cost to Fort Frances, while the parties continued discussions behind closed doors.

In June 2009, I returned to the district and asked residents about the Point Park dispute. An older white woman said, "I have heard nothing. I mean *nothing*. It's like it's not even an issue anymore." The difficult discussions had been deferred again, and the status quo restored. In April 2010, an Ontario Superior Court judge granted the town's request to maintain control of the park until the legal question of ownership was decided in court or a settlement was reached. Sporadic negotiations (between federal, provincial, and municipal representatives and local First Nations leaders and lawyers) continued in private.

Overall, the Point Park land dispute, like the video incident, illustrates the tendency to avoid publicly discussing political issues – especially those rooted in racism and colonialism. When the norm is finally breached, Indigenous and white residents become polarized in their views, and the tensions, bottled up for so long, risk exploding. Yet so long as residents follow the avoidance norm, it enables many to interact cordially as they go about their daily routines – even as inequities persist and conflicts and prejudices simmer backstage, always threatening to burst through and expose the façade.[13]

Local Context Matters: Settler Colonialism and Small-Town Dynamics

Although subtyping, ideology-based homophily, and political avoidance could occur anywhere, these processes may be especially salient in Fort Frances and other "border towns" due to historical and structural conditions. They are synergistic forms of "boundary work" (Lamont and Molnár 2002) facilitated by colonization, particularly in small-town contexts.

In this case, Indigenous individuals who historically were denied status by the Indian Act often tried to assimilate, in part, by distancing themselves from status Indians. Until 1982, the Métis were not even recognized

Figure 7.3 Closed for the Season. "It is more than the physical park closed because of winter. Winter has descended even on public discussion of the arrangements of how this land will be used in the future." – Dorothy, non-Indigenous woman, age fifty-nine. Photo courtesy of Dorothy.

as Indigenous peoples. In the Rainy River District, some joined the First Nations and legally became "Indian" (thanks to the unique "half-breed adhesion" in Treaty No. 3), while others lived in town and identified as white. Residential schools further divided Indigenous people, between those who internalized the assimilationist messages and those who resisted. Economic dependence has generated additional ideological rifts. Indigenous residents who have economically benefited from forestry or mining may be less willing to "rock the boat." Such intragroup divisions create opportunities for subtyping and ideology-based homophily.

Meanwhile, residential schools and conservative church/missionary teachings have fostered political avoidance by emphasizing obedience to authority. The demographic reality of minority status and the history of state-sanctioned violence against Indigenous peoples have further discouraged public discussions of racism and colonialism. Yet the current Indigenous population boom, the Indigenous cultural and political resurgence, and recent court decisions affirming Aboriginal and treaty rights (even as federal and provincial governments routinely ignore them) may enhance Indigenous peoples' proclivity to assert their interests and openly challenge the system. In the post–Idle No More era, this is increasingly the case (see chapter 10).

Nevertheless, the lack of anonymity in a small-town setting is a powerful countervailing force. In my research, I observed that Indigenous and white residents alike call Fort Frances home. They agree it is a great place to raise a family; they love the lakes, forests, and seasons; and they often have deep roots in the region. As much as some Indigenous people wish the "Whiteman" never "discovered" Turtle Island, most realize that settlers are here to stay. As much as some whites want to believe "real" Indians have vanished, many realize that Indigenous peoples and their cultures also are here to stay. And as macho as it is to "tell it like it is" in "a working man's town" (Dunk 1991), most residents avoid "sensitive issues," because they know they have to live with the neighbours they offend. As a result, racism and colonization are rarely discussed. Both the video incident and the Point Park land dispute stirred controversy for a time, but, as usual, the broader issues were "swept back under the rug," and the structural inequities and supporting ideologies remain intact.

The Limits of Contact under Settler Colonialism

This chapter confirms central tenets of Allport's contact hypothesis, while highlighting the limits of contact for combatting group position prejudice and laissez-faire racism. In a small-town, settler colonial context, amid widespread intergroup marriage and friendship, I found that many whites still blamed Indigenous people for various social problems and opposed policies to rectify injustices, and over 90 per cent of Anishinaabe reported personal experiences with racial discrimination. Thus, although contact may reduce old-fashioned prejudice, it does not diminish whites' sense of superior group position. As Jackman and Crane (1986, 481) put it:

> If prejudice does not derive from feelings of personal animosity but from an implicit sense of group position, then dominant groups will seek to defend their privileges no matter what brand of affect they feel towards subordinates.

In other words, so long as the settler colonial system persists, many dominant group members – including whites with Indigenous friends and family members – will be motivated to maintain their power, resources, and status. This wider context infringes on contact situations, inhibiting the generalization of contact effects, even when Allport's conditions otherwise appear to hold within the setting (such as in AA groups and on sports teams).

Building on group position theory and the subcategorization model of intergroup contact, and selectively utilizing critical-discursive analytic tools, this chapter has shown how three mutually reinforcing social processes contribute to the reproduction of group position prejudice: subtyping, whereby individuals who violate stereotypes are seen as exceptions that prove the rule; ideology-based homophily, whereby individuals befriend others who appear to share their racial ideologies; and a political avoidance norm, whereby the interpersonal is separated from the systemic and public discussions of racism are taboo. In the Rainy River District, these processes jointly enabled many whites to maintain a sense of superior group position, despite daily and often positive contact with Indigenous individuals. Specifically, whites tended to subtype Indigenous friends, especially those who seemed to share (and thereby validate) their racial ideologies, while political avoidance in daily interactions exaggerated the appearance of ideological affinity, preventing whites from ever seriously questioning their own beliefs and assumptions. Ultimately, the silence around racism and colonialism kept intergroup tensions bottled up backstage, so that when the avoidance norm was breached in a crisis, most whites (and a few "good Indians") denied and minimized the racial implications and urgently attempted to restore "order."

According to some theories, contact may reduce prejudice because it personalizes "the other" (Miller and Brewer 1984) or facilitates recognition of similarities and development of a common superordinate identity (Gaertner and Dovidio 2000). But this is insufficient in a settler colonial context where group position prejudice is expressed in part through refusal to acknowledge cultural diversity and Indigenous and treaty rights. The subcategorization model's emphasis on inter*group* interaction (Brown and Hewstone 2005) seems more pertinent here.

As my research shows, the norm within mixed sports teams, treatment settings, and workplaces, as well as many intermarriages and friendships, is that such differences are irrelevant and should be set aside. While this may create a sense of "we-ness," thereby undermining old-fashioned prejudice, it also tends to reinforce the view that "we" are all Canadian and should be treated "the same." Such outcomes may be desirable where marginalized groups are simply seeking acceptance in mainstream society, but they are inadequate to the struggle for Indigenous and treaty rights. Institutional support for contact and integration *does not* necessarily mean support for antiracism, let alone decolonization. So, what else can be done?

Chapter Eight

Education, Group Positioning, and Ideological Refinement

The time may come when I will ask you to lend me one of your daughters and one of your sons to live with us; and in return I will lend you one of my daughters and one of my sons for you to teach what is good, and after they have learned, to teach us.

Chief Sakatacheway, Lac Seul First Nation, upon signing Treaty No. 3, 1873 (quoted in Morris 2009 [1880], 64)

Upon signing Treaty No. 3, local Anishinaabe leaders emphasized the importance of *mutual* education, whereby Indigenous and settler peoples would teach each other their ways and learn from one another. Although crown representatives verbally agreed to these terms, the federal government instead implemented a residential school system. Indigenous children were forced into prison-like institutions that often involved child labour, punishment for speaking their language and practising their traditions, religious indoctrination, and physical, sexual, and emotional abuse (see chapters 1 and 9). Both they and non-Indigenous children, in their separate schools, were taught about the "superiority" of European culture and the "inferiority" of Indian ways (TRC 2015). Although Indigenous and settler children often attend school together today, including in the Rainy River District, Indigenous peoples have never had the opportunity to educate settlers in ways envisioned by the treaty signatories.

Despite this history, education, along with intergroup contact, remains one of the most commonly proposed "bridges" between Indigenous and settler peoples. Many residents I spoke with assumed that, with more accurate information, settlers would reject racial stereotypes and embrace egalitarian principles. At the same time, they suggested, making education more relevant for Indigenous children might reduce dropout rates and improve academic performance, leading to greater opportunities and social acceptance in Canada. However, the relationship between education, racism, and colonialism is complex, and education, especially of the variety promoted by most Rainy River District residents, is limited as a remedy for structural inequity.

One problem is that when Indigenous and white residents described education as a bridge, they often meant different things by it or had different ideas about how it would work. While some whites saw it as their duty to "help" Indigenous children succeed in mainstream schools, others resented the "special treatment" that Indigenous students allegedly received. Indigenous residents, meanwhile, were more likely to advocate for the learning of local Indigenous cultures, languages, and histories (by *all* students), and many Indigenous parents were distrustful of the mainstream system, due to the legacy of residential schooling and ongoing problems of exclusion, misrepresentation, and discrimination. Second, the forms of education that residents most often promoted do not adequately address the underlying problems of racism and colonialism. Reaffirming the political avoidance norm described in chapter 7, many settlers – displaying not so much ignorance as *wilful* ignorance – resisted such discussions altogether. Third, consistent with past research in other contexts, my interview and survey data show that although higher formal education reduces old-fashioned prejudice and is even associated with slight reductions in laissez-faire attitudes, it alone (like contact) does not overcome whites' sense of superior group position or some of the more subtle ideas, assumptions, and actions that perpetuate settler colonialism.

Perhaps the greatest challenge is motivating settlers to initially engage with the relevant issues – Indigenous histories and cultures, but also the contemporary relevance of treaties, racism, and colonization. Once they do engage, they must keep an open mind and have access to an effective pedagogical approach (e.g., experiential learning may have distinct benefits over lecturing or other conventional approaches). Moreover, as some Indigenous and Western critical scholars (Lee and Yerxa 2014; Regan 2010; Waziyatawin 2009) emphasize, it is not enough to understand racism, white supremacy, and settler colonialism on an abstract level; such learning must be accompanied by a sense of injustice that informs our daily actions and political choices, in a conscious ongoing process of antiracist and decolonizing practice. This process, in turn, may bring about more accountable relationships with Indigenous peoples.

Does Education Enlighten?

As outlined by Wodtke (2012), there are two major perspectives on the impact of education on intergroup attitudes. The conventional "enlightenment" view (consistent with classical social psychology) is that education has a liberalizing effect: individuals with more advanced education have a more enlightened worldview, including "commitment to democratic norms of equality and tolerance of racial outgroups" (Wodtke 2012, 80). Indeed, survey research shows that "highly educated whites are more likely to reject negative racial stereotypes, agree with structural explanations for black-white inequality, and endorse principles of equal treatment" (80). The premise is that prejudice arises from ignorance, irrationality, and narrow-mindedness; therefore, education may reduce prejudice by providing knowledge about the historical, social, and economic roots of inequality, reducing fear of the unknown, promoting egalitarian norms, and facilitating intergroup contact (Hyman, Wright, and Reed 1975; McClelland and Linnander 2006).

However, research also shows that highly educated whites are no more likely to support specific policies designed to overcome racial inequality, such as affirmative action (Jackman and Muha 1984; Schuman, Steeh, and Bobo 1997). The alternative "ideological refinement" view is that education enhances dominant groups' awareness of group interests, and their cognitive skills, thereby enabling them to articulate a more "astute defense of their privileged position" (Wodtke 2012, 81). Stemming from group position theory, this view suggests that dominant groups, such as white settlers in Canada, have "a vested interest" in maintaining their resources and privileges, and therefore "develop ideologies that legitimize their social position and mollify subordinate group challenges to the status quo" (83). Since overt prejudice is no longer socially acceptable, more educated whites may articulate "a more refined legitimizing ideology based not on assertions of categorical group differences but on the ostensibly race-neutral values of individualism and meritocracy," which provide "a seemingly principled means to deny the validity of group-based remedial policies" (83).

As for non-white groups, including Indigenous peoples, education may have either an "empowering" effect, fostering critical awareness of racism and inequality and commitment to their group interests, or an "ideological alignment" effect, whereby exposure to individualistic and meritocratic values in the mainstream system only strengthens commitment to the dominant (white) ideology. Based on large-scale US surveys, Wodtke's (2012, 80) research supports a revised ideological refinement/alignment perspective, whereby "education unevenly promotes different elements of the dominant group's legitimizing ideology" among both whites and non-whites, "depending on their position in the racial hierarchy." Specifically, higher levels of education are associated with rejection of categorical racial stereotypes and increased awareness of discrimination, but not with support for racial preferences in hiring and promotion; if anything, higher education is associated with more negative attitudes (among whites and blacks) towards affirmative action and other group-based remedial policies.

Based on the above one might expect that, for white residents of the Rainy River District, education would reduce overt prejudice and stereotyping but have little or no effect on their sense of group position/ perceptions of group threat, policy preferences, or more subtle expressions of racist ideology. And for Indigenous residents, while formal education might enhance awareness of (or willingness to report) discrimination, it could have little impact on their support of Indigenous and treaty rights – or perhaps even a negative impact if the ideological alignment hypothesis is correct.

One limitation of this approach to studying the relationship between education and intergroup attitudes, however, is that education is measured simply as one's overall *level* of formal education. The reality is that education takes multiple *forms*, and some forms may be more conducive to challenging racist and colonialist mentalities than others. For example, in higher education, social sciences and humanities majors, on average, may have more awareness and more progressive attitudes than business or engineering majors (Sidanius and Pratto 1999).[1] There is also mixed evidence regarding the efficacy of more targeted forms of diversity training (Bezrukova, Jehn, and Spell 2012). While cultural sensitivity/competence training seeks to teach majority group members about "other" cultures, values, and religions, often through exposure to "ethnic" food, music, and customs, antiracist education aims to expose issues of power and (white) privilege, emphasizing how everyday assumptions, decisions, and actions may perpetuate racial inequity, regardless of intentions. Consistent with group position theory, however, such programs often generate backlash, "making those in power take a defensive stance" (Satzewich 2011, 106). Perhaps the deeper problem is "the assumption that racism stems from a lack of knowledge," as opposed to competition over scarce resources (ibid.). If the real issue is power and privilege, then more radical change, such as legislation to outlaw discrimination, enforce a more equitable distribution of resources, and respect Indigenous jurisdiction, also may be necessary.

Nevertheless, some "alternative" types of education have been shown to improve settlers' awareness of and attitudes towards Indigenous peoples, including support for Indigenous and treaty rights. For example, transformative and experiential learning, which are rooted in the emancipatory pedagogy of Paulo Freire and critical communication theories of Jurgen Habermas, may involve "direct engagement with Indigenous peoples – in Indigenous spaces and places – to understand their (multiple) situated perspectives" (Castleden et al. 2013, 488). In these spaces, students are actively immersed in and engaged with worldviews that often challenge their beliefs, and must critically reflect on their own assumptions, attitudes, and actions. Common techniques include artistic expression, journal writing, dialogue circles, and digital storytelling, and the process is often described as unsettling yet deeply meaningful and even life altering.

Similarly, Paulette Regan (2010, 15) advocates an "unsettling pedagogy" in which settlers must step outside their comfort zones, reflect on (rather than escape from) the discomfort, and listen not only to the stories of Indigenous peoples but also to the questions they find themselves asking as they "bear witness" to these stories. Ultimately, she says, settlers must "challenge the peacemaker myth" at the "heart" of settler-Canadian identity, which suggests that we have good relations with "our Indians" because we (or our ancestors) made treaties, had "good intentions," and brought "civilization" (14). Settlers also need to make space for "historical counter-narratives of Indigenous diplomacy, law, and peacemaking," respect Indigenous self-determination, and take responsibility for our actions (14). Without unsettling settlers, disturbing their emotions, and challenging their assumptions, little significant learning will occur. In other words, their sense of group position will remain intact, and social change will be unlikely. Yet such pedagogical processes are *not* currently a routine part of the mainstream education system, and most Canadian university undergraduates have shockingly low levels of awareness of Indigenous peoples and issues (Godlewska et al. 2013). This fact illustrates that conventional educational approaches are insufficient to transform Indigenous-settler relations.

In the rest of this chapter, I show that although many Rainy River District residents viewed education as a bridge – and as one of the most promising solutions to racism – white and Indigenous residents often gave different (and sometimes contradictory) reasons for this. Moreover, the forms of education they advocated were not necessarily those that the above theories and research suggest would be most effective. Rather than supporting directly learning about "racism as a tool of settler colonialism" (Lee and Yerxa 2014, n.p.) or engaging in long-term experiential learning and critical self-reflection (Regan 2010), many residents, especially whites, seemed to promote a "museum approach" to "learning more about Indians" (Henry and Tator 2006, 213; Lee 2015). Furthermore, consistent with the ideological refinement perspective, my data show that although formal education reduces old-fashioned prejudice and stereotyping, it alone, like contact, does not eliminate whites' sense of superior group position or justifications for racial inequity. While some forms of education can soften racial attitudes and open minds, a post-secondary degree does not necessarily eradicate the underlying assumptions and ways of thinking and acting that perpetuate settler colonial structures.

Perceptions of Education as a Bridge

When asked about bridges between Aboriginal and non-Aboriginal communities, approximately half of all interviewees referred to education or integrated schools. However, more than a dozen interviewees (mostly Indigenous) also described mainstream educational institutions as a boundary, and many criticized the local public school board for its handling of the video incident (see chapter 3).

As noted in chapter 6, some residents viewed the school system as a bridge because it brings Indigenous and non-Indigenous children together, enabling them to interact and become friends. Others emphasized the more direct educational function, whereby formal schooling is expected to (1) open minds, broaden horizons, and dismantle stereotypes and prejudice; and (2) level the playing field, enabling Indigenous people to compete on the same plane as settlers. According to a middle-aged non-status Indian man:

> I think the bridges that bring Native [and non-Native] people together and get rid of this old, stigmatized thing ... is the school systems and the young people ... If you teach people to be accepting and understanding and you teach it to them young enough ... then, of course, they are going to carry that forward and it's going to create good relationships.

At the time of my study, more than 30 per cent of students in the Rainy River District School Board identified as Indigenous; similar percentages attended the (publicly funded) Catholic elementary schools. Like white youth from surrounding municipalities, Indigenous youth from nearby First Nations were bussed daily to and from Fort Frances High School (and some elementary schools). Thus, when asked, a middle-aged white woman in town perceived that Indigenous children were "all integrated into the school system with everybody else"[2] and that it had "built a lot of bridges."

Although education was one of the most commonly cited bridges, Indigenous and white residents often described it as such for different reasons. For some whites, it was a potential tool to "raise" Natives "up" to their own (presumed superior) level. From the perspective of a white school administrator, for example:

We need to get more of our First Nation population educated so that they see the education system as a crutch rather than a baseball bat ... that they're being hit over the head with ... Because I think – and this could go back to the residential schools – there still remains a huge distrust of the education system ... We've also gotta make sure that ... when these kids finish high school ... that they're suitably literate and numerate ... to be able to go on to post-secondary [education].

While undoubtedly well intentioned, these comments also convey an implicit sense of group superiority, a sort of white man's burden to teach "our First Nations" to trust and compete in "our" esteemed institutions. Although stated here in seemingly benign terms, such attitudes long buttressed the residential school system, which, rather than being a bridge, was one of the most destructive tools of colonialism (Miller 1996; Milloy 1999; TRC 2015). Yet such attitudes remained widespread in the Rainy River District. An older blue-collar worker put it more bluntly: "you can educate [Indigenous people] over however many generations it might take. It will get better." A white nurse, meanwhile, believed that "going to our schools" has "helped" Indigenous youth "join" mainstream society: "they see the better side of life."

From a more competitive "us verus them" (as opposed to a paternalistic "we teach them") perspective, a retired white businessman resented how "the government has given [Indigenous people] a lot of opportunities for education and employment" and when "it don't work out ... some of them play the 'trump card,' which is Native." Although he too viewed education as a possible bridge, he, like many other residents, blamed Indigenous people for allegedly squandering opportunities to "better themselves."

In fact, most Indigenous people highly value formal education (Environics 2010) and are concerned about the significant (but gradually narrowing) gaps between Indigenous and non-Indigenous students in high school completion rates, post-secondary attendance, and academic test scores (Frideres 2011; O'Sullivan 2011).[3] Yet framing the issue as a need for charitable whites to "help" the poor Natives – rather than a need for settlers to reflect on their own beliefs, actions, and policies, including the fact that on-reserve schools receive two to three thousand dollars less funding per pupil (Blackstock 2011), or the implications of multiple generations of non-Indigenous Canadians having grown up with a one-sided, often racist curriculum (TRC 2015) – reinforces the inequitable sense of group positions and perpetuates settler colonial relations.

In this light, many Indigenous residents emphasized that whites need to learn more about Indigenous peoples' historical and contemporary experiences and cultures and about treaty relations. According to a local First Nation chief, settlers are "not aware of the conditions that we have to live under" yet are quick to blame the victim and endorse racist stereotypes: "non-Native people have to be educated to understand what goes on here, but how to achieve that education process, I don't know," because neither he nor other community leaders have time to teach them. An older non-status Indian said, "you can't start with the generation that's biased already" because "no matter what you tell them," their minds are shut. However, he thought education would help improve relations among the youth if teachers went "to the point of educating about the treaty." A middle-aged Anishinaabe man agreed:

> I think it's just lack of education in the non-Native community. But I also think we could improve in our own community ... we've got to educate our kids a little bit better ... about our language, our treaty, our history. There's not too many kids that know about that.

Similarly, a self-described "half-breed" woman in her thirties said:

> A lot of people on both sides ... aren't aware fully. [Some Indigenous] people blame the "white man" for all their problems ... but they don't really know everything ... On the flipside ... those taxpayers that are mad ... don't know the history of the reserves being ripped off [or that] people are only getting five dollars [in annual treaty annuities] ... They're all mad, but they don't know what they're mad about! ... like I never went to a history class where they talked about the treaties ... What we're looking for is just acknowledgment that, "Yeah, you guys were ripped off. We're really sorry. What can we do to fix it?"

She concluded that "to bridge anything, it has to start with the little kids in school" and "Natives have to be a big part of the history."

Some white residents agreed that learning more (and more accurate) information about Indigenous peoples could be a bridge. However, they tended to emphasize education about "Aboriginal culture" rather than history or treaty rights, let alone racism and colonialism or critical reflection on their own role in sustaining and benefiting from these ongoing processes. For example, a white man in his thirties said:

> I think they should be doing way more education about ... their [Indigenous] culture and stuff. I would *way* rather my kid learn about that than about some stupid battle that Napoleon won, which has absolutely no bearing whatsoever on his life.

For a white man in his fifties:

> I think the culture barrier is something that we could start teaching people very early ... we don't need every child ... to learn to speak Oji-Cree or Ojibwa or whatever, but to get them to culturally understand that there's two predominant populations around here ... So, why don't we teach these kids ... what it is that makes up Aboriginal culture and what's important [because] peoples' cultures are what set their behaviours, right? If you're Italian or Greek, it's a big family, loud ... But that doesn't make 'em bad or different ... And it's no different for Aboriginals. They have certain behaviour modes that are driven by their culture and the way they're raised.

While teaching about the major traditions and worldviews of the "two predominant populations" certainly has merit, one danger of the approach described here is that it may perpetuate cultural stereotypes and essentialist explanations for human behaviour (see the following section, "Critical Analysis"). To the extent that learning about Indigenous cultures is incorporated into the curriculum, it must be done in a more nuanced way, with attention to how *all* cultures, even while having (relatively stable) core principles and values, are fluid and dynamic.

In response to the growing Indigenous population, continuing frustrations over the disproportionately high dropout rates among Indigenous students, lingering mistrust from the residential school era, and more recent racialized incidents (described in previous chapters), both school boards in the Rainy River District recently had taken steps to reach out to the First Nations, acknowledge their concerns, and develop curricula and policies that would better reflect the cultural backgrounds and needs of their students. For example, they introduced and expanded Anishinaabemowin language classes, recruited Indigenous teachers (and, at Fort Frances High School, an Indigenous vice-principal and Indigenous guidance counsellors), and instituted cultural awareness days, featuring, among other things, powwows on school grounds. While many residents praised such initiatives as "positive steps," others felt they had not gone far enough, and still others (especially whites) felt they had gone "overboard."

One senior white public school board administrator proudly described his board's recent initiatives to meet Indigenous students' needs and improve intergroup relations:

> We've hired, in the last year, two or three permanent Aboriginal people as teachers – predominantly Native as a Second Language [NSL] 'cause they're really hard to come by and we're trying to build our NSL because we know

Figure 8.1 Welcome in Three Languages. "Visitors to the Fort Frances High School are greeted in three languages [English, French, and Anishinaabemowin]." – Native Canadian, age sixteen. Photo courtesy of the caption speaker.

that our [Aboriginal] population is increasing. And we offer ... Native as a Second Language [from grade 4 through high school]; we would encourage *any* student to take [it]. You're living in northwestern Ontario; it would be a great opportunity to be involved in the language and the culture.

Beyond language classes, he continued, the Rainy River District School Board had incorporated the Seven Grandfather Teachings (see chapter 6) into its character education program: "How can anybody ever argue with those?" Moreover, he said, "We're heavy into pow-wows." In 2008, "J.W. Walker [a kindergarten to grade 8 school in Fort Frances] took every staff member, every student, up to Stanjik-oming for a powwow." He believed this was a "powerful" learning experience: in addition to being "immersed in the culture and the food and the dancing," non-First Nations students who "did the bus ride ... realized how far these [First Nations] kids come from Stanji every day," perhaps increasing empathy for their daily challenges. Stanjikoming First Nation members, meanwhile, were "absolutely thrilled to be able to host a whole school." In another case of experiential learning:

Fall Harvest is something Seven Gens [Seven Generations Education Institute] puts on ... Our western schools go up to Big Grassy and many of our other schools go to the Fall Harvest here [on Agency One grounds], and that's a *huge* cultural event ... there's winnowing of rice, plucking of geese, and soup, bannock, fish – the whole shebang ... you get the historical perspective; you get to sit down and talk with the Elders. Those are the kinds of things that keep us connected.

Despite these many initiatives, he and other educators acknowledged that more local history – including more accurate and detailed information about residential schools and treaties – should be incorporated into the curriculum.[4] According to one administrator, "it's an area that we're working on," and the 2008 Indian residential school apology "has probably made it easier for boards of education [and] the general public to be able to talk openly about this now."

Nevertheless, some interviewees expressed concerns about how these initiatives were perceived in the broader community. For instance, a local white teacher believed the hanging of Indigenous artwork and the holding of powwows at school, while viewed positively by some, may be perceived as window dressing or even provoke backlash from others:

We're trying to bridge, and we're trying to integrate ... but I don't know if we're doing it in the right way ... You can have a powwow and some [Indigenous] people are gonna say "This is great ... Thanks for doing this." [But others] say, "They're just doing it because they think they *have* to" ... And then you've got the white people who, like myself, say, "Okay, this powwow, as long as we're doing it for the right reasons, it's a great thing." But then [others] are saying, "We're just doing it because we *have* to. It's where we live." [So] what's the point if ... there's no explanation behind it? That's gonna create animosity.

Confirming these suspicions, a middle-aged white woman recalled an extended family member describing a recent school powwow as "a little overdone, don't ya think?" Such reactions reiterate the importance of ongoing experiential learning, rather than one-time events that may be perceived as tokenizing and that may exacerbate whites' perceptions of group threat. Moreover, although the school board administrator insisted that Anishinaabemowin language classes were open to all students, a retired NSL teacher reported that "a lot of non-Native students didn't want to take the course because they didn't view it as important." Yet several white parents said that when their children asked to enrol in

Anishinaabemowin language classes, they were discouraged by a local principal, who responded, "that's really for the Aboriginal kids" and "if you're white, you take French." Nevertheless, at least one of these children did enrol in Anishinaabemowin and "loved every aspect of it."[5] This shows how some residents try to police group boundaries in the education system and how others (even children) may challenge those boundaries and, thereby, the sense of group positions.

Ultimately, many residents were optimistic that the school system would improve intergroup relations by increasing awareness of Indigenous history and culture, by facilitating cross-group friendships, and by expanding opportunities for Indigenous and non-Indigenous children alike. However, some Anishinaabe were distrustful of the mainstream system, especially given the residential school legacy, recurrent encounters with racist teachers and students, and biased curricula, and some whites – dismissing Indigenous peoples' unique (nation-to-nation) relationships with Canada – believed that "Aboriginal culture" now received undue attention.

Still other interviewees asserted that formal education might not even be necessary, and that what is really needed is ongoing dialogue about meaningful issues. At times, this might take the form of one-on-one conversations, like my open-ended interviews. Other times, the necessary learning might occur through Indigenous-led educational events or institutions, such as the above-mentioned National Treaties No. 1 to 11 Gathering (August 2008), Naicatchewenin First Nation's cultural gatherings (spring and fall of 2008), and the Kay-Nah-Chi-Wah-Nung Historical Centre (a national historic site, managed by RRFN, that contains sacred burial mounds). According to a middle-aged Métis man, for example, "At the all-treaties conference ... I probably learned more in a week than I'd learned in fifty years." As mentioned in chapter 6, the few white interviewees who said they had changed their views on Indigenous peoples or issues also emphasized the importance of learning the "real" history, usually *outside* the formal education system (through books, movies, conversations, and participation in social justice groups). However, the biggest obstacle might be bringing all parties to the table. According to an older white man who was born and raised in Fort Frances:

> I think the communication is getting better, so the relationship is getting better. And I think we can do more as far as the education side of it – and I don't mean in a *formal* sense. I mean just ... having a discussion like this [*back-and-forth hand gesture*] ... I don't think that we have a problem that needs anything more than more education, more communication, a sense of fairness, and to keep plugging away at it.

Some Indigenous interviewees agreed. For an older Anishinaabe man who lived on reserve:

> To build that solid foundation, we need to do this, like what we're doing here right now [*back-and-forth hand gesture*] and what we've done in the past, having walks and meetings together ... with church people and traditional people ... to be able to understand one another ...

However, some residents questioned their neighbours' willingness to engage in such dialogue. A middle-aged First Nations woman described the Treaties Gathering as a bridge with unfulfilled potential. Since many residents "don't know about the treaties," she thought it was an opportunity to learn about "the true history." So, although "the event was good," she said, "it would have been nice to see a lot more non-Natives there." A younger non-status Indian agreed that "communication" and "education" are key, but convincing white people to engage is a challenge:

> A lot of white people say, "Well, they're getting everything free." [*laughter*] They don't understand. And ... until people can be educated and until we can properly communicate, that's gonna be a problem. But as long as you have that *fear*, you're not going to ... make that connection.

An older white man, originally from the United States, noted a further challenge: the lack of institutional infrastructure to facilitate such dialogue beyond the public schools:

> *There's just not an intellectual centre; there's no place for conversations to happen.* This is a real weakness in the white community ... You've got to deal with people's minds ... And to put it all on the high school, it's not only unfair, it's impossible ... I don't know where the leadership is going to come from. [Right now] it's coming from this tiny Right Relations Circle [see chapter 10] and a few other individuals who are kinda concerned, *most* of whom are Native. I mean, that's embarrassing! (Emphasis added)

A middle-aged Anishinaabe man, who was once homeless but who now worked full time and lived in town, elaborated:

> The fact that we don't talk to each other seems to be an issue ... We'll go to Wal-mart and [say], "Oh, the weather's good today." "Yeah, it might rain tonight." "Well, I hope it doesn't because I wanna go fishing" ... [But] if we communicated as a people on a *deeper* level and with much more *frequency*,

I think that would remove the boundaries ... I need to understand what you're thinking and you need to understand what I'm thinking. I need to understand your religion, beliefs, and values, and you need to understand mine. We need to explore each other's similarities and differences so that you and I can ... live together in a society where racism ... is not so prevalent ... But ... do we have the wherewithal to do that? I think the only time that happens is when there's incidents like this high school video; that's when we talked, and it's a knee-jerk reaction ... We live in a geographic location where we can do something for the good of everybody and we've got to start examining those things – politically, economically, socially, philosophically ... That's a big order though. Who's going to do that? The mayor? No. The chiefs? Probably not. A homeless person? Maybe. [*laughs*]

In short, many residents believed that education and communication held great promise as a bridge between Indigenous and settler peoples, but felt that, due to fear, ignorance, apathy, and the lack of "intellectual centre[s] for [meaningful] conversations to happen," these mechanisms had so far failed to fulfil their potential.

Critical Analysis

From a critical perspective, the forms of education promoted by most Rainy River District residents would do little to address, and in some cases would perpetuate, the underlying problems. What is rarely mentioned – except by a few politically engaged Anishinaabe, Métis, and non-Indigenous residents – is the need for direct education on and critical reflection about white privilege and settler complicity in ongoing racism and colonialism. Instead, most residents, including school officials, emphasized either "helping" Indigenous students "catch up" to white students or incorporating more "Aboriginal culture" into the local school system.

On one hand, many of these initiatives had been fought for and commended by local Indigenous residents and might be associated with increased academic performance by Indigenous students. A local First Nation chief said that "putting language into the curriculum" helps Indigenous students "understand their identity, who they are and where they come from." Empirical studies confirm that learning one's Indigenous language can boost self-esteem and improve academic achievement (Northwest Indian Language Institute 2015). As well, symbolic gestures such as hanging First Nations flags in the school atrium and welcoming students in multiple languages (English, French, and Anishinaabemowin) (see figures 3.3 and 8.1) may enhance Indigenous students' sense of "ownership," as one Indigenous educator put it.

However, these initiatives are insufficient for transforming group positions, and the standard approach to educating non-Indigenous students is problematic. For instance, the emphasis is usually on Indigenous culture, as opposed to Indigenous knowledges or Indigenous contributions to society, meaning that Indigenous peoples are still framed as the exotic "other." According to an Anishinaabe man who used to work at a local school, for example:

> When we'd have Native Awareness [Day] or bring in some dancers and singers, it kind of felt like going to a zoo, and you're the animal, and everyone is sort of staring at you; you're parading around in your outfits and whatnot.

While this "Indians in a jar" approach to cultural education may be "comfortable" and even "fun" for settlers, "fracturing Indigenous realities into safe pieces of information commodifies lived Indigenous experiences" (Lee 2015). More generally, as Damien Lee of Fort William First Nation and Jana-Rae Yerxa of Couchiching First Nation explain, it is inadequate to simply "learn more about Indians." Settlers also need to "flip the lens" and learn more about racism as a tool of settler colonialism, and about how white people in particular benefit from and are complicit with colonization – that is, how settlers maintain (or challenge) the system through their daily words, actions, and inactions (Lee and Yerxa 2014). We therefore must be wary of "projects that aim to learn more about the Other without substantive self-reflection ... learning more about Indigenous peoples is easy because it doesn't question positions of power" (n.p.). Although examining our own positions, assumptions, and behaviours may be deeply uncomfortable for settlers, it is a necessary part of the (un)learning process (Leonardo and Porter 2010; Regan 2010).

On rare occasions when such issues were raised, however, local (especially white) leaders tended to shut them down as "too divisive." For example, when two residents asked their church minister to host a workshop on decolonization, they were told "we don't want to make people feel uncomfortable." As Lee and Yerxa observe, whites often resort to "check-back messages" to thwart unsettling conversations: "That was a long time ago ... Get over it ... Not all white people are like that." Part of the problem, then, is not merely ignorance, but also *wilful* ignorance. As a First Nations woman quoted in chapter 3 put it, "People aren't informed *and* they don't care to be informed." This was illustrated most clearly to me at a private, all-white dinner party, when a thirty-five-year-old man with an undergraduate degree said the high school video incident was being "blown out of proportion" and no one would have cared if Indigenous youth had mocked a Finnish dance. When a younger woman (not from the region) suggested that he view the incident in light of residential school trauma, he covered his ears and said, "I don't want to hear it. I know what I know and I don't want to learn anything new." He then left the room and opened another beer (Field notes, February 2008). The fact is, some individuals may never change their minds; they cannot be reached through either contact or education because their sense of group position is too entrenched.

As Canadian philosopher Trudy Govier (2003, 78) puts it in the context of the historical and ongoing mistreatment of Indigenous peoples:

> We have chosen to ignore many facts, problems, and cries of pain. As a result ... we know little. Then, if we are charged with responsibility, we are apt to protest that we did not know. But we did know ... enough to ignore the situation in the first place ... enough to know that we did not want to know more ... because the truths we would face would be unpleasant and incompatible with our favoured picture of ourselves, and they imply a need for restitution and redress, threatening our rather comfortable way of life.

Although many settlers could benefit from targeted education about residential schools, treaties, and contemporary racism and colonialism, they have chosen to cover their eyes and ears because they know, deep down, that it might threaten their sense of superiority and entitlement.

That said, when a local white male resident, who had expressed racist views to me in private, was later forced to attend an Indigenous-led cultural sensitivity course at work where the impact of residential schools was addressed, he began to change his tune. A few days later, he remarked to me, "Now I know why Natives are so fucked up ... I'd kill anyone who tried to take my daughter away!" (Field notes, June 2008). It is true that this statement still perpetuates stereotypes about "fucked up" Natives, ignoring the many Native people who are healthy and successful in both mainstream and traditional ways, and fails to reflect on his own role as a settler in maintaining contemporary colonialism. Nevertheless, this change of heart reveals political growth and insight and suggests that even a one-day workshop, if well delivered, can begin to generate learning and empathy from some of the most bigoted white settlers.

Perhaps, though, as some interviewees suggested, the most efficient approach is to start with the youth, with mandatory, age-appropriate curricula. Yet if non-Indigenous adults are so resistant to change, if a critical mass of settlers do not "get it," and if Indigenous adults are too busy teaching their own children and rebuilding their own communities (as the First Nations chief above suggested), then developing and teaching such curricula can be a daunting challenge. Moreover, even if the right kind of material can be taught in the right kind of way, it must be accompanied by meaningful *action* to address the underlying structural inequities, including land dispossession, infringements on political autonomy, and inequalities in material living conditions and health and well-being. There still would be a need to *act* differently and to transform policies and institutions, that is, "to link knowledge and critical reflection to action" in order to bring about "deep social and political change" (Regan 2010, 23). Learning about injustice does not automatically produce just social relations.

Education and Intergroup Attitudes

Notwithstanding these caveats and critiques, it still may be worthwhile to examine the statistical associations between formal education and intergroup attitudes. Is higher education, as currently constituted, associated with reduced prejudice?

In my research, among the fifty-one non-Indigenous interviewees with complete survey data, fifteen (29 per cent) had a high school diploma or less (seven had not graduated from high school, eight had a high school diploma but no post-secondary), and thirty-six (71 per cent) had at least some college or university education (nineteen had a college or university degree, seven had a graduate degree) (see table 8.1).[6] According to enlightenment theory, higher levels of formal education, perhaps especially exposure to post-secondary education, should be associated with more progressive racial attitudes. In contrast, ideological refinement theory suggests that the impact of education is limited to more overt measures of prejudice, but that highly educated whites retain, and may be even more adept at expressing, subtle forms of racism.

As expected, my interview and survey data show that education does improve attitudes towards Indigenous peoples on measures of overt categorical prejudice. On indicators of the sense of group position and more covert justifications for racial inequity, however, the results are less straightforward and generally more supportive of ideological refinement theory. To a large extent, highly educated whites tend to retain a sense of group superiority and entitlement.

On the feeling thermometer, for example, whites with a high school diploma or less gave a median rating of 3 out of 5 or "neutral" to First Nations and Métis people in general (compared to 5 out of 5 or "very

Table 8.1 Education Attainment among Indigenous and Non-Indigenous Interviewees

Highest level of formal schooling completed	Indigenous interviewees ($N = 55$)	Non-Indigenous interviewees ($N = 51$)
% less than high school	27.3	13.7
% high school diploma	7.3	15.7
% some college or university	38.2	19.6
% college or university degree	21.8	37.3
% graduate or post-graduate degree	5.5	13.7

positive" for Canadians) (see table 8.2). Among whites with at least some college or university, median ratings increased to 4. Similarly, the median rating of Indigenous political leaders was 3 among whites with high school or less, but 3.45 among whites with post-secondary education. How to interpret this result is somewhat ambiguous, however, as some of the listed leaders may have been perceived as relatively "safe" and non-threatening ("sell-outs" working more in *settlers'* interests, according to some Indigenous activists).

On the other hand, the median rating of status Indians receiving tax exemptions was 3 and the median rating of Indigenous protesters was 2 among white interviewees at *all* levels of education. If anything, non-Indigenous residents with a post-secondary education (but not a graduate degree) were slightly more negative towards Indigenous protesters than those with a high school education or less. On the most direct quantitative measures of group threat, therefore, formal education had made no significant difference in settlers' attitudes, among residents interviewed.

These findings are consistent with the ideological refinement perspective within group position theory, which suggests that education alone does not alter dominant groups' interest in maintaining power and privileges. Although education may soften overall attitudes towards Indigenous people, many white residents with college or university degrees continued to oppose Indigenous and treaty rights and react especially negatively to Indigenous protests that challenge the status quo.

Nevertheless, turning to my more qualitative interview data, education *was* associated with at least slight reductions in laissez-faire racist attitudes. When asked about attributions for Indigenous poverty, for example, 60 per cent of whites with high school or less said Indigenous people themselves were mainly to blame, compared to 48 per cent of whites with at least some college or university. The finding that higher

Table 8.2 Selected Attitudes among Non-Indigenous Interviewees by Level of Education

Highest level of formal schooling completed	Non-Indigenous interviewees with high school or less (N = 15)	Non-Indigenous interviewees with some college or university (N = 36)
Median ratings on feeling thermometer (from 1, "strongly negative," to 5, "strongly positive")		
Canadians	5	5
First Nations	3	4
Métis	3	4
Indigenous political leaders	3	3.45
Indigenous people who receive tax exemptions	3	3
Indigenous protesters	2	2
Main explanation for Indigenous-white poverty gap		
% victim-blaming	60	48
Main reaction to residential school apology		
% saying "move on"	67	44

education increases the tendency to agree with structural or historical explanations for poverty is consistent with past research in other contexts (Wodtke 2012). Does this necessarily mean that highly educated whites are more likely to endorse redistributive policies or more far-reaching structural change?

When asked how Indigenous poverty could be reduced, if at all, more highly educated whites were less likely to endorse simplistic solutions, such as that Indigenous people must work harder or assimilate, or that social assistance should be abolished. Such individuals were more likely to say that government funding for Indigenous peoples should be increased; several recommended reviving the Kelowna Accord.[7] However, most of the proposed reforms would have minimal impact on settlers' own power, resources, or way of life. The most common proposal, by far, was to improve the public education system and, in turn, Indigenous peoples' academic achievement, which many saw as the key to success in the mainstream economy. Only a few non-Indigenous interviewees (all with university degrees) proposed more radical solutions, such as support for Indigenous self-determination and treaty rights and the rebuilding of sustainable local economies rooted in Indigenous values.

When asked if anything should be done to follow up on the residential school apology, 67 per cent of non-Indigenous interviewees with high school or less said no ("move on"), compared to 44 per cent of those with at least some college or university. In other words, the settler-Canadians with higher education were more likely to understand that residential school survivors cannot simply "get over it" and that action must accompany apology (see chapter 9). Nevertheless, it is impossible to know from these data whether more progressive attitudes on this question were due to education per se *or* to self-selection bias (progressive people self-select into higher education, as Gross [2013] argues). Further, a substantial minority of whites with college or university degrees still rejected follow-up action, and there was wide variation in what *specifically* they thought should be done. Most interviewees were referring to greater individual monetary compensation, more funding for mental health and addictions programs, or better educational opportunities for Indigenous youth. The majority were not calling for significant structural transformation, such as recognizing Indigenous sovereignty, honouring treaties, or returning land, and therefore arguably still displayed a form of ideological refinement; however, they did tend to be more open to the idea that reconciliation and redress are ongoing processes.

In short, more educated settlers were somewhat less likely to endorse victim-blaming attributions for poverty or to take an entirely laissez-faire stance on residential schools, and they expressed more positive overall attitudes towards First Nations and Métis people. However, they were no less likely than those without post-secondary education to resent Indigenous protesters or oppose treaty rights. As noted above, some highly educated whites also expressed racist views in private, among other whites (or others they assumed would agree with them), this despite being well-mannered in public and in formal interviews. Overall, these data suggest that the sense of group positions, while not completely impervious to change, is indeed resistant to change via the path of formal education.

As for thoughts on the impact of education on Indigenous residents, some (Indigenous and white) interviewees asserted that as Indigenous people acquire more formal education, they might gain more respect and acceptance from non-Indigenous Canadians. According to a white man married to a Métis woman:

> The education system is improving for the Aboriginal people, so there are a lot more of them getting good educations, and that starts setting the example for others ... And I think for the non-Aboriginals ... if they see them

being more successful and getting educations, they tend to ease up and feel a bit better about what's going on.

Although mainstream education may help some Indigenous people gain recognition and respect, from a group positioning perspective it also may provoke a sense of competition or threat among some settlers, thereby eliciting more (or different forms of) discrimination. As Wodtke (2012) suggests, it also may sensitize Indigenous peoples to such discrimination.

Among the fifty-five Indigenous interviewees with complete survey data, nineteen (35 per cent) had high school or less (fifteen had no diploma) and thirty-six (65 per cent) had at least some post-secondary education (fifteen had a college or university degree).[8] The self-report discrimination survey (described in chapter 4) reveals that more highly educated Indigenous interviewees reported higher numbers of racist incidents: those with high school or less reported an average of 7.8 incidents (median of 8.5), whereas those with at least some college or university reported an average of 12.6 incidents (median of 9). Among both groups, reported incidents ranged from subtle innuendos and exclusion to verbal and physical assaults. These findings do not necessarily mean that more highly educated Indigenous people *experience* more discrimination; perhaps they are just more aware of it or are better able to articulate it. Either way, these findings show that higher education does not prevent Indigenous people from facing discrimination.

Moreover, contrary to the ideological alignment hypothesis (Wodtke 2012), it seems that formal education does not diminish Indigenous peoples' support for radical or group-based strategies for change. If anything, Indigenous interviewees with post-secondary education had more positive attitudes towards Indigenous protesters, with the median rating increasing from 4 to 5 and the mean from 3.82 to 4.56. Well-educated Indigenous interviewees also expressed more elaborate justifications for Indigenous and treaty rights, including concepts like sovereignty, more detailed historical and structural explanations for poverty and health gaps, and numerous actions that should be taken to follow up on the residential school apology. While many Indigenous residents with less formal education agreed with such views, the point is that mainstream education does *not* appear to "heighten commitment to the dominant legitimizing ideology" (Wodtke 2012, 100), at least for most Indigenous interviewees (though, again, this may be a function of self-selection rather than education itself).

Overall, then, among the Rainy River District residents interviewed, formal education was associated with some significant improvements in settler attitudes, especially on measures of old-fashioned prejudice but also on more subtle measures, such as attributions for Indigenous poverty and opinions on follow-up action on the residential school apology. However, there was virtually no change on the most direct measures of perceived group threat (attitudes towards treaties and Indigenous protesters), suggesting that whites' sense of group position remained largely intact. Consistent with the ideological refinement perspective, moreover, some university-educated whites appeared congenial in public and responded to formal interviews in diplomatic ways, but they maintained their sense of superiority and entitlement and sometimes revealed racist attitudes "backstage" when they thought they could get away with it. Meanwhile, it appears mainstream education does little to diminish (and may even exacerbate) Indigenous peoples' encounters with racial discrimination. Contrary to the ideological alignment hypothesis, formal education was associated with greater rejection of the dominant white ideology, more support for Indigenous protesters, and more astute defences of Indigenous and treaty rights.

A New Kind of Education

> Much of the current state of troubled relations between Aboriginal and non-Aboriginal Canadians is attributable to educational institutions and what they have taught, or failed to teach, over many generations. Despite that history, or, perhaps more correctly, because of its potential, the Commission believes that education is also the key to reconciliation. (TRC 2015, 285)

Within and beyond the Rainy River District, education (like contact) is often portrayed as a virtual panacea. In its 2015 final report, the TRC, which spent six years organizing national events, conducting archival research, and gathering statements from more than six thousand residential school survivors, recommended, among other things, developing and implementing mandatory "age-appropriate curriculum on residential schools, Treaties, and Aboriginal peoples' historical and contemporary contributions to Canada," for all kindergarten to grade 12 students across the country (Call to Action 62). It also recommended funding for post-secondary institutions to train teachers on these subjects and on how to integrate Indigenous knowledges and teaching methods into the classroom. Further, it called on the federal government to eliminate the funding gap for on- and off-reserve schools and to "draft new Aboriginal education legislation with the full participation and informed consent of Aboriginal peoples" (Call to Action 10).

Many Rainy River District residents likely would support these recommendations. However, some described education as a bridge for different reasons. For some whites, education was a means to "help" Indigenous people succeed in mainstream Canada, a view that positions whites as the (superior) knowers/teachers. For many Indigenous residents, education could help *all* residents understand one another by enhancing knowledge about Indigenous cultures, treaties, and local histories. But many also distrusted the school system, especially given the legacy of attempted cultural genocide and Indigenous students' ongoing encounters with racism. Some believed that informal/extracurricular education and ongoing dialogue are more effective ways to improve group relations.

Yet none of these approaches may be sufficient to fully address the problem. At some point, settlers also need to "flip the lens" (Lee 2015) and examine their own assumptions and actions. Settlers need to understand that many of their beliefs help perpetuate or condone systemic racism and colonialism, something they often benefit from. Unless education leads to a deeper shift in attitudes, behaviours, and policies, it will not eliminate these structural inequities.

According to my data, then, formal education was associated with decreased old-fashioned prejudice and some reduction in laissez-faire attitudes among white residents. However, it had little or no impact on their underlying sense of group position. Whites with less formal education (who tended to work in forestry, agriculture, and other blue-collar sectors) were somewhat more agreeable to interviews; they prided themselves on their honesty and claimed to "tell it like it is"; some openly expressed racial slurs and stereotypes. Whites with a college or university education (who tended to work in white-collar or professional occupations) were more likely to decline interviews or refuse to return surveys, saying they wished to keep certain information "private." This is curious, given that more-educated, middle-class people are generally *more* likely to participate in research (Palys 1997). In this case, however, because I was upfront about my research topic, and because these more highly educated whites probably realized that some of their views might be interpreted by an educated outsider as "politically incorrect," they may have been less likely to participate and less forthcoming when they did.[9] Indeed, a few whites with post-secondary degrees who expressed positive attitudes towards Indigenous peoples in interviews later displayed laissez-faire or paternalistic attitudes or even overt prejudice in informal interactions (such as at parties or bars). On surveys, moreover, they were no less likely than whites with a high school education or less to resent Indigenous protesters and treaty rights asserters. If anything, on some measures, higher-educated whites displayed a *greater* sense of entitlement and threat.

Overall, these findings support the ideological refinement perspective within group position theory, which suggests that mainstream education does not enlighten, but rather "confers upon members of the dominant group an enhanced ability to justify current relations of inequality and subvert more radical challenges to their privileged social position" (Wodtke 2012, 83). However, it also must be noted that most of the (few) outspoken white advocates for Indigenous rights (including Right Relations Circle members) did have a post-secondary education, and all had learned, through university studies or by voluntarily seeking out information (from books, films, or Indigenous friends), a great deal about Indigenous peoples' historical and contemporary experiences and their own responsibilities as treaty people. Thus, education alone is insufficient, but certain forms of education – especially, perhaps, experiential learning – are plainly necessary for enabling settlers to think and act in antiracist, anticolonial ways.

Finally, there were important class and educational differences in the attitudes and behaviours of Indigenous peoples. Contrary to the ideological alignment hypothesis (Wodtke 2012), Anishinaabe and Métis residents with more formal education (i.e., university degrees) tended to be the staunchest defenders of Indigenous and treaty rights and provided compelling justifications for Indigenous sovereignty and group-based reparations. In contrast, the minority of Indigenous residents who endorsed laissez-faire ideologies (believing that everyone should be treated "the same" and that no follow-up action on the residential school apology is necessary) tended to be less well educated (having a high school diploma or less).[10]

Meanwhile, the economic success of some Indigenous people did not seem to deter white prejudice. Although some (Indigenous and non-Indigenous) residents suggested that, through mainstream education and economic success, Indigenous people might gain recognition and respect from whites, such achievements can also elicit feelings of competition and threat. Indeed, Indigenous interviewees with post-secondary education reported *more* experiences with discrimination than those with high school or less. Moreover, some white residents resented more educated Indigenous people for having "unfair advantages." Others expressed stereotypes about "greedy" and "corrupt" First Nations chiefs allegedly making millions while most of their band members languished in poverty.[11] While living in Fort Frances, I also heard at least half a dozen negative remarks by whites about a successful local Indigenous lawyer; meanwhile, successful white businessmen were routinely lauded as "Citizens of the Year." At the same time, more educated and affluent Indigenous residents, while respected by many fellow Indigenous community members, also reportedly faced jealousy and resentment from others who would "try to bring them down" – a phenomenon known as "crab syndrome" (see, e.g., Alfred 2009).

As noted in chapter 7, one reason why intergroup contact is insufficient to overcome whites' sense of group position and justifications for racial inequity is that Indigenous-settler interactions rarely involve direct conversations about "political" issues, including racism and colonialism. Perhaps better education and ongoing communication about such issues would make a difference. Yet, although interviewees frequently cited education as a bridge, the forms of education that most residents advocated are inadequate. Transformative and experiential education – which together provide a deeper understanding of Indigenous peoples' diverse experiences and cultures and of how historical injustices contribute to contemporary inequities, and which force settlers to reflect on their own assumptions and actions and ongoing treaty obligations – are necessary. But if the ultimate problem is the uneven balance of *power* rooted in settler colonialism, then simply "learning more about Indians" or "helping" Indigenous children assimilate to mainstream institutions will fail to transform the sense of group positions or the underlying structural inequities.

Chapter Nine

Racial Contestation and the Residential School Apology[*]

Two primary objectives of the Residential Schools system were to remove and isolate children from the influence of their homes, families, traditions and cultures, and to assimilate them into the dominant culture. These objectives were based on the assumption aboriginal cultures and spiritual beliefs were inferior and unequal. Indeed, some sought, as it was infamously said, "to kill the Indian in the child." Today, we recognize that this policy of assimilation was wrong, has caused great harm, and has no place in our country.

Prime Minister Stephen Harper, House of Commons, 2008

So said Prime Minister Stephen Harper as he stood before the House of Commons on 11 June 2008, to apologize to Indigenous peoples in Canada for the Indian residential school (IRS) system that the federal government funded and Christian churches operated across the country for more than a century.

Although rarely described as a bridge in my interviews, public apologies and reparations payments are often portrayed in academic and political discourse as vehicles for reconciliation. This chapter investigates how Rainy River District residents interpreted and responded to the federal government's IRS apology. In principle, an apology is an admission of guilt, an acknowledgment of wrongdoing. An official state apology therefore may undermine settlers' sense of group superiority. But what did this apology mean to Indigenous and non-Indigenous residents? To what extent did it alter the sense of group positions or repair relations at the local community level? To begin to answer these questions, I interviewed Indigenous and settler residents about their

---

[*] Excerpts from this chapter previously appeared in *Reading Sociology: Canadian Perspectives*, 2nd ed. (Denis 2011).

views on the apology, the associated monetary settlement, and ways to facilitate healing and reconciliation.

Despite some overlap in perspectives and within-group variations, Indigenous and white residents tended to frame the apology in incompatible ways. Although most residents agreed an apology was necessary, whites tended to view it as a final act of "closure," whereas Indigenous residents saw it as an early step in an ongoing "healing journey."[1] While most agreed that monetary compensation cannot erase survivors' pain, many whites felt it was excessive whereas Anishinaabe and Métis felt it was insufficient. Finally, when asked if follow-up action should be taken, a majority of whites said we should "stop dwelling on the past" and "just move on." In contrast, most Indigenous residents offered practical suggestions for healing, such as enhancing support for Indigenous-controlled health care, education, and cultural and language programs.

Theoretically, these conflicting interpretations can be understood as manifestations of a Canadian system of racial contestation (Bonilla-Silva 2003, 2010), an ongoing struggle for group positions (Blumer 1958; Bobo 1999) that is rooted in settler colonialism (Lowman and Barker 2015; Tuck and Yang 2012; Veracini 2010; Wolfe 2006). Many whites interpreted the apology in ways that supported their sense of group superiority; they suggested that Canada had acted morally by apologizing and offering compensation, and that if Indigenous people were still struggling, it was their own fault. The dominant Indigenous frame, by contrast, suggests that words alone are not enough; an apology becomes real by the actions that follow. Thus, although the federal IRS apology was arguably well crafted and delivered – including virtually all the contents and stylistic elements of an "effective" apology, as defined by sociolinguists and psychologists (Blatz, Schumann, and Ross 2009; Scher and Darley 1997) – it fell short of its stated goals. Genuine reconciliation will require a deeper transformation in social policies and practices, including *ongoing* recognition (Jenkins 1994; Taylor 1992) and restitution (Alfred 2005; Waziyatawin 2009) and respect for Indigenous self-determination and treaties (Corntassel and Holder 2008; Mackey 2013).

Official Apologies

A spate of "official apologies" for historical injustices by governments, churches, and other authorities in Canada and around the world has spawned a corresponding literature on the social psychological and political dynamics of apology (see, e.g., Gibney et al. 2008; Henderson and Wakeham 2013; Mookherjee et al. 2009; Nobles 2008). Simply put, an apology is a "speech act" that "acknowledges responsibility for an offense or grievance and expresses regret or remorse" (Lazare 2004, 23). From a sociological perspective, it is a form of "remedial work" that smooths over a social disruption by reaffirming belief in the violated norm(s) (Tavuchis 1991).

Several factors likely mediate the effectiveness of apologies, that is, whether they will be accepted by the target group and lead to healing, forgiveness, and reconciliation. Some scholars argue that the *content* of apologies shapes their effectiveness (Blatz, Schumann, and Ross 2009; James 2008; Scher and Darley 1997). Others emphasize the *process* by which an apology is delivered; to be meaningful, they say, the apology must be distinguished from daily routine by "a grand and well-publicized ceremony that acknowledges how the current government recognizes and condemns th[e] injustice, and values the minority group" (Blatz, 2008, 38). Still others take a *conditional* approach, arguing that apologies heal when they meet the psychological needs of the offended party, such as recognition that the offences were not their fault, assurance of safety in their relationships, an opportunity to see the offender suffer, reparations for the harm caused, restoration of their respect and dignity, and initiation of constructive dialogue (Lazare 2004). As Blatz, Schumann, and Ross (2009, 237) conclude, "different groups make different demands," and apologies should be "tailored to match the concerns of the victim group." Further contextual factors, such as timing, severity of the offence, prior levels of intergroup trust, and majority and minority group reactions, also could influence apology effectiveness (Blatz and Philpot 2010).

Particularly relevant in this regard are *Indigenous* criteria for apology and restitution. Although not discounting Western criteria, Regan (2010) suggests that, for most Indigenous peoples, an "authentic" apology is a "sacred act" that involves "storytelling, ceremony, and ritual" and is "inscribed in the oral traditions of the feast hall, the big house, or the circle" (183). The wronged party must have an opportunity to share their truths in this sacred space, and the process must be witnessed by individuals who listen deeply, remember the stories, and have the responsibility and authority to hold the apologizer(s) accountable. Nevertheless, if apologies are not accompanied by "substantive and structural changes that deal with power imbalances, land and resources," then, as Cree Saulteaux scholar Val Napoleon (2004) says, such stories, ceremonies, and rituals may be mere "window-dressing" (176, 184).

Racial Contestation, Recognition Politics, and Decolonization

A crucial problem is that apologies often occur in the context of *ongoing* processes of racial contestation, group positioning, and (de)colonization. Indigenous peoples are not just "previously victimized" groups

(Blatz, Schumann, and Ross 2009); they are *still* fighting for their political autonomy and their inherent and treaty rights. As such, while many Indigenous individuals may view apologies and monetary compensation as steps in the right direction, such actions will not achieve meaningful reconciliation so long as structural inequities and barriers to self-determination persist. Thus, Indigenous and allied scholars and activists increasingly reject "state-dominated reconciliation mechanisms" (Corntassel and Holder 2008, 465; Coulthard 2014), and argue that restitution – including the return of land and respect for Indigenous law and jurisdiction – is a "precondition" for "true reconciliation" (Alfred 2005, 151; Mackey 2013; Short 2005; Watts and King 2015; Waziyatawin 2009). Meanwhile, settlers may accept an apology as warranted (at least after the fact), but also use it to justify subsequent *inaction*. In other words, apologies set a precedent that can potentially be used to alter power relations (Lawn 2008; Nobles 2008) and restore mutual trust and respect (Gibney et al. 2008). Settlers, however, may also use apologies to *resist* fundamental changes in social policies and practices.

As previously discussed, colonization has created a hierarchical racial structure in Canada whereby whites enjoy "economic, political, social, and even psychological ... advantages" (Bonilla-Silva 2003, 65), often at Indigenous peoples' expense. According to Bonilla-Silva's racial contestation perspective, which is highly compatible with group position theory,[2] structural racial inequities are supported by a dominant racial ideology. Yet "although ... the ideas of the dominant race *tend* to be the dominant ideas in society, ideological rule over the subordinate race(s) ... is always at best partial, and is always contested" (67). There is an ongoing process of racial contestation. Thus, whereas most whites endorse laissez-faire racism or other ideologies seeking to justify racial inequities, most marginalized group members contest these ideologies and advocate for the redistribution of resources.

In this case, many Indigenous peoples are struggling for not only material and political resources but also the symbolic resources of recognition and respect. The IRS system was an assault on their dignity, an attempt to destroy them as a people. Thus, interactionist theories of identity may provide additional leverage for understanding responses to the IRS apology. From an interactionist perspective, ethno-national identities are always formed in a dialectic process of internal and external definition (Jenkins 1994).[3] As Canadian political philosopher Charles Taylor (1992, 1) puts it:

Our identity is partly shaped by recognition or its absence, often by the *mis*recognition of others, and so a person or group of people can suffer real damage, real distortion, if the people or society around them mirrors back to them a confining or demeaning or contemptible picture of themselves.

Recognition and respect for self-definitions and lived experiences may be just as important to many Indigenous people as the distribution of resources. Although this point receives little attention in the racial contestation framework (as developed by Bonilla-Silva), it is not necessarily mutually exclusive; both models emphasize the importance of *power relations* – one in shaping the allocation of material resources, the other in shaping the (mis)recognition of identities. While the former might predict a more positive response to monetary reparations and the latter a more positive response to apologies, both would agree that racial contestation and (mis)recognition are *ongoing* social processes.

For Indigenous peoples, the situation is more complex in that their self-defined identities are *inextricably linked* to their homelands and the resources contained therein. As Alfred and Corntassel (2005, 597) put it, "being Indigenous" is defined by attachment to one's homeland and by "the consciousness of being in struggle against ... colonization." Forced relocation from and destruction of Indigenous lands *is also an assault on Indigenous identities* – just as much as physical punishment for speaking one's language or practising one's ceremonies. Residential schools *were also a means of securing access to Indigenous lands and resources* – by removing children from their communities and attempting to indoctrinate them with ideologies of settler state supremacy. As Short (2005, 275) says, drawing on Nancy Frazer, "genuine 'recognition' of indigenous peoples (colonised without consent) must involve a redistribution of both political power and resources, which terminates not only their economic and social subordination but also the colonial relationship itself." The politics of apology and recognition, therefore, cannot be separated from the ongoing processes of racial contestation and (de)colonization.

Granted, some Indigenous scholars argue that recognition by the oppressor is not and should not be the primary goal. As Coulthard (2007, 442), drawing on Frantz Fanon, puts it, if "recognition is conceived as something that is ultimately 'granted' (Taylor 1993, 148) ... to a subaltern group or entity by a dominant group or entity," it will fail to transcend colonial power relations. What is necessary is "personal and collective *self*-affirmation ... Rather than remaining dependent on their oppressors for their freedom and self-worth ... the colonized must struggle to critically reclaim and revaluate the worth of *their own* histories, traditions, and cultures" (Coulthard 2007, 453; emphasis original).

From a sociological perspective, however, the *structural* conditions of the surrounding society may facilitate or hinder this process of "anti-colonial empowerment." Most Indigenous peoples today are highly interconnected with settler societies, and, given the military, political, and economic imbalance of power, settlers' responses matter. Indigenous peoples may "turn away" from Canada and "struggle for freedom on their own terms" (Coulthard 2007, 454), but their freedom will be stymied – by, for example, government approval of pipelines, mines, or clear-cuts on Indigenous lands – *unless* a critical mass of settlers also challenges "the background legal, political and economic framework of the colonial relationship" (451) and supports Indigenous and treaty rights. If settlers' sense of group superiority and entitlement prevails, however, paternalistic policies will continue to be imposed and both decolonization and reconciliation will remain a pipe dream, with or without apologies and cash settlements.

Racial Contestation and Residential Schools in the Rainy River District

As outlined in previous chapters, settler-Canadians, especially whites, have benefited from centuries of colonization, enabling them to live on Indigenous lands with their own (settler) governments. Although Indigenous peoples continue to be affected by intergenerational trauma (Bombay, Matheson, and Anisman 2014; Duran and Duran 1995; Wesley-Esquimaux and Smolewski 2004), they have been resurgent, reclaiming their identities, revitalizing their languages and traditions, and re-empowering their nations through land reclamation, economic development, and the restoration of traditional governance structures (see, e.g., Kino-nda-niimi 2014). Although still privileged as a group on standard socio-economic indicators, many whites feel *threatened* by Indigenous peoples' gains, portraying themselves as "victims" of "reverse discrimination" (Bobo and Tuan 2006).

These trends are pronounced in the Rainy River District because the local racialized structure has always been highly inequitable. At the time of my research, apart from First Nation chiefs and the president of the Métis Nation of Ontario, local political leaders (town councillors, mayors, federal and provincial representatives) were all white, as were major business leaders and town administrators.[4] Indigenous residents had less formal education and higher unemployment rates (Statistics Canada 2007) than whites, were more highly represented in local jails and child welfare facilities, and had lower incomes and poorer health.

These structural inequities are rooted in local historical and ongoing processes of colonization, including land dispossession, treaty violations, and residential schooling (see chapter 1). In Treaty No. 3 territory, there were six residential schools with an average of 685 "students" per year. On the Agency One reserve, adjacent to Fort Frances and Couchiching First Nation, St. Margaret's Residential School was operated by the Missionary Oblates of Mary Immaculate from 1906 to 1974.[5] At the time of the 2008 apology, an estimated twenty-four thousand survivors and their immediate family members lived in the region – 80 per cent of all Indigenous residents (Grand Council Treaty No. 3 2010; D.M. Kelly 2008). Although not all IRS experiences were uniformly negative (some survivors fondly recalled hockey games against white kids in town, and some staff were reportedly kind), the institution as a whole was genocidal (Palmater 2015; TRC 2015). Government and church officials neglected systemic problems, such as poorly constructed buildings, overcrowding, underfunding, unqualified and abusive teachers, and curricula oriented more around unpaid labour than learning (Auger 2005). Most survivors live with painful memories, including, in the St. Margaret's case, public beatings, brothers and sisters being physically separated, and children from Couchiching being able to see their mother washing dishes in her house through a school window, yet forbidden to go home and hug her at night. In Kenora, nutrition experiments were conducted on starving children (Mosby 2013). Sexual abuse was rampant (McLaren 2008). There are stories of young girls being raped and newborns buried alive, children running away and being caught and killed or freezing to death trying to find their way home. Such gruesome details are documented elsewhere (TRC 2015). My point here is that these experiences deeply wounded Indigenous individuals, families, and nations,[6] and help explain the socio-economic and health disparities, as well as the persisting mistrust and tensions in Indigenous-settler relations today.

At the same time, the local racial structure has been changing in ways that are likely to enhance whites' perceptions of group threat. As emphasized throughout this book, the growing Indigenous population, the declining white population, the revitalization of Indigenous languages and ceremonies, the assertion of Indigenous laws and policies, the opening of First Nations businesses, the settlement of land claims, and the indefinite shutdown of the Fort Frances mill have shifted the balance of power and destabilized the sense of group positions.

This context is essential for understanding residents' responses to the IRS apology. Although many Indigenous and white residents may not view themselves as engaged in "racial contestation," their group positions help shape their interpretations of events. The revised racial contestation framework outlined above suggests that while the apology may be meaningful for some Indigenous people, including IRS

Drawn by
George Snowball/
Naicatchewenin
Age 14
June 22, 1934

Figure 9.1 St. Margaret's Residential School. At the borders of Fort Frances and Couchiching First Nation, St. Margaret's Residential School was operated by the Missionary Oblates of Mary Immaculate from 1906 to 1974. This watercolour painting was displayed at the Fort Frances Museum residential school exhibit in the summer of 2008. Photo courtesy of the author.

survivors, many will question its sincerity in the absence of concrete follow-up actions to alter power relations and provide ongoing recognition of their identities and rights. Conversely, some whites will deny the necessity of an apology altogether. Others may accept it as "the right thing to do," but use it to justify subsequent inaction. Endorsing an apology and limited monetary compensation might even *reinforce* their sense of group superiority by "closing the door" on history: in their minds, they have taken the moral high ground by apologizing (through the prime minister) and helping fund reparations (through their taxes), thereby washing their hands of responsibility to Indigenous peoples. These predictions are largely confirmed by the data.

Contrasting Views on Canada's IRS Apology and Settlement

The primary data for this chapter derive from my interviews with seventy-two First Nations and Métis residents, including fourteen residential school survivors, and fifty-six white residents of the Rainy River District.[7] As part of the broader study, I asked participants about their views on the IRS apology, the associated monetary settlement, and ways to facilitate healing and reconciliation. These interviews were supplemented by ethnographic observation in the Fort Frances area, including my attendance at a local banquet hall on 11 June 2008 where dozens of residents gathered to watch the apology live on TV. I also participated in monthly meetings of the Right Relations Circle, which featured regular discussions about residential schools and their effects, film screenings (including *Muffins for Granny*, a 2006 documentary about residential school survivors by Anishinaabe filmmaker Nadia McLaren), and sharing circles with Indigenous and non-Indigenous residents.

Perspectives on the Apology

In many respects, the federal government's 2008 "Statement of Apology to former students of Indian Residential Schools" was masterfully crafted and delivered. Unlike the 1998 "Statement of Reconciliation," this was no mere "quasi-apology" (James 2008, 141). It included all ten elements that sociolinguists and social psychologists identify as being needed in an "effective" apology (Blatz, Schumann, and Ross 2009).[8] It expressed remorse ("we are sorry"); accepted responsibility ("on behalf of the Government of Canada and all Canadians"); admitted injustice ("this policy of assimilation was wrong"); acknowledged harm ("has caused great harm"); and promised forbearance ("has no place in our country"). It was accompanied by $2.8 billion in monetary compensation, based on a 2006 settlement agreement between the federal government, four churches, the Assembly of First Nations and other Indigenous organizations, and thousands of survivors who had been suing for damages.[9] The apology also praised Aboriginal peoples for their "courage" and "resilience," praised all Canadians for their "strong families, strong communities, and vibrant cultures and traditions," and dissociated the present system from historical injustice ("we are now joining you on this [healing] journey" and will "move forward together in partnership").[10] It requested, but did not demand, forgiveness.

The ceremonial process also befitted "a historical landmark" (Thompson 2008, 42). The apology was delivered by the prime minister in the House of Commons and recorded in the parliamentary record. All three opposition leaders offered their own apologies. Five prominent Indigenous leaders, arranged in a circle at the centre of the House, had the opportunity to respond.[11] Survivors and their families were invited to bear witness. Smudging and other Indigenous rituals were permitted in the House. The event was covered extensively by the media. What did ordinary Indigenous and non-Indigenous people make of all this?

On the day of the apology, across Canada large groups gathered in community centres, hockey arenas, and band offices. In Fort Frances, I attended the "Hope, Honour, Healing" event at the Rendezvous banquet hall, just steps from the former St. Margaret's Residential School, with over one hundred Anishinaabe and Métis residents and a handful of white supporters, to collectively prepare for, watch, and reflect as the prime minister said "sorry" and Indigenous dignitaries responded on live national television. As the sweet scent of burning sage wafted across the hall, some cried, others cheered, and still others fled, too emotional to bear the words they had so longed to hear (Field notes, June 2008).

Down the street, at the local public health unit, my partner Lisa asked some white co-workers in the break room if they had seen the apology. "What apology?" one replied. "For the residential schools," she said. "Oh, that? We didn't go … What were residential schools again?" And they returned to their discussion of cookbooks.

This anecdote illustrates an important point: while most Indigenous residents viewed the apology as a historic event, were highly engaged with it, and made sure to watch or listen, many settlers were indifferent and only paid attention after the fact, if at all.[12] These contrasting levels of engagement reflect the extent to which each group viewed the apology as identity-relevant. The widespread belief among settlers that residential schools were merely an "Aboriginal issue" that did not concern them (other than the taxes used to fund reparations) only underscored Indigenous peoples' feelings of non-recognition and reinforced the status quo.

When later asked how they felt about the apology, some Indigenous interviewees were positive, others were negative, and the majority were ambivalent (see table 9.1). Approximately 19 per cent said it was what they wanted to hear and that it would help them heal. Another 13 per cent were so wounded by residential school or its intergenerational effects that, they said, no matter what anyone said or did, it might never be enough; they rejected the apology as "a bunch of BS." Yet, the vast majority of Anishinaabe and Métis (65 per cent) gave mixed and nuanced responses. They said things like:

1 The apology was "a long time coming," and is an "early step" in our "healing journey."
2 We'd like to believe it was "heartfelt," but will have to "wait and see" if the government "makes good" on it and assess its "sincerity" by the "actions" that follow.
3 If settler-Canadians live out the apology, over time, then perhaps we can "forgive but never forget."[13]

Table 9.1 Residential School Attendance and Perspectives on the Residential School Apology and Settlement among Indigenous and White Interviewees, N = 128

	Indigenous interviewees (N = 72) (%)	White interviewees (N = 56) (%)
Residential school attendance		
Attended residential school	19	0
At least one immediate family member (parent, sibling, or spouse) attended residential school	68	2
At least one extended family member attended residential school	85	8
Perspectives on the apology		
Predominantly positive (apology was "good" or should be accepted)	19	41
Predominantly negative (apology was meaningless or should be rejected)	13	3.6
Mixed (apology was an early step, necessary but insufficient, had good and bad aspects, or should be judged by follow-up action)	65	25
Indifferent (don't care, not paying attention)	1.4	13
Unnecessary (Why should PM apologize for something he didn't do?)	0	23
Perspectives on the settlement		
Compensation fair or adequate	8.3	43
Compensation not enough	47	13
Compensation too much	0	31
Indifferent about compensation	0	5.6
Compensation unnecessary (Why should taxpayers pay for something they didn't do?)	0	25
Money won't cure the pain	75	59
Negative stereotypes about uses of money	13	19
Applied for compensation – self	19	0
Applied for compensation – close family member	58	5.6
Eligible for compensation but did not apply – self or close family member	19	0
What, if anything, should be done to follow up on the apology?[1]		
Just move on	9.7	55
Governments, churches, and/or local residents should take specific follow-up actions	82	36
Don't know/vague response	8.3	8.9
Mentions TRC	13	7.1
Sceptical of TRC	13	1.8

Note: Some column subtotals do not sum to 100% because responses are not mutually exclusive.
[1] A Fort Frances Times online poll, 18–24 June 2008, similarly asked: "Does the residential school apology need to be followed by concrete action?" Out of 217 total responses, 37% said yes and 63% said no.

After centuries of broken promises, most Indigenous peoples were unwilling to accept a political apology at face value, no matter how "beautifully worded." While many considered it to be the first official acknowledgement of their suffering, for them recognition is an *ongoing* process and a state apology is only one component.[14]

Some whites (25 per cent) shared these mixed sentiments, viewing the apology as "necessary but insufficient." Another 41 per cent expressed surface acceptance.[15] However, their responses were often short and defensive and their wording negative. For example, a white male millwright said, "I don't have a problem with that." "When you do something wrong, you should apologize, right?" added a white female store manager.

What does this abruptness and defensiveness mean? When probed further, some of these "positive" responders said (paraphrasing): "We've apologized. It's done. What more do they want? Move on!" In other words, the apology was "good" because, in their minds, it put the issue to rest and, as mainstream media routinely described it and as Henderson and Wakeham (2013) argue it was designed to do, closed the door on a "sad chapter in history."

A substantial minority of whites expressed indifference (13 per cent) or rejected the need for an apology altogether (23 per cent). "Why should [the prime minister] apologize for something he didn't do?" asked a younger white millworker. A small businessman in his sixties turned visibly angry: "I never had nothin' to do with them going to that school!" For years, such "storylines" have helped justify the status quo.[16] The fact that all four federal parties (Conservative, Liberal, New Democratic, and Bloc Québécois) publicly apologized makes it increasingly difficult to sustain these storylines. As will become clear, however, such rationalizations may no longer be necessary, as settler-Canadians have constructed new ways to defend their power and privileges without necessarily rejecting the apology. Moreover, the surface acceptance or defensiveness of many whites contrasted sharply with the more critical or cautiously optimistic outlook of most Indigenous residents.

In short, although opinions varied within the Indigenous and white populations, the modal responses differed in content, tone, and style – in ways expected by the revised racial contestation framework.

Perspectives on the Settlement

Much the same can be said about reactions to the monetary settlement. Just as most white and Indigenous residents agreed an apology was necessary, there was a high consensus that money alone cannot relieve the pain. However, the *meaning* of the compensation differed between groups (see table 9.1).

Some Anishinaabe and Métis (<10 per cent) viewed it as a positive gesture, more important for its symbolic rather than monetary value. Far more (47 per cent) complained that it was "not enough" and still others (10 per cent) called it "hush money," saying "the government is just trying to buy us off." A few interviewees made direct comparisons to the case of Maher Arar (a Canadian citizen who was wrongfully detained and deported to Syria where he was tortured for alleged terrorist links), viewing it as unfair that he received $10.5 million in compensation, when IRS survivors received an average of $19,412 (through Common Experience Payments).[17] Some added that no amount of cash could ever replace their dignity, and that it would be insulting to think otherwise. As one survivor put it, "They don't have enough money in Ottawa to pay me."Such comments suggest an "incommensurability" problem (Espeland and Stevens 1998; Tuck and Yang 2012). Although governments and resource extraction companies may try to compensate for the destruction of life, land, and dignity with money, many Indigenous peoples believe this is impossible. To highlight this, I recorded in my October 2008 field notes a Cree (Nehiyawak) prophecy written on a poster in one resident's living room:

> Only after the last tree has been cut down,
> Only after the last river has been poisoned,
> Only after the last fish has been caught,
> Only then will you find that money cannot be eaten.

A minority of whites (13 per cent) agreed that the settlement was "too little, too late." Yet their modal response (43 per cent) was that the compensation was fair or adequate. As with the apology, however, their wording and tone were often defensive and negative. For example, a municipal councillor said, "I don't have an issue with that." Unlike Indigenous interviewees, many whites (31 per cent) also complained that the money was either "too much" or should not have been given at all because:

1 Why should we, as "taxpayers," pay for "our ancestors' mistakes"?
2 Residential school teachers had "good intentions."[18]
3 Indigenous peoples' stories of abuse are exaggerated.
4 Residential school attendees are "all dead now anyway."[19]

A substantial minority of white (19 per cent) and Indigenous (13 per cent) interviewees also opposed compensating individuals who might

Table 9.2 Reported Uses of Settlement Money by Indigenous Interviewees and/or Close Family Members Who Received Compensation[1]

Reported uses	No. of cases
Shared it with family members (e.g., helped pay for children or grandchildren's education, supported relatives with chronic health conditions)	12
Bought a new motor vehicle (car, truck, or van)	8
"Paid the bills"/ paid off debt	5
Made house repairs or bought new furniture	4
Took a family vacation	4
Deposited in savings account	4
Used it for daily living expenses (to supplement pension or employment income)	3
Bought a new canoe	1
Bought a new computer	1
Bought food for low-income community members	1
Went gambling	1
Bought a new television	1

[1] In order of prevalence, not mutually exclusive.

"drink or gamble it away," which reflects well-known stereotypes. Yet when asked what they had done (or would do) with the money, survivors' most common responses were sharing it with family and buying a new motor vehicle (see table 9.2).

Nearly one in five Indigenous interviewees – including a lawyer who assisted with claim forms – also criticized the application process, describing friends or relatives who were eligible for compensation but did not apply because it was "too painful": being forced to list the abuses one experienced as a child, and in some cases never openly discussed before, can be re-traumatizing. Some had decided it was more trouble than it was worth.[20]

In any case, the IRS "issue" is *not* about money for most Indigenous peoples. It is about recognition – not only of this wrongdoing, but of their identities and rights on an ongoing basis. It is about settlers acknowledging their complicity in colonialism and taking responsibility through corrective action. It is about healing emotional and spiritual wounds, restoring dignity and respect, and working towards reconciliation at individual, familial, and intergroup levels.

Thus, although apologies might be more effective when accompanied by monetary compensation (Minow 2002), sometimes even their combination is insufficient. While eloquent speeches and individual cheques might help some survivors heal, reconciliation requires meeting the specific needs of the wronged group (Blatz, Schumann, and Ross 2009). In this case, it cannot be separated from the wider system of racial contestation (Bonilla-Silva 2010) and the ongoing struggle for decolonization and self-determination (Corntassel and Holder 2008; Short 2012). Until Indigenous identities and rights are recognized on Indigenous terms, and until a critical mass of settler-Canadians commits to an ongoing process of just and equitable relationship-building, as per the original peace and friendship treaties, reconciliation will remain elusive.

Perspectives on Next Steps

> In a relationship that has included physical and emotional abuse, apologies are never enough. Action and atonement are required ... The measure of the Government's apology of June 11, 2008, and those of the churches, will be whether their past behaviours toward Aboriginal people will have changed beyond the closing of the schools, the words of sorrow, and the payment of money. (Justice Murray Sinclair, chair of the TRC, October 2012)

As part of the IRS settlement agreement, the federal government in 2009 appointed a Truth and Reconciliation Commission with a five-year mandate to "witness, support, promote and facilitate truth and reconciliation events" and "create as complete an historical record as possible of the [residential school] system" for "public ... use and study" (http:// www.trc.ca/about-us/our-mandate.html#one).[21] After a bumpy start, including the resignation of its first chair, the commission held its first national event in Winnipeg in June 2010.

Yet when asked if anything should be done to follow up on the apology, only one in ten interviewees mentioned the TRC.[22] Those who did were sceptical of its structure and mandate. Some worried that TRC events would be a form of "entertainment reconciliation," where Indigenous peoples tell sad stories and settlers pity them, but nothing really changes. Genuine truth and reconciliation, they said, would also involve confession by residential school teachers, priests and nuns, police officers and bush pilots who transported children from loving families to cold and lonely institutions, and policymakers who designed the schools or neglected to close them despite the reported abuse and abysmal living conditions. Settler Canadians must acknowledge how they have benefited from the system, at Indigenous peoples' expense, and find ways to apply the apology on a local level.[23] Otherwise, the work of truth and reconciliation will be incomplete.

More generally, the sharpest gap in understandings emerged around the question of "next steps" (see table 9.1). While a majority of white interviewees (55 per cent) said we should "stop dwelling on the past" and "just move on," most Anishinaabe and Métis (82 per cent) described specific actions that governments, churches, and other individuals and organizations should do to live out the apology. For a retired white teacher: "It's part of our history. They've done their apology. Why beat a dead horse?" Her adult daughter agreed: "Let it go and move on." A white male childcare worker similarly stated: "I think they should leave it alone and let it die. It's been dealt with. They've been compensated. It's done."

In contrast, many Indigenous and a few non-Indigenous residents said the apology would be seen as sincere *only if* the government honoured its treaties, implemented the UN Declaration on the Rights of Indigenous Peoples,[24] respected Indigenous self-determination, acknowledged the unmarked graves of children who died in residential schools, compensated survivors of day schools and the Sixties Scoop, filled the chasm in education and child welfare funding, and ensured clean drinking water in all First Nation communities. In their view, the IRS system and its intergenerational effects could not be separated from these persisting structural inequities or the wider process of (de)colonization.[25]

Many Indigenous interviewees also recommended increased funding for Indigenous healing services and cultural and language programs to revitalize the very things residential schools sought to destroy.[26] One woman of mixed descent said:

I think they could have spent the money on language camps or ways for people to revive their culture ... I think that in order to get it back children would have to be immersed in it 24/7, just like the way they were immersed in it in residential school to get rid of it.

At a local level, there were concerns that the Fort Frances public schools did not pause to watch the apology on TV and that town council and the local Catholic church had not offered their own apologies. When asked his views, a municipal leader replied:

No, I don't think we should [do anything else]. I think we [*pause*] – I think they've done a good job. They've apologized and, you know, we have to get on with life.

These responses exemplify laissez-faire racist ideology and illustrate the tendency of many settlers to distance themselves from the issue and deny responsibility. Further, when I requested an interview from an older white resident who had, according to two sources, worked at a residential school, she denied it and told me to "find somebody else" (Field notes, fall 2008).

In sum, white and Indigenous residents tended to express divergent views on how to deal with the IRS legacy. Many whites thought that if residential schools caused harm, Indigenous people should be paid off, once and for all, so that everyone could "get on with life." They believed that the federal and church apologies and monetary compensation should suffice and that demanding more was "greedy." Such laissez-faire views leave structural inequities intact, thereby supporting whites' sense of group superiority. Conversely, to say that more should be done to rectify inequities might undermine settler-Canadians' positive self-image as "fair" and "generous" people who have "worked hard" for their resources and privileges.

In contrast, most Anishinaabe and Métis residents said that healing and reconciliation are ongoing processes; rather than "once-and-for-all" payments, they sought fundamental changes in their relationships with Canada. For them, this meant both resource redistribution (including the return of land and political authority) and lasting recognition of their identities and rights. The two are intertwined. To honour treaties, for example, means acknowledging Indigenous peoples' unique relationships to Canada, but also fixing funding inequities and respecting Indigenous nations' right to make decisions about their own lands. These issues cannot be separated from residential schools because they all stem from the same settler colonial system that has sought not only to destroy Indigenous cultures and replace them with Euro-Christian alternatives, but also to seize Indigenous lands and debilitate Indigenous governments (Mackey 2013). The divergent perspectives of Indigenous and white residents on reconciliation were consistent with the revised racial contestation framework, which posits an ongoing struggle for material, political, and symbolic resources that is most clearly manifested in response to rare "big events" (Blumer 1958, 6), such as the 2008 IRS apology.

Within-Group Differences in Perspectives

Although many white residents said it was "time to move on" (55 per cent), a substantial minority (36 per cent) believed that more should be done to support residential school survivors and Indigenous communities generally. Conversely, although most Indigenous residents advocated follow-up action (82 per cent), a minority (9.7 per cent) agreed with their white neighbours that the "past is past" and should be left alone. What explains these intragroup variations?

Racial contestation theory cannot answer this question because it is formulated entirely at the intergroup level (Bonilla-Silva 2010). However, the complementary group position model (Blumer 1958; Bobo 1999) is amenable to individual-level predictions to the extent that the *sense* of group position varies within groups. Settlers who express a stronger sense of group position (i.e., more intense feelings of group superiority and perceived threat from Indigenous peoples) should be more likely to endorse the "move on" sentiment. Conversely, Indigenous people who express a stronger sense of group position should be more likely to advocate follow-up actions (i.e., resource redistribution).

Although a comprehensive analysis is beyond the scope of this chapter, I did calculate the raw correlations between interviewees' responses to the "next steps" question and a range of demographic and attitudinal measures. The former responses were collapsed into a dummy variable where "1" meant emphasizing the "move on" sentiment. The latter variables included age, gender, education, political party affiliation, spouse's race/ethnicity, intergroup friendships, experiences with racial discrimination, standard measures of prejudice, and, perhaps most relevant, a "group competition" survey, comprising five questions that assessed (on a seven-point scale) the extent to which interviewees perceived Indigenous and white values and interests as conflicting, and a "feeling thermometer," measuring how warm or cold they felt towards twenty relevant individuals and groups. According to past research, these questions are reliable and valid indicators of perceived group threat and are strongly associated with laissez-faire racist policy orientations (Bobo 1999; Bobo and Tuan 2006).

If group position theory is correct, white individuals with a stronger sense of group position should be more likely to view the apology as a final act of closure (or perhaps even as unnecessary) and thus endorse "moving on." The data support this prediction. Specifically, white residents who expressed higher levels of group threat were significantly more likely to advocate "moving on" rather than taking follow-up action. This finding held for both those with higher scores on the group competition survey and those with colder feelings towards "threatening" subgroups, such as Indigenous protesters.[27]

Although few Indigenous interviewees agreed it was time to "move on," the individuals who did express this view shared some common characteristics. In particular, all seven had close white friends and none had a post-secondary degree. Such individuals may be more susceptible to internalizing racist ideologies or colonial mentalities and therefore to endorsing the dominant white perspective on the IRS apology (among other issues). In contrast, Indigenous residents who reported more lifetime experiences with discrimination and who identified as "traditional" were significantly more likely to call for follow-up action. Such individuals may be more aware of the intergenerational effects of residential schools and more invested, identity-wise, in the ongoing struggle for decolonization.

Curiously, however, there was no association between Indigenous peoples' scores on the group competition survey and their response to the "next steps" question. This may have been because most Anishinaabe and Métis residents were not seeking to *reverse* group positions; their goal, rather, was to restore equity and balance to their relationships with Canada. The standard group position measures might have had a different meaning for them. Alternatively, perhaps too few Indigenous interviewees endorsed "moving on" for any association to appear in the data.

Overall, these findings provide partial support for group position theory, which may be applied at the individual level to complement the racial contestation perspective highlighted in this chapter.

The Influence of Opinion Leaders

According to Blumer (1958), the sense of group position underlying racial prejudice is formed mainly in the public arena, with a focus on big emotional events and the disproportionate influence of governments and interest groups. Thus, the "storylines" (Bonilla-Silva 2003, 2010) used by Indigenous and white residents to justify their positions on the IRS apology should tend to echo and build on those of political leaders and activists in their respective communities. Although the focus of this book precludes a detailed analysis, it is important to note that a brief review of newspaper articles from local (*Fort Frances Times, Kenora Daily Miner, Thunder Bay Chronicle*) and national (*CBC, Globe and Mail, Toronto Star*) sources in the weeks preceding and following the apology supports this assertion.

For example, in an open letter to the prime ministe, published in the *Toronto Star* on 22 April 2008, Assembly of First Nations national chief Phil Fontaine called the apology a "first step toward reconciliation." On the day of the apology, Treaty No. 3 grand chief Diane Kelly wrote, "The acknowledgement by the Federal Government provides us the prospect to *initiate* a meaningful dialogue and disclosure as the historic Truth and Reconciliation [Commission] *begins* the daunting task of recording the stories of those impacted by this destructive federal policy and to *work toward* a positive relationship of mutual respect" (D.M. Kelly 2008; emphasis added). In contrast, local Liberal member of Parliament (MP) Ken Boshcoff said he hoped the apology would bring "closure" (J. Kelly 2008). The day before the apology, Conservative MP Pierre Poilievre questioned whether Canada was "getting value for all of this money" being spent on IRS survivors: "My view is that we need to engender the values of hard work and independence and self-reliance ... More money will not solve it" (CBC 2008). As one Indigenous interviewee put it, such "backhanded" comments quickly raised doubts about the sincerity of the apology.

Thus, although it is impossible to specify with these data the extent to which political leaders follow or shape public opinion, there is a clear association between the dominant messages of Indigenous and settler politicians and those of Indigenous and white residents, respectively. In both cases, the modal interpretations of the apology and appropriate follow-up actions diverged in ways that reflect ongoing processes of racial contestation, group positioning, and (de)colonization.

The Limits of Racial Contestation Theory

Despite its merits, the racial contestation perspective cannot fully explain responses to official apologies. It must be revised to consider the (mis)recognition of identities, along with the (re)distribution of resources. As some survivors said, no amount of money could compensate for the assault on their dignity. In addition to increased funding for social programs and infrastructure, Indigenous peoples require ongoing acknowledgment of their unique identities and rights as a condition for their reconciliation with and trust in Canada. This is understandable from an interactionist perspective, where identities are formed through the dialectic interplay of internal and external definition and thus mediated by power relations.

Racial contestation theory also must consider that North American society is not only racialized but settler colonial. Beyond an equitable distribution of resources and opportunities within Canada, genuine recognition of Indigenous identities would mean honouring nation-to-nation treaties and respecting Indigenous sovereignty.

Finally, racial contestation theory does not explain the substantial minority of settlers who agree that an apology and compensation are insufficient and that more should be done to address the IRS legacy and colonization generally. Although settlers who express lower levels of group threat are more likely to endorse follow-up action, it is unclear how some individuals develop an alternative sense of group position in the first place.[28]

Conclusion: The Apology from a Social Psychological Perspective

Social psychological research suggests that apologies can heal by improving trust in and attitudes towards the offending party (Blatz and Philpot 2010). In this case, many Indigenous residents wanted to believe the apology was "heartfelt"; two days before, an Anishinaabe man told me the news of an apology was "music to my ears." Yet, after hearing the prime minister's speech, he and many other Indigenous people had difficulty believing it and said they would judge its sincerity by the government's actions. In many cases, interviewees' hopes were undermined by contradictory subsequent messages from the apologizing government, including Prime Minister Harper's claim at a September 2009 press conference that Canada has "no history of colonialism." Thus, although public acknowledgment of wrongdoing is important (both to correct the historical record and as a benchmark against which to judge future action), the sincerity of this apology will remain doubtful and its ability to restore trust limited, so long as both the government and settler-Canadians fail to live out the apology through action.

It is difficult to forgive historical atrocities. My data confirm past research showing little or no association between government apologies (or monetary reparations) and willingness to forgive (Blatz and Philpot 2010). Some IRS survivors said they had forgiven individual perpetrators long before the federal apology. One told a touching story of how his former abuser (a Roman Catholic nun) reached out to him on her deathbed, apologizing for her sins and begging for forgiveness; he said he already had forgiven her. Other Indigenous residents said they were not ready to forgive. As Lazare (2004) suggests, a period of withholding forgiveness, which leaves the offender temporarily vulnerable, can be important for restoring balance to relationships. Whether granted or withheld, the power to forgive is that of Indigenous peoples alone. Moreover, as Coulthard (2014) emphasizes, righteous anger can motivate collective action. From this perspective, forgiving settlers prematurely may be a mistake, as it could sap the motivation to fight for ongoing justice.

Finally, although apologies may have the potential to shift "historical consciousness and collective identity within settler society" (Lawn 2008, 20), such outcomes are unlikely if settlers remain disengaged or interpret apologies in ways that reinforce their sense of group position. Indeed, apologizing might relieve dominant group members' guilt (Blatz 2008), but also have the insidious effect of making it easier to justify subsequent *inaction*. Surface acceptance of apologies can mask this deeper problem. If collective guilt is a predictor of support for progressive social policies, as some research suggests (Branscombe and Doosje 2004), then alleviating guilt through apology may be counterproductive if it inhibits follow-up action. In this case, settlers with a sense of group superiority and entitlement might point to the apology and compensation to relieve their guilt and justify the remaining social problems faced by Indigenous peoples as "their own fault." Settlers may cling to stolen land and resources, failing to see the connection between residential schools and the wider process of colonization. In the long run, such reactions inhibit reconciliation, whatever the government's intentions.

Addendum

Since 2009, Indigenous residents with whom I have kept in touch have become increasingly frustrated with Canada's failure to live up to the IRS apology. As expressed during public presentations of this chapter in Fort Frances in 2012, many residents viewed the apology as yet another "broken promise" that raised hopes and then dashed them. Under the Harper government (2006–15), not only was there a lack of meaningful action to "make good" on the apology, but the government cut Indigenous health funding, gutted environmental assessment processes, rejected calls for a public enquiry into the nearly twelve hundred missing and murdered Indigenous women across Canada, withheld residential school documents from the TRC, delayed land claim negotiations, and spent millions on legal fees to defend its underfunding of First Nation schools and child welfare agencies. In early 2013, at the height of the Idle No More movement – triggered by unilateral federal legislation, including fourteen bills affecting Indigenous peoples without their consent, which some dubbed a twenty-first-century "White Paper" (Palmater 2013) – some Anishinaabe, including young activists from the Rainy River District, symbolically burned a copy of the IRS apology on the streets of Winnipeg.

At the same time, most Indigenous people distinguish potential supporters and allies from the ruling party and political system and emphasize the importance of ongoing relationship-building at the grass-roots level. Although no official TRC event was organized in Fort Frances, events took place in Sioux Lookout, Thunder Bay, and Winnipeg (all in 2010). Some survivors and family members from the Rainy River District participated in these gatherings and found it empowering to share their stories and (re)connect with other survivors; some families reportedly grew closer together (see, e.g., Kinew 2015).

Yet the impact of this process on the broader Canadian public remains unclear. Two years after the federal apology, nearly 50 per cent of non-Aboriginal urban Canadians (23 per cent in Thunder Bay and 25 per cent in Winnipeg) said they had never "read or heard anything about Indian residential schools" (Environics 2010, 11), and the percentage of Canadians who believed that "most of the problems of native peoples are brought on by themselves" increased to a record high of 60 per cent in 2013 (Ipsos Reid 2013, 2). The TRC's (2015, 5) final report, which described the IRS system as a tool of "cultural genocide" and issued ninety-four Calls to Action, received extensive media coverage and seemed to enhance public awareness (Angus Reid 2015). Although a new Liberal government was elected in 2015, and Prime Minister Justin Trudeau promised to implement all ninety-four Calls to Action, much remains to be done, and the government has backtracked on key promises (Palmater 2017). As of this writing, most white residents of the Rainy River District have not participated in healing and reconciliation initiatives. School curricula await significant changes to make local Indigenous histories, cultures, and languages a more central component for all students. And the Town of Fort Frances continues to litigate over Point Park, claiming ownership of land that it leased from the Agency One First Nations for ninety-nine years.

All these developments reiterate that the processes of racial contestation and (de)colonization are ongoing. While the apology and settlement were important steps for some, they have done little to address structural inequities or the attitudes and assumptions that underpinned the residential school system. Many settler-Canadians maintain an "us versus them" group-positioning lens and laissez-faire or paternalistic attitudes. Meanwhile, rather than awaiting validation from settlers, many Indigenous peoples – including Anishinaabe and Métis in the Rainy River District – are increasingly focused, as Coulthard (2014) would advocate, on rebuilding their own institutions, revitalizing their languages and traditions, asserting their rights, enforcing their laws on their lands, and recognizing and taking pride in themselves.

Chapter Ten

The Benefits and Challenges of Collective Action: "We Can Work Together If We Want to Work Together"

If the liberal strategies of contact, education, and apologies are insufficient for dismantling racism and colonialism in Canada, what are the prospects for social change through collective action in light of my analysis of the social psychology of settler perceptions of group threat? According to Cliff Atleo Jr, citing Dene scholar Glen Coulthard (2014), "every major 'victory,' concession, or negotiation in the history of Canadian-Indigenous relations has come as a result of some form of direct action" (Atleo 2014, 190). Although not without risks and limitations, organized protests and other forms of collective action have often been necessary to gain attention, bring governments to the table, and generate meaningful change in Indigenous-settler relations. It is Indigenous intellectuals and activists, of course, who have taken the lead in the current wave of resistance and resurgence as they have done for more than 150 years. This chapter employs data and insights from my local case study to engage larger debates about Indigenous-led activism with a focus on the possibilities and challenges of transforming group positions and engaging settlers in a politics of decolonization.

When asked about intergroup bridges, Rainy River District residents discussed at least two types of collective action: (1) joining together and supporting one another in times of crisis; (2) more explicit antiracist and anticolonial activism. The former type has been demonstrated on multiple occasions throughout the district's history. Under certain conditions, Indigenous and non-Indigenous residents have collaborated to resolve immediate crises. Yet while they build trust and respect and often generate solidarity against a common enemy (e.g., government), such actions have rarely changed the policies or institutions that systematically advantage settlers and marginalize Indigenous peoples. Although this form of collective action may reduce overt prejudice, it alone does not eliminate group positioning or structural inequities.

Activism that more directly targets racism and colonialism may have more potential to alter power relations and realign identities and interests, but it is historically less common in the Rainy River District. It also entails significant challenges, including (often) internal division over strategies and goals, the reproduction of paternalistic relations within Indigenous-settler alliances, and racist backlash from the settler public, as group position theory would predict. It sometimes fails to achieve concrete change; often, however, it is the only thing that does achieve change.

After briefly reviewing relevant literature on Indigenous resistance and resurgence and the potential of collective action, I will illustrate the above benefits and challenges by briefly describing several recent cases of collective action in the Rainy River District, including joint efforts to deal with floods and government meddling, as well as organized actions to specifically target racism, land dispossession, and other colonial injustices.

Indigenous Resistance and Resurgence and the Potential of Collective Action

Indigenous peoples have always resisted colonization and sought to maintain control over their lands and lives, usually peacefully at first and sometimes by taking up arms as a last resort. Before the mid-twentieth century, most resistance was highly localized, a response to attempted land theft and assimilation policies. Tactics ranged from overt confrontation (as in the Red River and Northwest rebellions), to group-based negotiation (as in the numbered treaty discussions), to the solicitation of domestic and international allies (as in Haudenosaunee Chief Deskaheh's trip to the League of Nations in 1923), to more surreptitious acts (such as continuing banned traditional governance practices and ceremonies underground).

After the Second World War, a pan-Indigenous movement began to emerge, not only in Canada but around the world. National and treaty-area Indigenous political organizations formed to protect Indigenous and treaty rights and promote better socio-economic conditions. These new organizations, and this new sense of pan-Indigenous identity, facilitated the cross-national response to the 1969 White Paper and solidarity actions by First Nations across Canada during the 1990 Oka standoff. Many Indigenous people in Canada also participated in the American Indian Movement in the United States and were inspired by decolonization movements abroad.

As noted in chapter 1, Indigenous peoples in Treaty No. 3 Territory have taken organized political action to assert and defend their rights.

Anishinaabe leaders bargained hard in treaty negotiations (1869–73) and formally complained to Ottawa, via letters and petitions, when their treaty was violated. More recently, every First Nation in the Rainy River District has filed at least one land claim, and several have had land returned or received monetary compensation. While First Nations in the north of Treaty No. 3 territory have a reputation for more militant action, including blockades and even an armed occupation (see below), organized protests and activist groups have been less prominent in the Fort Frances area, at least until recently.

The question to be considered here is whether such collective action can serve as an effective remedy for racism and colonialism, potentially realigning group positions and advancing social justice, or whether it burns more bridges than it builds.

One complication is that collective action takes multiple forms and may be pursued by Indigenous peoples alone or in collaboration with settler-allies. Beyond direct protests and social activism against racism and colonialism or for Indigenous and treaty rights, collective action also may include more general cases of residents working together in a crisis or organizing for a common purpose. As will be seen below, different forms of collective action may have different benefits and challenges with respect to improving Indigenous-settler relations.

An important ongoing debate germane to this discussion concerns the strategic value of disruption. According to Frances Fox Piven (2006; 2011), the only way that people who lack financial resources and influence in conventional politics can create meaningful change is through disruptive action. Although policy change and more constructive forms of engagement also may be required, at some point the poor and oppressed must

> rise up in anger and hope, defy the rules that ordinarily govern their lives, and ... disrupt the workings of the institutions in which they are enmeshed. The drama of such events, combined with the disorder that results, propels new issues to the center of political debate [and often stimulates reform]. (Piven 2006, 1)

Examples of such action include boycotts, sit-ins, traffic tie-ups, strikes, and mass rallies. In this view, these tactics are effective precisely *because* they create "commotion among bureaucrats, excitement in the media, dismay among influential segments of the community, and strain for political leaders" (Piven 2011, 17). Indeed, many of the gains of the labour, civil rights, LGBTQ, feminist, and other social movements were achieved only after the use of such strategies of disruption (granted, the gains have often been less radical than activists would have liked).

Still, Piven's thesis is controversial even among social movement scholars, who more often emphasize the need for formal organization, leadership, incentives for participation, and means for acquiring resources and support (Engler and Engler 2014). Lacking a wider coordinated social movement that involves long-term organizing, strategic planning, and compromise, disruptive tactics may be overwhelmed by backlash and doomed to fail. For these theorists, change is often slow and incremental, part of an ongoing political process, and it may be especially important for numerical minorities, such as Indigenous peoples in Canada, to exercise caution and groom allies.

Consistent with Piven, Indigenous scholar Glen Coulthard (2014, 165) emphasizes the "necessity of direct action." Most settlers and some moderate Indigenous leaders call for restraint, claiming it is "only through talk, not through blockades that progress will be made" (Ovide Mercredi, quoted in Coulthard 2014, 167). But talk alone has rarely been sufficient. In fact, Coulthard says, "all negotiations over the scope and content of Aboriginal peoples' rights in the last forty years have piggybacked off the assertive direct actions" of Indigenous activists from Oka to Ipperwash and beyond.

But does this approach alienate settlers, exacerbating racial tensions? From the perspective of group position theory, if collective action threatens settlers' resources and privileges, then increased expression of racial prejudice seems likely, at least in the short term. As Coulthard says:

> Land has been stolen, and significant amounts of it must be returned. Power and authority have been unjustly appropriated, and much of it will have to be reinstated. This will inevitably be very upsetting to some [and] inconvenient to others. But it ... needs to happen if we are to create a more just and sustainable life in this country for the bulk of Indigenous communities, and for the majority of non-Indigenous people as well. (168)

The question is *how* to take action in a way that minimizes backlash enough that it does not overwhelm Indigenous-led movements, but is sufficiently forceful to secure meaningful change. Below, I analyse the impact of recent collective actions in the Rainy River District, particularly as they concern power relations and the sense of group positions. While such actions may temporarily amplify perceptions of group threat, they are often necessary for securing concrete benefits for Indigenous nations and may help realign group positions in the long run.

Crisis Management

Crises often have the capacity to bring previously disconnected or even competing groups together – to make sense of events, offer support, and confront a common enemy (Sherif et al. 1961). In doing so, groups sometimes realize that their common interests outweigh their differences or begin to view their relationships differently. Under such conditions, the sense of group positions may be realigned. In my interviews, some residents explicitly described recent local crises as intergroup bridges. For example, a white woman in her sixties recalled a flood in 2002 that washed out two bridges near Bergland (107 kilometres northwest of Fort Frances, near the Big Island and Big Grassy reserves), and how the local First Nations and white farmers worked together on a makeshift solution:

> I know if there was ... a crisis ... the communities work together ... We had a flood here [where] the river washed out a couple of bridges ... and the two communities worked very closely together so that people could get in and out.

Similar collaborative responses were displayed in 2014 when, in response to the worst spring flooding in decades (due to heavy precipitation), Indigenous and non-Indigenous neighbours worked together to stack tens of thousands of sandbags along the Rainy Lake and Rainy River shorelines and protect important sites.[1]

Several interviewees who discussed the bridging potential of recent local crises referred to the "Emo meat incident" of 2006, when provincial inspectors tried to confiscate uninspected beef from local white farmers. Rainy River First Nations intervened, offering to store the meat on reserve where inspectors could not tread without federal permission, and the First Nation and the farmers worked together to process and distribute the meat to its owners. This neighbourly gesture not only saved hundreds of steak dinners, but also reportedly improved intergroup relations (see figure 10.1).

According to an older white farmer involved in the incident, "If there's problems in the area, you see the Native community come to bat for everybody, just as well as the non-Native." In this case, the farmers thought they had an agreement with the province to butcher beef locally, but "it was only a verbal agreement." Perhaps relating to this dilemma, the First Nation "stood behind the farmers [and] the two communities pull[ed] together." When asked about RRFN's motivation, the farmer replied that they were "friends and neighbours and ... you've

Figure 10.1 Neighbours Helping Neighbours: Emo Meat Crisis.
"Highway demonstration in Barwick during the November 2006 Meat
Crisis. Provincial inspectors seized all domestic and wild meat at Sunrise
Meat and Sausage because some had not been slaughtered in inspected
facilities – an impossibility since no facilities existed locally. Rather than
see their meat destroyed, the farmers blocked access to the inspectors and
turned the meat over to Rainy River First Nations ... This crisis will stand
as a high point in community cooperation and solidarity." – Rick, non-
Indigenous man, age fifty-nine. Photo by Heather Ogilvie, *Fort Frances
Times*, 15 November 2006.

got family involved ... I think they felt it was a good thing to do, a com-
munity-spirited thing." Rainy River First Nations chief Jim Leonard
confirmed these sentiments:

> This meat plant just west of Barwick, a lot of farmers had cows there and
> the government come along and closed that facility and seized all that
> meat because it wasn't inspected ... you're supposed to take the meat up

to Dryden [244 kilometres northeast of Barwick] and then have it killed and inspected and bring it down and then process it, but because of cost farmers are just killing it directly and then getting it processed ... So, they called me up: "Would you come and help?" Well, I don't know nothing about meat ... but I went ... to give moral support ... the farmers were worried about their meat because ... if you leave it it's gonna spoil ... So ... because it was the provincial government that closed it, I says, "Put that meat on the back of that truck and bring it to the reserve, a federal land; the province can't touch it there" ... So, we moved that truck to the local sawmill, and the following day we processed the meat ... The whole district was behind us. And it showed ... that we *can* work together if we *want* to work together, and in that case, we did. And I still get people thanking me on the street today over that.

These incidents clearly demonstrate the capacity of Indigenous and non-Indigenous residents to work together in a crisis and protect their mutual interests. As Chief Leonard and others noted, such actions have increased trust and respect. Notably, it is often the Indigenous communities organizing to assist the non-Indigenous – though sometimes mutual support is lent, as in the flooding crises as well as in voluntary groups such as Parents Against Illicit Narcotics, programs such as the Healthy Living Food Box, and joint fundraising efforts for La Verendrye Hospital and other organizations. A few residents also referred to impending environmental crises as something that could unite everyone on a larger scale. However, such cooperative efforts do not directly address the structural bases of racism and colonialism because they are generally focused on resolving immediate crises or on wider economic pursuits, from the fur trade to forestry to broadband connections (see chapters 1, 2, and 6). Their potential to permanently transform group positions therefore may be limited.

The Video Incident Revisited

But what happens when the crisis itself is racialized? At least ten interviewees explicitly referred to the Fort High video incident (described in the Introduction) as a bridge. The way it was handled, especially by Anishinaabe Elders who led the healing and reconciliation efforts, revealed the strong latent capacity for collective action. While most Indigenous interviewees felt the video was offensive, many also viewed it as an opportunity for learning and change. And although many whites denied the video's racial implications or called it "an isolated incident," some also engaged in promising discussions about racism. Anishinaabe

Elders held private healing circles with the girls involved and then with a larger public ceremony. A diversity committee, comprising represent- . atives of over a dozen local organizations (including police, hospital, schools, and town council), was formed. The school board was forced to reflect on its policies and curricula. A "walk against racism" was jointly organized by Indigenous and non-Indigenous members of the Right Relations Circle, and over three hundred residents participated (see below). For all these reasons, some Anishinaabe framed the video as "a gift." According to one Elder involved in the healing circles:

> There's always a reason for everything ... even though the girls didn't know [what they were doing] – I guess they were drinking – I thought of it in a positive sense ... for the Native people and the education of high school kids. [We] had a [community] meeting and everybody was invited and [I said], "It was a blessing in disguise and it's time for us to all get together and wake up to our surroundings."

This sentiment was shared by many Indigenous residents, including a non-status Indian in his twenties who said, "When something bad happens, we get together." A middle-aged First Nation man agreed that although the video "created a little tinder box" and showed that the youth had "rage in them that they wanted to dispel,"

> it also was a good thing because it brought about discussions [and] some inward looking on both sides ... It brought something to the surface that's always festering here in northwestern Ontario.

Likewise, a younger Anishinaabe woman said the video "was a good thing because it has opened people's eyes [and] gotten people talking"; it also motivated Indigenous residents to "take more pride in" their traditions and teach about their culture. When asked if she thought settlers were ready to learn, she replied that in the months after the incident there was "a significant increase in the amount of non-Aboriginal people ... attending powwows" and other Indigenous events.

While many interviewees agreed that the video incident was an opportunity to open dialogue and transform relations, some nonetheless felt that its potential was not fully realized. A middle-aged white woman, for example, thought it was a teachable moment, but "I don't know if it was really handled well." If anything, she had noticed an increase in racist comments by her white relatives. Thus, although the incident opened avenues for discussion, some residents resisted, and the underlying tensions persisted. As painful or conflictual as it might be, a middle-aged Anishinaabe man emphasized the need for continued dialogue:

> *I don't think it [the dialogue in wake of the video incident] went far enough, but ...*
> *it was a start ...* I would say it was the first time that [racism] has ever been
> a big issue in Fort Frances. We've all known it's there. But it's never gotten to this point. And I think the reason is because you see a lot of Native
> people now ... draw[ing] the line ... That's [what's] gonna bring *real* peace
> and harmony. It's not the denial or the hidin' of it. It's when these things
> come to the surface and we begin to talk ... We could've gone another two
> hundred years pretending, but ... the real issue came to light ... *I don't think*
> *conflict is really the issue; it's how we deal with the conflict that's going to pro-*
> *duce fruits if we want it to.* (Emphasis added)

Only one parent of one of the six white girls involved with the
video agreed to a formal interview. When asked at the end of our
two-and-a-half-hour conversation what her daughter had learned from
the incident, she replied:

> My daughter learned to be racist. She learned what racism was. Um, never
> knew it before. Had never – never entered her head ... And not as in *she's*
> now racist, 'cause she's *obviously* not – but, um, that it works both ways. I
> think there's a lot of racism from the other side, sometimes more so. And
> maybe that's how one fights for change. I don't know. But ... that's the really sad thing ... She's learned to be less trusting. But she has also learned,
> thanks to some really great Elders, to Bessie [Mainville], to Nancy [Jones],
> that ... you can screw up, and it's okay ... The school destroyed them. But the
> Elders understood and made them realize that, you know what? It's okay.

Given this response, it is questionable how much truly was learned from
the incident. Rather than appreciating why many Indigenous residents
were insulted by the video, or how racism reflects power relations, she
denied that her daughter even "knew" what racism was and claimed
that Indigenous people are "more" racist than whites.[2] Such "moves to
innocence" (Tuck and Yang 2012) are staples of settler colonialism and
white supremacy, enabling whites to maintain their sense of group superiority and entitlement. The evasion of responsibility is surely *not* the
lesson that healing circle organizers wished to convey. Nevertheless, the
interviewee also credited the forgiving ways of the Elders, who did not
scapegoat the girls but rather viewed the crisis as a teachable moment –
not only for the girls but for the wider community. The question is: to
what extent were residents listening and ready to change?

Antiracist and Anticolonial Action

Explicitly antiracist or anticolonial activities were less commonly mentioned in my interviews. Among the few interviewees who described them as bridges, some were referring to the largely individual process of decolonizing the mind or becoming aware of how racist beliefs and attitudes have been engrained in *everyone* through socialization, and actively questioning and combatting them. For example, an older white man, a peace activist originally from the United States, said the onus lies mainly on "white folks," who "have to learn to have a different and healthier relationship with Native people." He added that "the process of decolonializing white society" would be "very hard" and would require "pressure ... legislation [and] training."

Some of these interviewees also described the need for organized collective action to tackle racism and colonialism. Before the video incident, there were few such activities in the Rainy River District. This is not to say that Anishinaabe and Métis people have not resisted colonization or engaged in their own quiet resurgence. As noted above, local Indigenous leaders have spoken out about treaty violations since the nineteenth century. Anishinaabe families hid in the bush and physically fought RCMP officers who tried to take their children. Once in residential school, children routinely talked back, ran away, or resisted in other ways (one convinced the principal at St. Margaret's to give him a paper route, which gave him a few hours of freedom each week). Traditional people continued speaking the language and practising ceremonies in private. Today, several Indigenous residents are members of the Ojibway Warrior Society or have participated in Indigenous activism elsewhere. There is also a widespread belief in the eighth fire prophecy (see Introduction), or what Anishinaabe scholar Leanne Simpson (2011, 66–7) calls *Chibimoodaywin*, a long-term, spiritually rooted social movement "to pick up the pieces of our lifeways ... build a political and cultural renaissance and resurgence [and] transform settler society ... based on the Indigenous principles of peace, justice, and righteousness as embodied in mino bimaadiziwin."

But unlike in some regions, until recently there has been little organized, explicit antiracist activism, either by Indigenous residents alone or in partnership with non-Indigenous allies. For decades, many white residents prided themselves on the lack of social unrest, taking it as a sign of "good" relations with "our Natives." Over the past decade, however, there has been a sharp rise in such collective action. While it has not always generated concrete gains for Indigenous peoples, and while it has often amplified whites' sense of group threat, bringing more prejudice to the surface, it also may be a sign of meaningful change in power relations.

A Brief History of Indigenous Resistance in Treaty No. 3 Territory

On a cold, snowy day in November 1965, in what reporters dubbed "Canada's first civil rights march," four hundred Indigenous men and women in Kenora (220 kilometres northwest of Fort Frances) marched from the Indian Friendship Centre to the local legion where town council was meeting. There they read a list of grievances and persuaded councillors to establish a mayor's committee to address anti-Indigenous racism and violence in town, and to sign a petition calling on the federal and provincial governments to provide basic services on nearby reserves, lengthen the trapping season, and improve First Nations' living conditions. Although Kenora became known as "Canada's Alabama" (Rutherford 2011, 2), and deep problems remained, the march signified that Indigenous peoples could no longer be ignored.

A decade later, Anishinaabe youth remained frustrated by the lack of change in how they were treated. In summer 1974 (a year after the Wounded Knee occupation in South Dakota), the Ojibway Warrior Society, supported by American Indian Movement activists, staged a forty-one-day armed occupation of Anicinabe Park, a disputed fourteen-acre lakefront property in Kenora, which allegedly had been sold to the town without the First Nations' permission. The organizers wrote in the local paper that "racism, bigotry, and subtle discrimination is running wild in this town," demanded better living conditions, health care, and education and an end to police harassment, and framed the occupation as "a first step in reasserting Aboriginal sovereignty and redressing the structural inequities [rooted in] colonialism" (Cronlund Anderson and Robertson 2011, 181).

The dominant response from local whites was harshly negative. Eleanor Jacobson, a former nurse, published the infamous pamphlet *Bended Elbow*, which blamed Indigenous peoples' social problems on their own behaviour, particularly alcoholism, and alleged that the government's treatment of them was "too generous," thereby perpetuating their "irresponsible" lifestyle. She claimed that "a few troublemakers and outsiders" led the occupation and, further, that white people were the true victims:

> I ask you, reader, who is being discriminated against? Nobody is building me a house and furnishing it ... Let's see you work for a living and to build and buy your own homes and pay for your own education ... If we have

a problem we can't ... go to the "White Man's Affairs" for help – there is none ... step out into reality from your dream world.

Although the occupation ended with no shootings or deaths, as a "weapon of last resort" (GCT3 n.d., 4) it sparked media and government attention. Kenora mayor Jim Davidson blamed the federal and provincial governments and said he hoped the "demonstration" would lead to change for Indigenous people. The Grand Council Treaty No. 3 and other Indigenous organizations met with the Ontario premier and cabinet for discussions around land disputes, harvesting rights, pollution, and conservation – an unprecedented move for the province. And the Ojibway Warrior Society agreed to end the occupation when weapons charges were dropped and proposals for a negotiated land claim settlement were instituted. Nevertheless, racial conflict continued, and today, over forty years later, many of the same structural inequities persist and the Anicinabe Park land claim remains unresolved. Yet the occupation also generated solidarity and inspired many Indigenous people to stand up for their rights.

While Kenora was "a centre of Indigenous-led political protest" in Canada (Rutherford 2011, 1), white residents of Fort Frances rejoiced at having neither such demonstrations nor such overt racism and conflict. Although some Indigenous residents quietly supported the occupation, others distanced themselves. In short, it was business as usual: local relations remained inequitable and paternalistic, but relatively peaceful and stable. The most overt collective action came from the mostly white forestry workers who staged a series of (sometimes violent) strikes and walkouts in 1968, 1973, 1974, 1975, 1976, and 1978–80. Apart from the few Indigenous individuals who worked in forestry, First Nations and Métis communities in the Rainy River District were relatively uninvolved. Indigenous resistance was subtle and surreptitious until the late 1970s, when then chief Rudy Morrisseau of Couchiching First Nation threatened to blockade the main highway into Fort Frances with a row of outhouses unless water pipes were extended to the reserve. The threat promptly gained attention and an agreement was negotiated with the federal government. Yet although Couchiching now has clean running water, it is forced to pay the industrial rate – at least three times what Fort Frances residents pay, an ongoing source of grievance.

Land claims then began to be filed across the district. In 1990, at the height of the Oka Crisis, or Kanehsatake Resistance, Big Grassy (Mishkosiimiiniiziibing) First Nation in the northwest of the district blockaded a bridge on Highway 621. Their purpose was twofold: to show support for the Mohawks at Oka and to raise awareness of their own land disputes, including the Assabaska claim to sixteen hundred acres, most of which was in Lake of the Woods Provincial Park (a joint claim with the Ojibways of Onigaming filed in 1977), and another claim to the Big Grassy River. The OPP helped keep the peace between Anishinaabe protesters and angry white motorists who sought access to the park or summer cottages. Despite (or perhaps because of) the backlash, the blockade gained attention and helped move the land claims process along. In 2000, in one of the first land claims settled in Treaty No. 3 (the first involving Ontario), the park was converted into reserve lands co-managed by the two First Nations and renamed Assabaska Ojibway Heritage Park. The First Nations also received $4.2 million in compensation. Although the blockade irritated some settlers, and there is still lingering mistrust and resentment, many non-Indigenous residents continue to use the park; one white interviewee even remarked that the condition of the campgrounds had improved since the First Nations regained control. The same year, the Big Grassy River claim was settled, restoring ownership of a portion of the waterway and monetary compensation. Beyond protest, settling such claims requires skilled negotiation and/or litigation. But, as Coulthard (2014) suggests, collective action is often necessary before Indigenous peoples' claims are taken seriously.

Closer to Fort Frances, intergroup relations remained quite stable. Yet conflict was on the rise again near Kenora. In 2002, Grassy Narrows (Asubpeeschoseewagong) First Nation erected the longest-running road blockade thus far in Canadian history, to prevent logging trucks from entering their traditional territory and clear-cutting their forests. As the Grand Council Treaty No. 3 wrote in its submission to the Ipperwash Inquiry, the Grassy Narrows blockade, led primarily by women and youth, was "not the first option, but their last and final option, to stand up for their traditional land" (GCT3 n.d., 6). Although "every effort" was made to negotiate with multinational forestry companies and the province, the latter refused to stop clear-cutting; "the only process that has worked has been the blockade" (7). In 2006, the blockade was temporarily extended from the logging road to Trans-Canada Highway 17 near Kenora, a more drastic measure that annoyed thousands of motorists but rapidly gained attention. International organizations such as Amnesty International, Rainforest Action Network, and Christian Peacemaker Teams worked with the First Nation to educate the public and lobby the government and forestry companies. In 2007, the province finally came to the negotiating table; AbitibiBowater surrendered its forestry licence in the relevant area, and a moratorium was placed on logging in Grassy Narrows' traditional territory.[3] Moreover,

blockade participants experienced a renewed sense of community solidarity, and the blockade itself became a site for reviving traditional
ways of life and restoring respectful relations with one another and the
land – significant developments for a community severely affected by
forced relocations, residential schools, mercury poisoning, and other
external forces (Willow 2012).

When asked about these events in 2008, most white interviewees and
some Indigenous interviewees in the Rainy River District *disapproved*
of Grassy Narrows' tactics, even though large numbers agreed they
had a legitimate grievance. The notion of local protests and blockades
seemed unthinkable. And despite the long-standing existence of an
Anti-Racism Committee in Sioux Lookout, a Red and White Committee
in Kenora, and similar groups in Thunder Bay, there was no organized
group – certainly none involving settlers – explicitly seeking to address
racism or colonialism in the Rainy River District.

The Right Relations Circle and the Walk against Racism (2008)

One of the first coordinated local responses involving settlers was the
Right Relations Circle (RRC), the small multiracial group that organized the "walk against racism" in the wake of the video incident. The
RRC originated in the spring of 2007, when three local white female
members of the United Church of Canada[4] attended a general council meeting in Thunder Bay, where church leaders urged members
to learn about the church's role in the Indian residential school system and find ways to live out the church's (1986 and 1998) apologies
locally, to show First Nations that they truly were sorry and committed to working together for a better future.[5] One founding member
recalled:

> There were [about] six hundred people [at General Council] ... I had met
> Stan McKay [of the Fisher River Cree First Nation in Manitoba] and he's a
> very prominent Aboriginal who was moderator of the United Church ... I
> [asked him], "Stan, if you were starting a group of any kind for Native and
> Non-Native relationships, what would you do?" He said, "I'd start small
> and get educated." And that was very wise.

After an initial meeting with Rainy River First Nations Elder Annie
Wilson, a few United Church women – along with a local Mennonite
couple – decided to embark on a five-session educational program
adapted from a United Church resource manual on "justice and reconciliation." They called themselves the Right Relations Circle. Their first

official group activity was watching *The Poet and the Indians* (Cullingham 1995), a film about Duncan Campbell Scott, the notorious Canadian poet/bureaucrat who oversaw the residential school system as deputy superintendent of Indian Affairs from 1913 to 1932. This was followed by a group visit to Onigaming First Nation in the summer of 2007 to read aloud the United Church apologies to residential school survivors and to hear their stories. Several members described this experience as "emotional" and "life-changing"; many shed tears alongside their Anishinaabe neighbours.

In September 2007, my partner Lisa met one of the RRC members at a work-related event. After hearing my research plans, the member invited us both to attend the next meeting. Although we were not United Church members, we were accepted with open arms. I soon became the group's minute-taker, allowing me to perform a crucial function while also taking field notes in a non-intrusive way. During subsequent monthly meetings, we watched films about residential schools and survivors' experiences, shared our own family histories, read about the signing of Treaty No. 3, and discussed common racial stereotypes ("deadly statements") while brainstorming "life-giving responses." Group members found these activities enlightening. According to one:

> Having activities ... or goals in common is a real bridge, and this is what I'm looking for out of my involvement in the Right Relations Circle is how we can build more bridges. And it behooves me as a white person to take initiative ... As I've been learning more ... I think there are many government practices still today that are very discriminatory and not helpful to [Indigenous peoples].

After completing the five sessions, the RRC began searching for ways to apply its knowledge and values. We wrote a letter of support to Kitchenuhmaykoosib Inninuwug (KI) First Nation, a fly-in community six hundred kilometres north of Thunder Bay, whose leaders had been imprisoned for non-violently protesting a mining company that sought to drill on their lands without consent.[6] Then, in February 2008, the video incident became public. As the local sense of crisis grew, the RRC organized a community forum attended by nearly one hundred residents, three-quarters of whom were Indigenous. During this emotional three-hour meeting, an Anishinaabe man stood up and described how the video had triggered painful memories of the physical, sexual, and spiritual abuse he had experienced in residential school and in white foster homes:

The question I always ask myself is "How did I survive?" [*long pause; wipes away tears*] Then, the other question: "What am I doing to make my community better?"

He mentioned recently participating in an annual walk in Thunder Bay to raise awareness of and to honour the hundreds of missing and murdered Indigenous women across Canada – a topic that affected him dearly because his own mother and two aunts were among them.[7] He said the video was "a cry for help from our high school ... the young people want answers"; and although he did not know what it would take to end racism, he would be "willing to march down Scott Street [the main business strip in Fort Frances] ... if that's what it comes to."

After the meeting, a few RRC members and Indigenous attendees discussed this idea of an antiracism walk. Before long, I found myself on a behind-the-scenes organizing committee with an experienced Mennonite peace activist, an Anishinaabe male Elder, and a middle-aged Anishinaabe woman. The date was set for 21 March 2008 – the United Nations International Day for the Elimination of Racial Discrimination, but also Good Friday and the spring solstice. As RRC members said, "Everything fell into place." Flyers for the event were printed, distributed, and advertised in local media. Local First Nations chiefs, Métis leaders, federal, provincial, and municipal representatives, and school board officials were invited to participate. Monetary and in-kind donations were received from the United Church's Healing and Reconciliation Fund, the United Native Friendship Centre, the Fort Frances Chiefs Secretariat, and others.[8] A First Nations cook was hired to provide bannock and chili for an after-walk feast.

On 21 March, over three hundred residents – approximately two hundred of them Indigenous – showed up to walk. Some carried placards saying "Biimosetaa – Walking Together to Overcome Racism."[9] All were given "harmony bows" (red, white, black, and yellow ribbons donated by the Kenora Multicultural Association) and "Racism: Stop It!" brochures (from the Canadian Heritage and Multiculturalism Department). Although town officials denied permission to walk on the street – citing archaic by-laws that apparently do not apply during annual Canada Day and Santa Claus Parades – most of us did so anyway. After the half-hour walk, a free meal was offered at the Nanicost facility on Agency One land (the former residential school, now shared by four local First Nations) located between the Town of Fort Frances and Couchiching First Nation. There was Anishinaabe drumming, acoustic guitar playing, and church choir singing. Inspirational speeches were given. A white RRC member spoke of treaty rights and obligations. An Anishinaabe Elder emphasized the need for inclusive education. And published poet and former chief of Rainy River First Nations Mashkawegaabo (Al Hunter) gave a spontaneous and moving oration that sought to link the walk against racism to "the big picture" and build on the momentum. Some felt inspired. As his speech took on a critical "political" tone, however, others grew agitated and began to leave. In his words:

> We cannot meet anger with anger ... It doesn't solve anything. It just per-petuates a cycle of violence.
>
> If you're going to walk against racism and ... stand next to the Native people in support and solidarity, then ... it shouldn't stop there. We should also be saying "yes" to people who are defending their land from mining companies ... who want to rape [the land] and take the resources. We have to respect and learn about treaty rights. It doesn't stop at joining in a walk.
>
> It means supporting the farmers in our area who are losing their farms ... It means standing with our neighbours who are working the land, who are losing their homes to foreclosure. And I mean that we, as Native people, have to stand and support them as well ...
>
> You support me against a mining company that wants to come into my community – I support you in trying to find ways to bring agriculture back to this district ... Are there ways to make our businesses more envi-ronmentally friendly? Green business!
>
> It shouldn't just end with a walk. Because when we walk against rac-ism, we're walking against environmental racism, economic racism, polit-ical racism – together. That's what it should ... translate into – and mutual cultural respect.
>
> You are welcome in my home. I do not close my door to anyone.
>
> ... There's a prophecy that the Anishinaabe have: "Oshkimaadiziig" they're called.[10] And it doesn't say they're Native people. They're just called "The New People" who [will] work together to find solutions to protect the land ... and create a new life together. And that time is now.

Several interviewees not affiliated with the RRC – and unaware of my involvement – described the walk as a high point in community solidarity and an important type of "bridge work." For example, a lo-cal Métis leader called it a "positive" outcome of the video incident. He said he participated in the walk because the Métis association "wanted to show our support ... We may have some different interests, political and otherwise, but we are all part of one community." For an Anishinaabe high school student:

I think [the walk against racism] was good. It brought like every kind of person together. There was a lot of Anishinaabe people there and [towns] people did stop and ... look at the signs we were holding.

When asked to reflect on the walk, one core (white) RRC organizer said he was "ecstatic":

I was really worried that we wouldn't have white folks [but] we had them! I don't know if it was quite as many as Native people, but it was pretty close. And we made a mistake; we should've gotten the names and phone numbers of every person there, so that we could call on them. Because taking the step of going out and walking ... that's the *best* way to know who your friends are. So, I felt really positive about that. And there was just a sense of "we're in this together."

Several Indigenous residents were also intimately involved in planning and organizing the walk and the feast. Some began attending RRC meetings regularly, though none was affiliated with the United Church. In the following months, Indigenous and non-Indigenous members collaboratively developed a formal mission statement:

The Right Relations Circle of the Rainy River District is a group of ordinary people who have come together to promote *just and equitable relations* between Aboriginal and non-Aboriginal people so that together, step by step, we can effectively work for right relations with our economic, social and natural environment. We do this through *self-education, sharing and action*, with *mutual respect* for each other's spiritual and religious beliefs. Everyone, Aboriginal and non-Aboriginal, is welcome in the Circle. (emphasis original)

Nevertheless, as the RRC continued to meet and plan activities in the summer and fall of 2008, some of the initial (white) members stopped participating and internal conflicts arose over how "political" the group should be: some preferred to continue focusing on self-education; others sought to take direct action, suggesting, among other things, an open forum on the land claim dispute at Point Park and an "audit study" of local businesses to document racial discrimination. Yet even some Indigenous members balked at these suggestions. Others grew annoyed by the condescending tone and resistance to action displayed by some white members. After I left town in December 2008, the group held only two more meetings.[11]

Apart from internal disagreements over strategy, tactics, and style among those who claim to share antiracist or decolonizing goals, another limitation of such groups and activities is that some settlers do not regard them as bridges at all. If anything, they see them as boundaries and feel deeply threatened by them, as group position theory would predict. During the walk, I saw several white residents peering out their living-room windows. According to a blue-collar worker whom I later asked about the walk, "That's just a bunch of do-gooders trying to get their picture in the newspaper." Moreover, he said, in his view talking about racism only provokes *more* racism. A white businessman in his fifties described the walk as "over the line": "I don't think we have a racism problem here. I think we have people unhappy about certain things with the Natives, and rightfully so!"

Thus, although explicitly antiracist activities may be a bridge for individuals who are open to participating, they may have difficulty reaching – and further alienate – those who are not. As social movement theorists suggest, it also can be difficult to sustain momentum, especially in a town with a history of avoiding political discussions (see chapter 7). Such challenges are inevitable, however, because creating just and equitable relations will involve "a massive transformation of the political, legal, cultural, social, and economic orders" (Atleo 2014, 190), and this will be upsetting for many people. In short, while more is required than a small, internally divided group like the Right Relations Circle, it did make valuable contributions in organizing the walk, expanding intergroup ties, and educating some settlers.

The Couchiching First Nation Toll Booth (2010)

As discussed in chapter 7, the video incident and the walk against racism were followed by a return to the status quo – polite interactions and little overt "race talk," but continued subtle underlying tensions. As the lease on Point Park expired in April 2009, tensions briefly escalated again, but the rumoured threat of blockades came and went. That summer, when Wee-chi-it-te-win Family Services faced backlash due to the proposed relocation of its Training and Learning Centre to Alberton, it decided to neither take legal action nor protest, but rather search for a new home elsewhere (see chapter 5).

Many Fort Frances residents were therefore surprised when, in April 2010, Couchiching First Nation announced that on 21 May (the first long weekend of the summer) it would establish a toll booth on Highway 11 to expedite the resolution of two long-standing grievances.[12] First, the First Nation said it had never been properly compensated for the land on which Highway 11 was built. Second, there was an urgent need to relocate community members who had been living on reserve lands allegedly contaminated by the former J.A. Mathieu sawmill, and the federal government had a fiduciary obligation to fund the relocation and clean up the lands.

According to then chief Chuck McPherson, in the mid-1960s, the federal and provincial governments negotiated an exchange of the Couchiching "two-chain shore allowance" for the highway right-of-way, essentially paying the community with its own land. He asserted that the highway, the main one running through the reserve and connecting Fort Frances to the east, had helped generate "billions of dollars ... in the district economy," but First Nations people were largely excluded from that prosperity. Meanwhile, the contamination was confirmed in 2003, with soil testing revealing dangerous levels of dioxins and furans, yet eight families were still awaiting relocation. Until these issues were addressed, Couchiching First Nation would charge one dollar for every car passing through the reserve and a fee for every boat launched from the Five-Mile Dock – just as Couchiching residents are forced to pay non-resident fees for services such as the library, arena, and pool in Fort Frances: "if people are utilizing our property and our facilities, we want to be compensated for it," said Chief McPherson (Revell 2010a).

Rather than impose the toll immediately, the First Nation strategically gave nearly one month's notice for all parties to work out a solution. Local federal and provincial representatives tried to facilitate meetings with relevant ministers, as well as mediate between the town and the First Nation. As MPP Howard Hampton put it:

> I think this is an expression of frustration by Couchiching ... they have tried going through all the official channels over and over again on these issues, and they just feel like they are not getting a response. (Revell, 2010b)

Indeed, federal and provincial officials refused to engage, and even before the toll booth went up, the local backlash was harsh and swift. A *Fort Frances Times* (2010a) poll conducted from 29 April to 5 May found that, among 1,906 respondents, 68 per cent were "outraged" and another 12 per cent were "worried." Hundreds of angry comments were posted online. Fort Frances mayor Roy Avis fretted about the economic impact, and said:

> I strongly believe [the toll booth] will become quite contentious, in that it will put family against family. There's so much inter-marriage in this area. I hope it doesn't get to that. (quoted in Revell and Hicks 2010)

The 28 April *Fort Frances Times* editorial (Revell 2010a) called the toll booth a "troubling tactic" and cautioned the First Nation to reconsider, lest the "contentious disputes revolving around aboriginal grievances that have plagued other communities" make their presence felt in the Rainy River District. Although "one can sympathize with the band's frustration over endless talks that seem to go nowhere," the editors argued that the toll booth would unfairly penalize both locals and tourists, potentially jeopardize emergency services,[13] and "poison relations between our communities for perhaps years." They advised: "Negotiation may not be perfect, but it's far better than confrontation."

But, as Couchiching First Nation councillor Ed Yerxa said, the dominant message from band members was that "we've been nice too long." They were no longer willing to accept their inequitable position and were determined to proactively change it. In mid-May, band members began distributing information packets to passing vehicles, outlining the reasons for their planned actions. On 21 May, still lacking a satisfactory response from the federal and provincial governments,[14] they erected the toll booth (figure 10.2).

While some motorists paid the toll, others "chose to drive through, refusing to pay a cent." As Chief McPherson put it:

> We've had a number of well-wishers ... Some people actually gave tips ... But ... we've [also] had people that have made a number of derogatory remarks, mostly racist in nature. (quoted in Revell 2010d)

Each vehicle was given a letter to mail to the federal minister of Indian and northern affairs, urging action on the contaminated soil and the highway claim. Yet as group position theory would predict, many white residents felt threatened, and the backlash escalated.

Racial slurs were hurled at toll booth organizers. Couchiching First Nation members "almost came to blows" with former friends in town. At least one reported being physically attacked.[15] An anti–toll booth Facebook group with more than seven hundred members was created and investigated for hate speech. Some Indigenous people who lived in town feared for their family's safety. A trucker threatened to physically smash the toll booth. And the Couchiching chief and councillors received death threats via telephone.[16]

The Ontario Provincial Police declared the toll booth illegal, warning participants: "The public has a legal right to free and uninhibited passage on highways in the Province of Ontario"; "Your actions constitute a deliberate interference with traffic"; and "Criminal charges may

Figure 10.2 Couchiching First Nation Toll Booth, May 2010. Photo provided by Holly Bruyere.

result" (Revell 2010c). In response, Couchiching invoked section 30 of the Indian Act, which states that "A person who trespasses on a reserve is guilty of an offence" and may be charged a fine, imprisoned, or both. Ultimately no charges were laid.

As with the video incident, heated arguments continued in the *Fort Frances Times* online comments section.[17] While many settlers agreed that Couchiching had legitimate grievances, especially over the soil contamination, many opposed the toll booth tactic, saying it was too militant, inconvenienced the wrong people, alienated potential allies, and further endangered an already fragile economy. They accused the First Nation of "extreme behaviour" and "highway robbery," saying "they have to realize there are limits to what can be demanded" and portraying themselves as "victims." According to one anonymous commenter:

Why are there different laws for natives and non-natives. It is illegal to set up a toll booth on a provincial highway. I understand they have some concerns about soil contaimination [*sic*], but this is not the way to protest.

This will affect many innocent people [and] have a very negative affect [sic] on relationships between natives and non-natives.

Some disputed the basis of the highway claim, arguing either that the First Nation has benefited from the highway and should be grateful or that "It's too late to complain about a bad deal now." From Couchiching's perspective, these arguments missed the point. Indigenous people have not benefited to nearly the same extent as white people, and yet the highway was constructed on Indigenous land. Further, complaints were made years ago, with plenty of calls to Ottawa and Queen's Park, and yet, as another commenter said, "Couchiching has been pretty much ignored. They have to do something so the governments take them seriously!"

Still others used the issue to launch into more general anti-Indigenous tirades, accusing the First Nation of "reverse discrimination," "bullying," criminality, and laziness. According to one, the toll booth organizers were "just a bunch of greedy kids with your hands out, [who should] try contributing to society instead of just take take take." Some called for a reverse toll booth on Indigenous people entering Fort Frances. Others advocated boycotting Couchiching businesses. One writer proclaimed that they would "take the long way to Thunder Bay just to avoid loosing [sic] any more of my hard earned money." Such comments show that the conflict transcended economic interests: to maintain a sense of moral superiority, the writer would rather spend more time and (gas) money than support the First Nation's cause and pay the toll. Others went so far as to promote violence to enforce a sort of "colour-blind" equality that would only further entrench systemic inequities:

The time is now for ALL Canadians to be treated equally. No more freeloading. You want respect, earn it ... Maybe [the toll booth] is exactly what we need to enrage the people who actually ensure this country survives by paying taxes. Lets [sic] start a fund to give to the first logger who turns the toll booth into a hundred pieces of shattered lumber.

Many of these comments were countered by Couchiching First Nation members and toll booth supporters. For instance, in response to the claim that they were asking for "handouts," one Indigenous writer replied, "Are you not asking for a free ride through our land? Stop talking about handouts and then ask[ing] for one." Another supporter explained:

Couchiching ... has created a lot of attention around this toll booth issue. Whether this is the most effective way to have their voices heard is debatable, but this is the route that they have chosen, and it certainly has got our attention ... please take the energy that you were going to put into writing down some racist rant and instead inform yourself on the issues ... Then direct your anger into sending letters to all of the government officials that have for years decided to pretend these issues didn't exist. Fighting with our friends and neighbors won't make the toll booth go away faster, but standing with them to have their voices heard just might.

The widespread perception that First Nation people were being "radical" or "militant" for erecting a toll booth (after waiting decades for their grievances to be heard) and that there is a "double standard" (in that whites allegedly would be arrested for taking similar actions) is especially curious, given the history of much more violent and disruptive labour strikes by primarily white workers in Fort Frances. Throughout the twentieth century, labour action was frequently initiated by local loggers, mill workers, postal workers, rail workers, and others. As described in *Fort Frances: The Story of a Town and Its People*, published by local historian Neil McQuarrie (2003, 155) on the town's centennial:

> The longest, bitterest, and most violent strike in the town's history ... began on July 5, 1978 when loggers working for Boise Cascade's Woodlands Division refused to begin work.

They accused the company of violating the collective agreement by shifting to an owner-operator system (whereby loggers own their own equipment and work on a contract basis). Although the Ontario Labour Relations Board declared it an illegal strike, union members set up picket lines at the Shevlin yards to stop the flow of logs to the mill and clashed with tugboats on the river. This resulted in

> threats, intimidation and a growing police presence in the town. There was damage to company property and to strikers' shacks while CNR and CPR rail lines were blown up in what some said was an attempt to restrict the movement of logs to the Fort Frances mill. (McQuarrie 2003, 156)

Spikes were laid on highways to puncture the tires of non-union truckers. When some workers crossed the picket lines in 1979, police were required to prevent further violence. The strike lasted two years, and the company switched to an owner-operator system, leaving long-term bitterness and tensions. The point here is that, despite losing this battle, these and other labour activists are celebrated as heroes by many white residents who have long gained from higher wages and benefits and safer working conditions. Yet when First Nations people *non-violently* stand up for their rights, they are condemned by some of these same residents – a sign of what one Couchiching member explicitly called "white privilege."

The toll booth also generated tensions within Indigenous communities. Some First Nations and Métis people (including Grand Council Treaty No. 3 and Nishnawbe Aski Nation leaders) were supportive, whereas others tried to disassociate from it, and even some Couchiching band members (reportedly even some councillors) opposed the tactic. Nevertheless, it did succeed in gaining attention. Within a week of the toll booth being erected, meetings were set with federal and provincial representatives.

Altogether, the toll booth lasted for ten days. The Couchiching leaders agreed to remove it after receiving commitments to "relocate eight home owners from contaminated lands" to new lots on the reserve and to "negotiate suitable compensation for the highway claim." Although some community members were dissatisfied with mere "promises," and would have preferred to keep the toll booth up until more concrete action was taken, Chief McPherson claimed "victory" (*Fort Frances Times* 2010b) and then Councillor Sara Mainville said, "I don't think you'll find a more united First Nation community than Couchiching" (*Fort Frances Times* 2010c). Indeed, one of the most positive outcomes reported by toll booth participants was that it brought a historically divided community closer together, increasing their sense of solidarity and pride. As Mainville stated:

> The community has really come together around [the toll booth]. I think ... the communication between the youth and the Elders, it's strengthening our resolve to continue, to fight for those ... issues, to be resolved and negotiate a just settlement.

Meanwhile, Mayor Avis said he was pleased to see the toll booth removed, as it was "a deterrent to positive relationships." The *Fort Frances Times* editorial on 2 June acknowledged that "the band accomplished what it had set out to do," but warned that "repairing the rift" within the Rainy River District "will take much longer," and reprimanded band members for "joking" about taking similar action regarding Point Park. Indeed, the Point Park land claim had been in the background all along; a day after the toll booth was announced, an Ontario Superior Court judge ruled that the town could maintain the park, free of charge, until the claim was settled. The *Times* editors concluded:

We can breathe a little easier that a potential crisis thankfully passed without violence, but we've really nothing else to celebrate because the underlying problems that prompted this "last resort" by Couchiching, as well as the ongoing mistrust and resentment that obviously remains percolating just beneath the surface, are far from being resolved.

Ultimately, the federal government did fund the relocation of the eight families, but as of this writing, the contaminated lands have not been cleaned up. The Highway 11 claim reportedly was settled in 2011, but the details are confidential and unclear even to many band members. Some say the funds were used to build a new hockey arena on reserve and to pay for the construction of new walking trails. Others believe the claim is still being litigated. And the Point Park case remains unresolved.[18] Left at that, despite lingering tensions and "bad blood" with the town, as one Anishinaabe woman put it, the benefits of the toll booth likely outweighed the drawbacks for many Couchiching residents.

In 2014, however, the new chief of Couchiching Sara Mainville published a letter in the *Fort Frances Times* "to apologize for the unilateral action we had taken," stating that she was "committed to work with the entire district's leadership on economic development and common issues" and that "We can do better by working together." Many toll booth participants felt betrayed, saying she did not consult them and "had no right to apologize" because they did not do anything wrong: "that is our land." Although Chief Mainville may have appeased some Fort Frances residents, she re-opened divisions within Couchiching that, as one member said, are "very deep and going to take a long time to heal." Thus, although the toll booth began to shift the sense of group positions, and stimulated concrete benefits for Couchiching members, this controversial collective action itself is now another elephant in the room.

Still, the toll booth will always have special meaning for many Couchiching members. As one movingly stated on the toll booth Facebook page:

I know we will continue to revitalize who we are as a people. Sometimes that stand in life will come in our homes, at our schools, at ... work, or on Highway 11 ... The government does not get to take that from us. EVER ... Chi Miigwech for teaching me courage in the face of adversity. You should all be very proud ... Together we can see this through. Freedom became ours the moment we stood WITH one another.

Idle No More (2012–13) and Beyond

In the interim, the "round dance revolution" had begun. From December 2012 to March 2013, tens of thousands of Indigenous and non-Indigenous people joined together in round dances, rallies, and teach-ins across Canada – and, briefly, around the world – to promote Indigenous self-determination and a healthy shared environment. Initiated by four women in Saskatchewan to oppose the federal government's omnibus budget bill C-45 – which facilitated the surrender of reserve lands and removed environmental protections for millions of waterways – the Idle No More movement quickly became one of the largest mass mobilizations of Indigenous peoples in history (for detailed accounts, see Coates 2015; Coburn 2015; Kino-nda-niimi Collective 2014; Wotherspoon and Hansen 2013). The Rainy River District was no exception.

On 21 December 2012, more than three hundred Anishinaabe and Métis people of all ages, and some non-Indigenous supporters, marched from Couchiching First Nation to Fort Frances with banners reading "Anishinaabe Insurgence, Colonialism Disrupted!"; "We are all treaty people"; and "As long as the rivers flow, our rights will be honoured" (figure 10.3). The pent-up anger and frustration had burst again, and many Indigenous residents felt empowered and hopeful. As Couchiching youth councillor Jeremy Jordan said:

> I am not afraid today to take a stand because this is not only about my future, but there will be a day when I have children, and ... I want [them] to say, "Daddy was there. Daddy fought for your rights." (quoted in Hicks 2012)

He recalled manning the toll booth two years earlier, "being called 'a stupid little brown boy' ... getting change thrown at my face." But he felt it was important to stand up and speak out again, not only for Indigenous and treaty rights, but because the climate crisis is "only going to get worse if we continue ... to let people just walk over us and rape Mother Earth."

The walk was followed by a peaceful protest at Point Park on 11 January 2013, round dances in Fort Frances streets and parking lots, a march down Highway 71 near Onigaming First Nation, and teach-ins across the district. A Facebook page called "Idle No More, Rainy River District Treaty 3 Territory" attracted more than two thousand members. There was strong participation by Indigenous residents, higher than in the walk against racism and more widespread than with

Figure 10.3 Idle No More in the Rainy River District. On 21 December 2012, hundreds of Indigenous residents and their supporters walked from Couchiching First Nation to Fort Frances as part of an Idle No More "Day of Action." Photo provided by Sonny McGinnis.

the Couchiching toll booth (though engagement by white neighbours remained low). For communities that, in my earlier interviews, were almost uniformly described as unwilling to rock the boat, "afraid" to even "talk about" racism or colonialism, this was quite the transformation. "Our people are just so passive and orderly, it's like we don't want to hurt people's feelings," one Anishinaabe interviewee had said in 2008. But, according to Chief Mainville, Idle No More was "a spiritual and educational awakening." As Jana-Rae Yerxa of Couchiching First Nation explained in a 2015 article titled "Refuse to Live Quietly!":

Humility does not mean silence. Respect does not mean to not challenge. Love does not mean that feelings will not be hurt ... The rage I feel about the everyday acts of settler colonial violence which aims to silence me ... is a healthy rage rooted in love: self-love; love for the land; love for my family; love for my community; love for my nation. Even to challenge others with their colonial comfort are acts of respect, humility and love because it presents an opportunity to learn and grow together, moving towards liberation, and further humanizing ourselves.

The *Fort Frances Times* did not take a position on Idle No More, but paternalistically warned against direct action. Its 16 January 2013 editorial read:

Dialogue and negotiation remain the only option to resolving aboriginal issues. Confrontation, whether through blockades, "toll booths," or other disruptions, only serves to heighten tensions and open the door to potential violence.

In admonishing Indigenous people to "abide the law" and not "abandon" the bargaining table, the editors ignored the fact that the federal government had passed legislation without Indigenous peoples' free, prior, and informed consent (contrary to the UN Declaration on the Rights of Indigenous Peoples) and had repeatedly walked away from or unnecessarily delayed many land claims negotiations.

Overall, in the Rainy River District, there was somewhat less backlash to Idle No More than to the toll booth, perhaps because it represented less of a direct threat. Indeed, some non-Indigenous residents supported the movement, especially insofar as their desire for a clean, healthy environment also was at stake, and, as Pam Palmater (2013) said, treaty rights may be "our last best hope" to protect the earth. Increasingly, instances of backlash were publicly confronted and challenged – another sign of shifting local power relations.

For instance, on 24 December 2012, at a flash mob round dance outside the Walmart in Fort Frances, an older white man remarked, "Get a job for once!" In response, a younger man from Couchiching followed him into the store with a cell phone video recorder, asking him three times to "repeat your racist comment" and stating that he was offended by the remark because "I'll have you know I have a very good job." The older man blushed and mumbled, but he refused to answer and continued shopping. The video was posted on Facebook and applauded by Indigenous and some non-Indigenous neighbours. Confirming the thesis in chapter 7 that contact alone does not eliminate prejudice, an Indigenous relative of the older man stated:

So proud of you for confronting ... him and making him run away with his tail between his legs. Just pisses me off that someone who has lived with natives as part of his family could turn out to be such a nasty, mean racist.

Meanwhile, a former Right Relations Circle leader wrote:

> Big time congrats for your action. You modelled what we "settlers in solidarity" should be doing all the time, confronting this ignorance and supremacy assumptions among us, shifting the culture.

In another case, a younger man in a pickup truck, frustrated by a round dance on Scott Street in Fort Frances, began driving through the circle, physically ramming into dancers. This incident was also caught on video and posted on YouTube.

Meanwhile, in Thunder Bay, numerous cases of racist backlash were reported. At the extreme, an Anishinaabe woman was gang-raped and left for dead, and the white men who assaulted her reportedly said, "You native people don't deserve your treaty rights" (CBC 2013). Yet there too community members banded together. As Arlene Tucker of Couchiching First Nation put it on the local Facebook page:

> We are starting to have some turbulence with outright racial tensions and uneducated comments about the Idle No More movement. With the recent attack in Thunder Bay of our Aboriginal sister, we must protect our loved ones ... Idle No More calls for only peaceful acts of protests [to change the legislation] that will affect the environment, our way of life, land sold on reserve, [with] zero consultation ... Talk about things and reach out for help when someone hurts you. If you feel you are not strong enough to stand on the forefront then support the movement in other ways. Write letters, donate water, pray, or whatever. Don't be discouraged and remember we are not doing anything wrong.

Although some whites predictably felt threatened by the movement, and lashed out against it, the assertive yet non-violent ways in which Indigenous residents confronted and corrected them signifies the ongoing realignment in group positions. Moreover, the support offered by some non-Indigenous residents like the RRC member quoted above suggests that some settlers are moving beyond an "us versus them" mentality and finding alternative ways to understand their identities and interests.

Although Idle No More did not achieve its immediate objective of stopping Bill C-45, it did empower a new generation of Indigenous and (some) non-Indigenous youth. Locally, as with the walk against racism and the Couchiching toll booth, there was another peak in community camaraderie and a renewed sense of energy. As elsewhere in Canada, Indigenous peoples have now largely turned their energy inward to focus on revitalizing Indigenous institutions, languages, cultures, and economies and to continue the long, patient resurgence, or *Chibimoodaywin*, prophesied generations ago when the Anishinaabe first encountered white people in their territory.

Conclusion

This chapter has shown that, despite significant challenges, collective action can be a useful and often necessary tool in the struggle against racism and colonialism. Some forms of collective action do not tackle these forces directly, but they can bring Indigenous and non-Indigenous people together in cooperative, mutually supportive relationships, increasing trust and, at least temporarily, challenging the sense of group positions. This has been illustrated in community responses to recent crises, as well as in a range of economic and other endeavours throughout the Rainy River District's history. Yet such actions alone do not alter the systemic or institutional factors that, for centuries, have benefited settlers at Indigenous peoples' expense.

Alternatively, blockades, toll booths, and protests may be less likely to create bridges between Indigenous and non-Indigenous people (apart from participants). However, they may be more likely to challenge power relations and enhance social justice, which may contribute to more sustainable bridges in the long run. Although the Right Relations Circle did not secure concrete changes in school curricula or other policies, and the group itself was internally divided, the walk against racism that it organized with First Nations communities helped create new social ties and strengthen solidarity. It also showed, for "the first time" in Fort Frances, that hundreds of Indigenous and non-Indigenous residents were willing to publicly demonstrate against racism and for more just and equitable relations.

The Couchiching toll booth stimulated government action to relocate eight families from contaminated land and settle a long-standing land claim. It also largely united a historically divided community, while exacerbating tensions with many white neighbours. The Idle No More movement attracted more settler support, perhaps due to its emphasis on shared environmental concerns, but achieved fewer concrete gains. However, like Indigenous-led actions elsewhere, it also prefigured more just and sustainable ways of living together and relating to one another and showed that Indigenous people will continue to assert and defend their rights.

Although the Rainy River District does not have a history of "disruptive" Indigenous-led collective action, the recent spike in such activity is another sign that times are changing, that Indigenous people are not staying "in their places," and that group positions are realigning. Increased expression of racial prejudice may be expected in the short term, given the deeply entrenched structural inequities and colonial mentalities. But such upheaval also may be a necessary step towards building understanding between Indigenous and non-Indigenous residents and restoring the spirit and intent of the original peace and friendship treaties.

Canada at a Crossroads

It was foreseen ... that there would be different eras of life ... the prophecy of the seven fires ... And the generation that we're in now, the seventh fire, *we're at the turning point:* which way is our white brothers and sisters going to choose? ... Are you going to choose the spiritual path ... that will preserve the earth for future generations? Or are you going to keep going down this road of damaging and taking over everything ... that road which is finite?

Mashkawegaabo (Al Hunter), Rainy River First Nations

As Mashkawegaabo says, we are at a turning point, a time of momentous transition in Indigenous-settler relations, both in the Rainy River District and across Canada. The decisions we make today about how to live together and relate to one another and the earth will affect future generations and society at large. As emphasized throughout this book, one of the greatest social psychological barriers to settlers joining with Indigenous peoples to light the eighth fire that will "preserve the earth" is the sense of group positions that maintains and justifies structural racism and settler colonialism in Canada. While settlers, especially whites, have long benefited from these arrangements, the system is not only unjust but also economically and environmentally unsustainable. The survival and well-being of all human (and many non-human) beings depends on fundamentally changing our ways.

By analysing Indigenous-settler relations in the Rainy River District via interviews, surveys, fieldwork, a photovoice project, and historical analysis, I have shown how whites' sense of group superiority and entitlement is rooted in historical and ongoing processes of colonization. The dominant sense of group positions is increasingly being threatened, however, by large-scale political, economic, and demographic changes, and by a series of local racialized incidents, from the Fort Frances High

School video incident to the Couchiching First Nation toll booth and beyond.

This sense of group positions is clearly expressed today in the divergent ways in which Indigenous and non-Indigenous residents frame their relationships and in the laissez-faire and paternalistic attitudes of many settlers. The dominant white frame positions whites as entitled to their resources and privileges, and as threatened by such "boundaries" as Indigenous land claims and treaties that require settlers to take responsibility and share power. In contrast, many Indigenous residents (and a minority of settlers) challenge the presumed inferiority of Indigenous peoples and articulate an alternative vision of group relations, based on respect for Indigenous identities and rights and a mutual commitment to upholding our treaty responsibilities to one another and the earth. As Bonilla-Silva (2014, n.p.) puts it in the US race relations context, "we conceive of the problem [and the solution] differently and in ways that reflect our position and interests in the racial order." That is why we cannot "talk straight" about (anti)racism; it is a function of power, not simply ignorance or misunderstanding.

Although many residents and scholars alike point to contact, education, and apologies as ways forward, these approaches are limited and must be accompanied by a wider social movement to transform the *structure* of group relations. Unlike towns studied in earlier ethnographies of Indigenous-settler relations (Braroe 1975; Dunk 1991), intergroup interactions, friendships, and marriages have been common in Fort Frances. Yet even many whites who have Indigenous friends and family members routinely express laissez-faire racism, blaming Indigenous people for their social problems, rejecting concrete actions to improve their living conditions, and resenting Indigenous activists.

In 2017, for example, Conservative senator Lynn Beyak of Dryden, Ontario – who previously lived in Fort Frances, owned car dealerships and tourist camps there, and served on the Fort Frances–Rainy River Board of Education – made national headlines when she complained that the "good deeds" of "kindly and well-intentioned" residential school staff had been overshadowed by negative stories in the Truth and Reconciliation Commission's reports (Tasker 2017). While acknowledging that "mistakes were made" in residential schools, she claimed that Indigenous friends and neighbours had learned valuable skills and knowledge, including the Christian faith. She also called on First Nations people to "trade your status card for Canadian citizenship."[1] In response, the TRC chair, Senator Murray Sinclair, said he was "shocked" by Ms Beyak's ignorance, Liberal minister of Indigenous affairs Carolyn Bennett said Beyak was "ill-informed, offensive, and simply wrong," and NDP MP Romeo Saganash likened Beyak's views to Holocaust denial (Galloway 2017). When Beyak subsequently published, on her senate website, letters of support from fellow Canadians (Lum 2018), Conservative leader Andrew Scheer deemed some of the letters "racist" and "unacceptable" and removed her from the Conservative caucus. While the political establishment sought to distance itself from Beyak, the problem, as documented in this book, is that Beyak's comments do reflect the views of a substantial number of white settlers in northwestern Ontario (and elsewhere), who resent the turning of tides and are desperate to defend their resources and status.

Drawing on classical psychological, neo-Marxist, cultural sociological, and settler colonial theories, this book has fleshed out some of the micro mechanisms sustaining such settlers' sense of group position and justifications for racial inequity. These range from the more or less deliberate strategies and tactics that some settlers use to protect their position in "threatening" situations (such as the Alberton group home controversy) to the often taken-for-granted social processes (such as subtyping and political avoidance) that are part of the daily fabric of life and that reproduce structural inequities without anyone necessarily intending it.

My analysis also illustrates that once group positions are entrenched, transforming them is extremely difficult. Although old-fashioned prejudice is rare today, more subtle attitudes and interaction patterns that sustain group positions remain widespread. Contact and education, at least in their most prevalent current forms, do little to reduce whites' sense of group superiority and entitlement, leaving settler colonial structures intact. Although most residents agreed after the fact that a state apology for the IRS system was necessary, whites quickly developed new ways to defend their resources and privileges, viewing the apology as a sign of Canadians' moral righteousness and rejecting concrete follow-up action. In contrast, most Anishinaabe and Métis said the apology would be meaningful only if accompanied by substantive changes in policies and practices. More locally, even something as seemingly minor as the attempted purchase of a small plot of land for an Indigenous youth centre triggered (perceived) group threat, leading many whites to vigorously defend the status quo. Throughout the district's history, there has been a clear pattern where Indigenous-settler relations seem harmonious for a time and then a racialized crisis, such as the rumoured Indian uprising of 1900 or the rumoured Point Park occupation of 2009, quickly divides the community into an "us versus them" scenario. Just as quickly, however, the crisis fades, and it becomes taboo again to discuss the underlying issues.

As DiAngelo (2015, 3) suggests, many white people fear such discussions, lest their sense of being good, moral, and innocent persons with a right to "comfort" be challenged by any revelation of complicity with racism. Consistent with group position theory, she writes:

> Socialized into a deeply internalized sense of superiority and entitlement that we are either not consciously aware of or can never admit to ourselves, we become highly fragile in conversations about race. We experience a challenge to our racial worldview as a challenge to our very identities as good, moral people. It also challenges our sense of rightful place in the hierarchy. Thus, we perceive any attempt to connect us to the system of racism as a very unsettling and unfair moral offense.

Nevertheless, there have always been settlers who see things differently. If Idle No More is any indication, increasing numbers of settlers are joining with Indigenous peoples in antiracist and anticolonial efforts. How far they will go in challenging and transforming group positions and colonial structures remains to be seen.

Indigenous peoples, for their part, have always resisted colonization and sought to maintain (or regain) control over their lands and lives. In the Rainy River District, direct actions, such as the walk against racism in 2008 and the Idle No More rallies and round dances in 2012-13, have been on the rise. Although such actions predictably trigger racist backlash from some white residents, they are often necessary to achieve meaningful change. As Coulthard (2012, n.p.) puts it:

> If you want those in power to respond swiftly to Indigenous peoples' political efforts, start by placing Native bodies (with a few logs and tires thrown in for good measure) between settlers and their money, which in colonial contexts is generated by the ongoing theft and exploitation of our land and resource base.

Such actions can be difficult to sustain, however, especially in regions where Indigenous peoples and their allies are outnumbered. In this context, it is crucial for initiatives such as the Right Relations Circle to link up with Indigenous-led movements and groups across the country that are similarly oriented to reviving the spirit and intent of the original peace and friendship treaties and implementing more just and sustainable ways of being. Fortunately, such initiatives are also growing, including in northwestern Ontario, from the twenty-five-year-old Sioux Lookout Anti-Racism Committee to the nascent Biskaabiiyang Collective in Thunder Bay.

Theoretical Implications: Group Position Theory in a Settler Colonial Context

Before I elaborate on practical and policy implications, it is important to consider some theoretical implications of this study and directions for future research. To a large extent, my work complements that of critical Indigenous scholars such as Glen Coulthard, who argues that over the past forty years there has been a shift from "the directly coercive rule of the last two centuries" to a "more indirect rule that imposes political, economic, and psychological structures that maintain ongoing appropriation of Indigenous peoples' lands and resources" (quoted in Walia 2015, n.p.). Coulthard's focus is mainly on the politics of recognition at the state level, that is, how land claims and modern treaty processes perpetuate settler colonialism. Taking the Rainy River District in the first decade and a half of the twenty-first century as a case study, I have analysed the reproduction of racist and colonialist outlooks and behaviours at the interpersonal and local community levels, with a focus on intergroup boundaries and bridges.

My research demonstrates the utility of group position theory for understanding the persistence of anti-Indigenous prejudice in twenty-first-century small-town Canada. It also shows how the theory can be enriched with concepts from other theories by specifying social psychological, cultural, and political mechanisms whereby Indigenous and white people construct, negotiate, maintain, and challenge their respective senses of group position.

I have also shown that group position theory sheds more light on white than Indigenous attitudes and behaviours. Among whites, survey measures of perceived group threat correlated highly with conservative policy orientations, such as laissez-faire attitudes towards Indigenous poverty and rejection of follow-up action on the IRS apology. Indigenous interviewees, however, displayed little evidence of group threat on the feeling thermometer, and their survey responses bore little relation to other attitudes. As illustrated even more vividly during the powwow video, group home, Point Park, and toll booth controversies, many white residents see things in zero-sum, "us versus them" terms; they are still fighting "to win the war." In contrast, although many Indigenous people are seeking acknowledgment of their identities and rights and a redistribution of resources (including the return of land), they are not trying to reverse group positions, but rather to forge equitable, mutually supportive, nation-to-nation relationships. Absent a willing treaty partner, many are forging ahead with the revitalization of their own languages, laws, and institutions and, as a last resort, putting their bodies on the line to defend their lands and ways of life.[2] However, most remain open to working with settlers who choose the "spiritual" path, as referenced by Mashkawegaabo above.

When we extend group position theory to the settler colonial context, it also becomes clear how the relatively powerful may exert their dominance not only through boundary imposition, but also through the attempted *erasure* of boundaries (i.e., coercive assimilation). In turn, historically marginalized groups may resist oppression not only by seeking to eliminate boundaries, but also by demanding respect for their (cultural, political, and other) boundaries. Asserting treaty rights and exercising Indigenous self-determination, for example, can be a form of antiracism, while statements such as "we are all Canadian" and "everyone should be treated the same" can amount to laissez-faire racism.[3] Nevertheless, the common thread to all forms of racism is the normative assumption of group superiority and the use of this assumption to rationalize (or prescribe) the inferior treatment or position of another group.

My research also demonstrates that although the Canadian landscape has changed since the 1970s – including national political and legal developments that provide more recognition of Indigenous identities and rights (such as the Constitution Act, RCAP, TRC, and various Supreme Court rulings), dramatic ongoing changes in the local population and economy, and higher levels of intergroup contact (including intermarriage and friendship) in the Rainy River District than in past research settings – Indigenous and white residents are still living in largely separate worlds. The "apartheid" is not so much spatial (though First Nations reserves are 95 per cent or more Indigenous and Fort Frances is still over 80 per cent white) or even social (though a substantial minority of residents does not have close cross-group friends), but rather *an apartheid of the mind*. Many white residents continue to think and act in ways that bolster their sense of group position – feeling entitled to their resources and privileges, ignoring their treaty obligations, and opposing policies to rectify injustices. In contrast, although Indigenous residents, out of practical exigencies, often participate in structures that reproduce inequities (by, for example, conforming to political avoidance norms), many of them frame their relationships with settlers in ways that seek to transcend group positioning (such as referencing the medicine wheel in their visions for the future). As shown throughout this book, however, a substantial minority of members in each group also endorses the dominant frame of the other.

The fundamental divide, then, is not so much based on "blood" or "skin" as on clashing ideological frames that sustain or challenge the settler colonial system. Yet these clashing frames have profound implications for racial inequality, including access to land, resources, and health and well-being. As Onkwehonwe scholar Taiaiake Alfred (2009, 177) puts it:

> It is not inherently a racial or ethnic struggle so much as it is an ideological or philosophical one that has racial implications because of the distribution of power in the modern world.

Many Anishinaabe believe that this struggle was prophesied by their ancestors. They suggest that our common interest in protecting and preserving the earth for future generations (and for our own survival and well-being) is the only way forward. Until settlers can learn to reframe their identities and interests as interdependent with those of their Indigenous neighbours, however, settlers will continue to use a predictable set of tactics and justifications to uphold their sense of group position and protect their resources and privileges.

Future Research Directions

This raises the critical question of *how* some settlers come to challenge the dominant sense of group positions. Although my focus has been largely on how whites retain laissez-faire racist views, even amid intergroup contact, the fact is that some white residents perceived the video incident as deeply insulting. Moreover, some believed that the Anishinaabe are the rightful owners/stewards of Point Park and fully supported treaty rights; a few white residents challenged Alberton township on what they perceived to be a prejudicial bylaw; and a substantial minority of settlers felt that far more should be done to "make good" on the federal IRS apology. Indeed, a minority of settlers has always believed that Indigenous peoples have been treated unjustly. Some have even spoken out publicly about it, including Simon Dawson, who had hoped to negotiate a "fair" treaty with the Anishinaabe and later in the 1870s condemned the Indian Act and treaty violations in the Ontario legislature (Chute and Knight 2006), and Dr Peter Bryce, whose 1907 report for the federal Department of Indian Affairs called the residential school system a "national crime" and recommended urgent reform (Miller 1996; Milloy 1999).[4]

The question is: what social processes and experiences lead some settlers to frame their identities and interests in ways that support Indigenous and treaty rights? How do some settlers come to participate in movements like Idle No More? While answering this question is beyond the scope of this book, my research suggests at least two pathways. First, some settlers are born into families who emphasize social justice values, or social responsibilities, and encounter situations that help them recognize that the way Indigenous peoples have been treated violates those values; being a good person, in their mind, depends on fulfilling their responsibilities and seeking fairness for Indigenous peoples. Second, some settlers encounter personal crises (such as the loss of a loved one or struggles with addiction) that lead them to reassess their basic assumptions, attitudes, and ways of life. A common response to crisis is to find comfort in the familiar, but sometimes the familiar breaks down. When such earth-shattering moments coincide with other conditions, such as learning about racism and colonialism or experiencing gestures of love and kindness from Indigenous persons, settlers may begin to transform their sense of group position. While these may not be the only pathways, and they surely involve complexities and caveats, they are useful starting points for more systematic research.[5]

More targeted ethnographic research, in Fort Frances and elsewhere, would also help clarify the pervasiveness and nuances of some of the processes identified in this book. For example, although I supplemented in-depth interviews with field observations at community events and other public and private settings, it may be valuable to conduct more systematic observation in classrooms, schoolyards, and workplaces to develop a more thorough understanding of how group positions are enacted in daily life among residents of specific ages, occupations, and so forth. One intriguing lead came from a Kenora resident who told me about a time-segregation pattern at a local grocery store, where he said white and Indigenous people tended to shop at different times. A larger-scale survey of cross-group marriages, friendships, and organizational memberships would also provide more details on the extent of cross-group contact and its association with laissez-faire attitudes.

There is a need for more detailed within-group analyses as well. My focus has been on the Indigenous/settler divide, especially the processes whereby whites attempt to maintain and justify, and Anishinaabe and Métis attempt to transform, their respective group positions. I deliberately chose to privilege this relationship because it is so foundational to Canada and to the local social structure. However, there are important differences in the attitudes and behaviours of Indigenous and non-Indigenous residents of different ages, classes, genders, geographic locations, and legal statuses, and future research should investigate more directly how these intersect with the dynamics emphasized in this book.

For example, white male and female interviewees tended to express qualitatively different forms of prejudice. Perhaps consistent with gender stereotypes, white women were more likely to express paternalistic attitudes (feeling sorry for "poor Natives"), whereas white men were more likely to express competitive hostility or resentment (especially towards Indigenous activists and those perceived as "a burden on the taxpayer"). What these women and men shared, however, was a sense of group superiority: both felt entitled to their existing resources and privileges and opposed fundamental societal changes. To some extent, these gender differences in attitudes also may be a function of the gendered occupational structure in the district, with women more often working in "helping" professions (health care, education, social services) and men in economically fragile, blue-collar sectors (forestry, small-scale agriculture).

Gender variations were apparent among Indigenous residents, too. Some Indigenous women spoke of the "double burden" they experienced, including racial discrimination and gender-based exclusion and men's violence, which are rooted in colonialism and the Eurocentric gender roles taught by missionaries and in residential schools (Anderson, Campbell, and Belcourt 2018; National Inquiry into Missing and Murdered Indigenous Women and Girls 2019; Stevenson 1999). Some complained that conservative Elders excluded them from participating in ceremonies or practices that they believed their female ancestors were able to participate in (such as drum groups). Other women (and their descendants) who had regained Indian status (and hence eligibility for treaty rights) through Bill C-31 (1985) reported not feeling accepted on reserve; yet many also understood that these internal tensions had been exacerbated (if not entirely created) by government laws and policies that increased the formally recognized Indigenous population without proportionately expanding funding.

Finally, stereotypes specifically about Indigenous women were widespread in the district, reflecting and reinforcing both racist and patriarchal structures. After one meeting with the Right Relations Circle, for example, I joined my partner at a dinner party in town. When I arrived, a local white male acquaintance in his thirties (fully aware of my research topic) joked, "Where were you? Bangin' some chick on Kooch [Couchiching First Nation]?" As Dunk (1991, 114) says, some whites continue to view Indigenous women as "'easy' in sexual terms" or as "victims of the degenerate Indian male" and thus in need of white men's protection. Across Canada, more than twelve hundred Indigenous women have been murdered or have gone missing in the past three decades (RCMP 2014). Several Rainy River District residents have relatives among them. At the same time, Indigenous women have been leading their communities through dramatic positive transformations, setting the example by overcoming addictions, reviving cultural traditions, and defending their lands and rights. A case in point in Treaty No. 3 territory is the ongoing women- and youth-led clear-cutting blockade at Grassy Narrows First Nation (fifty-three kilometres northeast of Kenora) (Willow 2012). Indigenous women have also had some of the greatest labour market improvements in recent years, at a time when Indigenous men's and non-Indigenous Canadians' labour market outcomes have stagnated or declined (DePratto 2015). These gender differences and other within-group differences in attitudes, behaviours, and outcomes merit further attention. Nevertheless, it is important to reiterate that the salient patterns documented in this book cut across the "boundaries" of gender, class, age, location, and formal legal status.

Practical and Policy Implications: Towards the Eighth Fire

Bearing in mind the above needs for further research, I will conclude with some practical and policy implications. First, there is no simple fix to the divisions between Indigenous and non-Indigenous residents in the Rainy River District, or in Canada. Decolonization will play out differently in different regions. What is required, though, is a holistic, multi-pronged, and long-term approach to transforming the structure of group relations and living up to the spirit of the original peace and friendship treaties. Despite my critique of the contact hypothesis (see chapter 7), *contact* can play a role in breaking down the most overt forms of prejudice. We need to foster contact situations that promote empathy and perspective-taking, whether through integrated sports teams, cultural exchange programs, or the types of healing and treatment settings described in earlier chapters.

Likewise, *education* alone has limited impact on the sense of group positions, but specific types of education are necessary. Public opinion surveys (Environics 2010; Godlewska et al. 2013; Ipsos-Reid 2013) show that many – perhaps a majority of – Canadians are ignorant about the basic facts of treaties, residential schools, and contemporary issues facing Indigenous peoples. My research also shows that individuals who have changed their views about these issues have often done so, in part, through critical and historical education. For example, one young man of mixed descent who initially endorsed colour-blind ideology contacted me a year later to say he had changed some of his opinions, "by learning the things they don't teach you in school." Shortly after our interview, he had begun reading more about Indigenous-settler relations, including the political philosophies of Indigenous scholars. While his own self-reflection facilitated the process, he radically changed his views after learning the "real" history. Based on such stories, it is likely that better historical, critical, and experiential education would help overcome the dominant laissez-faire frame.

Yet my research also highlights the problem of not merely ignorance, but *wilful* ignorance. As emphasized in chapter 8, some white residents "know what [they] know and don't want to learn anything new." A major barrier to change is bringing settlers to the table; they know enough to know that furthering their education on these issues, particularly from an Indigenous or critical perspective, may be uncomfortable, and so they avoid it. If, as Regan (2010) suggests, they can sit with the unsettled feelings and reflect on them, they may begin to see another way. Nevertheless, some individuals may never change their minds; they cannot be reached through contact or education because their sense of group position is just too entrenched. This is why the types of education outlined above must be included, in age-appropriate ways, in mandatory public school curricula from an early age (TRC 2015).[6] However, the education system alone cannot be responsible for the necessary changes. Attitudes are developed through manifold experiences in various sectors, including the family, media, and workplaces. Thus, a widespread transformation in settlers' sense of group position will require not only better education but a fundamental shift among all institutions of socialization.

Governments and other organizations must also change their policies if public apologies are to become meaningful. Many *structural* changes can and should be made, and should be relatively straightforward to implement, given the political will. These include fixing the funding formula for on- and off-reserve schools and child welfare organizations and ensuring that all First Nations have access to clean drinking water (see chapter 3). Of course, such policies may generate backlash from settler-Canadians concerned about their taxes and "reverse racism." Yet if reactions to the residential school apology are any indication, many settlers will find ways to rationalize events after the fact (see chapter 9). Moreover, it may be harder for whites to retain a sense of group superiority when the social system changes more deeply; eventually, structural changes will necessitate a change in cultural frames – especially if such changes are accompanied by public awareness campaigns to highlight the common interests of all concerned.

Achieving such policy changes will require coordinated political action and ongoing pressure and lobbying from both Indigenous peoples and settlers. As John Ralston Saul (2014) suggests, a critical mass of

Canadians needs to make this an election issue, voting only for parties that commit to such changes and holding them accountable for doing so. Canadian governments (and corporations) must begin to feel responsible for honouring Indigenous and treaty rights. As King and Pasternak (2015, n.p.) emphasize, however, "the future will not be easy ... The type of change required includes dramatic economic and political shifts."[7]

To truly honour our treaty responsibilities, as settler-Canadians, means *radically transforming* our ways of relating to Indigenous peoples and the land. As Coulthard (2014) puts it, referencing the Two-Row Wampum,[8] the settler ship has toppled the Indigenous canoe, polluted the river, and killed the fish. Perhaps it is time for settlers to not only "sink the ship," but also get out our lifeboats, support the rebuilding of Indigenous canoes (and remediation of the river), and learn how to paddle alongside the canoes. In concrete terms, this means that, in addition to contact, education, and apologies, genuine "reconciliation" will require a more equitable sharing of resources, the transfer of large amounts of land back to Indigenous control (or in some cases co-management), recognition of Indigenous law and jurisdiction on Indigenous lands, and financial support for Indigenous peoples' own healing efforts, language and cultural programs, and economic development initiatives.[9] It also means settlers overhauling our own systems:

> Non-indigenous Canadians must recognize that any restoration of the relationship with indigenous nations will first require a "Canadian comeback," a reorientation of the political economy away from the mythologies of liberal capitalism toward a more sustainable and just economic and social system. (King and Pasternak 2015, n.p.)

In other words, settlers must mobilize not only to help Indigenous peoples or to reconcile with them, but to help and reconcile with ourselves. We must value our responsibilities to one another and the land over the desire to get ahead or outcompete. We must nurture one another's physical, mental, emotional, and spiritual well-being rather than focusing on personal profit. In doing so, we may transform settler society in ways that respect Indigenous sovereignty and fulfil our treaty obligations.

Reconciliation also entails *ongoing dialogue* about what it means to be treaty partners and how to implement treaties today. This last point is crucial. As Anishinaabe scholar Hayden King says:

> First Nations people have always viewed the treaties as long-term relationships that need to be revisited. The chain needs to be polished, as the

Iroquois would say. Sit down and have that discussion on what treaties mean and have a more equitable and just division of jurisdiction and [responsibility] to each other and the land. (quoted in Price 2015, n.p.)

In my research, many white interviewees said that, above all, they wanted certainty, including an end to land claims: "pay them off already, so we can get on with life."[10] But that is *not* how most Anishinaabe frame it. In their view, we have a treaty relationship; a treaty is a sacred covenant to share and care for the land, respect one another's autonomy, and support one another in times of need (see also Craft 2013; Mills 2017). What exactly that looks like must be negotiated on an ongoing basis. Treaties were signed "in perpetuity," "as long as the sun shines and the rivers flow." There is no endpoint. It is a relationship that must be nurtured – continuously. Non-Indigenous Canadians, including our elected representatives and policymakers, must be open to ongoing discussions and (un)learning and demonstrate respect through our actions. Recent developments at the national level, including Supreme Court rulings that better recognize Indigenous title, TRC events, which helped raise public awareness and model the kinds of conversations that need to happen across Turtle Island, and the Idle No More movement, in which tens of thousands of settler-Canadians spoke out for Indigenous self-determination and environmental protection, all may signal a gradual shift in attitudes and the beginnings of new and more equitable relationships.

At the local level, too, there are glimmers of hope amid resistance to change. The indefinite closure of the Fort Frances mill in 2014 was a devastating blow for many white residents. Businesses shuttered, and homes and cottages went up for sale. Yet this turn of events, in conjunction with the ongoing Anishinaabe and Métis resurgence, has also opened new opportunities for Indigenous and settler residents to reimagine and restore their treaty relations. Many settlers are starting to realize that their own survival and well-being depends on working with, not against, Indigenous peoples.

In 2012–13, around the height of Idle No More, thirty-five representatives from the Rainy River District Municipal Association and the Fort Frances Chiefs Secretariat met to develop a list of priorities, including a formal accord to work together on issues of mutual concern – an unprecedented event for the Rainy River District. On the other hand, a recent campaign by Indigenous and settler residents to change the name of Colonization Road – sparked by the 2016 release of a film by the same name concerning the role of such roads in colonization (see chapter 3) – was rejected by Fort Frances municipal council on grounds that it would be too costly. As a young Indigenous resident put it, sarcastically, too many whites still view "reconciliation [as] fiscally irresponsible."

Meanwhile, a large new gold mine north of Barwick (sixty-five kilometres northwest of Fort Frances) opened in 2015 after extensive consultations with Indigenous communities and the signing of impact and benefit agreements with several First Nations and the Métis Nation of Ontario. Many residents see mining as a potential saviour of the local economy, and this time Indigenous communities, perhaps in their best bargaining position since the signing of Treaty No. 3, expect to benefit from jobs, training, and resource revenue sharing. Nevertheless, some Anishinaabe have raised environmental concerns and instead advocate a more fundamental shift away from large-scale resource extraction towards economic and other activities that are not only more equitable but also environmentally sustainable. Indeed, the impending environmental crises posed by climate change may be the ultimate challenge to the sense of group positions, both locally and globally, forcing Indigenous and settler peoples to work together in new ways and reimagine our relationships and responsibilities to ensure our very survival. As these developments continue to unfold, the fork in the road has become clearer. It is up to all of us, Indigenous and settler peoples, to continue the dialogue and choose our directions carefully.

Notes

Preface

1 A "g" or "k" is sometimes added to indicate the plural.

Introduction: Boundaries and Bridges in Indigenous-Settler Relations

1 Between 1876 and 1951, various Indigenous ceremonies were banned by the Indian Act.

2 Indigenous people tend to identify as members of nations, not races. Yet they have also been racialized and subject to racism by settlers. I therefore use the term "race" with the understanding that it is a socially constructed and often externally imposed category.

3 Similarly, critical race theory emphasizes the role of power in race relations and advocates for political change. However, it focuses more on the level of institutional racism and seeks to deconstruct the legal premises and policy frameworks (including colour blindness) that uphold white supremacy (Delgado and Stefancic 2017).

4 In Bonilla-Silva's (1999, 899) view, "after race-based structurations emerge, definite socially existing races arise, which develop distinct objective interests." Therefore, he says, "race" is a legitimate category of analysis.

5 Of course, other forms of racism may operate here as well. Mvskoke sociologist Dwanna Robertson (2015) argues that much racism against Indigenous peoples remains overt – from Pocahontas costumes to derogatory sports team names and logos – but it "has been normalized and institutionally legitimized, thereby rendering it invisible" to most settlers. This is part of the reality in the Rainy River District, and it reflects and reinforces whites' sense of group superiority and entitlement.

6 I sometimes also refer to colour-blind racism, the ideology that if we don't see or talk about race, then racism will disappear, but that leaves structural

inequities intact because the current distribution of resources and existing laws and policies are never challenged (Bonilla-Silva 2003, 2010; Gallagher 2005). Like laissez-faire racism, this ideology stems from "actual or perceived group interests and threats to those interests" (Quillian 2006, 312).

7 One may wonder how group position theory differs from theories of whiteness/white privilege. In North America, all whites benefit, to varying degrees, from white privilege, or the political, economic, social, and psychological advantages of whiteness in a racist society (Lewis 2004; McKinney 2005). However, not all whites feel entitled to their resources and status or threatened by challenges to them. Some fight for racial justice, even as they sometimes also internalize racial stereotypes and act in ways that reproduce racial inequality (Warren 2010). Furthermore, group position theory is not just about white identity and its dynamics; Indigenous, Black, Asian, and other group members also may have a sense of group position relative to one another (Bobo and Hutchings 1996).

8 Interestingly, Bell (2014) notes an almost opposite double bind: to achieve legal recognition of Indigenous rights, Indigenous peoples must demonstrate their cultural difference, yet if they are too well off in settler terms (such asemployment and education), their authenticity is questioned.

9 The number of publications on these topics is too large to cite, but interested readers should consult the work of Canadian-based Indigenous scholars such as Taiaiake Alfred, Chris Andersen, Kim Anderson, Marie Battiste, Cindy Blackstock, Amy Bombay, John Borrows, Martin Cannon, Jeff Corntassel, Glen Coulthard, Aimée Craft, Olive Dickason, Chelsea Gabel, Lynn Gehl, Hayden King, Margaret Kovach, Bonita Lawrence, Leroy Little Bear, Charlotte Loppie, Dawn Martin-Hill, Patricia McGuire, Aaron Mills, Rick Monture, Patricia Monture-Angus, Val Napoleon, David Newhouse, Pam Palmater, Chantelle Richmond, Audra Simpson, Leanne Simpson, Raven Sinclair, Janet Smylie, Verna St. Denis, Eve Tuck, Vanessa Watts, Shawn Wilson, Chelsea Vowel, and Cora Voyageur.

10 Crow Lake is a pseudonym, but Stymeist's description seems to point to Sioux Lookout (286 kilometres northeast of Fort Frances), the main service centre for many fly-in First Nation communities in northwestern Ontario.

11 Constitution Act, 1982, being Schedule B of the Canada Act, 1982 (UK), 1982, c. 11.

12 Indian Residential Schools Settlement Agreement. 2007. http://www .residentialschoolsettlement.ca.

13 Treaty 3 between Her Majesty the Queen and the Saulteaux Tribe of the Ojibbeway Indians at the Northwest Angle on the Lake of the Woods with Adhesions. 1966 [1873]. Transcribed from Roger Duhamel. Ottawa: Queen's Printer and Controller of Stationery. https://www.aadnc-aandc .gc.ca/eng/1100100028675/1100100028679.

14 A small town whose economy has been based primarily on forestry (Lucas 1971).

15 I use 2006 Census data, rather than the 2011 "National Household Survey," because the latter was voluntary and less reliable (e.g., it shows a slight decrease in Indigenous population in Fort Frances, despite well-known trends in the opposite direction).

16 The Métis are "descendants of people born of relations between Indian women and European men" during the fur trade era, "a distinct Aboriginal people with a unique history, culture, language and territory that includes the waterways of Ontario, surrounds the Great Lakes and spans what was known as the historic Northwest" (Métis Nation of Ontario 2019; see http://www.metisnation.org/registry/).

17 Additionally, I gathered documents from the local library and museums, which provided much of the historical and contextual material informing chapter 1.

18 Of the sixty-eight First Nation interviewees, sixty-four were status Indians and four were non-status.

19 More than 80 per cent of the interviews were one-on-one, but when residents asked to be interviewed along with their spouse or friend(s), I obliged. Realizing how productive these interviews were – with residents elaborating on or challenging one another and providing alternative perspectives – I began to deliberately interview some couples to observe interactional dynamics.

20 Compared to 2006 Census data, my sample is somewhat older, more educated, and more likely to be male, employed, and married (see table I.1). This is largely due to the deliberate oversampling of political leaders, who, Blumer (1958) suggests, have disproportionate influence in shaping the sense of group positions. In addition, my research concern with antiracist strategies and the Right Relations Circle likely resulted in over-representation of whites who identify as progressive or antiracist. Conversely, conservative whites may be under-represented; those who expressed overt prejudice in informal interactions sometimes declined interviews. Finally, I did not interview Indigenous individuals whom I knew had experienced severe traumas and were not at a stage of healing where they felt comfortable talking about it. Thus, my data likely provide a *conservative* estimate of the degree of prejudice in the population.

21 The formal interview response rate was 81 per cent for Indigenous and 61 per cent for white residents. The modal reason for declining interviews was "too busy" (about half). Three Anishinaabe cited the history of poor research ethics in Indigenous communities and the desire to speak for themselves. Perhaps illustrating the political avoidance norm (see chapter 7), two whites said they did not want their views interpreted as

"racist," two others did not feel the topic was "relevant," and one said, "I'm not touching that with a ten-foot pole!"

22 For the complete set of interview and survey questions, please contact the author at denisj@mcmaster.ca.

23 Three factors likely explain the difference in interview length: (1) Indigenous interviewees shared more stories of racial discrimination; (2) "traditional" Anishinaabe, especially Elders, tended to have slow, deliberate storytelling styles; (3) many whites gave brief responses and avoided self-disclosure.

24 Regrettably, I left the survey with many interviewees and asked them to return it later. Although more than three-quarters did, others said they were "too busy" or did not respond to follow-up requests.

25 A more complete set of photos and captions may be viewed at https:// whowearerrd.weebly.com/index.html.

26 Some participants already knew each other, but others – especially those not born and raised in the district – met for the first time.

27 The popularity of the photovoice exhibit reiterates the practical importance of the topic. While, to my knowledge, it did not lead to policy changes, it did help raise awareness and facilitate dialogue in a town reticent about discussing the boundaries. For example, there has been recent discussion about renaming Colonization Road.

28 My research design also was approved by Harvard University's Committee on the Use of Human Subjects.

29 I therefore did not interview members of this First Nation.

30 In 2011, I publicly presented my research to about sixty residents at the Métis Community Hall in Fort Frances. In 2012, I gave more targeted presentations to local First Nations leaders, the Right Relations Circle, and the town's Diversity Committee. One key comment from Indigenous residents was that although my arguments resonated, they wanted to hear more about me, as the researcher, and how I fit into the story. They did not just want an academic analysis in a "voice from nowhere," as settler social scientists have often attempted. Much of the preface and periodic references to my own observations and experiences were included largely in response to this feedback.

1. Colonization and the Development of Group Positions

1 Historian Richard White (2011, x) describes the wider Great Lakes region at this time as a "middle ground," a physical and social space in which diverse peoples sought to negotiate their differences and often misunderstood one another, but also developed new systems of shared meaning and exchange.

2 A huge tract of land northwest of Lake Superior, including the Hudson Bay drainage basin and what is now most of northern Quebec, northern Ontario, Manitoba, Saskatchewan, Alberta, northern British Columbia, Yukon, Northwest Territories, and Nunavut.

3 In fact, multiple generations of white Christian settlers were socialized to believe – via government ads, media, and schools – that they were superior and entitled to land and resources, that their hard work as pioneers was building a great country, and that Indigenous ways of life were inferior. However, settlers' economic well-being – as farmers, miners, loggers, and so on – often came at the expense of Indigenous peoples and their ways of life. It is therefore logical that when Indigenous peoples stand up for their land and rights and seek to prevent or control resource-extraction activities on their lands, this is seen as a threat by settlers whose livelihoods have long depended on such activities.

4 When the Canadian government purchased Rupert's Land from the HBC in 1869 and appointed an Anglophone governor, the Métis, led by Louis Riel, forbid the governor from entering the territory and declared a provisional Manitoba government. Prime Minister Macdonald then sent a military expedition to enforce federal authority. For a Métis perspective, see Andersen (2014).

5 Although the Anishinaabe alone might not have defeated the Canadian armed forces, they would have inflicted serious damage, cost the government millions, and perhaps inspired more widespread insurrection, at a time when Canada was worried about securing its border with the United States.

6 A copy of the Paypom Treaty may be accessed at http://caid.ca /paypom010208.pdf.

7 Rainy River Free Grants and Homestead Act. 1886. S.O. 1886, c. 7.

8 For more on the significance of colonization roads for settler colonialism in Canada, see the 2016 film *Colonization Road* narrated by local Anishinaabe comedian Ryan McMahon (St. John 2016).

9 An Act to amend and consolidate the laws respecting Indians, S.C. 1876, c. 18. https://www.aadnc-aandc.gc.ca/eng/1100100010252/1100100010254.

10 For critical analyses of the Indian Act and its amendments, see Cannon (2006) and Lawrence (2004), among others.

11 Under this system, each band (which is usually, but not always, composed of a single First Nation community) must elect a chief and council following the Indian Act.

12 For more details, see the 2015 film *The Pass System* (Williams 2015).

13 Indian agents (almost invariably white men) were appointed by the federal Department of Indian Affairs to administer the Indian Act.

14 Between 1867 and 1996, the federal government funded a church-run res-
    idential school system, whereby over 150,000 Indigenous children were
    forcibly removed from their homes, placed in bleak dormitories, forbidden
    to speak their languages or practise their traditions, given new English or
    French names, and indoctrinated with Christianity. The explicit purpose
    was to "civilize" the "savages" and "assimilate" them to the mainstream
    working class. Survivors were often caught between worlds: denied good
    jobs in settler society because of discrimination and inadequate education
    and alienated from their own communities because they had been re-
    moved for so long and taught to disdain their ways of life.

15 For example, in the 1898 Battle of Sugar Point, the Leech Lake band fought
    US troops (over the arrest of tribal members and the lumber companies'
    over-harvesting of timber), killing six soldiers (Thompson 1979).

16 See, e.g., Cronlund Anderson and Robertson (2011).

17 The Agency One reserve was established "not ... for any particular chief
    or band, but for the Saulteaux Tribe, generally," or at least the Rainy Lake
    bands (Simon Dawn, quoted in Holzkamm and Waisberg 2000, 44). For
    many years, it was the site of the local Indian agent's headquarters.

18 Robert Pither served as Indian agent at Fort Frances between 1871 and
    1888. He remained the park's namesake until 2014 when, after repeated
    complaints by the Anishinaabe about Pither's unjust treatment of Indig-
    enous peoples (including excavating burial mounds at Point Park for
    his root cellar) – despite having an Indigenous wife – the town dropped
    "Pither" from the name.

19 St. Catherine's Milling and Lumber Co. v. The Queen (1888) 14 A.C. 46
    (J.C.P.C.), aff'g (1887), 13 S.C.R. 577 (S.C.C.).

20 The significance of this court decision cannot be understated. The Judicial
    Committee of the Privy Council (the highest court of appeal in the United
    Kingdom) essentially ruled that the crown could overturn Aboriginal title
    whenever it wished. This became the basis for "Aboriginal law" in Canada
    for more than a century. More recent rulings by the Supreme Court of Can-
    ada (such as the 1997 Delgamuukw and 2014 Tsilhqot'in decisions) define
    Aboriginal title more liberally; but, while they restrict the conditions under
    which the federal or provincial governments may override Aboriginal title,
    they still give the crown the final say (Alfred 2005; Pottie 2014; Tsilhqot'in
    Nation v. British Columbia (2014) S.C.C. 44).

21 Social Darwinism was an ideology that distorted Charles Darwin's theory
    of evolution and misapplied it to human societies. It claimed, for example,
    that some human "races" were physically and morally superior to other
    races and would (or should) naturally outcompete them. Such ideas were
    often used to justify late-nineteenth to early-twentieth-century European
    imperialism and, later, Nazism (Hofstadter 1992).

22 A more detailed history of Indigenous-settler relations in the mid-twenti-
    eth century could be gleaned from oral histories, church archives, employ-
    ment records, and census data. This would be another project in itself. The
    key point here is that, by now, the balance of power was in settlers' favour,
    their sense of group position was entrenched, and intergroup relations
    were generally pleasant so long as Indigenous people knew their "place."

23 For more on the Sixties Scoop (as it unfolded in Ontario) and the associ-
    ated class action lawsuit, see https://www.sixtiesscoopsettlement.info/.

24 As the TRC (2015, 138) explains, child apprehensions were also based on
    "prejudicial attitudes toward Aboriginal parenting skills and a tendency
    to see Aboriginal poverty as a symptom of neglect, rather than as a conse-
    quence of failed government policies."

25 Weechi-it-te-win strives to provide "care that is rooted in [Anishinaabe]
    customs, traditions and values" and "to repatriate children who have been
    brought into care outside of Weechi-it-te-win's jurisdiction and reunite
    them with their families, communities and culture" (www.weechi.ca).

26 While class, gender, and other such inequalities exist within "Indigenous"
    and "settler" groups (Satzewich and Wotherspoon 2000), the Indigenous/
    settler divide is especially salient in many regions, including northwestern
    Ontario. For analyses of between-group inequalities on a cross-Canada
    scale, see Denis (2018), Frideres and Gadacz (2011), and RCAP (1996),
    among others.

27 As explained by local Métis lawyer Clint Calder at a public forum in 2009,
    the land is technically held in trust by the Crown. Since the federal govern-
    ment reportedly would not authorize new arrangements on the land, the
    former golf course became an open field.

28 Delgamuukw v. British Columbia (1997) 3 S.C.R. 1010; R v. Marshall (1999)
    3 S.C.R. 456.

29 On the limitations of such legal decisions, see Alfred (2005) and Pottie
    (2014), among others.

30 A seventy-eight-day armed standoff between Mohawk warriors, the
    RCMP, and Quebec police (Simpson and Ladner 2010).

31 For more on these and other conflicts, see Coulthard (2012) and Hedican
    (2013).

32 Reasons for the population increase include a much higher birth rate, leg-
    islation such as Bill C-31, which enabled many First Nation women (who
    had lost status through intermarriage) and their descendants to regain sta-
    tus, and a growing number of residents tracing their ancestry and apply-
    ing for Métis citizenship (Cannon 2006; Statistics Canada 2007). Reasons
    for the decrease in white population include a lower birth rate and higher
    youth out-migration, especially with the collapse of the forestry sector
    (Ortiz-Guerrero 2010).

33 At the Ainsworth OSB (oriented strandboard) manufacturing plant in Barwick, between 1997 and 2010, an average of 2 of 155 employees identified as Indigenous.

34 Across Canada, twenty of fifty paper mills have closed since 2000, and 118,000 forestry jobs (one third) were slashed between 2004 and 2014. Reasons include decreased demand for paper, high energy costs, international competition, and fluctuating exchange rates (Keenan, Parkinson, and Jang 2014; Ortiz-Guerrer 2010).

35 The question of Métis identification is politically fraught. See, e.g., Andersen (2014) and Vowel and Leroux (2016).

36 R v. Powley (2003) S.C.C. 43.

37 Approximately half of Fort Frances residents who had identified as Métis on the census were MNO members.

38 Although MNO membership requires acceptance by the Métis community, some individuals of mixed descent have acquired Indian status through Bill C-31 without participating in any First Nation community.

2. Perceiving Group Relations, Constructing Group Positions

1 Ten of these residents were interviewed a second time in the summer of 2009, due to their involvement in the Alberton group home controversy (see chapter 5). I asked if their views had changed since six to fifteen months earlier, and treated their new responses as additional "cases," coding them separately from original responses. The total sample size in table 2.1, therefore, is 170. Excluding these cases from the analysis does not change the trends reported here. For a complete list of residents' descriptions, categorized by emotional valence and frequency of reporting, please contact the author at denisj@mcmaster.ca.

2 The ten follow-up interviewees received two "predominant" codes each. Four of them changed their overall assessments (all in a negative direction).

3 For many Indigenous people, the term "integration" has negative connotations because it seems indistinguishable from "assimilation." In cases where interviewees used these terms to portray relations in a *negative* light, I did not include them in the "positive" tally.

4 In 1985, the federal government passed Bill C-31, An Act to Amend the Indian Act, restoring eligibility for Indian status (and thereby entitlement to treaty rights) to thousands of women and their descendants. The stated goal was to remove discriminatory rules, whereby, since 1876, Indigenous women who married non-status men had lost status and all associated rights and benefits. For critical analyses of this legislation, see Cannon 2006; Palmater 2011.

5 Although this was the consensus of most Fort Frances residents, including many Indigenous people, Kenora residents did not necessarily agree. According to an Anishinaabe Elder who once lived in Fort Frances but now lived in Kenora, "They're both the same ... Fort Frances is more subtle, but it [racism] is still there."

6 As of writing, 31 of 127 First Nation communities in Ontario do not have year-round road access.

7 This explanation seems to assume that settlers otherwise have little exposure to Indigenous people – a questionable assumption, since similar percentages of Indigenous people live in Kenora (15.8 per cent) and even more in Sioux Lookout (28.2 per cent) than in Fort Frances (16.8 per cent) (Statistics Canada 2007).

8 An alternative, but not mutually exclusive, explanation for the perception that intergroup relations are worse in Kenora and Sioux Lookout is the different local histories. Some residents pointed to the armed occupation of Anicinabe Park in Kenora in 1974 and the publication of the racist *Bended Elbow* pamphlet by a Kenora nurse the next year. Such events are relatively rare in the history of Fort Frances.

9 Technically, the settlement included 14,945 acres of provincial Crown land, which government agreed to set aside as reserve land, and the opportunity to "purchase up to 31,300 acres (12,677 hectares) of replacement land on a willing-buyer/willing-seller basis over a 40-year period and propose that land for reserve status" (http://media.knet.ca/node/1436).

10 However, the modal response for both groups was "mixed" (good and bad, up and down).

11 In fact, none of the first dozen interviewees (February to April 2008), including five whites, described relations in predominantly positive terms.

12 There is no reason to conclude that these trends were driven by temporal differences in interviewee composition. Even whites interviewed within six months of the video incident and whites interviewed in 2009 were far less likely to describe relations in positive terms (20 per cent and 10 per cent, respectively) compared to whites interviewed in the "lull" period between August and December 2008 (53 per cent). The only demographic difference between interviewees across the three time periods was that those interviewed in 2009 were somewhat more highly educated and more likely to be working in economically fragile industries.

13 Some houses on local reserves might be "gorgeous," but they were no more luxurious than the homes of many white residents in the Rainy River District, and census data revealed higher overcrowding and more need for major housing repairs on reserve. The idea that "education is basically there for them if they want it" is also a stereotype. Although some First Nation students are eligible for the Post-Secondary Student Support

Program (PSSSP), they must apply through their band, and there are strict eligibility criteria and (often) waiting lists. Métis and non-status students are ineligible. Furthermore, on-reserve schools receive significantly less funding than off-reserve schools, and many students must move far away from home to complete high school, creating substantial barriers to even being in a position to access the limited post-secondary funding.

3. Boundary Work and Group Positioning

1 It should be noted here that interviewees interpreted the term "bounda-ries" in multiple ways. Some understood it in the Barthian sense of the cri-teria that define and distinguish groups, claiming, for example, that being Anishinaabe was not just a matter of blood or self-identification, but also one of cultural practices and community acceptance. Most interviewees, however, took the existence of Indigenous and non-Indigenous groups for granted and focused instead on the barriers to getting along or sources of conflict between these groups.

2 In asking this question, I assumed (as did most interviewees) that there was already an Indigenous/settler boundary, that is, that the categories "Aboriginal" and "non-Aboriginal" were *socially* real. The question was: what separates or divides them? What prevents mutually respectful rela-tionships? And how do the perceived sources of division support (or chal-lenge) the dominant sense of group positions?

3 For a complete list, please contact the author at denisj@mcmaster.ca.

4 Furniss (1999, 17) highlights how whites' understanding of history is shaped by the "frontier myth," wherein settlers are the protagonists, struggling with a harsh environment and facing unknown and poten-tially hostile Indians. Their accounts of historical events valorize inde-pendence, courage, freedom, materialism, and advancement through hard work. Moreover, "the categories of Indian and white are mutually exclusive and oppositional," and "Euro-Canadian cultural superiority, material privileges, and political authority are taken as unquestioned truths."

5 Some Indigenous interviewees said that many Indigenous people also lack historical knowledge. Before the Elders pass on, they are trying to impart this knowledge to the youth, through community gatherings, cultural con-ferences, story-telling sessions, and other means.

6 Dorothy was not representative of white residents in the region. She had spent most of her adult life as a peace activist abroad and was an active member of the Right Relations Circle.

7 This is incorrect. Under sections 87 and 90 of the Indian Act, status Indi-ans' employment and business income "earned on a reserve" and "goods

bought on, or delivered to, a reserve" are exempt from taxation. These exemptions do *not* apply to Métis, Inuit, or non-status Indians. Moreover, "Indian property not situated on a reserve will generally be subject to tax just like property held by other Canadians." Status Indians who work off reserve are subject to income tax, the same as non-Indigenous Canadians who work off reserve. Ultimately, tax exemptions only apply to about 10 per cent of Indigenous people in Canada (Spielmann 2009). For more details, see Canada Revenue Agency's "Information for Indians," available at http://www.cra-arc.gc.ca/brgnls/stts-eng.html#heading1.

8 This would only be true if the two nurses were employed on reserve or at a registered First Nation government organization *and* if one was a status Indian and the other was not.

9 A majority of white interviewees said they do not oppose harvesting rights. However, many felt that these rights were "abused," referring to fish and wildlife allegedly being wasted or sold for profit (rather than used for self-sustenance). Some also felt that if Indigenous people want to exercise harvesting rights they should not use modern equipment, thereby framing the issue as a mutually exclusive choice between tradition and modernity. Many Indigenous residents countered that traditional Anishinaabe are in fact the greatest conservationists; far from wasting fish or game, they "only take what they need" and "use all parts of the animal" (meat for food, hide for drums, bone marrow for medicines, etc.). Some also believed that they should be able to make a moderate living from selling fish or game – just as the Mi'kmaq have the Supreme Court–recognized right to sell lobster. Others cited another form of "abuse" where *white* residents invite a "token Native" hunting so that they can shoot as much game (or catch as many fish) as they want; then, if inspected by the Ministry of Natural Resources (MNR), they claim that the Native shot (or caught) them all. An MNR officer in the district said this was an ongoing problem.

10 As Thomas King (2012, 69) says in *The Inconvenient Indian*, most non-Indigenous North Americans love "Dead Indians" (noble savages, who fought the good fight but tragically lost), ignore "Live Indians" (living, breathing Indigenous people), and resent "Legal Indians" (who "because of the treaties ... are entitled to certain rights and privileges" and are a constant reminder of how this country was formed).

11 The only alternative is for Canada to claim statehood on the basis of the racist "doctrine of discovery," as Mashkawegaabu (Al Hunter) suggested above.

12 Some interviewees carefully distinguished between treaty rights and welfare benefits, specifically the introduction of social assistance programs in Canada in 1965. While defending treaties, some Indigenous people

criticized the welfare system for creating more problems than it has solved. According to an older Native couple, for example:

> HUSBAND: Before 1965, I can't help but think that there was more mutual respect. In 1965, the government opted to change the welfare system. That's when the trouble started ... now, people expect a lot for nothing. And I think a lot of that is on the shoulders of the government. We were a proud people ... What we had, we worked for and we owned it and –
> WIFE: And life was good. There was nobody running around with name-brand shirts, but ... you shared.

13 In 2011, the Mississaugas of the New Credit First Nation signed a larger ($145 million) settlement to compensate for the unscrupulous purchase of much of the Greater Toronto Area.

14 Rainy River First Nations Settlement Agreement. 2005. http://www .rainyriver.firstnation.ca/land-claims.

15 Specifically, the communities of Hungry Hall 1 and 2, Little Forks, Long Sault 1 and 2, and Manitou Rapids 1 and 2 were amalgamated at Manitou Rapids reserve.

16 Family farms across Canada have been struggling due to the rise of large-scale "agri-business." Like the collapse of forestry, this downturn has affected white residents far more than Indigenous residents because the former are more likely to work in these sectors. Their economic uncertainty – juxtaposed with the recent economic gains of local First Nations (including land claim settlements) – is yet another reason why whites might perceive a "realistic threat" to their group position.

17 The 1997 Delgamuukw case concerned First Nations in BC that had not signed treaties. However, the same principle that Indigenous nations retain Indigenous title unless it is explicitly surrendered in a legally binding treaty would apply.

18 In Canadian law, the federal government is essentially a trustee to the First Nations.

19 The "duty to consult and accommodate" is also recognized in Section 35(1) of the Constitution Act (1982). The sticking point is what should happen when parties disagree. Many First Nations believe that, as sovereign nations, they should have the right to veto resource extraction (or other) activities on their territories. The federal and provincial governments and most corporations tend to disagree.

20 Disagreements about membership criteria are a major source of division *within* Indigenous communities. But working out such conflicts for themselves is an essential aspect of self-determination.

21 In fact, the term "First Nation" was first used in the early 1980s when the National Indian Brotherhood changed its name to the Assembly of First Nations to emphasize their status as multiple independent nations, rather than a single ethnic group (Frideres 2011). While the European form of nation state may not have existed in North America prior to colonization, Indigenous peoples did live in highly organized, self-governing societies with their own political, economic, and cultural systems, and there are synonyms for "nation" in many Indigenous languages.

22 Three separate white interviewees spontaneously used this term.

23 This interviewee is not saying that Indigenous peoples are incapable of punctuality, but that they have different norms around time (such as the idea that meetings start when everyone is ready). While some Indigenous residents joked about "Indian time," the notion that they are inherently tardy is a harmful stereotype (Spielmann 2009).

24 To understand the context underlying these issues, see the final reports of the Royal Commission on Aboriginal Peoples (1996), the Truth and Reconciliation Commission of Canada (2015), and the National Inquiry on Missing and Murdered Indigenous Women and Girls (2019).

25 While the interviewee did not have permanent employment income, he was paid (in cash and in kind) for various short-term jobs. He also hunted, fished, and gathered for many of his family's needs.

4. Racism, Prejudice, and Discrimination

1 All names used in this chapter are pseudonyms.

2 Although this interviewee used the term "racist," here she is technically referring to prejudice – negative attitudes towards "the other." From a sociological view, racism requires structural power (Bonilla-Silva 2010; Feagin 2010).

3 When asked to share some "Native jokes" so that I could understand the humour, he glanced around the restaurant and said, "Um ... " "You can whisper," I assured him. He chuckled and said, "You know what? I don't have any off the top of my head."

4 On public opinion polls, 36 per cent of Canadians say that Indigenous peoples' economic problems are "mainly their fault." The percentage jumps to 52 per cent in Manitoba (Macdonald 2015).

5 Some also disputed the dominant definition of poverty, saying that while they may not be employed in the mainstream economy, they are "rich" in their ways – hunting, fishing, speaking their language, practising their traditions, and providing for their families.

6 Is opposition to treaty rights necessarily evidence of group position prejudice? Granted, many Canadians are ignorant about treaties and might

change their minds with better historical education. However, some residents were fairly knowledgeable about the subject and still rejected treaties with racially tinged rhetoric. In a Wisconsin case, Bobo and Tuan (2006) found perceived group threat to be the best explanation for white opposition to Chippewa fishing rights. Treaty rights opponents carried placards stating, "Spare a fish, spear an Indian." In such cases, treaty opposition cannot be separated from group position prejudice. More generally, attempts to found the country on anything other than an equitable nation-to-nation agreement may be seen as racist.

7 While I do not aim here to generalize about population distributions, my quantitative measures probably underestimate the overall degree of prejudice in the region. My participation in the Right Relations Circle led to interviews with some of the most vocal antiracists. Conversely, some overtly bigoted whites declined interviews. Many whites also expressed more prejudiced views during interviews and informal conversations than they did on questionnaires. Such discrepancies may result from impression management or distrust of the researcher.

8 Using Krieger et al.'s (2005) Experiences of Discrimination questionnaire, I asked respondents "Have you personally experienced discrimination, been prevented from doing something, or been hassled or made to feel inferior in any of the following [nine settings] because of your race, ethnicity, or color?" If the answer was yes, they were asked to share examples.

9 The mean (average) numbers were 13, 7.5, and 2.4, respectively. These findings are consistent with other surveys of racial discrimination in northwestern Ontario. For example, one study in Thunder Bay found that 56 per cent of Indigenous respondents had experienced racial discrimination *in the past year*, compared to 23 per cent of other racialized respondents and 14 per cent of the (majority-white) overall sample (N = 392) (Haluza-Delay 2002). While my percentages are somewhat higher, I asked about discrimination over the life course. The Urban Aboriginal Task Force (2007) also identified racial discrimination as a major barrier, especially in northern Ontario; in its survey of 159 Indigenous residents of Kenora, 94 per cent said they had experienced discrimination and 96 per cent believed it was an ongoing problem. A sceptic might wonder if Indigenous people are more inclined to report negative experiences, but this is unlikely; historically oppressed groups have often "internalized negative views of the dominant culture and accepted their subordinate status and related unfair treatment as 'deserved' and hence non-discriminatory" (Krieger 2000, 57). Shame and denial are also common (RCAP 1996; TRC 2015), making under-reporting likely. Moreover, I repeatedly observed anti-Indigenous discrimination, while I, as a white person, was treated with great respect by Anishinaabe and Métis residents.

10 Pseudonym for common surname in the region.
11 Pseudonym.

5. The Alberton Group Home Controversy

1 An "encounter" is a power-laden set of interactions between groups who are "forced to confront one another, make sense of each other's motives and differences, and [who are often] transformed in the process" (Espeland 2001, 407). Like the video incident described in the Introduction, the Alberton group home controversy was another "critical moment" with potential to reconfigure beliefs, attitudes, identities, and structures (Winship 2004).

2 Alberton's population fell to 864 in 2011 (a 9.8 per cent decline since 2006).

3 TLC clients are twelve to seventeen year olds who have been removed from home for assessment, treatment, and temporary residence due to problems such as parental neglect. They may have substance abuse or social/emotional issues. There are separate facilities for sex offenders and violent-crime-involved youth (see http://www.weechi.ca).

4 Under the Indian Act (1876), First Nations do not own their reserves; the land is held in trust by the federal government. In a settler colonial context, therefore, the question of land ownership has added significance.

5 The property had large buildings easily convertible into student dormitories, plentiful storage space, horses and stables, serene walking trails, a pond with wildlife, a central location, a reasonable price, and potential for future development (such as relocating administrative offices).

6 The Alberton municipal council consists of five locally elected residents who serve three-year terms and are eligible for re-election. They are accountable to the voters but also bound by federal and provincial legislation.

7 The alleged Native conspiracy to "take over" the township and turn it into a reserve was based on a few residents weaving together distinct recent activities, including the Rainy River First Nations buying a stake in a local business, a First Nations family purchasing a private home in the township, and WFS proposing to relocate its Training and Learning Centre. The only connection between these three actions was that they all involved First Nations people. There was no plan to convert any of the properties into reserve lands.

8 For instance, marginalized groups might emphasize morality rather than material wealth (Lamont 2000).

9 For instance, smudging is said to cleanse the spirit and shield it from negative energies.

10 The Seven Grandfather Teachings are respect, courage, wisdom, truth, honesty, humility, and love.

11 For more on the residential school system (including St. Margaret's Residential School, just east of Fort Frances), see chapters 1 and 9. Importantly, the Alberton group home controversy occurred just one year after the federal government's Indian residential school apology and promise to forge a new relationship based on "mutual respect." The reaction of Alberton residents seems to indicate a disjuncture between the national rhetoric of "truth and reconciliation" and the actual state of intergroup relations on the ground, at least in some communities.

12 Increasingly, Indigenous scholars and activists emphasize the struggle for self-determination over the "politics of [external] recognition" (Alfred and Corntassel 2005; Coulthard 2014; Simpson 2008). Many Anishinaabe and Métis residents do not see these pursuits as mutually exclusive. However, incidents like that described in this chapter may enhance the perception that seeking settlers' acceptance is futile, if not counterproductive.

13 There is also a growing body of social psychological research on individual interpretations of and responses to specific incidents of racial discrimination (Bombay, Matheson, and Anisman 2013; Ziersch et al. 2011). Another approach to studying antiracism focuses on the identities and actions of self-defined antiracist activists and organizations (Srivastava 2006; Warren 2010). In the Indigenous-settler relations context, several authors have examined alliance-building and solidarity work (Davis 2010; Grossman 2017; Lawrence and Dua 2005; Wallace 2013). See chapter 10 for more details on the local Right Relations Circle.

14 The OMB (reconfigured as the Local Planning Appeal Tribunal as of 1 January 2019) was "an independent tribunal subject to the rules of natural justice" and provincial legislation. It heard applications and appeals on land use planning, financial, and other municipal issues (https://elto.gov .on.ca/tribunals/lpat/about-lpat).

15 Some of these concerns, especially fears of crime, are associated with racial but also class- and age-based stereotypes.

16 Under sections 87 and 90 of the Indian Act, status Indians are, under specific conditions, exempt from certain forms of taxation – a major irritant for many white residents (see chapter 3).

17 Although some residents may have genuinely believed that the youth would be better off on reserve, any such arguments were undermined by angry caveats such as "Don't you get it? We don't want *you people* here!"

18 When asked privately, virtually every resident I spoke with acknowledged that at least "a few bad apples" were driven by prejudice. However, they insisted that their *own* opposition to the group home was not. The tendency to reduce the problem to the overt bigotry of a small minority, while ignoring structural inequities, is another process that contributes to the reproduction of systemic racism.

19 Denying the relevance of racism to political decision-making helps maintain the sense of group positions by implying that settlers are naturally entitled to their existing privileges.

20 While "playing the victim" might seem contrary to maintaining a sense of *superior* group position, it ultimately serves to protect dominant group privileges. By claiming the moral high ground ("I am innocent," "two wrongs don't make a right"), whites try to pre-empt claims to their resources (McKinney 2005).

21 If the property were zoned "rural residential," no rezoning application, and hence no public meeting, would have been required.

22 The official reason for denying the rezoning request was that it "[did] not follow the Township Official Plan," under which the property had been zoned a "business park" (despite being in residential use for decades). Yet some councillors themselves had ridiculed the official plan. At the 8 July meeting, one joked that the consultant who wrote it unknown years ago probably "took the same template for the whole of Ontario and sent it everywhere ... made a million dollars ... and then left for the Bahamas."

23 See http://celebratingdiversity.ca/.

24 The *Globe and Mail* also ran a feature story the following summer (White 2010).

25 Another option was appealing to the Ontario Human Rights Tribunal, which addresses discrimination complaints (http://www.hrto.ca/hrto/index.php?q=en). However, legal counsel worried that the human rights code deals more with individual than collective discrimination.

26 At the third meeting, MPP Hampton recounted similar cases of past resistance to and fears about group homes in the region that ultimately amounted to "a hill of beans." In his view, if WFS were given a chance, residents would hardly notice its presence.

27 Quoted from the Response of Dorothy Friesen and Mervin Eugene Stoltzfus to Alberton Township Council Motion to Dismiss Appeal of Interim Control By-Law No. 22/09, 4 November 2009.

28 The appellants insist that the documents were hand delivered to the township clerk.

29 Quoted from Ontario Municipal Board Decision, Case PL090831, 13 May 2010.

6. Bridge Work

1 For a complete list, please contact the author at denisj@mcmaster.ca.

2 Even the Métis celebration was part of an annual "Proud to be Canadian" Heritage Day event.

3 Although a few Indigenous interviewees were apathetic about language and culture loss, most Indigenous residents I spoke with were highly

interested in retaining their traditions and passing them on to future generations; some were taking language courses and many hoped that their children would be fluent in Anishinaabemowin.

4 Smaller percentages of whites and much smaller percentages of Indigenous residents attended Anglican, United, and evangelical churches in the district.

5 For more on the tensions and ties between Indigenous and settler spiritual beliefs and practices, see Heinrichs (2014).

6 In fact, nearly 80 per cent of First Nation interviewees (and 75 per cent of white interviewees) reported hunting or trapping.

7 The phrase "good and bad in all races" may seem less susceptible to such twisting. It is antiracist in that it rejects categorical stereotyping. As will be seen in chapter 7, however, it can also be a form of subtyping, which is often used to justify racial inequalities and bolster whites' sense of group superiority.

8 As mentioned above, long-standing Anishinaabe teachings on how to live a good life, based on wisdom, love, respect, bravery, honesty, humility, and truth (Benton-Banai 1988).

9 A teaching tool consisting of red, white, black, and yellow quadrants, which, inter alia, represent the striving for balance, equity, and respect among all peoples from "the four corners" of the world (e.g., Brant Castellano 2011).

10 Stones that may be used in a sweat lodge ceremony.

11 During the Idle No More movement, many Indigenous and some non-Indigenous activists made similar arguments at a national level (Axworthy and Kinew 2013; Palmater 2013).

12 Indeed, Couchiching First Nation already has its own golf course, bingo hall, and hockey arena, and has contemplated opening its own school and water treatment facility.

13 The woodlands division is responsible for supplying logs to the mills and monitoring and managing forestlands.

14 According to a senior manager at the Fort Frances mill, as of 2009 less than 2 per cent of the 700-plus employees identified as First Nations. At the Ainsworth plant in Barwick, only 3 of the 155 employees identified as Indigenous. Even at Manitou Forest Products (the RRFN-owned sawmill), approximately half of the sixty employees were white.

15 In 2011, AbitibiBowater changed its name to Resolute Forest Products. In 2014, the Fort Frances mill announced an indefinite shutdown, citing "poor market conditions" (CBC 2014). As of writing, only a few staff are employed to keep the plant clean, and Resolute is considering alternative products.

7. A Tenuous Balance

1 Other scholars also have observed that contact may coexist with conflict. Barth (1969, 10), for example, noted that "ethnic distinctions do not depend on an absence of social interaction ... but are quite to the contrary the very foundations on which embracing social systems are built." However, Barth did not directly theorize colonization or specify the social psychological mechanisms that maintain the sense of group positions.

2 About one-third of these were Métis and two-thirds were First Nations.

3 In addition, 12 per cent of First Nation interviewees had a Métis partner, and 25 per cent of Métis interviewees had a First Nation partner. Intermarriage rates in the broader population are not publicly available.

4 Some interviewees may have guessed about their friends' racial/ethnic backgrounds, but few said they did not know. There are, of course, ongoing debates about what constitutes Indigenous (and settler) identity and the criteria for determining race/ethnicity.

5 The median score for Indigenous leaders rose to 3.5.

6 Among these "antiracist" whites, nearly all who were born in the region had at least one close Indigenous friend. Of the three principled antiracists who were *not* born there, only one had a close Indigenous friend.

7 In Feagin and Vera's (1995) terms, many whites are "passive bystanders" who may not support discrimination, but do not actively oppose it; smaller numbers are "officiants" (who commit racist acts), "acolytes" (who support officiants), and "race traitors" (who actively confront racism).

8 A white conservation officer I spoke with did not confirm these stories. In his view, traditional Anishinaabe are more conservation minded than whites.

9 Exactly how many residents followed this norm is unclear, but it is most evident in its breach. In later interviews and public presentations, Indigenous and white residents agreed this description was "bang-on for this district."

10 Other researchers have observed a similar compartmentalization of life realms, highlighting how people find ways to "live together apart" (Durrheim and Dixon 2005, 60). Minard (1952), for example, showed how black and white American miners had harmonious interactions underground, but re-established racial divisions above ground.

11 This refusal is unlikely to be explained simply by "social desirability bias"; when 39 per cent of whites decline confidential interviews with a fellow white person, something deeper is at stake. If I had not disclosed my topic, the response rate likely would have been higher. For instance, one white store manager initially seemed interested in being interviewed, but when

told it was for a study of "Aboriginal–non-Aboriginal relations," she declined, saying "I'm not touching that with a ten-foot pole!"

12 At this fourth annual "National Treaties #1–11 Gathering," a resolution was passed to support the claim that stewardship should be restored to the Agency One First Nations.

13 Over the next few years, three more "critical incidents" briefly shattered the "veneer" of racial harmony: white backlash to the proposed establishment of an Anishinaabe group home in Alberton (see chapter 5), an even more intense backlash to Couchiching First Nation's construction of a toll booth on Highway 11 to protest government neglect (see chapter 10), and the Idle No More movement (see chapter 10). Each case was marked by a sudden rupture and rise in tensions, widespread denial, and apparent shock, active attempts by whites to restore "order," with collusion by some Indigenous people, and another period of political avoidance.

8. Education, Group Positioning, and Ideological Refinement

1 However, these attitudinal differences may be due as much to self-selection as to the impact of specialized education/training.

2 This is an overstatement. At the time, Big Grassy, Lac La Croix, and Onigaming First Nations all had their own schools, in part due to their distance from town. Big Grassy's school offered kindergarten to grade 8, and also served students from Big Island First Nation. The other two schools offered kindergarten to grade 12. But some youth from these communities also boarded with families in town and attended the Fort Frances high school. Meanwhile, growing numbers of Indigenous students were opting out of the "mainstream" system. A small number were pursuing traditional education through home schooling. A larger number had completed their high school diplomas through Seven Generations Education Institute, an organization operated by ten local First Nations since 1985.

3 Although the Rainy River District School Board declined to share the results of its Indigenous self-identification surveys, one school administrator estimated that Indigenous students constituted more than 30 per cent of the high school population, but that only one in six graduates (17 per cent) in 2009 was Indigenous (a record high for the school board). Moreover, another local educator said Indigenous students were already "two or three years behind" in basic literacy skills by grade 3. Some Indigenous and allied scholars dispute such claims on the basis that standardized tests are biased, or at least do not measure the knowledge and skills valued most by Indigenous people. To the extent that they are accurate measures of specific skill sets, they are the result of cumulated (dis)advantage.

4 Since my interviews in 2008–9, the Province of Ontario, in consultation
   with Indigenous community members, has revised portions of the public
   school history and Indigenous studies curricula to include more comprehensive accounts of residential schools and treaties. As of writing,
   however, much of this material is only covered in elective high school
   courses, rather than being mandatory for all children from kindergarten
   to grade 12. After the release of the TRC's (2015) final report, the province announced plans to respond to TRC Call to Action 62 and "ensure
   that the impact of residential schools, the history of colonization and the
   importance of treaties is incorporated into mandatory learning expectations in Ontario's public education system curriculum" (Government of
   Ontario 2016). In 2015, treaty education kits, developed by Kelly Crawford
   of M'Chigeeng First Nation, were made available for grades 1–8 teachers
   across the province (*Anishinabek News 2015*).
      At the post-secondary level, as of 2016, Lakehead University in Thunder
   Bay required all students to take at least one half-credit with "significant
   Indigenous knowledge" (CBC 2015a), and the University of Winnipeg
   introduced a mandatory Indigenous Studies course requirement (CBC
   2015b).
5 Conversely, another Anishinaabe woman (not from the district) argued
   that, given the history of forced assimilation and cultural appropriation,
   perhaps Indigenous language programs *should* be restricted to Indigenous children, at least until there is a greater number of fluent language
   speakers.
6 Compared to the Rainy River District population as a whole (Indigenous
   and non-Indigenous), interviewees were more highly educated, on average. As of the 2006 Census, 30.2 per cent of residents had not completed
   high school, 28.2 per cent had a high school diploma or GED, and 41.6 per
   cent had a post-secondary degree (9.3 per cent had a university degree).
   With a larger, more representative sample, it is possible that differences
   in attitudes between the highly educated and those with a high school diploma or less would be more pronounced.
7 The 2005 Kelowna Accord was an agreement between the federal government, all provinces and territories, and five national Indigenous organizations that would have significantly increased funding for Indigenous
   education, health care, housing, and economic development. It was unilaterally cancelled by the federal Conservatives in 2006.
8 Overall, Indigenous interviewees were slightly more educated than the
   Indigenous population in the Rainy River District. As of the 2006 Census,
   39.3 per cent of Indigenous residents had not completed high school,
   26.1 per cent had a high school diploma or GED, and 34.7 per cent had a
   post-secondary degree (5.8 per cent had a university degree).

Although overall education attainment levels were lower for Indigenous than for non-Indigenous residents, at the time of this study the gap was narrowing. In 2014, thirty-one students from Couchiching First Nation alone graduated from a post-secondary program, and more Indigenous than white students had reportedly graduated "on time" with a four-year university degree. This educational turnaround was a source of pride for many Indigenous residents.

9 Two white men with university degrees – one white collar, the other blue collar – later told me that they had "held back" in their interviews. One had close Indigenous friends.

10 However, the majority of Indigenous interviewees with less formal education also supported Indigenous and treaty rights.

11 While cases of extravagant remuneration and corruption exist (Popplewell 2010), they are at least as common among non-Indigenous leaders. The vast majority of First Nation chiefs make less than $100,000 (the median salary is $60,000, and 42 of 582 chiefs subject to the 2014 First Nations Financial Transparency Act made less than $10,000), and most work extremely hard for their communities (see Smith 2015; Warry 2007).

9. Racial Contestation and the Residential School Apology

1 For a local Anishinaabe approach to holistic healing, see Morrisseau (1998).

2 There are subtle differences between racial contestation and group position theories. Bonilla-Silva's theory stems from the realistic conflict tradition and focuses on material and political struggle between "real" competing racial groups, whereas group position theory stems from the interactionist tradition and emphasizes the social construction of status hierarchies, conceiving the latter in terms of conflicts over both "tangible" (money, land, political power) and "intangible" (prestige, honour, respect) resources (Blumer 1958; Bobo 1999).

3 Stuchlik (1979) illustrates the power of external definitions in identity formation by showing how Spanish colonizers' changing definitions of the Mapuche in Chile (from "brave and fearless warriors" to "lazy drunken Injuns" to "gentle savages who lack education") influenced Mapuche behaviour and self-definitions – while also providing insight into how the Spanish viewed themselves and their goals. The Spanish were able to impose (disproportionately) their definitions on the Mapuche because of their monopolization of violence and other resources; even in resisting external definitions, the Mapuche were responding to them.

4 In 2015 an Indigenous MP, Don Rusnak (Liberal), was elected in the Thunder Bay-Rainy River riding.

5 Most of the children who attended St. Margaret's were from First Nations in the Rainy River District. However, some were flown in from elsewhere in Canada. Early on, some white orphans also attended. Meanwhile, some local Indigenous children were sent to other institutions hundreds of kilometres away.

6 In interviews, many survivors and their children vividly described the impact of such experiences on their mental health, self-esteem, ability to parent, strained family relations, loss of language and identity, and more. For detailed analyses of such intergenerational effects, see Bombay, Matheson, and Anisman (2014), Aboriginal Healing Foundation reports (www.ahf.ca), and the TRC's (2015) final report.

7 The total number of interviews is 128 because some initial interviews were conducted before the apology, and some follow-up interviews in 2009 focused mainly on the Alberton group home controversy.

8 Nevertheless, a critical reader will note passages that reinforce paternalistic relations between the federal government and Indigenous peoples. For example: "we apologize for failing to *protect* you ... you were *powerless* to protect your own children" (emphases added).

9 Before the settlement, 18,000 class action lawsuits had been filed by Indian residential school survivors. Under the out-of-court settlement, each living survivor was eligible for a Common Experience Payment (CEP) of $10,000 for the first year of attendance, plus $3,000 for each additional year and the possibility of greater compensation through an independent assessment process in cases of physical or sexual abuse (see Indian Residential Schools Settlement Agreement, 2007, http://www.residentialschoolsettlement.ca). The deadline for applying for compensation was 19 September 2011 (later extended to 2012). As of 2015, more than 78,000 Indian residential school survivors' claims had been recognized for CEPs and more than 31,000 had been resolved by the independent assessment process (Schwartz 2015).

10 Arguably, the apology also met seven of James's (2008) eight criteria, the shortcoming being that it was judged by many Indigenous peoples (and some settlers) as "hypocritical," given ongoing government (in)actions.

11 "Voice" is also important in the apology process (Lazare 2004). Prior to lobbying by Indigenous peoples and allies, the Conservative government did not plan to let Indigenous leaders speak in the House.

12 Seven white interviewees said they were "indifferent" to the apology. Whites' responses were also shorter and less coherent, and a few whites declined interviews because the topic was "not relevant" to them.

13 A similar range of responses has been observed among Indigenous peoples in Australia in response to the Australian government's "Stolen Generations" apology (Mookherjee et al. 2009; Short 2012).

14 Few interviewees explicitly criticized the apology for failing to include Indigenous criteria. Some welcomed the attempt to incorporate selected Indigenous traditions (such as smudging and witnessing). However, many also emphasized the need for local healing and reconciliation initiatives that would follow Anishinaabe protocols, and many questioned the prime minister's sincerity on grounds that he was not emotionally engaged.

15 Combining "mixed" and "positive" responses, 66 per cent of non-Indigenous interviewees agreed an apology was necessary. If anything, this figure is slightly higher than that suggested by prior surveys. In a national poll three months before the apology (March 2008), 42 per cent of Canadians said they would support a prime ministerial apology for the state's role in the Indian residential school system. Two months after the apology (August 2008), 63 per cent of Canadians said they agreed with the apology (Regan 2010).

16 Racial storylines are "narratives that appear over and over in the justifications (or criticisms) used to maintain (or challenge) racial privilege" (Bonilla-Silva 2003, 72). They are "fable-like and incorporate a common scheme and wording" (e.g., "the past is past").

17 Both settlements were finalized in 2007.

18 In 2017, Conservative senator Lynn Beyak, who is from northwestern Ontario, stirred controversy across Canada when she made similar comments (see Conclusion).

19 In fact, more than eighty thousand are still alive.

20 These findings are largely consistent with a national study of the impact of the Common Experience Payment, based on interviews with 281 First Nations, Métis, and Inuit survivors by a research team commissioned by the Aboriginal Healing Foundation (Reimer et al. 2010). Like my interviewees, theirs had overwhelmingly mixed reactions: while some survivors found the process relatively straightforward and appreciated the compensation as a symbolic gesture, substantial numbers found the process "challenging both logistically and emotionally" (xiii). Many complained that support services were inadequate, some schools had been deemed ineligible, and there was an arbitrary cut-off date for deceased survivors' families to receive compensation on their behalf (the survivor had to be alive as of May 2005). Reimer et al. also found that survivors who were already on a "healing journey" before applying for the CEP had more positive experiences than those who were not (xv). For the latter, the application process sometimes exacerbated their pain, triggering "negative emotions or traumatic flashbacks" (xiv).

21 The TRC's mandate was later extended to six years, after a lengthy court battle to force the federal government to share necessary documents.

22 In fairness, my interviews were conducted before the first national TRC event. If asked the same question today, more residents might be aware of the TRC.

23 As the late Gene Stoltzfus – an older white resident not originally from the region, but an active member of the Right Relations Circle and a long-time Christian peace activist – wrote in an online blog in October 2007: "Those of us who are descendants of immigrants have been living in denial and will need to walk through the pain and deception of our own history to a new plane of truth and acknowledgement of unearned wealth and privilege. Although the settlement with victims of residential schools here suggests reconciliation, the content's details selectively call for a process that creates a safe space for the school victims to tell their story. *It says nothing about a process of transformation for the children of immigrants caught in our own addictions to subdue the earth for our economic benefit*" (emphasis added).

24 In November 2010, the Government of Canada announced it would endorse the UN Declaration, but only to the extent that it conformed to Canada's existing laws and Constitution. When asked on the Aboriginal Peoples Television Network if this endorsement signalled a shift in government policy toward Indigenous peoples, the then federal minister of Indian and northern affairs, John Duncan, replied that it did not.

25 As Mackey (2013, 50) argues, the scope of Harper's apology was too narrow; it ignored the connections between residential schools and "the breaking of treaties and the usurping of Aboriginal territories that were the basis of settling, building, and populating the [Canadian] nation."

26 Less than two years after the Indian residential school apology, the same federal government eliminated funding for the Aboriginal Healing Foundation, which, since 1998, had facilitated hundreds of community-based healing initiatives and dozens of research reports.

27 Several other variables were moderately associated with the likelihood of whites expressing the "move on" sentiment, including being worried about one's personal economic security, having less than a university education, being male, and supporting the Conservative Party. Whites who had a close Indigenous friend or spouse were somewhat more likely to advocate follow-up action.

28 For promising recent work on how settlers can become allies and work in solidarity with Indigenous peoples, see Davis 2010, Gehl 2012, Grossman 2017, Hiller 2017, McGuire and Denis 2019, and Regan 2010.

10. The Benefits and Challenges of Collective Action

1 Despite their efforts, several docks were damaged, roads washed out, basements flooded, sewers broken, events cancelled, and the Couchiching First Nation cemetery experienced significant erosion.

2 In general, this interviewee's views were representative of the majority white "laissez-faire" perspective – neither virulently hostile nor very

progressive. I am unsure about the views of the other parents and their daughters, but one Indigenous contact said, "They are exactly the sort of folk you talk about – deeply racist but revile the accusation, and certainly don't see themselves that way."

3 As legal challenges proceed, however, the threat of renewed clear-cutting has been repeatedly raised.

4 The United Church of Canada formed in 1925, merging the Methodist and Presbyterian churches, the Congregational Union of Ontario and Quebec, and the Association of Local Union Churches. The largest Protestant denomination in Canada, it has a bottom-up governance structure and a long history of social activism.

5 This institutional commitment to reconciliation was formalized at a 2009 national meeting in Pinawa, Manitoba.

6 The official charge was "obstruction of business," which KI First Nation did not deny. The province had granted the company a license to drill without KI's permission. Under the Constitution Act (1982), the crown has a "duty to consult and accommodate" First Nations about activities that potentially infringe on Aboriginal or treaty rights. Under the United Nations Declaration on the Rights of Indigenous Peoples, Indigenous peoples have a right to free, prior, and informed consent.

7 At least 1,181 Indigenous women were murdered or went missing between 1980 and 2012 (RCMP 2014).

8 A request for funding from the Rainy River Valley Safety Coalition was declined.

9 I have also seen this spelled "Bamoseda," but this was the spelling offered by a local Elder.

10 Here, he is referring to the eighth fire prophecy.

11 Wary of how my affiliation with the RRC might be perceived by non-affiliated residents, I tried to keep it private and did not discuss it with potential interviewees.

12 The toll booth action unfolded after my formal interviews and fieldwork, so my analysis here is based on media coverage, public Facebook discussions, and follow-up interviews.

13 Couchiching promised that all emergency vehicles and school buses would be exempt from the toll, but the editors posed the question of traffic tie-ups.

14 Despite Couchiching's announcement, four letters from MP John Rafferty, and a letter from Grand Council Treaty No. 3 Ogichidaakwe Diane Kelly, the federal government remained silent. The provincial government "initially offered to install street lights and street signs, and perhaps a bike trail ... to resolve the dispute," before promising "serious discussions" (*Fort Frances Times*, 19 May 2010).

15 The member was allegedly chased on his bike by three white residents who yelled racial insults.

16 The death threats were investigated by the OPP, but no charges were laid.

17 Eventually the newspaper created a login and registration system, after which the volume and intensity of comments declined.

18 The Superior Court ruled in 2014 that the two-chain allowance is not part of the Agency One reserve. In 2018, the First Nations and the federal and provincial governments reached a settlement regarding the Agency One lands. As of this writing, few details have been released, and Fort Frances continues to litigate for ownership of Point Park.

Conclusion: Canada at a Crossroads

1 In fact, First Nations were granted Canadian citizenship in 1956.

2 Certainly, some settlers also might seek to salvage the relationship and show that they respect Indigenous histories and rights, and some Indigenous people (impacted by colonial trauma) still may be fighting to win the war. My data suggest, however, that in general the group position model applies better to (white) settlers – a point that might seem counter-intuitive given Bobo and Hutchings' (1996) finding that more alienated racial groups tend to express greater perceived threat.

3 By contrast, given the history of slavery and segregation, the US civil rights movement has emphasized equality and integration; black Americans often seek access to the same jobs, schools, buses, and neighbourhoods as white Americans. Many Indigenous people also pursue such ends, but in a context of ongoing settler colonialism, Indigenous activists generally stress different goals, such as regaining control of their lands, securing recognition of their unique identities and cultures, and exercising their national sovereignty and treaty rights.

4 Both Dawson and Bryce faced attacks on their personal credibility, and the Canadian government failed to act on most of their recommendations.

5 For closer analysis of this issue, see Davis, Denis, and Sinclair (2018).

6 In the wake of the TRC, the then Liberal Ontario government promised to make such changes. However, when the Conservatives were elected in 2018, they almost immediately cancelled a related curriculum-writing session.

7 Saul also puts faith in the Canadian court system. However, as King and Pasternak (2015, n.p.) note, "no court in Canada has ever recognized the sovereignty of indigenous peoples. In fact, courts have taken careful steps to lay down a framework allowing provinces to infringe on aboriginal title if it is in the interests of the public good." As Asch (2014) suggests,

334   Notes to pages 304–5

the question that courts have been unwilling to address is how the Crown gained sovereignty.

8 The Two-Row Wampum is a treaty made in 1613 between the Dutch and the Haudenosaunee stating that the two nations would travel down the river of life side by side, each in their own vessel (respecting one another's political autonomy) and supporting one another in a spirit of peace, friendship, and respect.

9 Locally, in response to public presentations of my findings in 2011–12, Indigenous residents of the Rainy River District also called for structural and symbolic changes, such as renaming Colonization Road, increasing Indigenous representation on school boards, and including more positive stories about Indigenous peoples in the media.

10 The settler colonial desire for certainty was also emphasized in Mackey's (2016) study of land disputes in southern Ontario and upstate New York.

Works Cited

Alfred, Taiaiake. 2005. *Wasáse: Indigenous Pathways of Freedom and Action*. Peterborough: Broadview.

– 2009. *Peace, Power, Righteousness: An Indigenous Manifesto*, 2nd ed. Don Mills: Oxford University Press.

Alfred, Taiaiake, and Jeff Corntassel. 2005. "Being Indigenous: Resurgences against Contemporary Colonialism." *Government & Opposition* 9:597–614. https://doi.org/10.1111/j.1477-7053.2005.00166.x.

Allport, Gordon. 1954. *The Nature of Prejudice*. Boston: Beacon.

Andersen, Chris. 2014. *"Métis": Race, Recognition, and the Struggle for Indigenous Peoplehood*. Vancouver: UBC Press.

Anderson, Kim, Maria Campbell, and Christi Belcourt, eds. 2018. *Keetsahnak: Our Missing and Murdered Indigenous Sisters*. Edmonton: University of Alberta Press.

Angus Reid Institute. 2015. "Truth and Reconciliation: Canadians See Value in Process, Skeptical about Government Action." 24 June. http://angusreid .org/wp-content/uploads/2015/07/2015.06.24_TRC.pdf.

Anishinabek News. 2015. "'Teachers Kit Will Help Alleviate Racism and Support Areas of Treaty Education' – Madahbee." 7 May. http://anishinabeknews .ca/2015/05/07/8293/.

Asch, Michael. 2002. "From *Terra Nullius* to Affirmation: Reconciling Aboriginal Rights with the Canadian Constitution." *Canadian Journal of Law and Society* 17 (2): 23–40. https://doi.org/10.1017/s0829320100007237.

– 2014. *On Being Here to Stay: Treaties and Aboriginal Rights in Canada*. Toronto: University of Toronto Press.

Assembly of First Nations (AFN). 2004. *Federal Government Funding to First Nations: The Facts, the Myths, and the Way Forward*. Ottawa: Assembly of First Nations.

Atleo, Cliff, Jr. 2014. "Red Skin, White Masks: A Review." *Decolonization: Indigeneity, Education & Society* 3 (2): 187–94. https://jps.library.utoronto.ca /index.php/des/article/view/22037/17880.

Auger, Donald J. 2005. *Indian Residential Schools in Ontario*. N.p.: Nishnawbe Aski Nation.

Axworthy, Lloyd, and Wab Kinew. 2013. "Canada's Future: Let's Be Divided No More." *Globe and Mail*, 11 January. http://www.theglobeandmail.com /globe-debate/canadas-future-lets-be-divided-no-more/article7199421/.

Barth, Fredrik, ed. 1969. *Ethnic Groups and Boundaries: The Social Organization of Culture Difference*. Boston: Little, Brown.

Basso, Keith. 1979. Portraits of "the Whiteman": Linguistic Play and Cultural Symbols among the Western Apache. Cambridge: Cambridge University Press.

Bell, Avril. 2014. *Relating Indigenous and Settler Identities: Beyond Domination*. Basingstoke: Palgrave Macmillan.

Bell, Joyce M., and Douglas Hartmann. 2008. "Diversity in Everyday Discourse: The Cultural Ambiguities and Consequences of 'Happy Talk.'" *American Sociological Review* 72 (6): 895–914. https://doi.org/10.1177 /000312240707200603.

Benford, Robert D., and David A. Snow. 2000. "Framing Processes and Social Movements: An Overview and Assessment." *Annual Review of Sociology* 26 (1): 611–39. https://doi.org/10.1146/annurev.soc.26.1.611.

Benton-Benai, Edward. 1988. *The Mishomis Book: The Voice of the Ojibway*. Saint Paul: Red School House.

Bezrukova, Katerina, Karen A. Jehn, and Chester S. Spell. 2012. "Reviewing Diversity Training: Where We Have Been and Where We Should Go." *Academy of Management Learning & Education* 11 (2): 207–27. https://doi .org/10.5465/amle.2008.0090.

Biernacki, Patrick, and Dan Waldorf. 1981. "Snowball Sampling: Problems and Techniques in Chain Referral." *Sociological Methods and Research* 10 (2): 141–63. https://doi.org/10.1177/004912418101000205.

Blackstock, Cindy. 2011. "Jordan Shannen: First Nations Children Demand that the Canadian Government Stop Racially Discriminating against Them." Shadow Report: 3rd and 4th Periodic Report to the UNCRC. Ottawa: First Nations Child and Family Caring Society.

Blalock, Hubert M. 1967. *Toward a Theory of Minority-Group Relations*. New York: Wiley.

Blatz, Craig. 2008. "How Members of Majority and Victimized Groups Respond to Government Redress for Historical Harms." PhD diss., University of Waterloo.

Blatz, Craig W., and Catherine Philpot. 2010. "On the Outcomes of Intergroup Apologies: A Review." *Social and Personality Psychology Compass* 4 (11): 995–1007. https://doi.org/10.1111/j.1751-9004.2010.00318.x.

Blatz, Craig W., Karina Schumann, and Michael Ross. 2009. "Government Apologies for Historical Injustices." *Political Psychology* 30 (2): 219–41. https://doi.org/10.1111/j.1467-9221.2008.00689.x.

Blumer, Herbert. 1955. "Reflections on Theory of Race Relations." In *Race Relations in World Perspective*, edited by A.W. Lind, pp. 3–21. Honolulu: University of Hawaii Press.

– 1958. "Race Prejudice as a Sense of Group Position." *Pacific Sociological Review* 1 (1): 3–7. https://doi.org/10.2307%2F1388607.

Bobo, Lawrence. 1999. "Prejudice as Group Position: Microfoundations of a Sociological Approach to Racism and Race Relations." *Journal of Social Issues* 55 (3): 445–72. https://doi.org/10.1111/0022-4537.00127.

Bobo, Lawrence, and Vincent L. Hutchings. 1996. "Perceptions of Racial Group Competition: Extending Blumer's Theory of Group Position to a Multiracial Social Context." *American Sociological Review* 61 (6): 951–72. https://doi.org/10.2307/2096302.

Bobo, Lawrence, James Kluegel, and Ryan A. Smith. 1997. "Laissez-Faire Racism: The Crystallization of a Kinder, Gentler Anti-Black Ideology." In *Racial Attitudes in the 1990s*, edited by J.K. Martin and S.A. Tuch, 15–44. Westport: Greenwood.

Bobo, Lawrence D., and Mia Tuan. 2006. *Prejudice in Politics: Group Position, Public Opinion, and the Wisconsin Treaty Rights Dispute*. Cambridge, MA: Harvard University Press.

Bombay, Amy, Kimberly Matheson, and Hymie Anisman. 2013. "Appraisals of Discriminatory Events among Adult Offspring of Indian Residential School Survivors: The Influences of Identity Centrality and Past Perceptions of Discrimination." *Cultural Diversity and Ethnic Minority Psychology* 20 (1): 75–86. https://doi.org/10.1037/a0033352.

– 2014. "The Intergenerational Effects of Indian Residential Schools: Implications for the Concept of Historical Trauma." *Transcultural Psychiatry* 51 (3): 320–38. https://doi.org/10.1177/1363461513503380.

Bonilla-Silva, Eduardo. 2003. "Racial Attitudes or Racial Ideology? An Alternative Paradigm for Examining Actors' Racial Views." *Journal of Political Ideologies* 8 (1): 63–82. https://doi.org/10.1080/13569310306082.

– 2010. *Racism without Racists: Color-Blind Racism and Racial Inequality in Contemporary America*, 3rd ed. New York: Rowman & Littlefield.

– 2014. "The Problem of Racism in 'Post-Racial' America." The 2014 Bahá'í Chair for World Peace Annual Lecture, University of Maryland, 18 September.

Borrows, John. 2010. *Canada's Indigenous Constitution*. Toronto: University of Toronto Press.

Botsford, Wanda. 2013. *Our Local Métis Story*. Fort Frances Museum Special Exhibit.

Branscombe, Nyla R., and Bertjan Doosje, eds. 2004. *Collective Guilt: International Perspectives*. New York: Cambridge University Press.

Braroe, Niels Winther. 1975. *Indian and White: Self-Image and Interaction in a Canadian Plains Community*. Stanford: Stanford University Press.

Bray, Matt, and Ernie Epp. 1984. *A Vast and Magnificent Land: An Illustrated History of Northern Ontario*. Thunder Bay: Lakehead and Laurentian University.

Brown, Rupert, and Miles Hewstone. 2005. "An Integrative Theory of Intergroup Contact." *Advances in Experimental Social Psychology* 37:255–343. https://doi.org/10.1016/s0065-2601(05)37005-5.

Canadian Broadcasting Corporation (CBC). 2008. "Conservative MP Apologizes for 'Hurtful' Comments on Aboriginal People." 12 June. http://www.cbc.ca/news/canada/conservative-mp-apologizes-for-hurtful-comments-on-aboriginal-people-1.712106.

– 2012. *8th Fire: Aboriginal Peoples, Canada & the Way Forward* (4-part documentary). Seville Pictures.

– 2013. "Thunder Bay's Aboriginal Population Fears Racism and Violence." 20 February. http://www.cbc.ca/news/canada/thunder-bay-s-aboriginal-population-fears-racism-and-violence-1.1391361.

– 2014. "Resolute Halts Last Paper Machine at Fort Frances Mill." 14 January. http://www.cbc.ca/news/canada/thunder-bay/resolute-halts-last-paper-machine-at-fort-frances-mill-1.2496379.

– 2015a. "Lakehead University in Thunder Bay, Ont., to Mandate Indigenous Learning." 20 February. http://www.cbc.ca/news/canada/thunder-bay/lakehead-university-in-thunder-bay-ont-to-mandate-indigenous-learning-1.2963546.

– 2015b. "UWinnipeg Approves Mandatory Indigenous Course Requirement." 26 March. http://www.cbc.ca/news/canada/manitoba/uwinnipeg-approves-mandatory-indigenous-course-requirement-1.3011314.

Cannon, Martin. 2006. "First Nations Citizenship: An Act to Amend the Indian Act and the Accommodation of Sex-Discriminatory Policy." *Canadian Review of Social Policy* 56: 40–71. https://search.proquest.com/openview/930c68684f538fa65c95cfb2ab0722b2/1?pq-origsite=gscholar&cbl=28163.

Cardinal, Harold. 1969. *The Unjust Society*. Vancouver: Douglas & McIntyre.

Castleden, Heather T., Kiley Daley, Vanessa Sloan Morgan, and Paul Sylvestre. 2013. "Settlers Unsettled: Using Field Schools and Digital Stories to Transform Geographies of Ignorance about Indigenous Peoples in Canada." *Journal of Geography in Higher Education* 37 (4): 487–99. https://doi.org/10.1080/03098265.2013.796352.

Castleden, Heather, T. Garvin, and Huu-ay-aht First Nation. 2008. "Modifying Photovoice for Community-Based Participatory Indigenous Research." *Social Science and Medicine* 66 (6): 1393–405. https://doi.org/10.1016/j.socscimed.2007.11.030.

Chandler, Michael J., and Christopher Lalonde. 1998. "Cultural Continuity as a Hedge against Suicide in Canada's First Nations." *Transcultural Psychiatry* 35 (2): 191–219. https://doi.org/10.1177/136346159803500202.

Charmaz, Kathy. 2006. *Constructing Grounded Theory: A Practical Guide through Qualitative Analysis*. London: Sage.

Chute, Janet E., and Alan Knight. 2006. "Taking up the Torch: Simon J. Dawson and the Upper Great Lakes' Native Resource Campaign of the 1860s and 1870s." *With Good Intentions: Euro-Canadian and Aboriginal Relations in Colonial Canada*, edited by Celia Haig-Brown and David A. Nock, 106–31. Vancouver: UBC Press.

CIHR, NSERC, and SSERC (Canadian Institutes of Health Research, Natural Sciences and Engineering Council of Canada, and Social Sciences and Humanities Research Council of Canada). 2018. *Tri-Council Policy Statement: Ethical Conduct for Research Involving Humans*. http://www.pre.ethics.gc.ca/eng/policy-politique_tcps2-eptc2_2018.html.

Clink, Julie. 1997. *Between the Ripples ... Stories of Chapple*. Barwick: Chapple Heritage Committee.

Coates, Kenneth. 2015. *#IDLENOMORE and the Remaking of Canada*. Regina: University of Regina Press.

Coburn, Elaine, ed. 2015. *More Will Sing Their Way to Freedom: Indigenous Resistance and Resurgence*. Halifax: Fernwood.

Cornell, Stephen. 1988. "The Transformations of Tribe: Organization and Self-Concept in Native American Ethnicities." *Ethnic and Racial Studies* 11 (1): 27–47. https://doi.org/10.1080/01419870.1988.9993587.

Corntassel, Jeff. 2012. "Re-envisioning Resurgence: Indigenous Pathways to Decolonization and Sustainable Self-Determination." *Decolonization: Indigeneity, Education & Society* 1 (1): 86–101. https://jps.library.utoronto.ca/index.php/des/article/view/18627.

Corntassel, Jeff, and Cindy Holder. 2008. "Who's Sorry Now? Government Apologies, Truth Commissions, and Indigenous Self-Determination in Australia, Canada, Guatemala, and Peru." *Human Rights Review* 9 (4): 465–89. https://doi.org/10.1007/s12142-008-0065-3.

Coulthard, Glen S. 2007. "Subjects of Empire: Indigenous Peoples and the 'Politics of Recognition' in Canada." *Contemporary Political Theory* 6:437–60. https://doi.org/10.1057/palgrave.cpt.9300307.

– 2012. "#IdleNoMore in Historical Context." *Decolonization: Indigeneity, Education & Society*, 24 December. https://decolonization.wordpress.com/2012/12/24/idlenomore-in-historical-context/.

– 2014. *Red Skin, White Masks: Rejecting the Colonial Politics of Recognition*. Minneapolis: University of Minnesota Press.

Craft, Aimée. 2013. *Breathing Life into the Stone Fort Treaty: An Anishinabe Understanding of Treaty One*. Saskatoon: Purich.

Cronlund Anderson, Mark, and Carmen Robertson. 2011. *Seeing Red: A History of Natives in Canadian Newspapers*. Winnipeg: University of Manitoba Press.

Cullingham, James, dir. 1995. *Duncan Campbell Scott: The Poet and the Indians* (film). Tamarack Productions.

Daschuk, James. 2013. *Clearing the Plains: Disease, Politics of Starvation, and the Loss of Aboriginal Life*. Regina: University of Regina Press.

Daugherty, Wayne E. 1986. *Treaty Three Research Report*. Ottawa: Treaties and Historical Research Centre, Indian and Northern Affairs Canada.

Davis, Lynne, ed. 2010. *Alliances: Re/Envisioning Indigenous–Non-Indigenous Relationships*. Toronto: University of Toronto Press.

Davis, Lynne, Jeffrey S. Denis, and Raven Sinclair, eds. 2018. *Pathways of Settler Decolonization*. New York: Routledge.

Davis, Lynne, and Heather Yanique Shpuniarsky. 2010. "The Spirit of Relationships: What We Have Learned about Indigenous/Non-Indigenous Alliances and Coalitions." In *Alliances: Re/Envisioning Indigenous-Non-Indigenous Relationships*, edited by Lynne Davis, 334–48. Toronto: University of Toronto Press.

Dawson, Simon. 1859. "General Report on the Progress of the Red River Expedition." In *Report on the Exploration of the Country Between Lake Superior and the Red River Settlement, and Between the Latter Place and the Assiniboine and Saskatchewan*. Toronto: Legislative Assembly of Province of Canada.

Delgado, Richard, and Jean Stefancic. 2017. *Critical Race Theory*, 3rd ed. New York: NYU Press.

Denis, Jeffrey S. 2011. "Bridging Understandings: Anishinaabe and White Perspectives on the Residential School Apology and Prospects for Reconciliation." In *Reading Sociology: Canadian Perspectives*, 2nd ed., edited by Lorne Tepperman and Angela Kalyta, 257–62. Don Mills: Oxford University Press.

– 2012. "Transforming Meanings and Group Positions: Tactics and Framing in Anishinaabe-White Relations in Northwestern Ontario, Canada." *Ethnic and Racial Studies* 35 (3): 453–70. https://doi.org/10.1080/01419870.2011.589525.

– 2015. "Contact Theory in a Small-Town Settler-Colonial Context: The Reproduction of Laissez-Faire Racism in Indigenous-White Canadian Relations." *American Sociological Review* 80 (1): 218–42. https://doi.org/10.1177/0003122414564998.

– 2018. "Sociology of Indigenous Peoples in Canada." Online supplement to *SOC+*, 4th ed., edited by Robert J. Brym. Toronto: Nelson.

DePratto, Brian. 2015. "Aboriginal Women Outperforming in Labour Markets." *TD Economics: Special Report*, 6 July. https://www.td.com/document/PDF/economics/special/AboriginalWomen.pdf.

DiAngelo, Robin. 2015. "Why It's So Hard to Talk to White People about Racism." *Huffington Post*, 30 April. http://www.huffingtonpost.com/good-men-project/why-its-so-hard-to-talk-to-white-people-about-racism_b_7183710.html.

Dickason, Olive Patricia, and Moira Calder. 2006. *A Concise History of Canada's First Nations*. Don Mills: Oxford University Press.

Dixon, John, Kevin Durrheim, and Colin Tredoux. 2005. "Beyond the Optimal Contact Strategy: A Reality Check for the Contact Hypothesis." *American Psychologist* 60 (7): 697–711. https://doi.org/10.1037/0003 -066x.60.7.697.

Dovidio, John F., Samuel L. Gaertner, and Kerry Kawakami. 2003. "Intergroup Contact: The Past, Present, and Future." *Group Processes and Intergroup Relations* 6 (1): 5–21. https://doi.org/10.1177/1368430203006001009.

Drache, Hiram. 1983. *Koochiching: Pioneering along the Rainy River Frontier*. Apple Valley: IPP/Hobar.

Duneier, Mitchell. 2001. "On the Evolution of *Sidewalk*." In *Contemporary Field Research: Perspectives and Formulations*, 2nd ed., edited by Robert M. Emerson, 167–87. Long Grove: Waveland.

Dunk, Thomas W. 1991. *It's a Working Man's Town: Male Working-Class Culture*. Montreal: McGill-Queen's University Press.

Duran, Eduardo, and Bonnie Duran. 1995. *Native American Postcolonial Psychology*. Albany: State University of New York Press.

Durrheim, Kevin, and John Dixon. 2005. *Racial Encounter: The Social Psychology of Contact and Desegregation*. New York: Routledge.

Elias, Norbert, and John L. Scotson. 1965. *The Established and the Outsiders: A Sociological Enquiry into Community Problems*. London: Sage.

Eliasoph, Nina. 1999. "Everyday Racism in a Culture of Political Avoidance: Civil Society, Speech, and Taboo." *Social Problems* 46 (4): 479–502. https:// doi.org/10.2307/3097072.

Emo Historical Committee. 1978. *The River of Time: A History of Emo*. Emo: self-published.

Engler, Mark, and Paul Engler. 2014. "Can Frances Fox Piven's Theory of Disruptive Power Create the New Occupy?" *Waging Non-Violence*, 7 May. http://wagingnonviolence.org/feature/can-frances-fox-pivens -theory-disruptive-power-create-next-occupy/.

Environics Research Group. 2010. *Urban Aboriginal Peoples Study: Main Report*. Toronto: Environics Institute. http://www.uaps.ca/.

Espeland, Wendy. 2001. "Bureaucrats and Indians in a Contemporary Colonial Encounter." *Law and Social Inquiry* 26 (2): 403–33. https://doi.org/10.1111 /j.1747-4469.2001.tb00183.x.

Espeland, Wendy Nelson, and Mitchell Stevens. 1998. "Commensuration as a Social Process." *Annual Review of Sociology* 24 (1): 312–43. https://doi .org/10.1146/annurev.soc.24.1.313.

Feagin, Joe R. 2010. *The White Racial Frame: Centuries of Racial Framing and Counter-Framing*. New York: Routledge.

Feagin, Joe R., and Hernan Vera. 1995. *White Racism*. New York: Routledge.

Flanagan, Tom. 2000. *First Nations? Second Thoughts*. Montreal and Kingston: McGill-Queen's University Press.

Fontaine, Phil. 2008. "Apology to Native People Must End 'Denial of Truth': An Open Letter to the Prime Minister from Chief Phil Fontaine." *Toronto Star*, 22 April. https://www.thestar.com/opinion/columnists/2008/04/22 /apology_to_native_people_must_end_denial_of_truth.html.

Fort Frances Museum Permanent Exhibit. 2006/07. "Fort Frances: A History." Text by Emily Carr, Interpretive Development Intern.

Fort Frances Times. 2006. "Power Agreement Not in Jeopardy: Town, Mill." 8 November. http://www.fftimes.com/news/news/power-agreement -not-jeopardy-town-mill.

– 2008. "Online Poll: Does the Residential School Apology Need to Be Followed By Concrete Action?" 18–24 June. http://www.fftimes.com /node/299797/results.

– 2010a. "Online Poll: How Do You Feel about Couchiching's Plan to Set Up a Toll Booth on Highway 11?" 29 April–5 May. http://www.fftimes.com /polls/how-do-you-feel-about-couchiching%E2%80%99s-plan-set-toll -booth-highway-11.

– 2010b. "Couchiching Claiming 'Victory' with Toll Booth." 2 June. http:// www.fftimes.com/news/news/couchiching-claiming-%E2%80%98victory %E2%80%99-toll-booth.

– 2010c. "No Winners." Editorial, 2 June. http://www.fftimes.com/news /editorials/no-winners.

– 2013. "Abide Law." Editorial, 16 January. http://www.fftimes.com/news /editorials/abide-law.

Freire, Paulo. 1970. *Pedagogy of the Oppressed*. New York: Continuum.

Frideres, James S. 2011. *First Nations in the Twenty-First Century*. Don Mills: Oxford University Press.

Frideres, James S., and René R. Gadacz. 2011. *Aboriginal Peoples in Canada*, 9th ed. Don Mills: Pearson Education Canada.

Furniss, Elizabeth. 1999. *The Burden of History: Colonialism and the Frontier Myth in a Rural Canadian Community*. Vancouver: UBC Press.

Gaertner, Samuel L., and John F. Dovidio. 2000. *Reducing Intergroup Bias: The Common Ingroup Identity Model*. Philadelphia: Psychology Press.

Gallagher, Charles A. 2005. "Color-Blind Privilege: Social and Political Functions of Erasing the Color Line in Post-Race America." In *Rethinking the Color Line: Readings in Race and Ethnicity*, 2nd ed., edited by C.A. Gallagher, 575–88. New York: McGraw-Hill.

Galloway, Gloria. 2017. "Conservatives Disavow Tory Senator's Positive Views of Residential Schools." *Globe and Mail*, 9 March. https://www .theglobeandmail.com/news/politics/conservatives-disavow-tory -senators-positive-views-of-residential-schools/article34248144/.

Gaventa, John. 1980. *Power and Powerlessness: Quiescence and Rebellion in and Appalachian Valley*. Chicago: University of Illinois Press.

Gehl, Lynn. 2012. "Ally Bill of Responsibilities." https://www.lynngehl.com /ally-bill-of-responsibilities.html.

Gibney, Mark, Rhoda E. Howard-Hassmann, Jean-Marc Coicaud, and Niklaus Steiner, eds. 2008. *The Age of Apology: Facing Up to the Past*. Philadelphia: University of Pennsylvania Press.

Godlewska, Anne, Jennifer Massey, Jones K. Adjei, and Jackie Moore. 2013. "The Unsustainable Nature of Ignorance: Measuring Knowledge to Effect Social Change: First Results of an Online Survey of Aboriginal Knowledge at Queen's University." *Canadian Journal of Native Studies* 33 (1): 65–95. https:// search.proquest.com/openview/e77cf8a61d9e44bb15f79719d45302d4 /1?pq-origsite=gscholar&cbl=44018.

Goffman, Erving. 1974. *Frame Analysis*. New York: Harper Colophon.

Government of Ontario. 2016. "Ontario Implementing New Indigenous Training and Education Requirements." Press release, 17 February. https:// news.ontario.ca/opo/en/2016/02/ontario-implementing-new-indigenous -training-and-education-requirements.html.

Govier, Trudy. 2003. "What Is Acknowledgement and Why Is It Important?" In *Dilemmas of Reconciliation: Cases and Concepts*, edited by Carol A.L. Prager and Trudy Govier, 65–89. Waterloo: Wilfrid Laurier University Press.

Grand Council Treaty No. 3 (GCT3). N.d. *Submission to the Ipperwash Inquiry*. https://www.attorneygeneral.jus.gov.on.ca/inquiries/ipperwash/policy _part/projects/pdf/Chiefs_of_Ontario-Grand_Council_Treaty_3.pdf.

Gross, Neil. 2013. *Why Are Professors Liberal and Why Do Conservatives Care?* Cambridge: Harvard University Press.

Grossman, Zoltán. 2017. *Unlikely Alliances: Native Nations and White Communities Join to Defend Rural Lands*. Seattle: University of Washington Press.

Habermas, Jürgen. 1984. *The Theory of Communicative Action*. Cambridge: Polity.

Haluza-Delay, Randolph. 2002. "A Community of Acceptance: Respect for Thunder Bay's Diversity." Report prepared for Diversity Thunder Bay. http://www.diversitythunderbay.ca/uploads/documents/A-Community -of-Acceptance.pdf.

Hedican, Edward. 2013. *Ipperwash: The Tragic Failure of Canada's Aboriginal Policy*. Toronto: University of Toronto Press.

Heinrichs, Steve, ed. 2013. *Buffalo Shout, Salmon Cry: Conversations on Creation, Land Justice, and Life Together*. Waterloo and Harrisonburg: Herald Press.

Henderson, Jennifer, and Pauline Wakeham, eds. 2013. *Reconciling Canada: Critical Perspectives on the Culture of Redress*. Toronto: University of Toronto Press.

Henry, Frances, and Carol Tator. 2006. *The Colour of Democracy: Racism in Canadian Society*, 3rd ed. Scarborough: Thomson-Nelson.

Hewstone, Miles, and Rupert Brown. 1986. *Contact and Conflict in Intergroup Encounters*. Oxford: Basil Blackwell.

Hicks, Duane. 2012. "'Idle No More' Takes Hold Here." *Fort Frances Times*, 24 December. http://www.fftimes.com/news/news/%E2%80%98idle -no-more%E2%80%99-takes-hold-here.

Hiller, Chris. 2017. "Tracing the Spirals of Unsettlement: Euro-Canadian Narratives of Coming to Grips with Indigenous Sovereignty, Title, and Rights." *Settler Colonial Studies* 7 (4): 415–40. https://doi.org/10.1080 /2201473x.2016.1241209.

Hofstadter, Richard. 1992. *Social Darwinism in American Thought*. Boston: Beacon.

Holzkamm, Tim E., and Leo G. Waisberg. 2000. "Agency Indian Reserve 1: Selection, Use, and Administration." Draft report prepared for Grand Council Treaty No. 3, 19 September.

Holzkamm, Tim E., Leo G. Waisberg, and Joan A. Lovisek. 1995. "'Stout Athletic Fellows': The Ojibwa During the 'Big-Game Collapse' in Northwestern Ontario, 1821–71." In *Papers of the Twenty-Sixth Algonquian Conference*, edited by David H. Pentland, 169–82. Winnipeg: University of Manitoba.

Hyman, Herbert H., Charles R. Wright, and John S. Reed. 1975. *The Enduring Effects of Education*. Chicago: University of Chicago Press.

Ipsos Reid. 2013. "Fast Fallout: Chief Spence and Idle No More Movement Galvanizes Canadians around Money Management and Accountability." 15 January. http://www.ipsos-na.com/news-polls/pressrelease.aspx?id=5961.

Jackman, Mary R. 1994. *The Velvet Glove: Paternalism and Conflict in Gender, Class and Race Relations*. Berkeley: University of California Press.

Jackman, Mary R., and Marie Crane. 1986. "'Some of My Best Friends Are Black ... ' Interracial Friendship and Whites' Racial Attitudes." *Public Opinion Quarterly* 50 (4): 459–86. https://doi.org/10.1086/268998.

Jackman, Mary R., and Michael J. Muha. 1984. "Education and Intergroup Attitudes: Moral Enlightenment, Superficial Democratic Commitment, or Ideological Refinement?" *American Sociological Review* 49 (6): 751–69. https://doi.org/10.2307/2095528.

James, Matt. 2008. "Wrestling with the Past: Apologies, Quasi-Apologies, and Non-Apologies in Canada." In *The Age of Apology: Facing Up to the Past*, edited by Mark Gibney, Rhoda E. Howard-Hassmann, Jean-Marc Coicaud, and Niklaus Steiner, 137–53. Philadelphia: University of Pennsylvania Press.

Jenkins, Richard. 1994. "Rethinking Ethnicity: Identity, Categorization, and Power." *Ethnic and Racial Studies* 17 (2): 197–223. https://doi.org/10.1080 /01419870.1994.9993821.

Keenan, Greg, David Parkinson, and Brent Jang. 2014. "Paper Trail: The Decline of Canada's Forestry Industry." *Globe and Mail*, 5 December. https://www.theglobeandmail.com/report-on-business/economy/paper-trail-the-fall-of-forestry/article21967746/.

Kelly, Diane M. 2008. "Residential School Apology: Statement to the Gatherings of Treaty #3 Citizens." Grand Council Treaty No. 3, 11 June. Handout.

Kelly, Jim. 2008. "Step Taken in Healing Process." *Chronicle-Journal* (Thunder Bay), 12 June. https://www.chroniclejournal.com/step-taken-in-healing-process/article_4cd949e8-e1f6-5643-b586-b646b983bfbc.html.

Kinew, Wab. 2015. *The Reason You Walk: A Memoir*. Toronto: Viking Canada.

King, Hayden, and Shiri Pasternak. 2015. "Don't Call It a Comeback: While Indigenous People Keep Resisting Assimiliation, It's Canada That Needs to Catch Up." *Literary Review of Canada*, January. http://reviewcanada.ca/magazine/2015/01/dont-call-it-a-comeback/.

King, Thomas. 2012. *The Inconvenient Indian: A Curious Account of Native People in North America*. Toronto: Doubleday Canada.

Kino-nda-niimi Collective. 2014. *The Winter We Danced: Voices from the Past, the Future, and the Idle No More Movement*. Winnipeg: Arbeiter Ring.

Kovach, Margaret. 2010. *Indigenous Methodologies: Characteristics, Conversations, and Contexts*. Toronto: University of Toronto Press.

Krieger, Nancy. 2000. "Discrimination and Health." In *Social Epidemiology*, edited by Lisa F. Berkman and Ichiro Kawachi, 36–75. New York: Oxford University Press.

Krieger, Nancy, Kenneth H. Smith, Deepa Naishadham, Cathy Nelson Hartman, and Elizabeth M. Barbeau. 2005. "Experiences of Discrimination: Validity and Reliability of a Self-Report Measure." *Social Science and Medicine* 61 (7): 1576–96. https://doi.org/10.1016/j.socscimed.2005.03.006.

Lamont, Michèle. 2000. *The Dignity of Working Men: Morality and Boundaries of Race, Class, and Immigration*. Cambridge: Harvard University Press.

– 2001. "Symbolic Boundaries." In *International Encyclopedia of the Social and Behavioral Sciences*, edited by Neil J. Smelser and Paul B. Baltes, 15341–7. Amsterdam: Elsevier.

– 2009. "Responses to Racism, Health, and Social Inclusion as a Dimension of Successful Societies." In *Successful Societies: How Institutions and Culture Affect Health*, edited by Peter A. Hall and Michèle Lamont, 151–68. Cambridge: Cambridge University Press.

Lamont, Michèle, and Nissim Mizrachi, eds. 2012. *Responses to Stigmatization in Comparative Perspective*. London: Routledge.

Lamont, Michèle, and Virág Molnár. 2002. "The Study of Boundaries in the Social Sciences." *Annual Review of Sociology* 28:167–95. https://doi.org/10.1146/annurev.soc.28.110601.141107.

Lawn, Jennifer. 2008. "Settler Society and Postcolonial Apologies in Australia and New Zealand." *Sites: New Series* 5 (1): 20–40. https://doi.org/10.11157/sites-vol5iss1id.

Lawrence, Bonita. 2004. *"Real" Indians and Others: Mixed-Blood Urban Native Peoples and Indigenous Nationhood.* Vancouver: UBC Press.

Lawrence, Bonita, and Enakshi Dua. 2005. "Decolonizing Antiracism." *Social Justice* 32 (4): 120–43. https://www.racialequitytools.org/resourcefiles/bonita-lawrence-decolonizing-anti-racism.pdf.

Lazare, Aaron. 2004. *On Apology.* New York: Oxford University Press.

Lee, Damien. 2015. "Indian in a Jar?" *Zoongde* (blog), 21 February. https://zoongde.com/.

Lee, Damien, and Jana-Rae Yerxa. 2014. "Fighting Racism and Settler-Colonialism in Thunder Bay." NCRA radio interview by Scott Neigh, 27 July. http://previous.ncra.ca/exchange/dspProgramDetail.cfm?programID=152044.

Leonardo, Zeus, and Ronald K. Porter. 2010. "Pedagogy of Fear: Toward a Fanonian Theory of 'Safety' in Race Dialogue." *Race Ethnicity and Education* 13 (2): 139–57. https://doi.org/10.1080/13613324.2010.482898.

Levine, Robert A., and Donald T. Campbell. 1972. *Ethnocentrism: Theories of Conflict, Ethnic Attitudes, and Group Behavior.* New York: Wiley.

Lewis, Amanda. 2004. "'What Group?' Studying Whites and Whiteness in the Era of 'Color-Blindness.'" *Sociological Theory* 22 (4): 623–46. https://doi.org/10.1111/j.0735-2751.2004.00237.x.

Lithman, Yngve Georg. 1984. *The Community Apart: A Case Study of a Canadian Indian Reserve Community.* Winnipeg: University of Manitoba Press.

Little Bear, Leroy. 2000. "Jagged Worldviews Colliding." In *Reclaiming Indigenous Voice and Vision,* edited by Marie Battiste, 77–85. Vancouver: UBC Press.

Loveman, Mara. 1999. "Is 'Race' Essential?" *American Sociological Review* 64 (6): 891–8. https://doi.org/10.2307/2657409.

Lovisek, Joan A., Leo G. Waisberg, and Tim E. Holzkamm. 1995. "'Deprived of Part of Their Living': Colonialism and Nineteenth-Century Flooding of Ojibwa Lands." In *Papers of the Twenty-Sixth Algonquian Conference,* edited by David H. Pentland, 1–12. Winnipeg: University of Manitoba.

Lowman, Emma Battell, and Adam J. Barker. 2015. *Settler: Identity and Colonialism in 21st Century Canada.* Halifax: Fernwood.

Lucas, Rex A. 1971. *Minetown, Milltown, Railtown: Life in Canadian Communities of Single Industry.* Toronto: University of Toronto Press.

Lum, Zi-Ann. 2018. "Lynn Beyak's 'Letters of Support' Could Be Grounds For Human Rights Complaint." *Huffington Post,* 4 January. https://www.huffingtonpost.ca/2018/01/04/lynn-beyak-s-letters-of-support-could-be-grounds-for-human-rights-complaint-indigenous-senator_a_23324263/.

Macdonald, Nancy. 2015. "Welcome to Winnipeg: Where Canada's Racism Problem Is at Its Worst." *Maclean's*, 22 January. http://www.macleans.ca /news/canada/welcome-to-winnipeg-where-canadas-racism-problem-is -at-its-worst/.

Mackey, Eva. 2013. "The Apologizers' Apology." In *Reconciling Canada: Critical Perspectives on the Culture of Redress*, edited by Jennifer Henderson and Pauline Wakeham, 47–62. Toronto: University of Toronto Press.

− 2016. *Unsettled Expectations: Uncertainty, Land and Settler Decolonization.* Halifax: Fernwood.

Macoun, Alissa, and Elizabeth Strakosch. 2013. "The Ethical Demands of Settler Colonial Theory." *Settler Colonial Studies* 3 (3–4): 426–43. https:// doi.org/10.1080/2201473x.2013.810695.

Maghbouleh, Neda. 2017. *The Limits of Whiteness: Iranian Americans and the Everyday Politics of Race*. Stanford: Stanford University Press

Mainville, Sara J. 2007. "*Manidoo Mazina'igan*: An *Anishinaabe* Perspective of Treaty 3." Master's thesis, University of Toronto.

− 2014. "Building Trust." *Fort Frances Times*, 21 May. http://www.fftimes .com/news/letter-editor/building-trust.

Margaret, Jen. 2010. *Working as Allies*. Winston Churchill Fellowship Report. http://www.awea.org.nz/sites/awea.org.nz/files/Jen%20Margaret %20Winston%20Churchill%20Report%202010.pdf.

Maxwell, Krista. 2011. "Making History Heal: Settler Colonialism and Urban Indigenous Healing in Ontario, 1970s–2010." PhD diss., University of Toronto.

McClelland, Katherine, and Erika Linnander. 2006. "The Role of Contact and Information in Racial Attitude Change among White College Students." *Sociological Inquiry* 76 (1): 81–115. https://doi.org/10.1111/j.1475-682x .2006.00145.x.

McGuire, Mollie C., and Jeffrey S. Denis. 2019. "Unsettling Pathways: How Some Settlers Come to Seek Reconciliation with Indigenous Peoples." *Settler Colonial Studies* 9 (4): 505–24. https://doi.org/10.1080/2201473X. 2019.1598701.

McKinney, Karyn. 2005. *Being White: Stories of Race and Racism*. New York: Routledge.

McLaren, Nadia, dir. 2006. *Muffins for Granny* (film). Mongrel Media.

McPherson, Miller, Lynn Smith-Lovin, and James M. Cook. 2001. "Birds of a Feather: Homophily in Social Networks." *Annual Review of Sociology* 27 (1): 415–44. https://doi.org/10.1146/annurev.soc.27.1.415.

McQuarrie, Neil. 2003. *Fort Frances: The Story of a Town and Its People*. Fort Frances: Centennial Committee of the Town of Fort Frances.

Miller, J.R. 1996. *Shingwauk's Vision: A History of Native Residential Schools*. Toronto: University of Toronto Press.

– 2000. *Skyscrapers Hide the Heavens: A History of Indian-White Relations in Canada,* 3rd ed. Toronto: University of Toronto Press.

– 2009. *Compact, Contract, Covenant: Aboriginal Treaty-Making in Canada.* Toronto: University of Toronto Press.

Miller, Norman, and Marilyn B. Brewer, eds. 1984. *Groups in Contact: The Psychology of Desegregation.* Orlando: Academic Press.

Milloy, John S. 1999. *A National Crime: The Canadian Government and the Residential School System, 1879 to 1986.* Winnipeg: University of Manitoba Press.

Mills, Aaron. 2017. "What Is a Treaty? On Contract and Mutual Aid." In *The Right Relationship: Reimagining the Implementation of Historical Treaties,* edited by John Borrows and Michael Coyle, 208–47. Toronto: University of Toronto Press.

Minow, Martha. 2002. *Breaking the Cycles of Hatred.* Princeton: Princeton University Press.

Mookherjee, Nayanika, Nigel Rapport, Lisette Josephides, Ghassan Hage, Lindi Renier Todd, and Gillian Cowlishaw. 2009. "The Ethics of Apology: A Set of Commentaries." *Critique of Anthropology* 29 (3): 345–66. https://doi.org/10.1177/0308275x09336703.

Morris, Alexander. 2009 [1880]. *The Treaties of Canada with the Indians of Manitoba and the North.* Ottawa: Archives Canada.

Morrisseau, Calvin. 1998. *Into the Daylight: A Wholistic Approach to Healing.* Toronto: University of Toronto Press.

Mosby, Ian. 2013. "Administering Colonial Science: Nutrition Research and Human Biomedical Experimentation in Aboriginal Communities and Residential Schools, 1942–1952." *Histoire Sociale/Social History* 46 (1): 145–72. https://hssh.journals.yorku.ca/index.php/hssh/article/viewFile/40239/36424.

Murphy, Jessica. 2016. "Canada Pledges to Overhaul Broken Welfare Program for Indigenous Children." *The Guardian,* 26 January. https://www.theguardian.com/world/2016/jan/26/canada-discriminated-against-indigenous-children-welfare-services.

Nagel, Joane. 1995a. "American Indian Ethnic Renewal: Politics and the Resurgence of Identity." *American Sociological Review* 60 (6): 947–65. https://doi.org/10.2307/2096434.

– 1995b. "Resource Competition Theories of Ethnicity." *American Behavioral Scientist* 38 (3): 442–58. https://doi.org/10.1177/000276429 5038003006.

Napoleon, Val. 2004. "Living Together: Gitksan Legal Reasoning as a Foundation for Consent." Paper presented at Consent as the Foundation for Political Community, inaugural conference of the Consortium on Democracy and Constitutionalism, University of Victoria, 1–3 October.

National Inquiry into Missing and Murdered Indigenous Women and Girls. 2019. *Reclaiming Power and Place: Final Report, Volumes 1a–1b.* 3 June. https://www.mmiwg-ffada.ca/final-report/.

Newcomb, Steve. 2008. *Pagans in the Promised Land: Decoding the Doctrine of Christian Discovery.* Fulcrum.

Newton-Taylor, Brenda, and Kathleen Larion. 2009. "Rainy River District Aboriginal Needs Assessment Survey Report." Centre for Addictions and Mental Health and Couchiching First Nation, Treatment and Support Services Project. https://www.scribd.com/document/30358790/Rainy -River-District-Aboriginal-Addiction-Needs-Assesment-Survey-Report -Couchiching-First-Nation.

Nobles, Melissa. 2008. *The Politics of Official Apologies.* New York: Cambridge University Press.

Northwest Indian Language Institute. 2015. "Benefits of Indigenous Language Learning." https://cpb-us-e1.wpmucdn.com/blogs.uoregon.edu/dist/8 /15685/files/2015/09/Benefits-fact-sheet-for-webpage.pdf.

Ontario Forestry Coalition. 2007. "Sawmill Closures since 2002." https://www150.statcan.gc.ca/n1/pub/11-621-m/2011089/part-partie1-eng.htm.

Ortiz-Guerrero, Cesar. 2010. "A Region in Transition: The Role of Networks, Capitals, and Conflicts in the Rainy River District." PhD diss., University of Waterloo.

O'Sullivan, Erin. 2011. "The Community Well-Being Index (CWB): Measuring Well-Being in First Nations and Non-Aboriginal Communities, 1981–2006." Report submitted to Aboriginal Affairs and Northern Development Canada. http://publications.gc.ca/site/eng/427778/publication.html.

Palmater, Pamela. 2011. *Beyond Blood: Rethinking Indigenous Identity.* Saskatoon: Purich.

– 2013. "Idle No More: What Do We Want and Where Are We Headed?" *Rabble.ca*, 4 January. http://rabble.ca/blogs/bloggers/pamela-palmater /2013/01/what-idle-no-more-movement-really.

– 2015. "Canada's Residential Schools Weren't Killing Culture, They Were Killing Indians." *Rabble.ca*, 9 June. http://rabble.ca/blogs/bloggers /pamela-palmater/2015/06/canadas-residential-schools-werent-killing -culture-they-were-.

– 2017. "Justin Trudeau Has Forgotten His Promises to Indigenous Peoples." *CBC News*, 8 February. http://www.cbc.ca/news/opinion/promise-to -indigenous-1.3972965.

Palys, Ted. 1997. *Research Decisions: Quantitative and Qualitative Perspectives,* 2nd ed. Toronto: Harcourt Canada.

Paulsen, Ralph. 2015. "Was There Smoke? One Man Asks Why He Didn't Know about Residential Schools." *CBC News*, 29 June. http://www.cbc.ca /news/aboriginal/was-there-smoke-one-man-asks-why-he-didn-t-know -about-residential-schools-1.3132522.

Peruniak, Shirley F. 2000. *Quetico Provincial Park: An Illustrated History*. Atikokan: Friends of Quetico Park.

Pettigrew, Thomas F., and Linda R. Tropp. 2006. "A Meta-analytic Test of Intergroup Contact Theory." *Journal of Personality and Social Psychology* 90 (5): 751–83. https://doi.org/10.1037/0022-3514.90.5.751.

Phung, Malissa. 2011. "Are People of Colour Settlers Too?" In *Cultivating Canada: Reconciliation through the Lens of Cultural Diversity*, edited by Ashok Mathur, Jonathan Dewar, and Mike DeGagné, 289–98. Ottawa: Aboriginal Healing Foundation.

Pickard, Andy, and Cindy Pickard, dirs. 2007. *The 8th Fire* (film). Imagica Pictures. https://www.imdb.com/title/tt1533091/.

Piven, Frances Fox. 2006. *Challenging Authority: How Ordinary People Change America*. New York: Rowman & Littlefield.

– 2011. *Who's Afraid of Frances Fox Piven?* New York: New Press.

Popplewell, Brett. 2010. "Rotting First Nation, Wealthy Chief." *Toronto Star*, 29 October. https://www.thestar.com/news/investigations/2010/10/29/rotting_first_nation_wealthy_chief.html.

Pottie, Erin. 2014. "American Law Professor: Aboriginal Title Decision Is No Game-Changer." *Halifax Chronicle Herald*, 23 July.

Price, Scott. 2015. "Hayden King on Treaties and Treaty Relations in Canada." *Intercontinental Cry*, 21 January. https://intercontinentalcry.org/hayden-king-treaties-treaty-relations-canada/.

Putnam, Robert. 2000. *Bowling Alone: The Collapse and Revival of American Community*. New York: Simon & Schuster.

Pyke, Karen D. 2010. "What Is Internalized Racial Oppression and Why Don't We Study It? Acknowledging Racism's Hidden Injuries." *Sociological Perspectives* 53 (4): 551–72. https://doi.org/10.1525/sop.2010.53.4.551.

Quillian, Lincoln. 2006. "New Approaches to Understanding Racial Prejudice and Discrimination." *Annual Review of Sociology* 32 (1): 299–328. https://doi.org/10.1146/annurev.soc.32.061604.123132.

RCMP (Royal Canadian Mounted Police). 2014. *Missing and Murdered Aboriginal Women: A National Operational Overview*. http://www.rcmp-grc.gc.ca/en/missing-and-murdered-aboriginal-women-national-operational-overview.

Regan, Paulette. 2010. *Unsettling the Settler Within: Indian Residential Schools, Truth Telling, and Reconciliation in Canada*. Vancouver: UBC Press.

Reimer, Gwen, Amy Bombay, Lena Ellsworth, Sara Fryer, and Tricia Logan. 2010. *The Indian Residential Schools Settlement Agreement's Common Experience Payment and Healing: A Qualitative Study Exploring Impacts on Recipients*. Ottawa: Aboriginal Healing Foundation.

Revell, Peggy. 2010a. "Couchiching Vows to Set Up Toll Booth." *Fort Frances Times*, 28 April. http://www.fftimes.com/news/news/couchiching-vows-set-toll-booth.

– 2010b. "'Serious Response' to Issues Needed: Politicians." *Fort Frances Times*, 5 May. http://www.fftimes.com/news/news/%E2%80%98serious -response%E2%80%99-issues-needed-politicians.

– 2010c. "Toll Booth Goes Up." *Fort Frances Times*, 21 May. http://www .fftimes.com/news/news/toll-booth-goes.

– 2010d. "Toll Booth Subject of Praise, Threats: Chief." *Fort Frances Times*, 26 May. http://www.fftimes.com/news/news/toll-booth-subject-praise -threats-chief.

Revell, Peggy, and Duane Hicks. 2010. "Band Sets Fees for Toll Booth." *Fort Frances Times*, 19 May. http://www.fftimes.com/news/news/band -sets-fees-toll-booth.

Rifkin, Mark. 2013. "Settler Common Sense." *Settler Colonial Studies* 3 (3–4): 322–40. https://doi.org/10.1080/2201473x.2013.810702.

Robertson, Dwanna L. 2015. "Invisibility in the Color-Blind Era: Examining Legitimized Racism against Indigenous Peoples." *American Indian Quarterly* 39 (2): 113–53. https://doi.org/10.5250/amerindiquar.39.2.0113.

Roediger, David. 1991. *The Wages of Whiteness: Race and the Making of the American Working Class*. London: Verso.

Royal Commission on Aboriginal Peoples (RCAP). 1996. *Highlights from the Report of the Royal Commission on Aboriginal Peoples*. Ottawa: Government of Canada. http://ainc-inac.gc.ca/ap/pubs/rpt/rpt-eng.asp.

Rutherford, Scott. 2011. "Canada's Other Red Scare: Rights, Decolonization, and Indigenous Political Protest in the Global Sixties." PhD diss., Queen's University, Kingston, ON.

Satzewich, Vic. 2011. *Racism in Canada*. Don Mills: Oxford University Press.

Satzewich, Vic, and Terry Wotherspoon. 2000. *First Nations: Race, Class, and Gender Relations,* 2nd ed. Scarborough: Nelson.

Saul, John Ralston. 2014. *The Comeback*. Toronto: Viking.

Scher, Steven J., and John M. Darley. 1997. "How Effective Are the Things People Say to Apologize? Effects of the Realization of the Apology Speech Act." *Journal of Psycholinguistic Research* 26:127–40. https://doi.org/10.1023 /A:1025068306386.

Schuman, Howard, Charlotte Steeh, and Lawrence Bobo, eds. 1997. *Racial Attitudes in America: Trends and Interpretations*. Cambridge: Harvard University Press.

Schwartz, Daniel. 2015. Truth and Reconciliation Commission: By the Numbers. *CBC News*, 2 June. http://www.cbc.ca/news/aboriginal/truth -and-reconciliation-commission-by-the-numbers-1.3096185.

Scott, James C. 1990. *Domination and the Arts of Resistance: Hidden Transcripts*. New Haven: Yale University Press.

Sherif, Muzafer, O.J. Harvey, B.J. White, William R. Hood, and Carolyn W. Sherif. 1961. *Intergroup Cooperation and Competition: The Robbers Cave Experiment*. Norman: University Book Exchange.

Short, Damien. 2005. "Reconciliation and the Problem of Internal Colonialism." *Journal of Intercultural Studies* 26 (3): 267–82. https://doi.org/10.1080/07256860500153534.

– 2012. "When Sorry Isn't Good Enough: Official Remembrance and Reconciliation in Australia." *Memory Studies* 5 (3): 293–304. https://doi.org/10.1177/1750698012443886.

Sidanius, James, and Felicia Pratto. 1999. *Social Dominance: An Intergroup Theory of Social Hierarchy and Oppression*. Cambridge: Cambridge University Press.

Simpson, Audra. 2014. *Mohawk Interruptus: Political Life across the Borders of Settler States*. Durham: Duke University Press.

Simpson, Leanne, ed. 2008. *Lighting the Eighth Fire: The Liberation, Resurgence, and Protection of Indigenous Nations*. Winnipeg: Arbeiter Ring.

– 2011. *Dancing on Our Turtle's Back: Stories of Nishnaabeg Re-creation, Resurgence and a New Emergence*. Winnipeg: Arbeiter Ring.

– 2017. *As We Have Always Done: Indigenous Freedom through Radical Resistance*. Minneapolis: University of Minnesota Press.

Simpson, Leanne, and Kiera Ladner. 2010. *This Is an Honour Song: Twenty Years Since the Blockades*. Winnipeg: Arbeiter Ring.

Smith, Joanna. 2015. "First Nations Financial Transparency Act: Median Salary for a Chief Is $60,000." *Hamilton Spectator*, 8 February. https://www.thespec.com/news-story/5328804-first-nations-financial-transparency-act-median-salary-for-a-chief-is-60-000/.

Smith, Linda Tuhiwai. 1999. *Decolonizing Methodologies: Research and Indigenous Peoples*. London: Zed Books.

Spielmann, Roger. 2009. *Anishinaabe World: A Survival Guide to Building Bridges between Canada and First Nations*. Sudbury: Scrivener.

Srivastava, Sarita. 2006. "Tears, Fears, and Careers: Anti-racism and Emotion in Social Movement Organizations." *The Canadian Journal of Sociology* 31 (1): 55–90. https://doi.org/10.1353/cjs.2006.0028.

Steinman, Erich. 2012. "Settler-Colonial Power and the American Indian Sovereignty Movement: Forms of Domination, Strategies of Transformation." *American Journal of Sociology* 117 (4): 1073–130. https://doi.org/10.1086/662708.

Stephan, Walter G., and Cookie White Stephan. 2000. "An Integrated Threat Theory of Prejudice." In *Reducing Prejudice and Discrimination*, edited by Stuart Oskamp, 23–46. Mahwah: Lawrence Erlbaum Associates.

Stevenson, Winona. 1999. "Colonialism and First Nations Women in Canada." In *Scratching the Surface: Canadian Anti-Racist Feminist Thought*, edited by Enakshi Dua and Angela Robertson, 49–80. Toronto: Canadian Scholars Press.

St. John, Michelle, dir. 2016. *Colonization Road* (film). Frog Girl Films. https://www.colonizationroad.com/.

Stuchlik, Milan. 1979. "Chilean Native Policies and the Image of the Mapuche Indians." In *Queen's University Papers in Social Anthropology, Vol. 3: The Conceptualization and Explanation of Processes of Social Change*, edited by D. Riches, 33–54. Belfast: Queen's University Press.

Stymeist, David. 1975. *Ethnics and Indians: Social Relations in a Northwestern Ontario Town*. Toronto: P. Martin Associates.

Sue, Derald Wing. 2010. *Microaggressions in Everyday Life: Race, Gender, and Sexual Orientation*. Hoboken: John Wiley & Sons.

Swidler, Ann. 1986. "Culture in Action: Symbols and Strategies." *American Sociological Review* 51 (2): 273–86. https://doi.org/10.2307/2095521.

Tajfel, Henri, and John Turner. 2001. "An Integrative Theory of Intergroup Conflict." In *Intergroup Relations*, edited by M.A. Hogg and Dominic Abrams, 94–110. London: Psychology Press.

Talaga, Tanya. 2017. *Seven Fallen Feathers: Racism, Death, and Hard Truths in a Northern City*. Toronto: Anansi.

Tasker, John Paul. 2017. "Conservative Senator Defends 'Well-Intentioned' Residential School System." *CBC News*, 8 March. http://www.cbc.ca /news/politics/residential-school-system-well-intentioned-conservative -senator-1.4015115.

Tavuchis, Nicholas. 1991. *Mea Culpa: A Sociology of Apology and Reconciliation*. Stanford: Stanford University Press.

Taylor, Charles. 1992. *Multiculturalism and "The Politics of Recognition."* Princeton: Princeton University Press.

Thobani, Sunera. 2007. *Exalted Subjects: Studies in the Making of Race and Nation in Canada*. Toronto: University of Toronto Press.

Thompson, Janna. 2008. "Apology, Justice, and Respect: A Critical Defense of Political Apology." In *The Age of Apology: Facing Up to the Past*, edited by Mark Gibney, Rhoda E. Howard-Hassmann, Jean-Marc Coicaud, and Niklaus Steiner, 31–44. Philadelphia: University of Pennsylvania Press.

Thompson, Marg. 1979. *Rainy River: Our Town, Our Lives*. Rainy River: self-published.

Truth and Reconciliation Commission of Canada (TRC). 2015. *Honouring the Truth, Reconciling for the Future: Summary of the Final Report of the Truth and Reconciliation Commission of Canada*. Winnipeg: TRC. http://www.trc.ca/.

Tuck, Eve, and K. Wayne Yang. 2012. "Decolonization Is Not a Metaphor." *Decolonization: Indigeneity, Education & Society* 1 (1): 1–40. https://jps.library. utoronto.ca/index.php/des/article/view/18630.

United Nations. 2008. *United Nations Declaration on the Rights of Indigenous Peoples*. Resolution 61/295. https://www.un.org/development/desa /indigenouspeoples/wp-content/uploads/sites/19/2018/11/UNDRIP_E _web.pdf.

Urban Aboriginal Task Force. 2007. "Kenora: Final Report." Report commissioned by the Ontario Federation of Indian Friendship Centres, the Ontario Métis Aboriginal Association, and the Ontario Native Women's Association. http://ofifc.org/sites/default/files/docs /UATFKenoraFinalReport.pdf.

Vasquez, Jessica M., and Christopher Wetzel. 2009. "Tradition and the Invention of Racial Selves: Symbolic Boundaries, Collective Authenticity, and Contemporary Struggles for Racial Equality." *Ethnic and Racial Studies* 32 (9): 1557–75. https://doi.org/10.1080/01419870802684232.

Veracini, Lorenzo. 2010. *Settler Colonialism: A Theoretical Overview*. Basingstoke: Palgrave Macmillan.

Vowel, Chelsea. 2016. *Indigenous Writes: A Guide to First Nations, Métis, and Inuit Issues in Canada*. Winnipeg: Highwater Press.

Vowel, Chelsea, and Darryl Leroux. 2016. "White Settler Antipathy and the *Daniels* Decision." *TOPIA: Canadian Journal of Cultural Studies* 36:30–42. https://doi.org/10.3138/topia.36.30.

Waisberg, Leo G. 1983. "The Rainy River Ojibway: An Ethnographical and Historical Outline." Unpublished manuscript, Fort Frances Museum Archives.

Waisberg, Leo G., and Tim E. Holzkamm. 1993. "'A Tendency to Discourage Them from Cultivating': Ojibwa Agriculture and Indian Affairs Administration in Northwestern Ontario." *Ethnohistory* 40 (2): 175–211. https://doi.org/10.2307/482201.

– 1998. "'Peaceful Pursuit of Happiness': Anishinabeg Resources in the Boundary Waters after Treaty #3." Paper presented at the American Society for Ethnohistory Conference, 13 November.

Waisberg, Leo G., Joan A. Lovisek, and Tim E. Holzkamm. 1996. "Ojibwa Reservations as 'An Incubus upon the Territory': The Indian Removal Policy of Ontario, 1874–1982." In *Papers of the Twenty-Seventh Algonquian Conference*, edited by David H. Pentland, 337–52. Winnipeg: University of Manitoba.

Walia, Harsha. 2015. "'Land Is a Relationship': In Conversation with Glen Coulthard on Indigenous Nationhood." *Rabble*, 21 January. http://rabble .ca/columnists/2015/01/land-relationship-conversation-glen-coulthard -on-indigenous-nationhood.

Wallace, Rick. 2013. *Merging Fires: Grassroots Peacebuilding between Indigenous and Non-Indigenous Peoples*. Halifax: Fernwood.

Wang, Caroline, and Mary Ann Burris. 1997. "Photovoice: Concept, Method, and Use for Participatory Needs Assessment." *Health Education and Behaviour* 24 (3): 369–87. https://doi.org/10.1177/109019819702400309.

Warren, Mark R. 2010. *Fire in the Heart: How White Activists Embrace Racial Justice*. New York: Oxford University Press.

Warren, William. 1984 [1885]. *History of the Ojibway People*. Saint Paul: Minnesota Historical Society.

Warry, Wayne. 2007. *Ending Denial: Understanding Aboriginal Issues*. Toronto: Broadview.

Watts, Vanessa, and Hayden King. 2015. "TRC Report a Good Start, but Now It's Time for Action." *Globe and Mail*, 5 June. http://www.theglobeandmail .com/news/national/trc-report-a-good-start-but-now-its-time-for-action /article24824924/.

Waziyatawin. 2009. "You Can't Un-ring a Bell: Demonstrating Contrition through Action." In *Response, Responsibility, and Renewal: Canada's Truth and Reconciliation Journey*, edited by Gregory Younging, Jonathan Dewar, and Mike DeGagné, 191–202. Ottawa: Aboriginal Healing Foundation.

Wesley-Esquimaux, Cynthia, and Magdalena Smolewski. 2004. *Historic Trauma and Aboriginal Healing*. Ottawa: Aboriginal Healing Foundation.

White, Patrick. 2010. "Native Group-Home Proposal Sparks Racial Tension in Ontario Town." *Globe and Mail*, 14 July. http://www.theglobeandmail .com/news/national/native-group-home-proposal-sparks-racial-tension -in-ontario-town/article1387155/.

White, Richard. 2011. *The Middle Ground: Indians, Empires and Republics in the Great Lakes Region, 1650–1815*, 20th anniversary ed. Cambridge: Cambridge University Press.

Widdowson, Frances, and Albert Howard. 2008. *Disrobing the Aboriginal Industry: The Deception behind Indigenous Cultural Preservation*. Montreal and Kingston: McGill-Queen's University Press.

Wien, Frederic. 2009. *The State of the First Nation Economy and the Struggle to Make Poverty History*. Ottawa: Assembly of First Nations.

Wilder, David A. 1984. "Intergroup Contact: The Typical Member and the Exception to the Rule." *Journal of Experimental Social Psychology* 20 (2): 177–94. https://doi.org/10.1016/0022-1031(84)90019-2.

Williams, Alex, dir. 2015. *The Pass System* (film). Tamarack Productions. http://www.tamarackproductions.com/the-pass-system/.

Williams, Robert A., Jr. 2012. *Savage Anxieties: The Invention of Western Civilization*. Basingstoke: Palgrave Macmillan.

Willow, Anna J. 2012. *Strong Hearts, Native Lands: Anti-Clearcutting Activism at Grassy Narrows First Nation*. Winnipeg: University of Manitoba Press.

Wilson, William Julius. 1999. *The Bridge over the Racial Divide: Rising Inequality and Coalition Politics*. Berkeley: University of California Press.

Wilson, William Julius, and Anmol Chaddha. 2009. "The Role of Theory in Ethnographic Research." *Ethnography* 10 (4): 549–64. https://doi.org /10.1177/1466138109347009.

Wimmer, Andreas. 2008. "The Making and Unmaking of Ethnic Boundaries: A Multilevel Process Theory." *American Journal of Sociology* 113 (4): 970–1022. https://doi.org/10.1086/522803.

Wingfield, Adia Harvey, and Joe R. Feagin. 2010. *Yes We Can? White Racial Framing and the 2008 Presidential Campaign*. New York: Routledge.

Winship, Christopher. 2004. "Veneers and Underlayments: Critical Moments and Situational Redefinition." *Negotiation Journal* 20 (2): 297–311. https:// doi.org/10.1111/j.1571-9979.2004.00024.x.

Wodtke, Geoffrey T. 2012. "The Impact of Education on Intergroup Attitudes: A Multiracial Analysis." *Social Psychology Quarterly* 75 (1): 80–106. https:// doi.org/10.1177/0190272511430234.

Wolfe, Patrick. 2006. "Settler Colonialism and the Elimination of the Native." *Journal of Genocide Research* 8 (4): 387–409. https://doi.org/10.1080 /14623520601056240.

Wotherspoon, Terry, and John Hansen. 2013. "The 'Idle No More' Movement: Paradoxes of First Nations Inclusion in the Canadian Context." *Social Inclusion* 1 (1): 21–36. https://doi.org/10.17645/si.v1i1.107.

Yeigh, Frank. 1892. *The Rainy River District, province of Ontario, Canada: A description of its soil, climate, products, agricultural capabilities and timber and mineral resources, together with the laws pertaining to free grants and homesteads, to mining and to the preservation of forests from destruction by fire*. Toronto: Warwick. Microform.

Yerxa, Jana-Rae. 2015. "Refuse to Live Quietly!" *Settler Colonial Studies* 5 (1): 100–2. https://doi.org/10.1080/2201473x.2014.909961.

Ziersch, Anna M. Gilbert Gallaher, Fran Baum, and Michael Bentley. 2011. "Responding to Racism: Insights on How Racism Can Damage Health from an Urban Study of Australian Aboriginal People." *Social Science and Medicine* 73 (7): 1045–53. https://doi.org/10.1016/j.socscimed.2011.06.058.

Index

The letter *f* following a page number denotes a figure; the letter *t* denotes a table.